RECURRENT NEURAL NETWORKS AND SOFT COMPUTING

Edited by **Mahmoud ElHefnawi** and **Mohamed Mysara**

Recurrent Neural Networks and Soft Computing
Edited by Mahmoud ElHefnawi and Mohamed Mysara

Published by InTech

Janeza Trdine 9, 51000 Rijeka, Croatia

Publishing Process Manager Sasa Leporic

Technical Editor Teodora Smiljanic

Cover Designer InTech Design Team

Additional hard copies can be obtained from orders@intechopen.com

Recurrent Neural Networks and Soft Computing,
Edited by Mahmoud ElHefnawi and Mohamed Mysara
p. cm.
ISBN 978-953-51-0409-4

For EU product safety concerns:
IN TECH d.o.o., Prolaz Marije Krucifikse Kozulić 3, 51000 Rijeka, Croatia,
info@intechopen.com or visit our website at intechopen.com.

Meet the editors

Dr Mahmoud ElHefnawi is the the Biomedical informatics and Chemoinformatics group leader at the Centre of Excellence for Advanced Sciences(CEAS) and Informatics and Systems Department, National Research Centre NRC). Also, he was a part-time Researcher and adjunct faculty at the American University in Cairo and Egyptian JapaneseUniversity for Science and Technology (EJUST). He cofounded the Information Technology Institute (ITI) bioinformatics track. Many publications on topics including rational drug design, docking, and optimizing gene therapy for Influenza, Hepatitis C Virus (HCV), and different cancers, structural bioinformatics and motif predictions applications in virology, and applications of phylogenetic analysis. These were in reputed journals like Bioinformatics (Oxford University Press), PLOS1 (Public library of science), journal of molecular recognition, European journal of medicinal chemistry, and Virology Journal.

Mr Mohamed Mysara, MSc graduate from the University of Nottingham, Dec/2010, acquiring the ITI prize for the best dissertation. Mr Mysara is working in the field of Bioinformatics and computational biology, has done various work in the field of post-transcriptional gene regulation and in chemoinformatics. Mr Mysara has several applications in the field of machine learning and its application, either in RNA interference, as in MysiRNA-Designer software for siRNA prediction or in chemoinformatics classifiers. He has been working in National Research Center, Bioinformatics and Chemoinformatics group, as an assistant researcher; currently he is junior scientist at Nile University in Bioinformatics research group.

Contents

Preface XI

Part 1 Soft Computing 1

Chapter 1 **Neural Networks and Static Modelling 3**
Igor Belič

Chapter 2 **A Framework for Bridging the Gap Between Symbolic and Non-Symbolic AI 23**
Gehan Abouelseoud and Amin Shoukry

Chapter 3 **Ranking Indices for Fuzzy Numbers 49**
Tayebeh Hajjari

Chapter 4 **Neuro-Fuzzy Digital Filter 73**
José de Jesús Medel, Juan Carlos García and Juan Carlos Sánchez

Part 2 Recurrent Neural Network 87

Chapter 5 **Recurrent Neural Network with Human Simulator Based Virtual Reality 89**
Yousif I. Al Mashhadany

Chapter 6 **Recurrent Neural Network-Based Adaptive Controller Design for Nonlinear Dynamical Systems 115**
Hong Wei Ge and Guo Zhen Tan

Chapter 7 **BRNN-SVM: Increasing the Strength of Domain Signal to Improve Protein Domain Prediction Accuracy 133**
Kalsum U. Hassan, Razib M. Othman, Rohayanti Hassan, Hishammuddin Asmuni, Jumail Taliba and Shahreen Kasim

Chapter 8 **Recurrent Self-Organizing Map for Severe Weather Patterns Recognition 151**
José Alberto Sá, Brígida Rocha, Arthur Almeida and José Ricardo Souza

Chapter 9 **Centralized Distributed Parameter Bioprocess Identification and I-Term Control Using Recurrent Neural Network Model 175**
Ieroham Baruch,
Eloy Echeverria-Saldierna and Rosalba Galvan-Guerra

Chapter 10 **Optimization of Mapping Graphs of Parallel Programs onto Graphs of Distributed Computer Systems by Recurrent Neural Network 203**
Mikhail S. Tarkov

Chapter 11 **Detection and Classification of Adult and Fetal ECG Using Recurrent Neural Networks, Embedded Volterra and Higher-Order Statistics 225**
Walid A. Zgallai

Chapter 12 **Artificial Intelligence Techniques Applied to Electromagnetic Interference Problems Between Power Lines and Metal Pipelines 253**
Dan D. Micu, Georgios C. Christoforidis and Levente Czumbil

Chapter 13 **An Application of Jordan Pi-Sigma Neural Network for the Prediction of Temperature Time Series Signal 275**
Rozaida Ghazali, Noor Aida Husaini,
Lokman Hakim Ismail and Noor Azah Samsuddin

Preface

Section 1: Soft Computing

This section illustrates some general concepts of artificial neural networks, their properties, mode of training, static training (feedforward) and dynamic training (recurrent), training data classification, supervised, semi-supervised and unsupervised training. **Prof. Belic Igor's** chapter that deals with ANN application in modeling, illustrating two properties of ANN: universality and optimization. **Prof. Shoukry Amin** discusses both symbolic and non-symbolic data and ways of bridging neural networks with fuzzy logic, as discussed in the second chapter including an application to the robot problem. **Dr. Hajjari Tayebeh** discusses fuzzy logic and various ordering indices approaches in detail, including defuzzification method, reference set method and the fuzzy relation method. A comparative example is provided indicating the superiority of each approach. The next chapter discusses the combination of ANN and fuzzy logic, where neural weights are adjusted dynamically considering the fuzzy logic adaptable properties.

Dr. Medel Jeus describes applications of artificial neural networks, both feed forward and recurrent, and manners of improving the algorithms by combining fuzzy logic and digital filters. Finally **Dr. Ghaemi O. Kambiz** discusses using genetic algorithm enhanced fuzzy logic to handle two medical related problems: Hemodynamic control & regulation of blood glucose.

Section 2: Recurrent Neural Network

Recurrent Neural Networks (RNNs), are like other ANN abstractions of biological nervous systems, yet they differ from them in allowing using their internal memory of the training to be fed recurrently to the neural network. This makes them applicable for adaptive robotics, speech recognition, attentive vision, music composition, hand-writing recognition, etc. There are several types of RNNs, such as Fully recurrent network, Hopfield network, Elman networks and Jordan networks, Echo state network, Long short term memory network, Bi-directional RNN, Continuous-time RNN, Hierarchical RNN, Recurrent multilayer perceptron, etc. In this section, some of these types of RNN are discussed, as well as application of each type. **Dr. Al-Mashhadany Yousif** Illustrates types of ANN providing a detailed illustration of RNN, types and advantages with application to human simulator. This chapter discusses time-delay recurrent neural network (TDRNN) model, as a novel approach. **Prof. Ge Hongwei's** chapter demonstrates the advantages of using such an approach over other approaches using a graphic illustration of the results. Moreover, it illustrates its usage in non-linear systems. **Dr Othman Razib M.** describes in his chapter the usage of a combination of Bidirectional Recurrent Neural Network and Support vector machine (BRNN-SVM) with the aim of protein domain prediction, where BRNN acts to predict the secondary structure as SVM later processes the produced data to classify the domain. The chapter is well constructed and easy to understand. **Dr. Rocha Brigida**'s chapter discusses using Recurrent self-organizing map (RSOM) for weather prediction. It applies Self-Organizing Map (SOM), single layer neural network. To deal with the dynamic nature of the data, Temporal Kohonen Map (TKM) was implemented including the temporal dimension, which is followed by applying Recurrent Self-Organizing Map (RSOM) to open the window for model retraining. It proceeds to describe data preprocessing, training and evaluation in a comparative analysis of these three approaches. **Dr. Baruch Ieroham** describes the usage of different RNN approaches in aerobic digestion bioprocess featuring dynamic Backpropagation and the Levenberg-Marquardt algorithms. It provides sufficient introductory information, mathematical background, training methodology, models built, and results analysis. **Dr. Tarkov Mikhail** discusses using RNN for solving the problem of mapping graphs of parallel programs, mapping graph onto graph of a distributed CS as one of the approaches of over heading and optimization solutions. They used different mapping approaches, as Hopfield, achieving improvement in mapping quality with less frequency, Splitting that achieved higher frequency, Wang was found to achieve higher frequency of optimal solutions. Then they proposed using nesting ring structures in "toroidal graphs with edge defect" and "splitting method". **Dr. Zgallai Walid A** discusses the use of RNN in ECG classification and detection targeting different medical cases, adult and fetal ECG as well as other ECG abnormalities. In **Prof. Micu Dan Doru's** work, Electromagnetic Interference problems are described and how they could be solved using artificial intelligence. The authors apply various artificial intelligence techniques featuring two models, one for evaluation of magnetic vector potential, and the other for self & mutual impedance matrix determination. **Finally Dr. Ghazali Rozaida** discusses the use of Jordan Pi-Sigma Neural Network (that featuring RNN) for weather forecasting, providing sufficient background information, training and testing against other methods, MLP and PSNN.

We hope this book will be of value and interest to researchers, students and those working in the artificial intelligence, machine learning, and related fields. It offers a balanced combination of theory and application, and each algorithm/method is applied to a different problem and evaluated statistically using robust measures like ROC and other parameters.

Mahmoud ElHefnawi
Division of Genetic Engineering and Biotechnology, National Research Centre &
Biotechnology, Faculty of Science, American University in Cairo,
Egypt

Mohamed Mysara (MSc).
Biomedical Informatics and Chemoinformatics Group, National Research Centre, Cairo,
Egypt

Part 1

Soft Computing

1

Neural Networks and Static Modelling

Igor Belič
Institute of Metals and Technology
Slovenia

1. Introduction

Neural networks are mainly used for two specific tasks. The first and most commonly mentioned one is pattern recognition and the second one is to generate an approximation to a function usually referred to as modelling.

In the pattern recognition task the data is placed into one of the sets belonging to given classes. Static modelling by neural networks is dedicated to those systems that can be probed by a series of reasonably reproducible measurements. Another quite important detail that justifies the use of neural networks is the absence of suitable mathematical description of modelled problem.

Neural networks are model-less approximators, meaning they are capable of modelling regardless of any knowledge of the nature of the modelled system. For classical approximation techniques, it is often necessary to know the basic mathematical model of the approximated problem. Least square approximation (regression models), for example, searches for the best fit of the given data to the known function which represents the model.

Neural networks can be divided into dynamic and static neural (feedforward) networks, where the term dynamic means that the network is permanently adapting the functionality (i.e., it learns during the operation). The static neural networks adapt their properties in the so called learning or training process. Once adequately trained, the properties of the built model remain unchanged - static.

Neural networks can be trained either according to already known examples, in which case this training is said to be supervised, or without knowing anything about the training set outcomes. In this case, the training is unsupervised.

In this chapter we will focus strictly on the static (feedforward) neural networks with supervised training scheme.

An important question is to decide which problems are best approached by implementation of neural networks as approximators. The most important property of neural networks is their ability to learn the model from the data presented. When the neural network builds the model, the dependences among the parameters are included in the model. It is important to know that neural networks are not a good choice when research on the underlying mechanisms and interdependencies of parameters of the system is being undertaken. In such cases, neural networks can provide almost no additional knowledge.

The first sub-chapter starts with an introduction to the terminology used for neural networks. The terminology is essential for adequate understanding of further reading.

The section entitled "Some critical aspects" summarizes the basic understanding of the topic and shows some of the errors in formulations that are so often made.

The users who want to use neural network tools should be aware of the problems posed by the input and output limitations. These limitations are often the cause of bad modelling results. A detailed analysis of the neural network input and output considerations and the errors that may be produced by these procedures are given.

In practice the neural network modelling of systems that operate on a wide range of values represents a serious problem. Two methods are proposed for the approximation of wide range functions.

A very important topic of training stability follows. It defines the magnitude of diversity detected during the network training and the results are to be studied carefully in the course of any serious data modelling attempt.

At the end of the chapter the general design steps for a specific neural network modelling task are given.

2. Neural networks and static modelling

We are introducing the term of static modelling of systems. Static modelling is used to model the time independent properties of systems which implies that the systems behaviour remains relatively unchanged within the time frame important for the application. (Fig. 1). In this category we can understand also the systems which do change their reaction on stimulus, but this variability is measurable and relatively stable in the given time period. We regard the system as static when its reaction on stimulus is stable and most of all repeatable - in some sense - static.

The formal description of static system (Fig. 1) is given in (1)

$$Y_m(X_n, t) = f(X_n, P_u, t) \tag{1}$$

Where Y_m is the m - dimensional output vector,

X_n is the n – dimensional input – stimulus vector,
P_u is the system parameters vector,
t is the time.

In order to regard the system as static both the function f and the parameters vector P_u do not change in time.

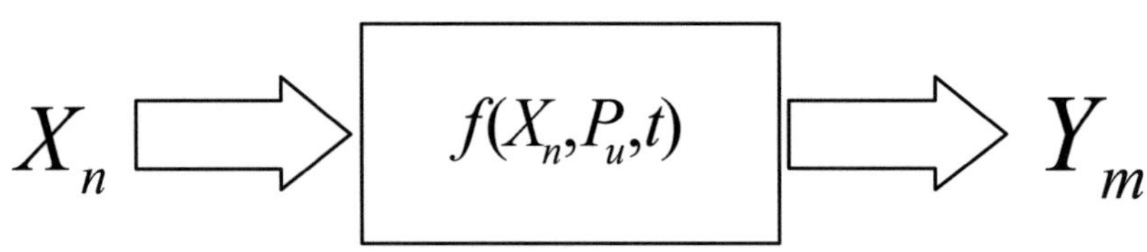

Fig. 1. The formal description of static system.

Under the formal concept of static system we can also imply a somewhat narrower definition as described in (1). Here the system input - output relationship does not include the time component (2).

$$Y_m\ (X_n) = f(X_n,\ P_u) \tag{2}$$

Although this kind of representation does not seem to be practical, it addresses a very large group of practical problems where the nonlinear characteristic of a modelled system is corrected and accounted for (various calibrations and re-calibrations of measurement systems).

Another understanding of static modelling refers to the relative speed (time constant) of the system compared to the model. Such is the case where the model formed by the neural network (or any other modelling technique) runs many times faster than does the original process which is corrected by the model[1].

We are referring to the static modelling when the relation (3) holds true.

$$\tau_m << \tau_s \tag{3}$$

Where τ_m represents the time constant of the model, and τ_s represents the time constant of the observed system. Due to the large difference in the time constants, the operation of the model can be regarded as instantaneous.

The main reason to introduce the neural networks to the static modelling is that we often do not know the function f (1,2) analytically but we have the chance to perform the direct or indirect measurements of the system performance. Measured points are the entry point to the neural network which builds the model through the process of learning.

3. The terminology

The basic building element of any neural network is an **artificial neural network** cell (Fig. 2 left).

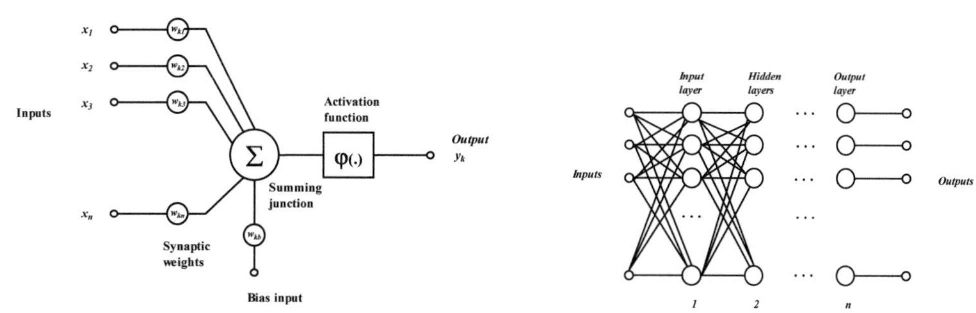

Fig. 2. The artificial neural network cell (left) and the general neural network system (right)

---

[1]The measurement systems usually (for example vacuum gauge) operate indirectly. Through measurement of different parameters the observed value of the system (output) can be deduced. Such is the case with the measurement of the cathode current at inverted magnetron. The current is in nonlinear dependence with the pressure in the vacuum system. In such system the dependence of the current versus pressure is not known analytically – at least not good enough - to use the analytical expression directly. This makes ideal ground to use neural network to build the adequate model.

Each artificial neural network consists of a number of **inputs (synapses)** that are connected to the **summing junction**. The values of inputs are multiplied by adequate weights **w** **(synaptic weights)** and summed with other inputs. The training process changes the values of connection weights, thus producing the effect of changing the input connection strengths. Sometimes there is a special input to the neural cell, called the **bias input**. The bias input value is fixed to 1, and the connection weight is adapted during the training process as well. The value of summed and weighted inputs is the argument of an **activation function** (Fig. 3) which produces the final output of an artificial neural cell. In most cases, the activation function $\varphi(x)$ is of **sigmoidal**[2] type. Some neural network architectures use the mixture of sigmoidal and linear activation functions (radial basis functions are a special type of neural network that use the neural network cells with linear activation functions in the output layer and non-sigmoidal functions in the hidden layer).

Artificial neural network cells are combined in the **neural network architecture** which is by default composed of two layers that provide communication with "outer world" (Fig. 2 right). Those layers are referred to as the **input and output layer** respectively. Between the two, there is a number of **hidden layers** which transform the signal from the input layer to the output layer. The hidden layers are called "hidden" for they are not directly connected, or visible, to the input or output of the neural network system. These hidden layers contribute significantly to the adaptive formation of the non-linear neural network input-output transfer function and thus to the properties of the system.

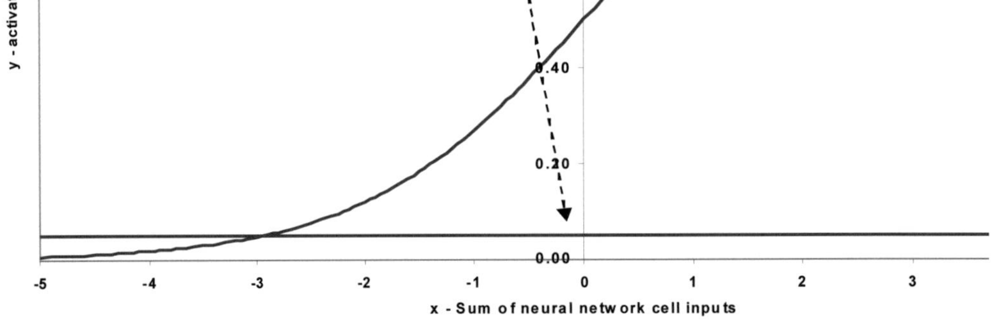

Fig. 3. The activation function $\varphi(x)$ of an artificial neural network cell.

[2] One of the sigmoidal type functions is $\varphi(x) = 1/(1+e^{-x})$.

3.1 Creation of model – The training process

The process of adaptation of a neural network is called "training" or "learning". During supervised training, the input - output pairs are presented to the neural network, and the training algorithm iteratively changes the weights of the neural network.

The measured data points are consecutively presented to the neural network. For each data point, the neural network produces an output value which normally differs from the **target value**. The difference between the two is the approximation error in the particular data point. The error is then propagated back through the neural network towards the input, and the correction of the connection weights is made to lower the output error. There are numerous methods for correction of the connection weight. The most frequently used algorithm is called the **error backpropagation algorithm**.

The training process continues from the first data point included in the training set to the very last, but the queue order is not important. A single training run on a complete training data set is called an **epoch**. Usually several epochs are needed to achieve the acceptable error (**training error**) for each data point. The number of epochs depends on various parameters but can easily reach numbers from 100,000 to several million.

When the training achieves the desired accuracy, it is stopped. At this point, the model can reproduce the given data points with a prescribed precision for all data points. It is good practice to make additional measurements (**test data set**) to validate the model in the points not included in the training set. The model produces another error called the **test error**, which is normally higher than the training error.

4. Some critical aspects

Tikk et al. (2003) and Mhaskar (1996) have provided a detailed survey on the evolution of approximation theory and the use of neural networks for approximation purposes. In both papers, the mathematical background is being provided, which has been used as the background for other researchers who studied the approximation properties of various neural networks.

There is another very important work provided by Wray and Green (1994). They showed that, when neural networks are operated on digital computers (which is true in the vast majority of cases), real limitations of numerical computing should also be considered. Approximation properties like universal approximation and the best approximation become useless.

The overview of mentioned surveys is given in (Belič, 2006).

The majority of works have frequently been used as a misleading promise, and even proof, that neural networks can be used as the general approximation tool for any kind of function. The provided proofs are theoretically correct but do not take into account the fact that all those neural network systems were run on digital computers.

Nonlinearity of the neural network cell simulated on a digital computer is realized by polynomial approximation. Therefore, each neural cell produces a polynomial activation function. Polynomial equivalence for the activation function is true even in the theoretical sense, i.e., the activation function is an analytical function, and analytical functions have their polynomial equivalents.

The output values of the neural network can be regarded as the sum of polynomials which is just another polynomial. The coefficients of the polynomial are changed through the adaptation of neural network weights. Due to the finite precision of the numeric calculations the contributions, of the coefficients with higher powers become lower from the finite precision of the computer. The process of training can no longer affect them. This is also true of any kind of a training scheme.

The work of Wray and Green (1994) has been criticized, but it nevertheless gives a very important perspective to the practitioners who cannot rely just on the proofs given for theoretically ideal circumstances.

There are many interesting papers describing the chaotic behaviour of neural networks (Bertels, et.al., 1996), (Huang, 2008), (Yuan, Yang, 2009), (Wang, et.al., 2011). The neural network training process is a typical chaotic process. For practical applications this fact must never be forgotten.

Neural networks can be used as a function approximation (modelling) tool, but they neither perform universal approximation, nor can the best approximation in a theoretical sense be found.

A huge amount of work has been done trying to find proofs that a neural network can provide approximation of continuous functions. It used to be of interest because the approximated function is also continuous and exists in a dense space. Then came the realization that, even if the approximated function is continuous, its approximation is not continuous since the neural network that performs the approximation consists of a finite number of building blocks. The approximation is therefore nowhere dense, and the function is no longer continuous. Although this does not sound promising, the discontinuity is not of such a type that it would make neural network systems unusable. This discontinuity must be understood in a numerical sense.

Another problem is that neural networks usually run on digital computers, which gives rise to another limitation mentioned earlier: as it is not always possible to achieve the prescribed approximation precision, **the fact that neural networks can perform the approximation with any prescribed precision does not hold**.

Furthermore, another complication is that continuity of the input function does not hold. When digital computers are used (or in fact any other measurement equipment), the denseness of a space and the continuity of the functions cannot be fulfilled for both input and output spaces. Moreover, when measurement equipment is used to probe the input and output spaces (real physical processes), denseness of a space in a mathematical sense is never achieved. For example, the proofs provided by Kurkova (1995) imply that the function to be approximated is in fact continuous, but the approximation process produces a discontinuous function. This is incorrect in practice where the original function can never be continuous in the first place.

A three layer neural network has been proved to be capable of producing a universal approximation. Although it is true (for the continuous functions), this is not practical when the number of neural cells must be very high, and the approximation speed becomes intolerably low. Introducing more hidden layers can significantly lower the number of neural network cells used, and the approximation speed then becomes much higher.

Numerous authors have reported on their successful work regarding the neural networks as approximators of sampled functions. Readers are kindly requested to consult those reports and findings to name but a few (Aggelogiannaki, et.al. 2007), (Wena, Ma, 2008), (Caoa, et.al., 2008), (Ait Gougam, et.al., 2008), (Bahi, et.al., 2009), (Wanga, Xub, 2010).

4.1 Input and output limitations

Neural networks are used to model various processes. The measurements obtained on the system to be modelled are of quite different magnitudes. This represents a problem for the neural network where the only neural network output (and often input) range is limited to the [0,1] interval. This is the case since the neural network cell activation function $\varphi(x)$ (Fig. 3) saturates output values at values 0 and 1. The users should be well aware of the processes as these are often the cause of various unwanted errors.

For some neural network systems this range is expanded to the [-1,+1] interval.

This is the reason why the input and output values of the neural network need to be preconditioned. There are two basic procedures to fit the actual input signal to the limited interval to avoid the saturation effect. The first process is scaling, and the second is offsetting.

First, the whole training data set is scanned, and the maximal $y_{\max}$ and minimal $y_{\min}$ values are found. The difference between them is then the range which is to be scaled to the [0-1] interval. From all values y the value of $y_{\min}$ is subtracted (this process is called offsetting). The transformation of the values is obtained by the equation

$$y'_i = \frac{y_i - y_{\min}}{y_{\max} - y_{\min}} \tag{4}$$

Here y'_i represents the offset and scaled value that fits in the prescribed interval. The reverse transformation is obtained by the equation

$$y_i = y_{\min} + y'_i \left(y_{\max} - y_{\min} \right) \tag{5}$$

The process is exactly the same for the neural network input values, only the interval is not necessarily limited to the 0 - 1 values.

This is not the only conditioning that occurs on input and output sides of the neural network. In addition to scaling, there is a parameter that prevents saturation of the system and is called **scaling margin**. The sigmoidal function tends to become saturated for the big values of inputs (Fig. 3). If the proper action is to be assured for the large values as well, then the scaling should not be performed on the whole [0,1] interval. The interval should be smaller for the given amount (let us say 0.1 for 10% shrinking of the interval). The corrected values are now

$$y'_i = \frac{S_m}{2} + \frac{(1 - S_m)(y_i - y_{\min})}{y_{\max} - y_{\min}} \tag{6}$$

where S_m represents the scaling margin.

The reverse operation is obtained by the equation

$$y_i = y_{\min} + \frac{\left(y'_i - \frac{S_m}{2}\right)\left(y_{\max} - y_{\min}\right)}{\left(1 - S_m\right)} \tag{7}$$

When selecting the value of $S_m = 0.1$, this means that the actual values are scaled to the interval [0.05 , 0.95] (see Fig. 3).

The training process is usually stopped when the prescribed accuracy is achieved on the training data set. However, there is still an important issue to discuss in order to understand the details. The parameter "training tolerance" is user set, and it should be set according to the special features of each problem studied.

Setting the training tolerance to the desired value (e.g. 0.1) means that the training process will be stopped when, for all training samples, the output value does not differ from the target value by more than 10 % of the training set range. If the target values of the training set lie between 100 and 500, then setting the training tolerance parameter value to 0.1 means that the training process will stop when, for all values, the differences between the target and the approximated values will not differ by more than 40 (10% of 500-100). Formally this can be written with the inequality:

$$for\ all\ i \ ; \quad \left|y_i^T - y_i\right| \ < \ \Delta_T\left(y_{\max} - y_{\min}\right) \tag{8}$$

Here y_i^T represents the target value for the ith sample, y_i is the modelled value for the ith sample, Δ_T is the training tolerance, and $y_{\max}$, $y_{\min}$ are the highest and the lowest value of the training set.

It is not common practice to define the tolerance with regard to the upper and lower values of the observation space. For the case when neural networks are used to approximate the unipolar functions, the absolute error E_d is always smaller than the training tolerance

$$E_d \le \Delta_T \tag{9}$$

The absolute error produced by the neural network approximation for the ith sample becomes:

$$E_i^d = \frac{\left|y_i - y_i^T\right|}{y_{\max}} \tag{10}$$

while the relative error is:

$$E_i^r = \frac{\left|y_i - y_i^T\right|}{y_i^T} \tag{11}$$

and the relation between the absolute and relative error is:

$$E_i^r = E_i^d \frac{y_{\max}}{y_i^T} \tag{12}$$

And furthermore

$$E_i^r \leq \Delta_T \frac{y_{\max}}{y_i^T} \tag{13}$$

An important conclusion follows from the last inequality. At the values where y_i^T is much smaller than $y_{\max}$, the relative error becomes very high, and, therefore, the results of the modelling become useless for these small values. **This implies that the span between $y_{\max}$ and $y_{\min}$ should not be too broad (depending on the particular problem but, if possible, not higher then two decades), otherwise the modelling will result in a very poor performance for the small values.**

To avoid this problem other strategies should be used.

4.2 Approximation for wide range functions

The usual study of neural network systems does not include the use of neural networks in a wide range of input and output conditions.

As shown in the previous section, neural networks do not produce a good approximation when the function to be approximated spans over a wide range (several decades).

The quality of approximation (approximation error) of small values is very poor compared with that of large ones. The problem can be solved by means of:

a. Log/Anti Log Strategy; the common and usual practice is to take the measured points and to perform the logarithm ($\log_{10}$) function. The logartihmic data is then used as input and target values for the neural network; or
b. segmentation strategy; the general idea is to split the input and output space into several smaller segments and perform the neural network training of each segment separately. This also means that each segment is approximated by a separate neural network (sub network). This method not only gives much better approximation results, but it also requires a larger training set (at least 5 data points per segment). It is also a good practice to overlap segments in order to achieve good results on segment borders.

5. Training stability analysis

The training process of a neural network is the process which, if repeated, does not lead to equal results. Each training process starts with different, randomly chosen connection weights so the training starting point is always different. Several repetitions of the training process lead to different outcomes. Stability of the training process refers to a series of outcomes and the maximal and minimal values, i.e., the band that can be expected for the particular solution. The narrower the obtained band, the more stable approximations can be expected (Fig. 4).

The research work on the stability band has been conducted on 160 measured time profile samples. For each sample, 95 different neural network configurations have been systematically tested. Each test has included 100 repetitions of the training process, and each training process required several thousand epochs. From the vast database obtained, statistically firm conclusions can be drawn. So much of work was necessary to prove the importance of the stability band. In practice users need to perform only one or two tests to get the necessary information.

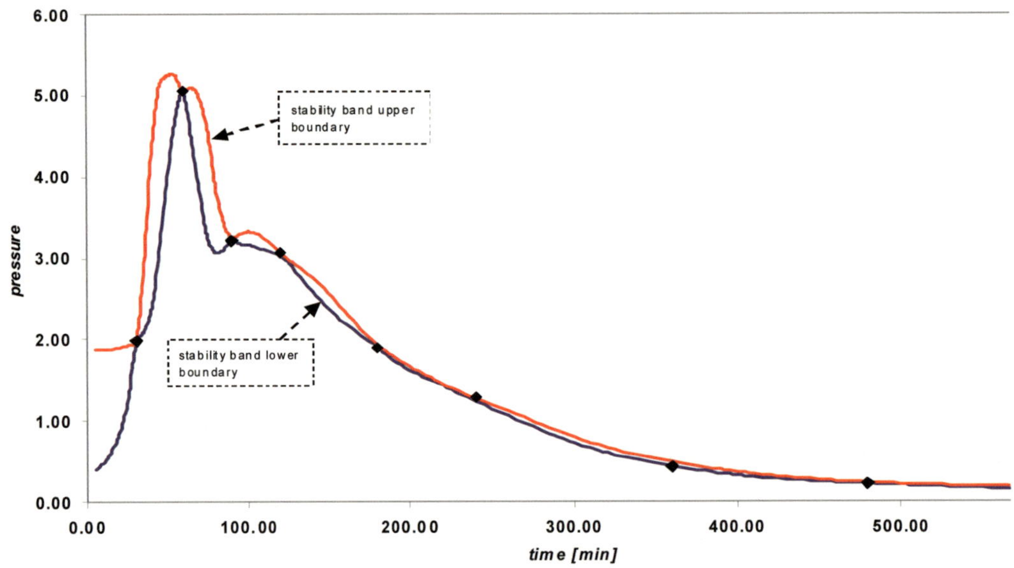

Fig. 4. The different training processes produce different models. A possible outcome of an arbitrarily chosen training process falls within the maximal and minimal boundaries which define the training "stability band".

The procedure for the determination of the training stability band is the following:

1. Perform the first training process based on the training data set and randomly chosen neural network weights.
2. Perform the modelling with the trained neural network in the data points between the training data points.
3. The result of the modelling is the first so-called reference model. This means that the model is used to approximate the unknown function in the space between the measured points. The number of approximated points should be large enough so the approximated function can be evaluated with sufficient density. Practically this means the number of approximated points should be at least 10 times larger than the number of measured data points (in the case presented, the ratio between the number of measured and the number of approximated points was 1:15).
4. Perform the new training process with another set of randomly chosen weights.
5. Compare the outcomes of the new model with the previous one and set the minimal and maximal values for all approximated points. The first band is therefore obtained and bordered by the upper and lower boundaries.

6. Perform the new training process with another set of randomly chosen weights.
7. For each approximated point perform the test to see whether it lies within the established lower or upper boundary. If this is not the case, extend the particular boundary value.
8. Repeat steps 6, 7 and 8 until the prescribed number of repetitions is achieved.

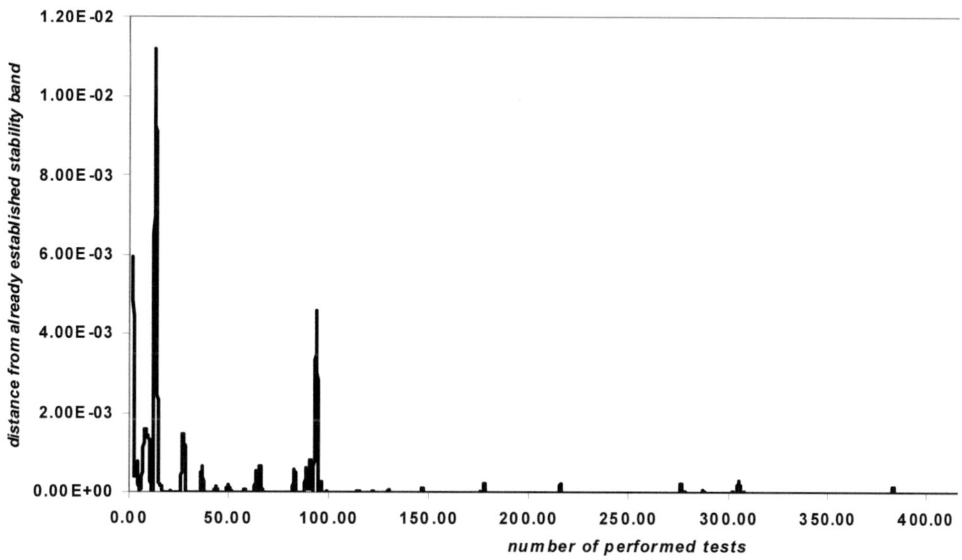

Fig. 5. The training stability upper boundary change vs. the number of separate training experiments. The training stability band does not change significantly after the 100th training experiment.

The practical question is how many times should the training with the different starting values for the connection weights, be performed to assure that the training stability band no longer changes in its upper and lower boundaries. Fig. 5 shows the stability band upper boundary changes for each separate training outcome (the distance from existing boundary and the new boundary). The results are as expected, and more separate trainings are performed, lesser the stability band changes. The recording of the lower boundary change gives very similar results. Fig. 5 shows clearly that the changes after the 100th repetition of training do not bring significant changes in the training stability band. In our further experiments the number of repetitions was therefore fixed to 100. When dealing with any new modelling problem, the number of required training repetitions should be assessed.

Only one single run of a training process is not enough because the obtained model shows only one possible solution, and nothing is really known about the behaviour of the particular neural network modelling in conjunction with the particular problem. In our work, the spinning rotor gauge error extraction modelling was performed and results were very promising (Šetina, et.al., 2006). However, the results could not be repeated. When the training stability test is performed, the range of possible solutions becomes known, and further evaluation of adequacy of the used neural network system is possible. The training stability band is used instead of the worst case approximation analysis. In the case where the complete training stability range is acceptable for the modelling purposes, any trained neural network can be used.

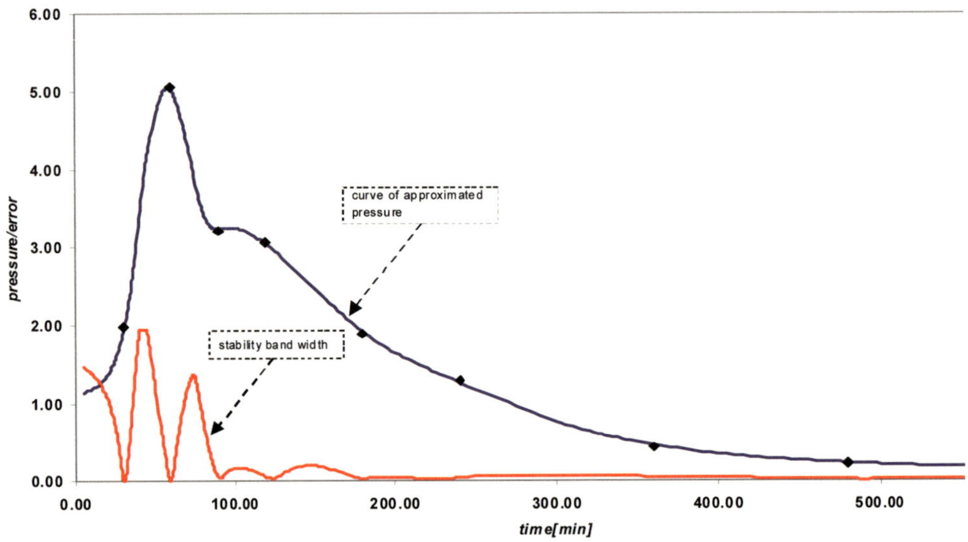

Fig. 6. The upper curve represents the band centre line, which is the most probable model for the given data, and the lower curve represents the band width. The points depict the measured data points that were actually used for training. The lower curve represents the width of the training stability band. The band width is the smallest at the measured points used for training.

When the band is too wide, more emphasis has to be given to find the training process that gives the best modelling. In this case, genetic algorithms can be used to find the best solution (or any other kind of optimization) (Goldberg, 1998).

Following a very large number of performed experiments it was shown that the middle curve (centre line) (Fig. 6) between the maximal and minimal curve is the most probable curve for the observed modelling problem. The training stability band middle range curve can be used as the best approximation, and the training repetition that produces the model closest to the middle curve should be taken as best.

Some practitioners use the strategy of division of the measured points into two sets: one is used for training purposes and the other for the model evaluation purposes. This is a very straightforward strategy, but it works well only when the number of the measured points is large enough (in accordance with the dynamics of the system-sampling theorem). If this is not the case, all measured points should be used for the training purposes, and an analysis of the training stability should be performed.

6. The synthesis (design) of neural networks for modelling purposes

Neural network modelling is always based on the measurement points which describe the modelled system behaviour. It is well known from the information theory that the observed function should be sampled frequently enough in order to preserve the system information. Practically, this means that the data should be gathered at least 10 times faster than the highest frequency (in temporal or spatial sense) produced by the system (Shannon's theorem). If the sampled data is too sparse, the results of the modelling (in fact any kind of modelling) will be poor, and the modelling tools can not be blamed for bad results.

The synthesis of a neural network should be performed in several steps:

1. Select the training data set which should be sampled adequately to represent the observed problem. Input as well as output (target) parameters should be defined.
2. Check the differences between the maximal and minimal values in the training set (for input and output values). If the differences are too high, the training set should be segmented (or logarithmed), and for each segment the separate neural network should be designed.
3. Set the first neural network which should consist of three layers (one being the hidden layer). Set the training tolerance parameter that satisfies the modelling needs. Choose an arbitrary number of neural cells in the hidden layer (let's say 10) and start the training procedure. Observe the way in which the neural network performs the training. If the training process shows a steady decrease of the produced training error, the chosen number of neural cells in the hidden layer is sufficient to build the model. If the output error shows unstable behaviour and it does not decrease with the number of epochs then the number of cells in the hidden layer might be too small and should be increased. If the speed of the neural network output error decreases too slowly for practical needs, then another hidden layer should be introduced. It is interesting that the increase of number of neural cells in one hidden layer does not significantly improve the speed of training convergence. Only addition in a new hidden layer can lower the training convergence speed. Addition of too many hidden layers also can not guarantee better training convergence. There is a certain limit to a training convergence speed that can be reached with an optimal configuration, and it depends on the problem at hand.
4. Perform the training stability test and decide whether further optimization is needed. It is interesting that the training stability band mostly depends on the problem being modelled and that the various neural network configurations do not alter it significantly.
5. At step 4, the design of the neural network is completed and it can be applied to model the problem

Usually, one of the modelled parameters is time. In this case, one of the inputs represents the time points when the data samples were taken. Fig. 6 shows the model of degassing a vacuum system where the x axis represents the time in minutes and the y axis represents the total pressure in the vacuum system (in relative numerical values). In this case, the only input to the neural network was time and the target was to predict the pressure in the vacuum chamber.

7. The example of neural network modelling

Suppose we are to model a bakeout process in a vacuum chamber. The presented example should be intended for industrial circumstances, where one and the same production process is repeated in the vacuum chamber. Prior to the production process, the entire system must be degassed using an appropriate regime depending on the materials used. The model of degassing will be used only to monitor the eventual departure of the vacuum chamber pressure temporal profile. Any difference in the manufacturing process as it is the introduction of different cleaning procedures might result in a different degassing profile. A departure from the usual degassing profile should result in a warning signal indicating possible problems in further production stages.

For the sake of simplicity, only two parameters will be observed, time t and pressure in the vacuum chamber p. Practically, it would be appropriate to monitor temperature, heater current, and eventual critical components of mass spectra as well.

First, it has to be determined which parameters are primary and which are their consequences. In the degassing problem, one of the basic parameters is the heater current, another being time. As a consequence of the heater current, the temperature in the vacuum chamber rises, the degassing process produces the increase of pressure and possible emergence of critical gasses etc. Therefore, the time and the heater current represent the input parameters for the neural network, while parameters such as temperature, pressure, and partial pressures are those to be modelled.

In the simplified model, we suppose that, during the bakeout process, the heater current always remains constant and is only switched on at the start and off after the bakeout. We also suppose that there is no need to model mass spectra and temperature. Therefore, there are two parameters to be modelled, time as the primary parameter and pressure as the consequence (of constant heater current and time).

Since the model will be built for the industrial use, its only purpose is to detect possible anomalies in the bakeout stage. The vacuum chamber is used to process the same type of objects, and no major changes are expected to happen in the vacuum system as well. Therefore, the bakeout process is supposed to be repeatable to some extent.

Several measurements are to be made resulting in the values gathered in Table 1..

Time [min]	Numeric values of pressure
30	0.51
60	0.95
90	0.96
120	1.40
180	2.40
240	2.13
360	1.00
480	0.56
600	0.30

Table 1. Measurements of bakeout of the vacuum system. The time–pressure pairs are the training set for the neural network.

The model is built solely on the data gathered by the measurements on the system. As mentioned before, neural networks do not need any further information on the modelled system.

Once input (time t) and output (pressure p) parameters are determined, the neural network architecture must be chosen. The undertaking theory suggests that one hidden layer neural network should be capable of producing the approximation. Nevertheless, from the practical point of view, it is a better choice to start with a neural network with more then one hidden layer. Let us start with two hidden layers and with 10 neurons in each hidden layer. One neuron is used for the input layer and one for the output layer. The configuration architecture can be denoted as **1 10 10 1** (see Fig 2 right).

The measured values are the training set, therefore, the neural network is trained to reproduce time-pressure pairs and to approximate pressure for any point in the space between them.

Once the configuration is set and the training set prepared, the training process can start. It completes successfully when all the points from the training set are reproduced within the set tolerance (1% or other appropriate value). A certain number of training epochs is used for the successful training completion.

The result of training is a neural network model which is, of course, only one of many possible models. For any serious use of such model, the training process should be repeated several times and the outcomes should be carefully studied. With several repetitions of training process on the same training set, the training stability band can be determined. Fig. 7 shows the training stability band for the training set from the Table 1 and for the neural network configuration 1 10 10 1, where dots represent the measured points included in the training set.

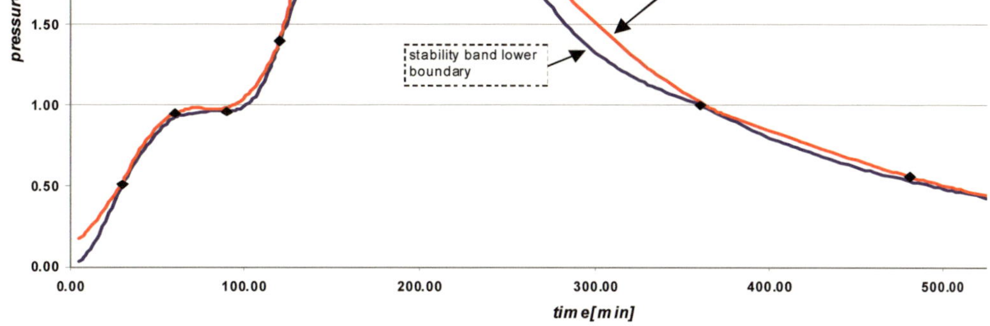

Fig. 7. The training stability band for the presented example. The measured points are depicted with dots, and their numeric values are given in Table 1.

If the training stability band is narrow enough, there is no real need to proceed with further optimisation of the model, otherwise the search for optimal or, at least, a sufficient model should continue.

It is interesting to observe the width of the training stability band for different neural network configurations. Fig. 8 provides the results of such study for the training set from the Table 1. It is important to notice that the diagram on Fig. 8 shows the average stability band-width for each neural network configuration. Compared to the values of the measured dependence, the average widths are relatively small, which is not always the case for maximal values of a training stability band. It would be more appropriate for certain problems to observe the maximal value of training stability band width instead of the average values.

On the other hand, the width of the training stability band is only one parameter to be observed. From the practical point of view, it is also important to know how time consuming the training procedure for different configurations really is. Fig. 9 provides some insights into this detail of neural network modelling. Even a brief comparison of Fig. 8 and Fig. 9 clearly shows that neural networks that enable a quick training process are not necessary those which also provide the narrowest training stability band.

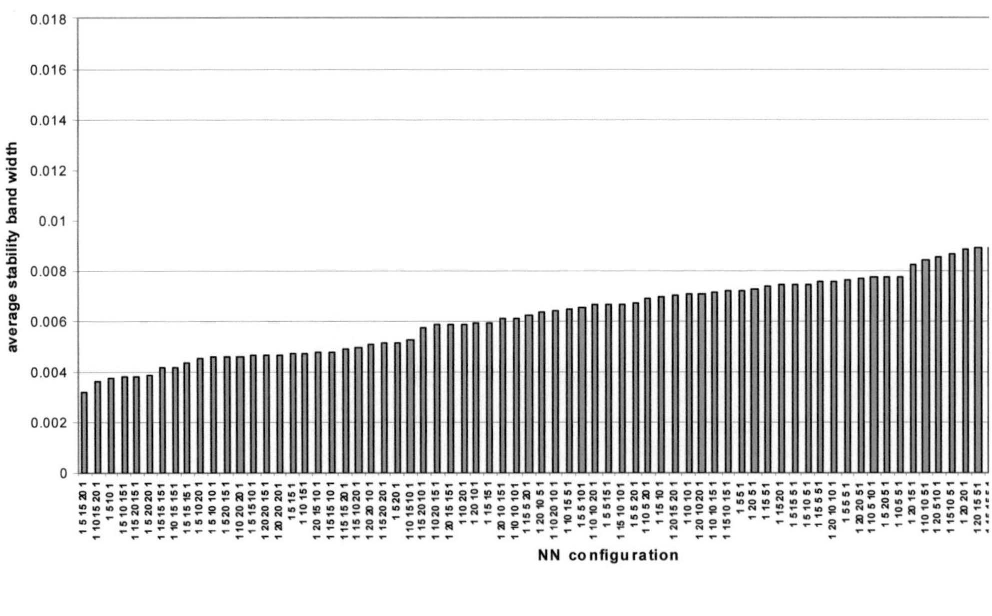

Fig. 8. Dependence of the average width of the training stability band versus the neural network configuration.

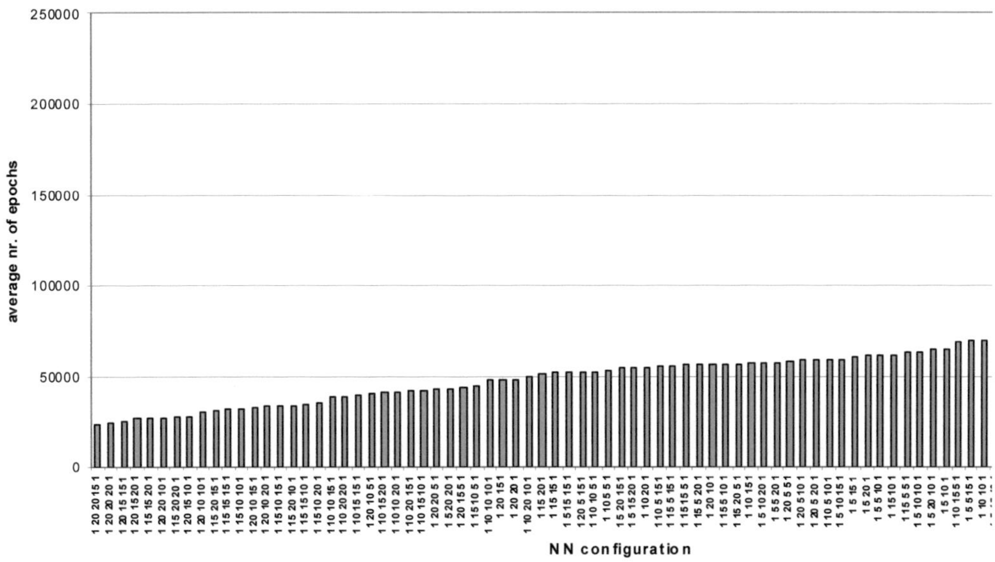

Fig. 9. Dependence of the average number of epochs versus the neural network configuration. The higher number of epochs needed usually means faster.

Fig. 10 is a representation of two properties: the average number of epochs (x axis), and the average training stability band width (y axis). Each point in the graph represents one neural network configuration. Interesting configurations are specially marked. It is interesting that the configuration with only one hidden layer performs very poorly. Even an increased number of neurons in the neural network with only one hidden layer does not improve the situation significantly.

If we seek for the configuration that will provide best results for the given trainig data set, we will try to provide the configuration that trains quickly (low number of epochs) and features the lowest possible training stability band width. Such configurations are 1 20 20 20 1 and 1 15 20 15 1. If we need the lowest possible training stability band-width then we will choose the configuration 1 5 15 20 1.

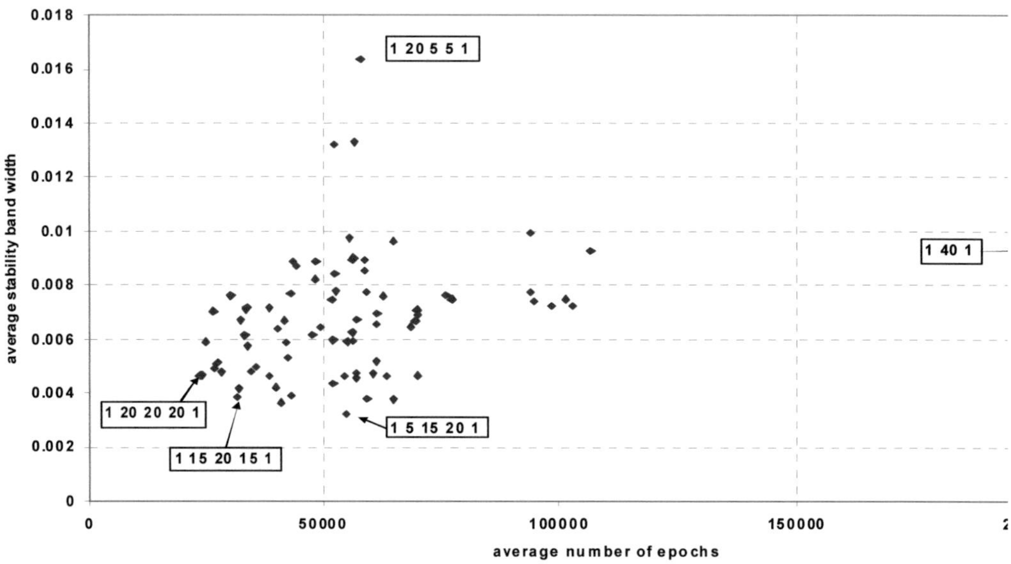

Fig. 10. The optimisation process seeks the neural network that uses both the lowest possible number of epochs while producing an approximation with the narrowest training stability band. Each dot on the graph represents one neural network configuration. Interesting configurations are highlighted.

8. Conclusions

The field of neural networks as a tool for approximation (modelling) is very rapidly evolving. Numerous authors have reported their research results on the topic.

In this chapter, two very important issues of the theory of approximation are questioned. One is the universality of approximation, and the second is the best approximation property. Both properties are not applicable to the neural networks that run on digital computers.

Theoretically, it has been proven that a three layer neural network can approximate any kind of function. Although this is theoretically true, it is not a practical situation since the number of epochs needed to reach the prescribed approximation precision drops significantly with the increase in the number of hidden layers.

The newly introduced concept of approximation of wide-range functions by using logarithmic or segmented values gives the possibility to use neural networks as approximators in special cases where the modelled function has values spanning over several decades.

The training stability analysis is a tool for assessment of training diversity of neural networks. It gives information on the possible outcomes of the training process. It also provides the ground for further optimization.

The important conclusions from the presented example are that the nature of the modelled problem dictates which neural network configuration performs the most appropriate approximation, and that, for each data set to be modelled, a separate neural network training performance analysis should be performed.

9. References

Aggelogiannaki, E., Sarimveis, H., Koubogiannis, D. (2007). Model predictive temperaturecontrol in long ducts by means of a neural network approximation tool. *Applied Thermal Engineering.* 27 pp 2363–2369

Ait Gougam, L., Tribeche, M. , Mekideche-Chafa, F. (2008). A systematic investigation of a neural network for function approximation. *Neural Networks.* 21 pp 1311-1317

Bahi, J.M., Contassot-Vivier , S., Sauget, M. (2009). An incremental learning algorithm for function approximation. *Advances in Engineering Software.* 40 pp 725–730

Belič, I. (2006). Neural networks and modelling in vacuum science. *Vacuum.* Vol. 80, pp 1107-1122

Bertels, K, Neuberg, L., Vassiliadis, S., Pechanek, D.G. (1998). Chaos and neural network learning - Some observations. *Neural Process. Lett.* 7, pp 69-80

Caoa, F., Xiea, T., Xub, Z.(2008). The estimate for approximation error of neural networks: A constructive approach. *Neurocomputing* . 71 pp 626–630

Goldberg, D.E. (1998). *Genetic Algorithms in Search, Optimization, and Machine Learning.* Addison-Wesley

Huang, W.Z., Huang, Y. (2008). Chaos of a new class of Hopfield neural networks. *Applied Mathematics and Computation.* 206, (1) pp 1-11

Kurkova, V. (1995). Approximation of functions by perceptron networks with bounded number of hidden units. *Neural Networks.* 8 (5), pp 745-750

Mhaskar, H.N. (1996). Neural Networks and Approximation Theory. *Neural Networks,* 9, (4), pp 721-722

Šetina, J., Belič, I. (2006). Neural-network modeling of a spinning-rotor-gauge zero correction under varying ambient temperature conditions. In: *JVC 11, 11th Joint Vacuum Conference,* September 24 - 28, 2006, Prague, Czech Republic. Programme and book of abstracts, pp 99-100

Tikk, D., Kóczy, L.T., Gedeon, T.D. (2003). A survey on universal approximation and its limits in soft computing techniques. *International Journal of Approximate Reasoning.* 33(2), pp 185-202

Yuan, Q., Li, Q., Yang, X.S. (2009). Horseshoe chaos in a class of simple Hopfield neural networks. *Chaos, Solitons and Fractals* 39 pp 1522–1529

Wang, J., Xub, Z. (2010). New study on neural networks: The essential order of approximation. *Neural Networks.* 23 pp 618-624

Wang, T., Wang, K., Jia, N. (2011). Chaos control and associative memory of a time-delay globally coupled neural network using symmetric map. *Neurocomputing* 74 pp 1673–1680

Wena, C., Ma, X. (2008). A max-piecewise-linear neural network for function approximation. *Neurocomputing* . 71 pp 843–852

Wray, J., Green, G.G.R. (1994). Neural Networks, Approximation Theory and Finite Precision Computing. *Neural Networks*. 8 (1)

2

A Framework for Bridging the Gap Between Symbolic and Non-Symbolic AI

Gehan Abouelseoud[1] and Amin Shoukry[2]
[1]*Alexandria University*
[2]*Computer Science and Eng. Dept, Egypt-Japan University of Science and Technology (EJUST), Alexandria, Egypt*

1. Introduction

FRS (Fuzzy Rule Systems) and ANNs (Artificial Neural Networks) have gained much popularity due to their capabilities in modeling human knowledge and in learning from data, respectively. Fuzzy systems have the advantage of allowing users to incorporate available experts' knowledge directly in the fuzzy model [2]. Thus, decisions made by fuzzy systems are transparent to the user (i.e. the reasons behind the decisions made are clearly understood by tracing the decision and finding out which rules fired and contributed to it). However, there are many parameters whose values are arbitrary. These values have to be "guessed" by a fuzzy system designer, yet they largely influence the system behavior. Thus, a fuzzy system is as good as its programmer.

On the other hand, ANNs have the advantage of being universal functions approximators, requiring only sample data points and no expert knowledge [3]. Despite their advantages, they are essentially black box models. This means that the reasons behind their decisions are concealed in the knowledge acquired in the trained weights. However, these usually have no clear logical interpretation. Thus, their reliability is questionable.

To combine the advantages of both systems while overcoming their disadvantages, two approaches have been proposed in literature. The first is rule extraction from weights of trained ANNs [4]-[7]. However, the proposed approaches often yield some "un-plausible" rules, thus rule pruning and retraining is often required. For examples, some rules may be impossible i.e. their firing depends on conditions that can never occur in reality (*impossible antecedents*). For example, a rule dictating that a certain action is to be taken in case time is negative. The second approach is ANFIS [8], which attempts to cast the fuzzy system as an ANN with five layers. Although, only two of these layers are adaptable, this model is still more complicated to build and train than a conventional feed-forward ANN for two main reasons. First, the user's expertise is required to choose appropriate consequent (output) membership functions. Second, the desired output needs to be known a priori. This may not be possible for several applications including design problems, inverse problems and high dimensional problems. For example, in a robot path tracking problem, the ANN is required to predict the correct control input. In such application, the desired performance is known but no real-solid rules exist, especially, if the robot is required to be self-adaptive. Similarly, consider a car shape optimization problem. The ANN is required to estimate the shape parameters required to achieve certain air resistance during car motion. Constraints on the shape parameters exist; however, no clear rule database exists relating shape parameters to the desired performance.

The present work proposes a new approach that combines the advantages of fuzzy systems and ANNs through a simple modification of ANN's activation calculations. The proposed approach yields weights that are readily interpretable as logical consistent fuzzy rules because it includes the "semantic" of both input and output variables in the learning/optimization process.

The rest of the chapter is organized as follows. Section II describes the proposed framework. Section III demonstrates its effectiveness through a case study. Section IV shows how it to can be generalized to solve optimization problems. An illustrative example is given for this purpose. Finally, Section V concludes the chapter with a summary of the advantages of the proposed approach.

2. The proposed approach

Fig.1 shows a typical feed-forward ANN with a single hidden layer of sigmoid neurons. Conventionally, the output of such an ANN is given by:

$$o_k = \sum_{j=1}^{N_h} w_{jk} sig\left(\sum_{i=1}^{N_i} w_{hij} x_i^p + b_j \right) \tag{1}$$

where $w_{hij}, b_j, w_{jk}, x_i^p, N_h, N_i, o_k$ are the weight of the connection between the ith input to the jth hidden neuron, the bias of the jth hidden neuron, the weight of the connection between the jth hidden neuron and the kth output neuron, the number of hidden neurons, the number of inputs (elements in each input pattern), the kth output, respectively. The number of output neurons is N_o.

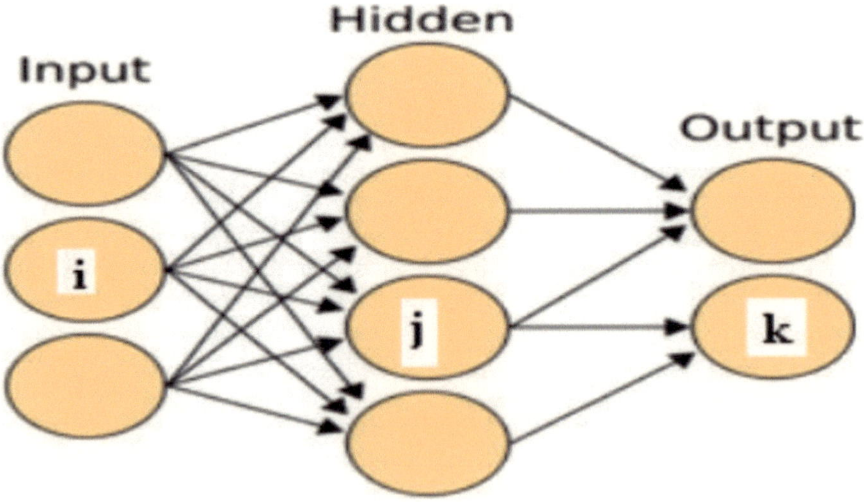

Fig. 1. Architecture of a typical feed-forward ANN

It has been proved in [1] that the sigmoid response to a sum of inputs is equivalent to combining the sigmoid response to each input using the fuzzy logic operator "ior" (interactive or). The truth table of the "ior" operator is shown in table 1. The truth table can be readily generalized to an arbitrary number of inputs. Eq.(1) can, thus, be interpreted as the output of a fuzzy inference system, where the weight w_{jk} is the action recommended by fuzzy rule *j*. However, this w_{jk} does not contribute directly to the ANN output. Instead, its contribution to the output is weighted by the sigmoid term $sig\left(\sum_{i=1}^{N_i} w_{hij} x_i^p + b_j\right)$.

The sigmoid term corresponds to the degree of firing of the rule, which judges to what extent rule 'j' should participate in the ANN final decision. Moreover, the inference is based on 'ior' rather than the product/'and' fuzzy operator used in ANFIS. It is clear from the 'ior' truth table that the 'ior' operator decides that a rule fully participate in the ANN final decision if all its inputs satisfy their corresponding constraints or if some of them does, while the others are neutral. On the other hand, it decides that the rule should not participate if one or some of the inputs do not satisfy their constraints, while the others are neutral. In the case that some of the inputs completely satisfy the constraints; while others completely violate them, the rule becomes neutral participating by half-weighted recommended action in the final ANN output. The mathematical expression for "ior" is as follows [1]:

$$ior(a_1, a_2, \ldots\ldots\ldots, a_n) = \frac{a_1.a_2 \ldots\ldots\ldots\ldots a_n}{(1-a_1).(1-a_2)\ldots\ldots\ldots(1-a_n) + a_1.a_2\ldots\ldots\ldots a_n} \quad (2)$$

In linguistic terms, an antecedent formed by "ior-ing" several conditions, is equivalent to replacing the conventional phrase: "*if* A & B & --- then" with "So long as none of the conditions A, B, ... are violated --- then". Throughout the paper we will use the Mnemonic "SLANCV" as a shortcut for this phrase. Thus we can say that Eq. 1 can be restated as a set of rules taking the following format:

$$SLANCV \quad x_i^p > -\left(b_j / N_i\right) / w_{hij} \quad then \quad o_{jk} = w_{jk}$$
$$i = 1,2,\ldots,N_i$$

Despite the successful deployment of the "ior" based rule extraction in several applications ([1], [6] and [7]), it has several disadvantages. For example, the weights and biases of a hidden neuron have no direct clear logical interpretation. This makes the incorporation of available knowledge difficult. Such knowledge is of great use in accelerating the ANN training procedure. Besides, leaving weights and biases values unconstrained often lead to some un-plausible rules (rules with impossible antecedent) that need pruning. Therefore, to overcome these disadvantages, our approach is to modify Eq.(1) as follows:

$$o_k = \sum_{j=1}^{N_h} w_{jk}^c sig\left(\sum_{i=1}^{N_i} w_{hij}^c (x_i^p - b_{ij}^c)\right) \quad (3)$$

where, w_{hij}^{c} are the weights joining input *i* to hidden neuron *j*, and w_{jk}^{c} are the weights joining hidden neuron *j* to output neuron *k*.

The superscript '*c*' denotes that these weights are constrained. In general, a constrained variable Par^{c} that directly appears in Eq. (3) is related to its corresponding free optimization variable *Par* by the following transformation:

$$Par^{c} = (Parmx - Parmn)\, sig\left(\frac{Par}{\max(Parmx, (Parmn())} \right) + Parmn \quad (4)$$

where, $Parmx, Parmn$ are the maximum and minimum values of the parameter, respectively.

Comparing Eqs. (1) and (3), it is clear that our approach introduces two simple, yet effective, modifications:

- First, in Eq. (3), w_{hij} is taken as a common factor to the bracket containing the input and bias. Second, there is a bias corresponding to each input (b_{ij}). Using these two modifications, Eq.(3) has a simple direct fuzzy interpretation.

$$SLANCV \quad x_i^p > b_{ij}^c\left(ifw^c{}_{hij} > 0\right), x_i^p < b_{ij}^c\left(ifw^c{}_{hij} < 0\right) \quad then$$

$$o_{jk} = w^c{}_{jk}, where\ i = 1,2,...,N_i$$

First Input	Second Input	IOR Output
0	0	0
0	0.5	0
1	0.5	1
0.5	0.5	0.5
1	0	0.5
0	1	0.5
1	1	1
0.5	1	1
0.5	0	0

Table 1. Truth Table of the IOR- Operator.

This direct interpretation makes it easy for the designer to incorporate available knowledge through appropriate weight initialization; as will be made clear in the adopted case study.

- The weights and biases included in Eq. (3) are constrained according to limits defined by the system designer. This ensures that the deduced rules are logically sound and consistent.

Furthermore, often, the nature of a problem poses constraints on the ANN output. Two possible approaches; are possible; to satisfy this requirement:

- Modifying Eq.(2) by replacing the sigmoid with a normalized sigmoid.

$$o_k = \sum_{j=1}^{N_h} w_{jk}^c \frac{sig\left(\sum_{i=1}^{N_i} w_{hij}^c (x_i^p - b_{ij}^c)\right)}{\sum_{j=1}^{N_h} sig\left(\sum_{i=1}^{N_i} w_{hij}^c (x_i^p - b_{ij}^c)\right)} \quad (5)$$

- Adding a penalty term to the objective function used in the ANN training so as to impose a maximum limit to its output.

In this research, we adopted the first approach.

To apply the proposed approach to a particular design problem, there are essentially three phases

1. Initialization and knowledge incorporation: In this phase, the designer defines the number of rules (hidden neurons) and chooses suitable weights and biases constraints.
2. Training phase.
3. Rule Analysis and Post-Rule-Analysis Processing: The weights are interpreted as fuzzy rules. A suitable method is used to analyse the rules and improve the system performance based on the insight gained from this rule analysis.

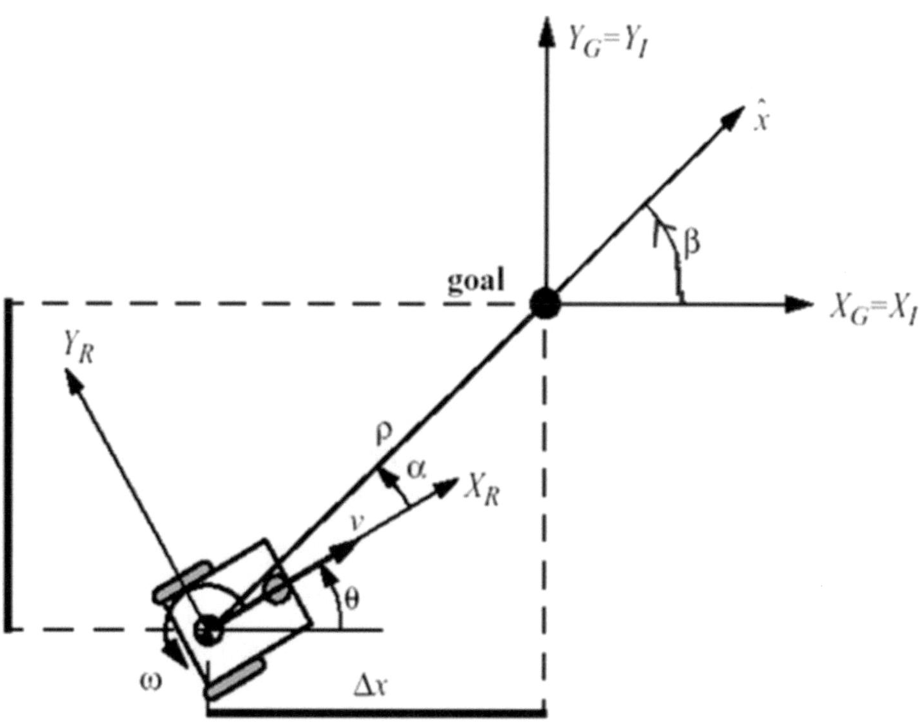

Fig. 2. Parameters used to describe the path tracking problem.

3. Case study: Robot path tracking

In this example, an ANN is adapted to assist a differential-wheel robot in tracking an arbitrary path. Fig. 2 illustrates the geometry of the problem. The robot kinematic model, the need for a closed loop solution, the choice of a suitable representation for the ANN's inputs and outputs as well as the initialization, training and interpretation of the weights of the obtained ANN, are discussed below.

3.1 The robot kinematic model

The kinematic model of the robot is described by the following equations:

$$\begin{aligned} \dot{X}_R &= v \quad \cos\theta \\ \dot{Y}_R &= v \quad \sin\theta \\ \dot{\theta} &= \omega \end{aligned} \tag{6}$$

Where

$$\dot{X}_R, \dot{Y}_R, \theta, \omega$$

represent the horizontal, vertical components of the robot linear velocity v, its orientation angle and its angular velocity, respectively. Once a suitable control algorithm determines v and ω , it is straightforward to determine the corresponding v_r , v_l values by solving the following 2 simultaneous equations:

$$v = \frac{v_r + v_l}{2} \qquad \omega = \frac{v_r - v_l}{l} \tag{7}$$

where l is the distance between the right and left wheels to yield:

$$v_r = \frac{2\mathrm{v} + \omega l}{2}, v_l = \frac{2\mathrm{v} - \omega l}{2} \tag{8}$$

It is clear from (7) that an average positive (negative) velocity indicates forward (reverse) motion along the robot current axis orientation. Similarly, it is clear from (8), that a positive (negative) difference between v_r and v_l indicates a rotate-left or counter-clockwise (rotate-right or clockwise) action. In case both wheels speeds are equal in magnitude and opposite in sign, the robot rotates in-place.

3.2 Open vs closed loop solutions of the path tracking problem

Consider a path with known parametric representation $\left(x(t), y(t)\right)$. In this case, the robot reference linear and angular velocities (denoted v_{ref} and ω_{ref}) can be calculated based on the known desired performance. For the robot to follow the desired path closely, its velocity should be tangent to the path. Thus the reference velocities can be computed using:

$$v_{ref} = \sqrt{\dot{x}(t)^2 + \dot{y}(t)^2}$$
$$w_{ref} = \frac{d}{dt}\sin^{-1}\left(\frac{\dot{y}(t)}{v_{ref}}\right) \tag{9}$$

Applying the control inputs (v_{ref} and ω_{ref}) (or equivalently (v_r and v_l)) to the robot would enable it; in the absence of noise and other types of inaccuracies; to follow the required path. This open loop design will be called the "*direct forcing case*".

However, to assist the ANN in learning the concept of a path (not an instance of a path) as well as making it robust against disturbances, we need to find a closed-loop control law. This is not straightforward because the kinematics model is nonlinear. In what follows, our objective is to show how the proposed ANN-based framework can provide reliable closed-loop control; of the form shown in Fig. (3); compared to the direct forcing case. In Fig. (3), the role of the Robot kinematics simulator is to predict the robot location at the current time step given its current control inputs.

For the purpose of illustration, we will restrict our case study to the following family of paths:

$$x(t) = bt; 0 < b < 1 \quad \text{and} \quad y(t) = ct^3; -1 < c < 1$$

where 't' is the time vector= [0 (start time):0.05(time step):1 (final time)].

The ANN is trained on randomly chosen 11 members of this family and tested on different 11 members of the same family. To demonstrate the robustness of the proposed approach an additive disturbance (of uniform distribution) is added to both v and ω. The value of the disturbance can reach up to 200% of v value and 100% of ω value.

3.3 Choice of the ANN's inputs and outputs

Several possible input-output choices exist. The first has been reported in [11]. The time is the input and the speeds are the output. An alternative choice is to consider the coordinates (x, y) of each point on the path; as inputs; and the corresponding actions (speeds); as output. The third choice is to input the path as a whole as a single input vector and the corresponding sequence of actions (speeds) as a single output vector. All these choices share two fundamental disadvantages. First, it is impossible to interpret the trained weights as fuzzy rules. Furthermore, the ANN does not learn the "concept" of path tracking in general. Instead, it learns to track a single path only. In addition, the first and second choices do not explicitly capture the relation between consecutive path points. To overcome these limitations, we investigated different combinations of ANN inputs and outputs.

Only the two input-output combinations, that produced the best results, are discussed:

i. Case "A":

The inputs to the ANN are chosen to be:

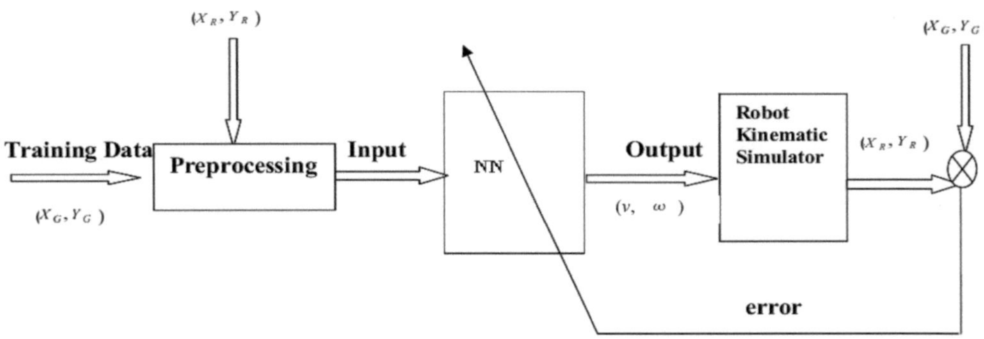

Fig. 3. A typical closed loop Block diagram for the flow of information in the Robot Path Tracking Problem

- the distance 'ρ' to the goal point, $\rho = \sqrt{(X_G - X_R)^2 + (Y_G - Y_R)^2}$
- the angle 'α' that the robot needs to rotate to orient itself in the direction of the goal.

Refering to Fig. (2), α is calculated using the following equations:

$$\beta = \tan^{-1}\left(\frac{Y_G - Y_R}{X_G - X_R}\right), \alpha = -\theta + \beta$$

- the deviations between the actual and reference robot linear and angular velocities $(v_{ref} - v_{rob})$ and $(\omega_{ref} - \omega_{rob})$

The outputs are the corrections (increase/ decrease) (v_{inc}, ω_{inc}) needed for (v, ω) to keep following the required path. Fig. 4 shows the block diagram of this system.

ii. Case "B"

The inputs and outputs are as in case A, with the following two additional inputs:

- the previous control inputs (v, ω).

Fig. 5 shows the block diagram of this system.

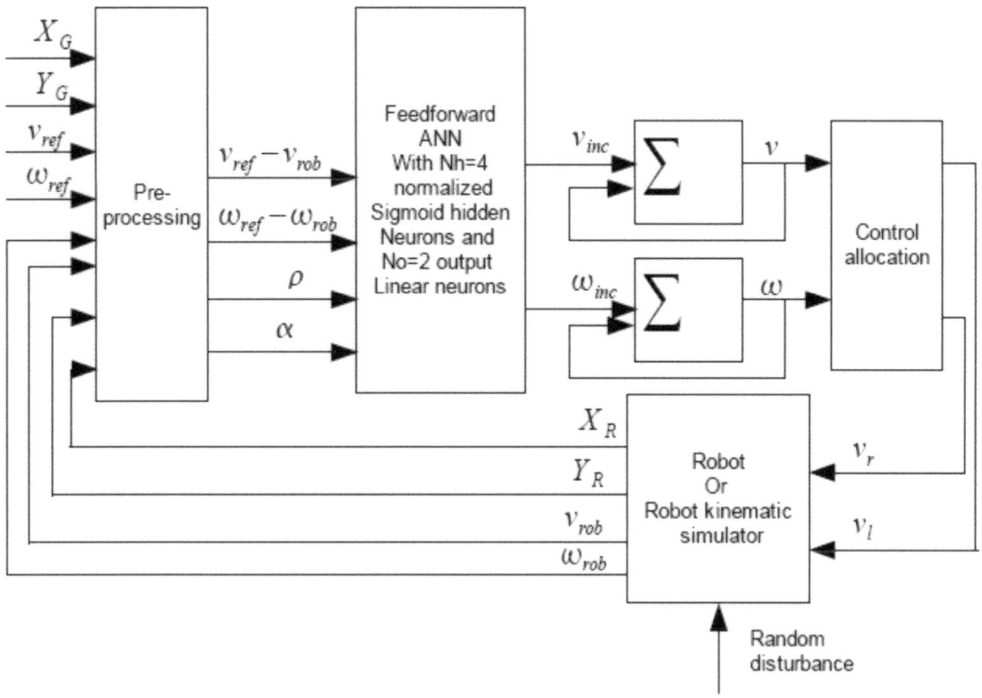

Fig. 4. Block diagram of the system in case study case A

3.4 Initialization and knowledge incorporation phase

Knowledge of the range of each input and output variables helps in the proper initialization of both the weights and biases. Recall that N_i is the number of inputs, N_o is the number of outputs, N_h is the number of hidden neurons (which corresponds to the number of rules used by the ANN in decision making). Biases are stored in a matrix B^c of dimensions N_i x N_h : Thus, each column of B^c corresponds to a certain rule. Each entry (row number, column number), in B^c, contains the threshold to which the corresponding input is compared in a particular rule (corresponding to that column). The weights connecting the inputs to the hidden neurons are stored in a matrix Wh^c of dimensions N_i x N_h . As before, each column corresponds to a certain rule. This time, however, the sign of the number in each entry (row number , column number), in Wh^c, controls the comparison operator with the corresponding threshold stored in B^c (negative corresponds to "less than", while positive corresponds to "greater than"). Thus, each column from B^c together with the corresponding column from Wh^c determine the antecedent of a 'SLANCV' rule. The weights connecting the hidden neurons to the output neurons are stored in a matrix Wo^c of dimensions N_h x N_o . The numbers in each row of Wo^c indicate the outputs (consequents) suggested by a certain rule. Such an interpretation of the weights/bias matrices as rules antecedents/ consequents helps in selecting suitable initial values for the ANN's parameters as well as understanding its decisions after training. For example, at initialization, the values in each row of B^c should be constrained to lie within the range of possible values for this input. For instance, if the third input is ρ , then the entries in the third row of B^c should all be positive. Similarly, if the first output is the velocity correction v_{inc} then the first column of Wo^c can take both negative /positive small values to allow the ANN to increase or decrease the robot speed while avoiding instability.

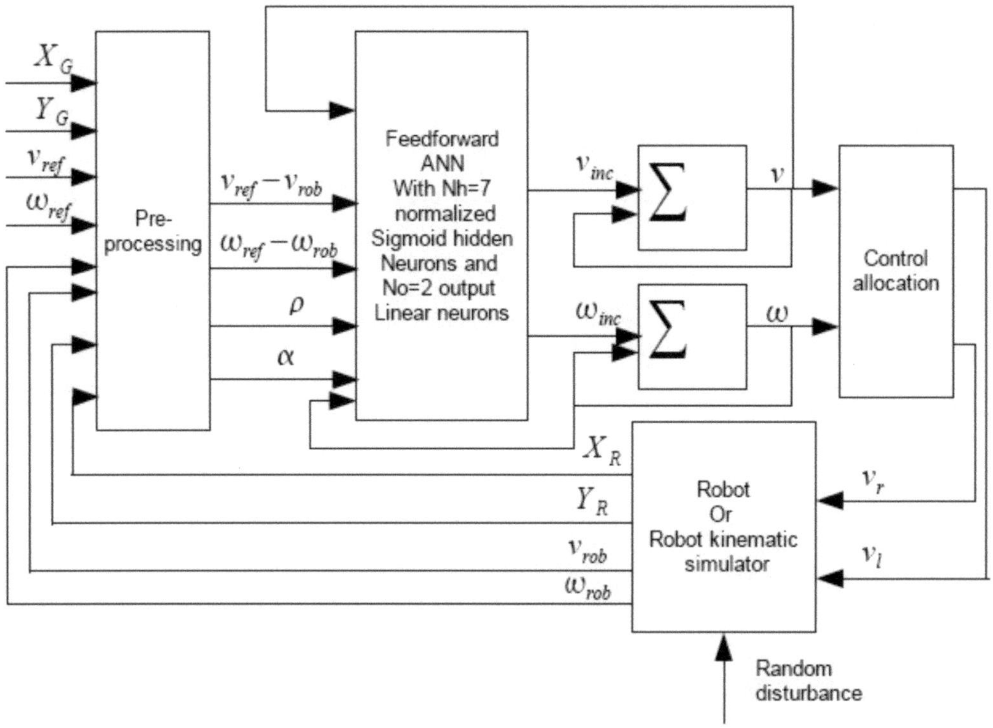

Fig. 5. Block diagram of the system in case study case B

3.5 Training phase

To train the ANN, the following objective function is minimized:

$$objg = \frac{1}{N_p} \sum_{p=1}^{N_p} \sum_{i=1}^{K_i} \rho_i^p \tag{10}$$

where ' ρ_i^p ' is the distance between the desired location on the pth path and the corresponding robot's actual location at the ith time instant, K_i is the number of points along the path to be tracked and N_p is the number of paths used in training. Since the objective function is not a closed form function (in the ANN weights and biases) and can only be computed through a simulator, a numerical optimization algorithm is used [10], [11], where gradients are computed using a numerical version of the Broyden–Fletcher–Goldfarb–Shanno (*BFGS*) optimization algorithm. The gradients are calculated numerically using the following formula:

$$\frac{\partial Objg}{\partial Par_i} = \frac{Objg(Par_i + \varepsilon) - Objg(Par_i - \varepsilon)}{2\varepsilon} \tag{11}$$

where ε is a very small number, typically $\varepsilon = 10^{-11}$. Par_i is the ith element of the vector *Par*

For case 'A', the number of adjustable parameters is 2* (4 (inputs) * 4 (hidden neurons/ rules)) + 4 (hidden neurons)* 2 (outputs), which equals 40 parameters. For case B, the number of adjustable parameters is 2* (6 (inputs) * 7 (hidden neurons/ rules)) + 7 (hidden neurons)* 2 (outputs), which equals 98 parameters . Figs. (6 and 7) show the results for cases 'A' and 'B', respectively.

It is clear that case 'B' is more robust to disturbance. However, both cases clearly outperform the open loop (direct forcing) case.

The fact that case 'B' produced better results is to be expected. Certainly, feedback provides memory to the system and helps in accumulating knowledge, which is an essential aspect of learning. We tried two types of feedback; direct feedback in which the ANN learns the link between its own outputs (v_{inc}, ω_{inc}) and the errors in performance and indirect feedback in which the ANN learns the link between a certain action (v, ω) and the errors in performance. The second memory type produced better results. Appendix A compares these results obtained using our approach with those obtained using conventional ANN [1,6,7] and ANFIS [8].

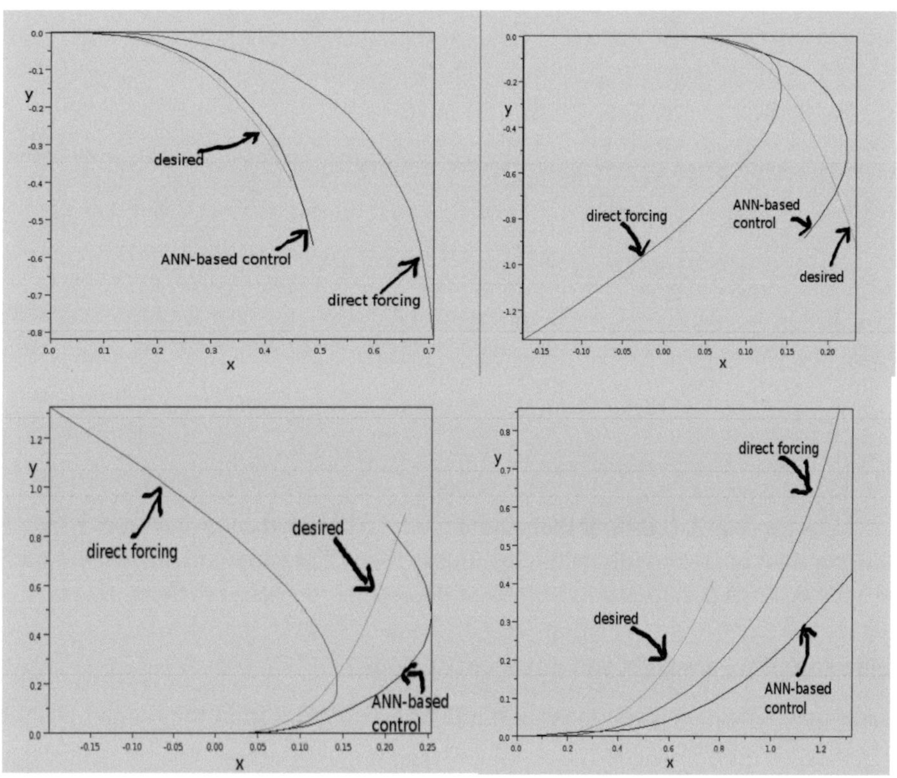

Fig. 6. Results for case A. It is clear that closed loop ANN-based control is more robust to disturbances than open-loop direct forcing

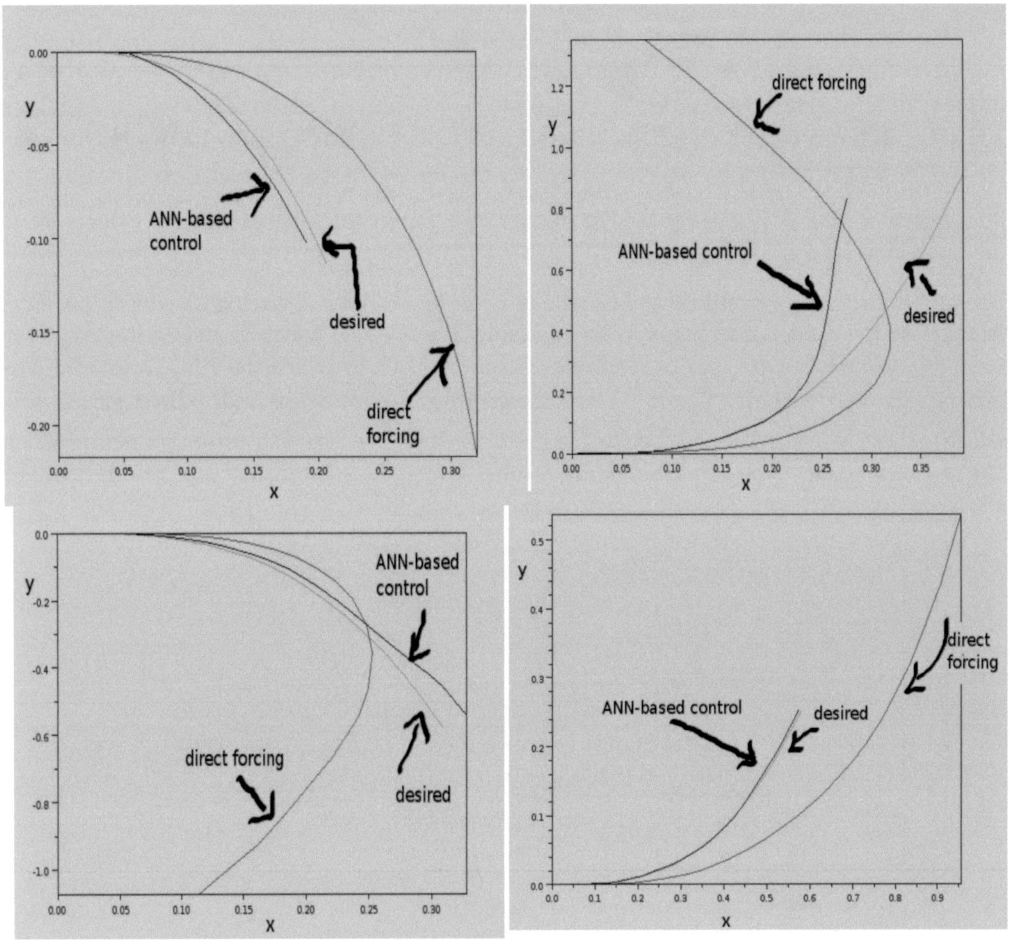

Fig. 7. Results for case B. It is clear that closed loop ANN-based control is more robust to disturbances than open-loop direct forcing. It is evident that adding to the ANN inputs the control actions at the previous step improved the results compared to those of case A.

3.6 Rule extraction, analysis and post-processing

Following the guidelines given in section 3.4, rule extraction from the trained weights and biases becomes straightforward.

Fig. (8) illustrates how the rules, for case 'A', have been extracted. The discovered rule-base is summarized as follows :

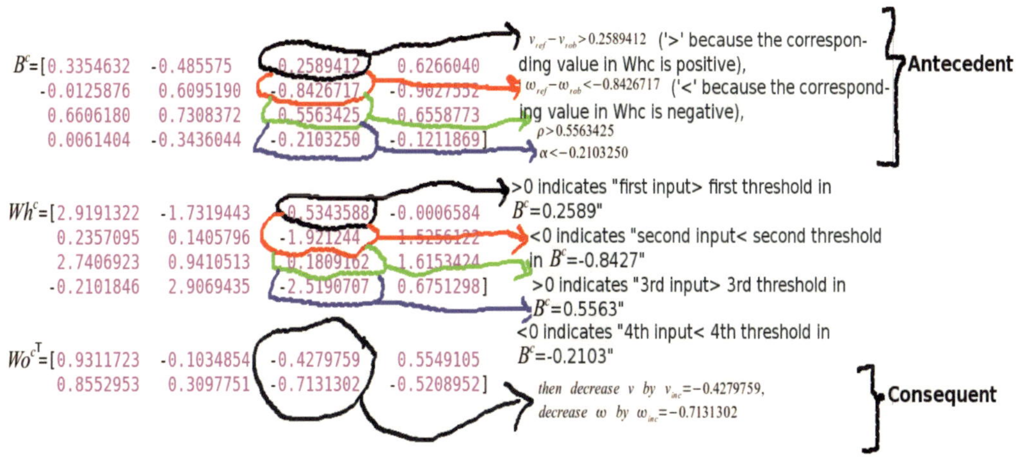

Fig. 8. An illustration of the rules extraction from weights and biases matrices.

$$\begin{aligned}
&SLANCV \quad v_{ref} - v_{rob} > 0.3354632, \quad \omega_{ref} - \omega_{rob} > -0.0125876, \quad \rho > 0.6606180, \quad a < 0.0061404 \\
&\quad then \quad increase \quad v \quad by \quad v_{inc} = 0.9311723, \quad increase \quad \omega \quad by \quad \omega_{inc} = 0.8552953 \\
&SLANCV \quad v_{ref} - v_{rob} < -0.485575, \quad \omega_{ref} - \omega_{rob} > 0.6095190, \quad \rho > 0.7308372, \quad a > -0.3436044 \\
&\quad then \quad decrease \quad v \quad by \quad v_{inc} = -0.1034854 \quad increase \quad \omega \quad by \quad \omega_{inc} = 0.3097751 \\
&SLANCV \quad v_{ref} - v_{rob} > 0.2589412, \quad \omega_{ref} - \omega_{rob} < -0.8426717, \quad \rho > 0.5563425, \quad a < -0.2103250 \\
&\quad then \quad decrease \quad v \quad by \quad v_{inc} = -0.4279759, \quad decrease \quad \omega \quad by \quad \omega_{inc} = -0.7131302 \\
&SLANCV \quad v_{ref} - v_{rob} < 0.6266040, \quad \omega_{ref} - \omega_{rob} < -0.9027552, \quad \rho > 0.6558773, \quad a > -0.1211869 \\
&\quad then \quad increase \quad v \quad by \quad v_{inc} = 0.5549105, \quad decrease \quad \omega \quad by \quad \omega_{inc} = -0.5208952
\end{aligned}$$

Similarly, the rule-base for case 'B' is summarized as follows:

$$\begin{aligned}
&SLANCV \quad v > 1.1800783, \quad \omega < 0.5797996, \quad v_{ref} - v_{rob} > 0.3283071, \quad \omega_{ref} - \omega_{rob} > -0.1895662, \\
&\quad \rho > 1.2352848, \quad a > -0.3088343 \quad then \\
&\quad increase \quad v \quad by \quad v_{inc} = 0.6156011 \quad increase \quad \omega \quad by \quad \omega_{inc} = 0.8038080 \\
&SLANCV \quad v > 1.258573, \quad \omega > 0.817993, \quad v_{ref} - v_{rob} < -0.4339714, \quad \omega_{ref} - \omega_{rob} > 0.0552364, \\
&\quad \rho > 1.246724, \quad a > 0.2514984 \quad then \\
&\quad decrease \quad v \quad by \quad v_{inc} = -0.6117282, \quad increase \quad \omega \quad by \quad \omega_{inc} = 0.4437878 \\
&SLANCV \quad v < 0.2235206, \quad \omega > 0.7800814, \quad v_{ref} - v_{rob} < -0.7777185, \quad \omega_{ref} - \omega_{rob} < -0.7120344, \\
&\quad \rho > 1.5151515, \quad a < -0.0003327 \quad then \\
&\quad decrease \quad v \quad by \quad v_{inc} = -0.4927100, \quad decrease \quad \omega \quad by \quad \omega_{inc} = -0.0680181 \\
&SLANCV \quad v > 1.4049258, \quad \omega < -0.3766352, \quad v_{ref} - v_{rob} < 0.0756778, \quad \omega_{ref} - \omega_{rob} < -0.7105109, \\
&\quad \rho < 0.1169906, \quad a < -0.2358675 \quad then \\
&\quad decrease \quad v \quad by \quad v_{inc} = -0.2173556, \quad decrease \quad \omega \quad by \quad \omega_{inc} = -0.3592529 \\
&SLANCV \quad v < 0.9930632, \quad \omega > 0.8202830, \quad v_{ref} - v_{rob} > -0.1180958, \quad \omega_{ref} - \omega_{rob} < -0.6506539, \\
&\quad \rho > 0.1156700, \quad a < 0.2116636 \quad then \\
&\quad increase \quad v \quad by \quad v_{inc} = 0.3642978 \quad decrease \quad \omega \quad by \quad \omega_{inc} = -0.8061992
\end{aligned}$$

$$SLANCV \quad v < 0.7807096, \quad > 0.4849204, \quad v_{ref} - v_{rob} > 0.4796375, \quad \omega_{ref} - \omega_{rob} > 0.5922044,$$
$$\rho > 1.2921157, \quad a > 0.2758564 \quad then$$
$$increase \quad v \quad by \quad v_{inc} = 0.3424317, \quad increase \quad \omega \quad by \quad \omega_{inc} = 0.8207999$$
$$SLANCV \quad v < 0.5131913, \quad \omega > -0.2240559, \quad v_{ref} - v_{rob} < -0.4493099, \quad \omega_{ref} - \omega_{rob} > 0.7691425,$$
$$\rho < 1.0904348, \quad a > 0.2174491 \quad then$$
$$decrease \quad v \quad by \quad v_{inc} = -0.5255254, \quad increase \quad \omega \quad by \quad \omega_{inc} = 0.8943484$$

In order to improve system performance and remove any inconsistencies, the rules above must be analysed. The following rule analysis procedure is limited to case 'B'. This procedure is assisted by a plot of the DOF (Degree-Of-Firing) of each rule (output of sigmoid) versus time. Such plots help in visualizing which rules the ANN is applying at each time instant and judging the decision/ performance made at this particular time. In particular, it is highly useful to identify dominant rules (rules having relatively high outputs) at the time a wrong decision is made. Correction is then possible by retraining the ANN keeping all rules fixed except the faulty dominant one. For example, as shown in Fig. 9, at the time the deviation from the desired path becomes maximum, rule 5 is dominant followed by rule 4. Accordingly, three different strategies, have been attempted, to retrain the ANN, to improve its performance. In all three strategies, all rules have been kept fixed except:

- for the first strategy: rule 5 (5th column of Wh^c ,5th column of B^c and the 5th row of Wo^c),
- for the second strategy: both the degrees of firing of rules 4 and 5 (4th and 5th column of Wh^c), and their then part (4th and 5th row of Wo^c),
- for the third strategy: the degree of firing of rule 5 and its then part (5th column of Wh^c and the 5th row of Wo^c), with the addition of a new rule (rule 8) whose SLANCV part is the same as that of rule 5 (8th column of B^c is same as its 5th column) but whose DOF (8th column of Wh^c) and consequent part (or then part) (8th row of Wo^c) are to be determined by the training algorithm. The idea is to insert a new rule that co-fires with the malfunctioning rule to provide some correcting action. For our case study, this last strategy gave us the best results. The results after retraining are shown in Fig. 10.

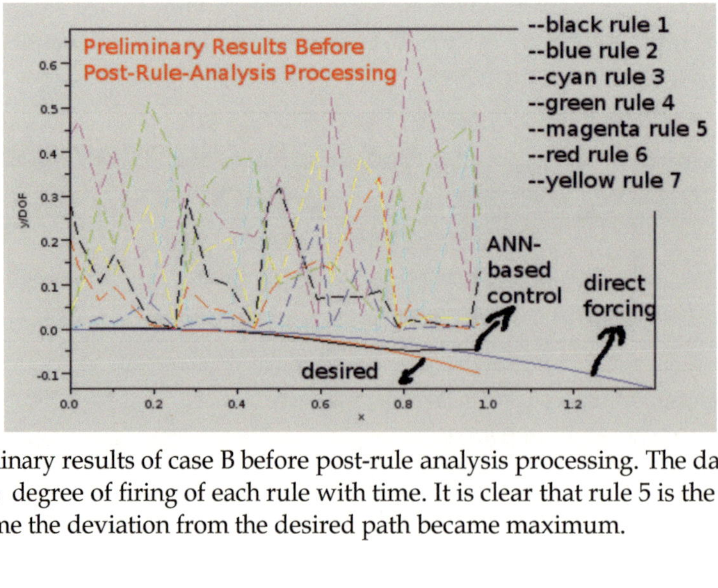

Fig. 9. Preliminary results of case B before post-rule analysis processing. The dashed curves represent the degree of firing of each rule with time. It is clear that rule 5 is the dominant rule at the time the deviation from the desired path became maximum.

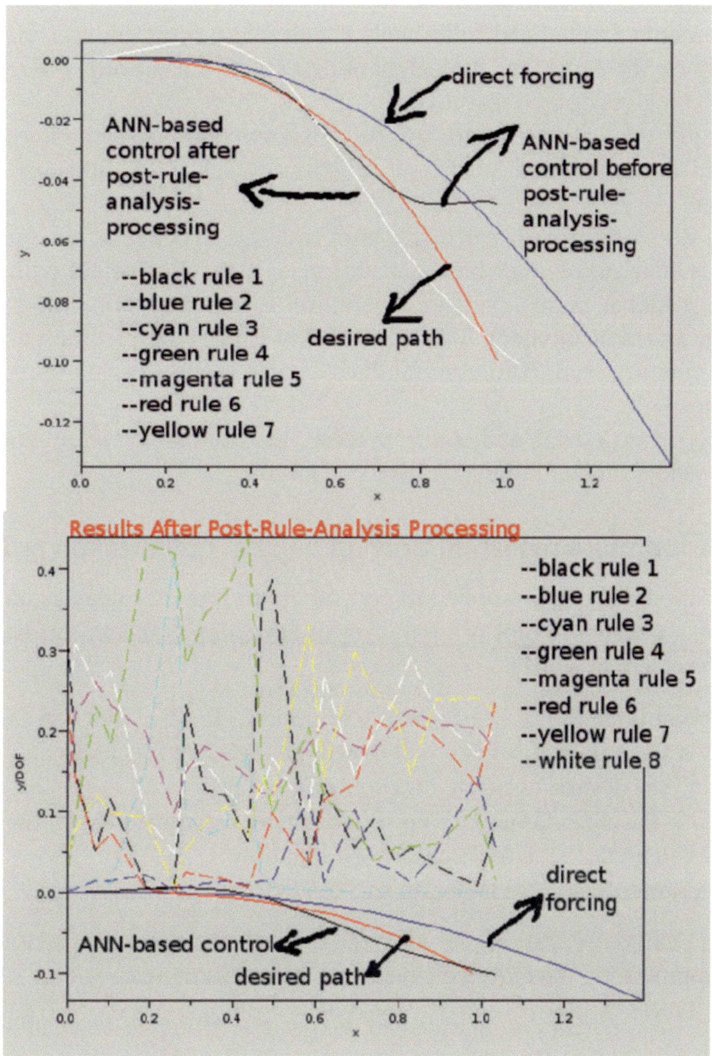

Fig. 10. Results of case B after retraining with only the parameters corresponding to rules 5 degree of firing and its "then" part allowed to vary in addition to adding a new rule 8 with the same SLANCV part as rule 5 to co-fire with it and to provide corrective action. It is clear that this retraining improved the results.

3.7 Discussion

Although the rule analysis method presented, helped in improving the results, it still needs improvement. In fact, rule analysis is a rather complex task. Understanding the logic behind the rules (why each rule recommends a particular consequent given a certain antecedent) is not simple for the following reasons:

1. Rules operate in parallel and collectively. Each rule recommends a certain consequent depending on the context of the neighbouring rules. Collectively, the overall decision helps achieving the desired objective.
2. According to the training algorithm, rules recommend certain consequents in order to minimize the desired objective function which is a function of the robot kinematics.
3. Rules are derived through batch (off-line) training. Therefore, the overall objective function is minimized over time and not at a particular instant (rules are derived based on a global point of view). Therefore, a rule may not sound reasonable to employ at a certain moment. This what makes it necessary to train an ANN over a certain family of curves. Different families of curves are expected to require different global rules.
4. Rule analysis is a trial and error process. Its complexity is proportional to the dimensionality (number of independent variables).

4. Directions for future research: Solving general optimization problems

The proposed approach can be applied to general optimization problems and not just path-tracking. From an abstract point of view, any optimization problem can be mapped to a goal-tracking problem in which:

- The goal point is the desired performance or desired objective function value.
- The input is the absolute difference between the objective function value at the current solution and the desired objective function value.
- The output is the correction, to the current solution, recommended by the ANN. This is fed-back as an input to the ANN at the next iteration.
- Time evolution corresponds to iterations.

Hence, over the different iterations the ANN is expected to suggest a sequence of corrections that helps in approaching the required objective function value.

This approach to optimization is expected to be less prune to local minima trapping, provides better insight into the nature of the investigated problem and can easily deal with multi-objectives/ errors optimization. For example, in the robot path tracking problem, $\alpha, \rho, v_{ref} - v_{rob}, \omega_{ref} - \omega_{rob}$ were error measures that, ideally are required to be all zeros. In this case, the robot perfectly tracks the desired path and remains tangent to it at all times. This property (being tangent at all times) is desirable, from a practical point of view, because even if the robot path is close to the desired path but with too many frequent changes of orientation, wear out will occur to the robot parts and it will be questionable whether the robot can, practically, makes these moves).

4.1 Illustrative example: Minimizing the camel benchmark function

The camel objective function is defined as follows

$$f_{Sixh}(x_1, x_2) = \left(4 - 2.1x_1^{\ 2} + \frac{x_1^{\ 4}}{3}\right)x_1^{\ 2} + x_1 x_2 + \left(-4 + 4x_2^2\right)x_2^2; -3 \le x_1 \le 3, -2 \le x_2 \le 2.$$

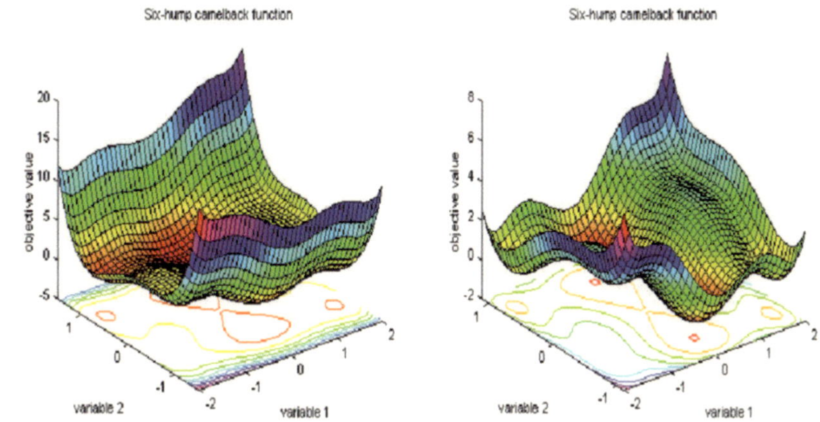

Fig. 11. Camel function objective function.

The global minimum is $f(x_1, x_2) = -1.0316; (x_1, x_2) = (-0.0898, 0.7126), (0.0898, -0.7126)$. Fig. 11 shows a plot of the camel objective function.

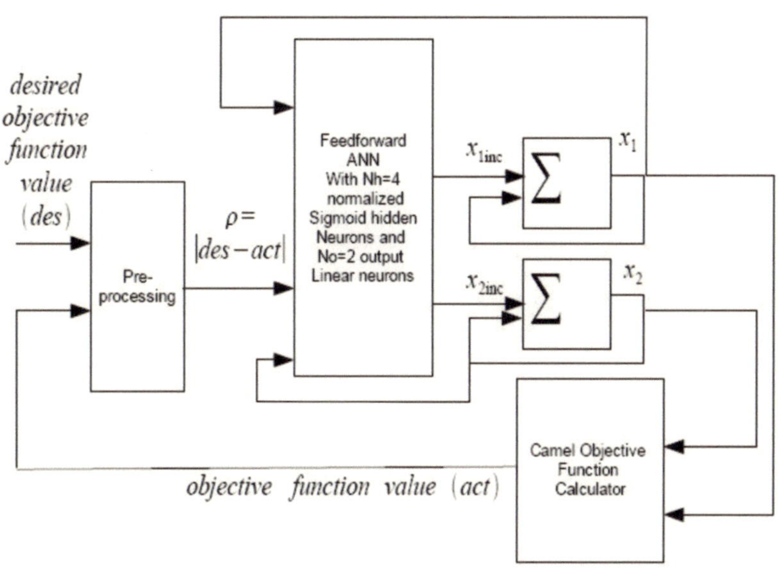

Fig. 12. Block diagram of the system used to find the global minimum of the camel objective Function.

To apply the proposed ANN-based approach to find the global minimum of this function, the closed loop system in Fig. 12 has been adopted. The inputs to the ANN are the values of x_1 and x_2 at the previous iteration, the absolute difference between the desired value of the objective function at the current iteration and its current actual value. The outputs of the ANN are the recommended corrections to x_1 and x_2 (increase or decrease). The ANN weights and biases were estimated numerically as before such that the ANN minimize the camel objective function. The desired value for the objective function at any iteration is chosen to be slightly less than its current value (For example, for decrratio=0.85, the desired objective function at a certain iteration =decrratio* the actual objective function value corresponding to the current solution). This idca is borrowed from [13], where it has been recommended to be adopted with any optimization method. The ANN has been trained, as before, using a numerical BFGS algorithm, where the objective function to be minimized is defined as :

$$Objg = \rho_F \tag{12}$$

where, ρ_F is the absolute difference between the desired objective function value and its actual value at the last iteration. The rules extracted from the trained ANN are as follows:

$$SLANCV \quad x_1 > 0.6755704, \quad x_2 > 1.5209156, \quad \rho > 0.0161157,$$
$$decrease \quad x_1 \quad by \quad x_{1inc} = -0.0668506 \quad decrease \quad x_2 \quad by \quad x_{2inc} = -0.0203858$$
$$SLANCV \quad x_1 > 1.4023561, \quad x_2 > 0.4688876, \quad \rho > 0.1058053,$$
$$increase \quad x_1 \quad by \quad x_{1inc} = 0.0617143 \quad decrease \quad x_2 \quad by \quad x_{2inc} = -0.0195689$$
$$SLANCV \quad x_1 > 0.6147782, \quad x_2 < 0.1270187, \quad \rho < 1.504679,$$
$$increase \quad x_1 \quad by \quad x_{1inc} = 0.0301060 \quad decrease \quad x_2 \quad by \quad x_{2inc} = -0.0128413$$
$$SLANCV \quad x_1 > 0.0459426, \quad x_2 > 0.3802873, \quad \rho < 0.5840457,$$
$$decrease \quad x_1 \quad by \quad x_{1inc} = -0.0279751 \quad decrease \quad x_2 \quad by \quad x_{2inc} = -0.0338863$$

Fig. 13 shows the results (the objective function value versus iteration number). Clearly, the ANN-based optimization technique found the global optimal (The initial solution was $x_1 = -2.5, \quad x_2 = 2.5$). When using the BFGS technique to minimize the camel objective function, with the same learning rate, the algorithm completely diverged. For a lower learning rate, direct BFGS reached the global optimal. However, ANN-based optimization offers greater promise for higher dimensions/ multi-objective/ error problems and provides insight into the solution through the analysis of the derived rules. A key reason for the robustness of the ANN-based optimization over direct optimization is that it explores the objective function and derives problem-dependent heuristics (as opposed to meta-heuristics).

An important direction for future investigation is the use of concepts borrowed from "robust optimization" to enhance the quality of the rules extracted from the ANN. Robust optimization concepts can be applied at two different levels:

- At the action level, we can include noise during ANN training. The error in path-tracking can be defined as a function of the difference between the average expected location and the desired location as well as the variance (or standard deviation of this error). This will make the ANN develop a decision strategy that is more prudent and is less likely to cause divergence from the desired path, in case of disturbance.

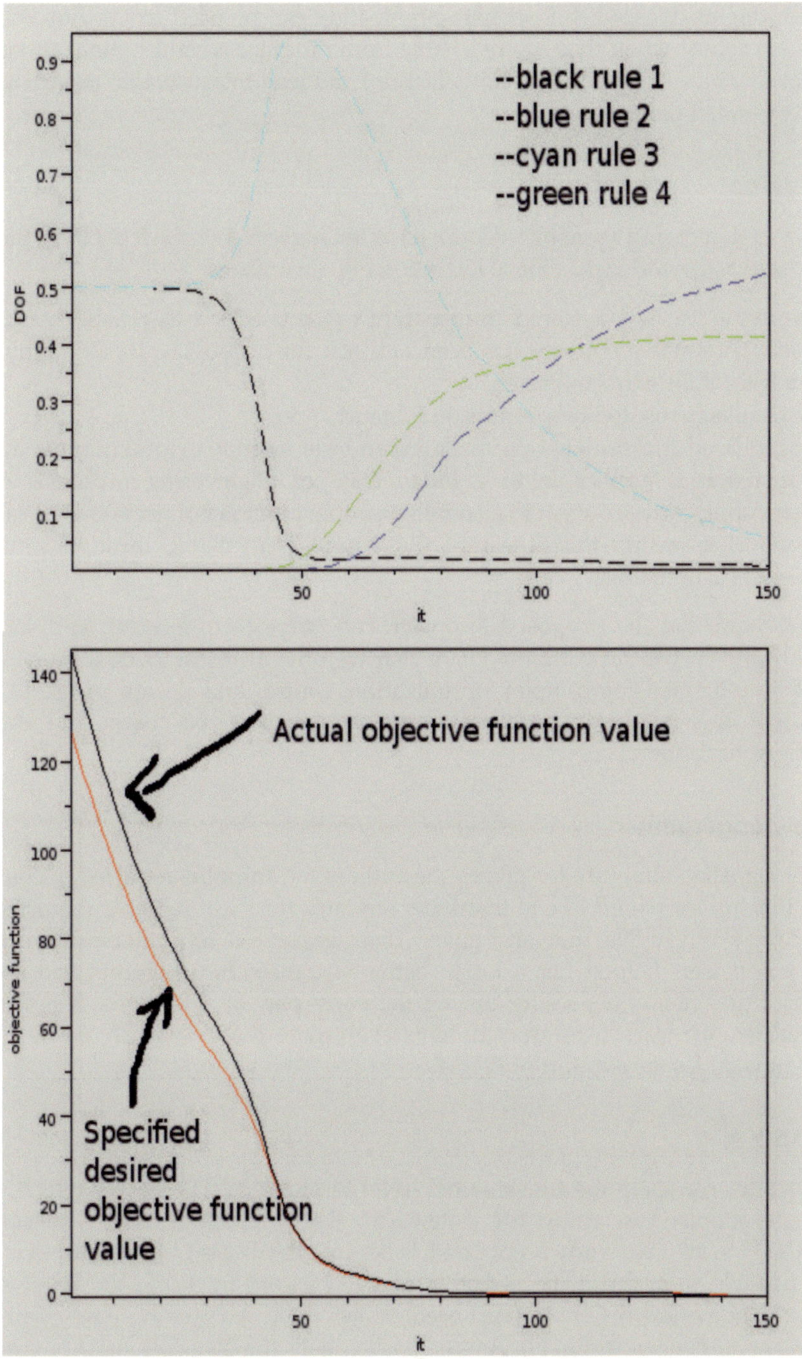

Fig. 13. The results of using the proposed approach to find the global minimum of the camel objective function. The top figure shows the degree of firing of the different rules versus iteration number. The bottom figure depicts the objective function value versus iteration number. The approach successfully converged to the global minimum.

- At the weights/biases level, robust optimization can be used to develop robust rules. Rules are robust when they are reachable from different weight initializations (i.e. they are not sensitive to a particular initialization) and lead to acceptable performance when subject to small perturbations.

5. Conclusion

We believe that merging symbolic AI (logic) with non-symbolic AI (ANNs) through our new proposed framework can achieve the following advantages:

1. The resulting learning system is transparent to the user and its reliability can be easily assessed. A suitable strategy has been outlined for improving its reliability based on the analysis of the extracted rules.
2. The system is robust to noisy inputs and disturbances.
3. The logic-based approach to optimization can be less prune to local minima trapping.
4. The approach is applicable to a broad class of engineering problems where the corresponding correct output to a certain example input is not necessarily available (but a means of assessing the fitness of the output is available through simulation or practical measurements).

We do not claim that the proposed approach can outperform existing approaches in all problems, however, we can certainly claim that we offered researchers, a framework truly worthy of investigation for complex optimization, control and design problems. The best approach will always remain problem-dependent which is the charm and challenge of engineering optimization.

6. Acknowledgement

After thanking Allah almighty for giving the authors the stimulus required to complete this work, the first author would like to thank her students for their valuable inquiries during a summer course on ANNs that she gave. Their eagerness to understand, queries and continuous criticisms helped her a lot to better formulate her thoughts and served as a valuable encouragement, especially during the early part of this work. It is true that, at many occasions, we learn from our students even more than we teach them! The second author acknowledges the support of EJUST.

7. Appendix A

In this appendix, we apply the conventional ANN formulation ([1] ,[6] ,[7]) and ANFIS [8] to case 'B' of the adopted case study. It is noteworthy that strict application of the conventional ANN or ANFIS to this case study is not possible because the desired system output is unknown (it is not possible to evaluate the objective function except by using the robot simulator). Therefore, the numerical BFGS has been used, as before, in the training phase with the same objective function defined in Eq. (9). As said earlier, with the conventional ANN formulation the output of the ANN described in Eq. (1) can be interpreted as fuzzy rules of the form:

$$SLANCV \quad x_i^p > -\left(b_j / N_i\right) / w_{hij} \quad then \quad o_{jk} = w_{jk}$$
$$i = 1,2,\ldots,N_i$$

The fact that the antecedent of a rule depends on both the bias of the corresponding hidden neuron and the weights from inputs-to this hidden neuron makes it difficult the use of known inputs constraints in weights/biases initialization. Thus, we are forced to use small random weights and biases initially, train the ANN, extract the rules and then re-train in case some of the rules yield un-plausible antecedents. For our case study, 3 out of the 7 rules had un-plausible antecedents. For example, one of the rules stated:

$$SLANCV \quad v < -1.1959689, \quad w > 0.1675315, \quad v_{ref} - v_{rob} > 0.8878251, \quad \omega_{ref} - \omega_{rob} > 0.1353403,$$
$$\rho < -2.7918388, \quad a < -0.2060677,$$
$$decrease \quad v \quad by \quad v_{inc} = -6.6637447, \quad decrease \quad \omega \quad by \quad \omega_{inc} = -5.8271221$$

Clearly comparing ρ to a negative threshold is not logical.

Fig. 14 illustrates a typical ANFIS architecture for the case of a 2 inputs $(x_{1,}x_2)$ single output, 2 rules example. A_{ij} is the membership function of the ith input in the jth rule. The DOF of a rule is computed using the 'Product' operator, i.e. it is the product of the output of the membership functions of a certain rule (Layer 2). NORM units (Layer 3) divides the individual DOF of each rule by the sum of DOF of all rules to produce a normalized degree of firing $\overline{w}_j$. Layer 4 computes the consequent of each rule j for each output k, f_{jk} as a function of the inputs $f_{jk} = \sum_{i=1}^{Ni} p_{ijk} + r_{jk}$. The overall system output is computed as a weighted sum of the different rules consequents ($f_k = \sum_{j=1}^{N_h} \overline{w}_j f_{jk}$, N_h is the number of rules which equals 2 in Fig. 14). Similarly, to be able to compare our approach to ANFIS [8], we use the same block diagram given in Fig. 5 but replacing the typical feed-forward ANN with an ANFIS. The ANFIS formulation does not impose restrictions on membership function's choices. Therefore, sigmoid membership functions have been chosen, for the purpose of comparison with our approach. In this case, the membership function of the jth rule takes the form:

$$A_{ij} = \text{sig}\left(a_{ij}\left(x_i - c_{ij}\right)\right)$$

Our approach can be viewed as a modified ANFIS system with the '*Product*' operator replaced by the 'ior' operator and with $p_{ijk} = 0$. As indicated by the results (Fig. 15), these modifications enhance the performance considerably. ANFIS training involves the estimation of the parameters p_{ijk}, r_{jk} for each rule contributing to the output as well as the membership functions parameters a_{ij}, c_{ij} of each rule. The extracted rules after training are as follows:

If $v < 0.7060525$ and $\omega < -0.2171979$ and $(v_{ref} - v_{rob}) > -0.4880470$ and $(\omega_{ref} - \omega_{rob}) < -0.3037414$ and $\rho < 0.5722985$ and $\alpha < -0.2705797$ then

$$v_{inc} = -0.4977126*v + -0.2252019*\omega + -0.2252019*(v_{ref} - v_{rob}) + 0.6536675*(\omega_{ref} - \omega_{rob}) + -0.9451361*\rho + 0.4929671*\alpha + 0.5642881 + 0.2698283,$$

$$\omega_{inc} = -0.2601446*v + -0.0526525*\omega + -0.0526525*(v_{ref} - v_{rob}) + -0.0256069*(\omega_{ref} - \omega_{rob}) + 0.2929497*\rho + -0.6628894*\alpha + 0.6927095 + 0.5608534$$

If $v > 0.9536605$ and $\omega < -0.3640576$ and $(v_{ref} - v_{rob}) > 0.3635925$ and $(\omega_{ref} - \omega_{rob}) > -0.5739730$ and $\rho < 1.0224728$ and $\alpha > 0.2518629$ then

$$v_{inc} = -0.2252019*v + 0.5305053*\omega + 0.5305053*(v_{ref} - v_{rob}) + 0.5254107*(\omega_{ref} - \omega_{rob}) + 0.6691905*\rho + 0.1321803*\alpha + -0.4524829 + 0.5491040,$$

$$\omega_{inc} = -0.0526525*v + -0.1341857*\omega + -0.1341857*(v_{ref} - v_{rob}) + -0.4909975*(\omega_{ref} - \omega_{rob}) + -0.2141134*\rho + -0.2020394*\alpha + -0.1888051 + 0.0712943$$

If $v < 0.7970844$ and $\omega > 0.2311402$ and $(v_{ref} - v_{rob}) > -0.2606914$ and $(\omega_{ref} - \omega_{rob}) > 0.3577566$ and $\rho > 0.5432450$ and $\alpha > 0.3045580$ then

$$v_{inc} = -0.4283727*v + 0.5254107*\omega + 0.5254107*(v_{ref} - v_{rob}) + -0.1505240*(\omega_{ref} - \omega_{rob}) + 0.8359596*\rho + -0.0326892*\alpha + 0.3081844 + -0.0003588,$$

$$\omega_{inc} = 0.3454005*v + -0.4909975*\omega + -0.4909975*(v_{ref} - v_{rob}) + -0.2778212*(\omega_{ref} - \omega_{rob}) + 0.6994976*\rho + 0.4886705*\alpha + 0.2289957 + 0.5789568$$

If $v < 1.0159674$ and $\omega > 0.1276233$ and $(v_{ref} - v_{rob}) < -0.2720805$ and $(\omega_{ref} - \omega_{rob}) > -0.0879307$ and $\rho > 0.7092691$ and $\alpha > -0.1685077$ then

$$v_{inc} = -0.9451361*v + 0.4569717*\omega + 0.4569717*(v_{ref} - v_{rob}) + 0.8359596*(\omega_{ref} - \omega_{rob}) + 0.6869079*\rho + 0.7200467*\alpha + 0.7449960 + 0.8263730,$$

$$\omega_{inc} = 0.2929497*v + 0.2791020*\omega + 0.2791020*(v_{ref} - v_{rob}) + 0.6994976*(\omega_{ref} - \omega_{rob}) + 0.1821506*\rho + 0.6257491*\alpha + 0.4543635 + 0.2199392$$

$$\begin{aligned}
&\textit{If}\quad v>1.205344 \text{ and } \omega>-0.0968983 \text{ and } (v_{ref}-v_{rob})>0.0373195\\
&\text{and}\quad (\omega_{ref}-\omega_{rob})<0.1962357 \text{ and } \rho>1.2538755 \text{ and } \alpha<0.1218786\\
&\text{then}\quad v_{inc}= 0.5642881*v + -0.2429051*\omega + -0.2429051*(v_{ref}-v_{rob}) +\\
&\qquad 0.3081844*(\omega_{ref}-\omega_{rob}) + -0.6377921*\rho +\\
&\qquad 0.2372806*\alpha + 0.3039157 + -0.7144687,\\
&\quad \omega_{inc}= 0.6927095*v + 0.7480350*\omega + 0.7480350*(v_{ref}-v_{rob}) +\\
&\qquad 0.2289957*(\omega_{ref}-\omega_{rob}) + 0.5583952*\rho +\\
&\qquad -0.4286680*\alpha + 0.2080972 + -0.4508324
\end{aligned}$$

$$\begin{aligned}
&\textit{If}\quad v>1.205344 \text{ and } \omega>-0.0968983 \text{ and } (v_{ref}-v_{rob})>0.0373195\\
&\text{and}\quad (\omega_{ref}-\omega_{rob})<0.1962357 \text{ and } \rho>1.2538755 \text{ and } \alpha<0.1218786\\
&\text{then}\quad v_{inc}= 0.5642881*v + -0.2429051*\omega + -0.2429051*(v_{ref}-v_{rob}) +\\
&\qquad 0.3081844*(\omega_{ref}-\omega_{rob}) + -0.6377921*\rho +\\
&\qquad 0.2372806*\alpha + 0.3039157 + -0.7144687,\\
&\quad \omega_{inc}= 0.6927095*v + 0.7480350*\omega + 0.7480350*(v_{ref}-v_{rob}) +\\
&\qquad 0.2289957*(\omega_{ref}-\omega_{rob}) + 0.5583952*\rho +\\
&\qquad -0.4286680*\alpha + 0.2080972 + -0.4508324
\end{aligned}$$

$$\begin{aligned}
&\textit{If}\quad v>0.6196452 \text{ and } \omega<0.2323706 \text{ and } (v_{ref}-v_{rob})>0.5647629\\
&\text{and}\quad (\omega_{ref}-\omega_{rob})>-0.0327666 \text{ and } \rho>0.4904380 \text{ and } \alpha>-0.1630150\\
&\text{then}\quad v_{inc}= -0.0378747*v + -0.3878541*\omega + -0.3878541*(v_{ref}-v_{rob}) +\\
&\qquad 0.1955760*(\omega_{ref}-\omega_{rob}) + 0.0637325*\rho +\\
&\qquad -0.1970121*\alpha + -0.2060373 + 0.4825770,\\
&\quad \omega_{inc}= 0.1229261*v + 0.1073914*\omega + 0.1073914*(v_{ref}-v_{rob}) +\\
&\qquad -0.2504428*(\omega_{ref}-\omega_{rob}) + 0.6417333*\rho +\\
&\qquad 0.2868955*\alpha + 0.1431067 + 0.1357565
\end{aligned}$$

It is clear from Fig. 15, that both the conventional ANN and ANFIS produce inferior results to those obtained using the proposed approach (refer to Fig. 7). Thus, the proposed modifications to conventional ANNs succeeded in producing an improved ANFIS system capable of outperforming both conventional ANNs and ANFIS for problems where the desired ANN output is not known a priori (like in the path tracking case study).

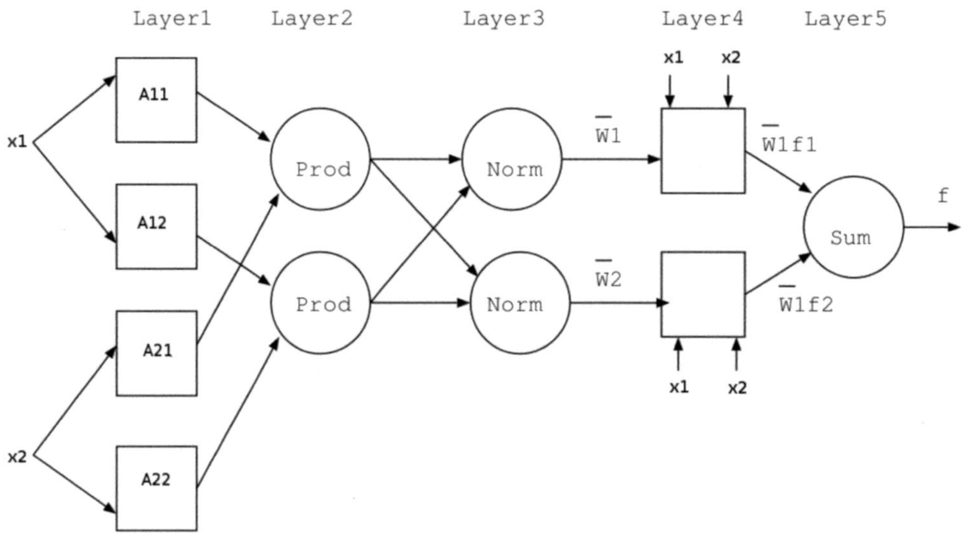

Fig. 14. Architecture of a typical ANFIS system for a 2 inputs single output example

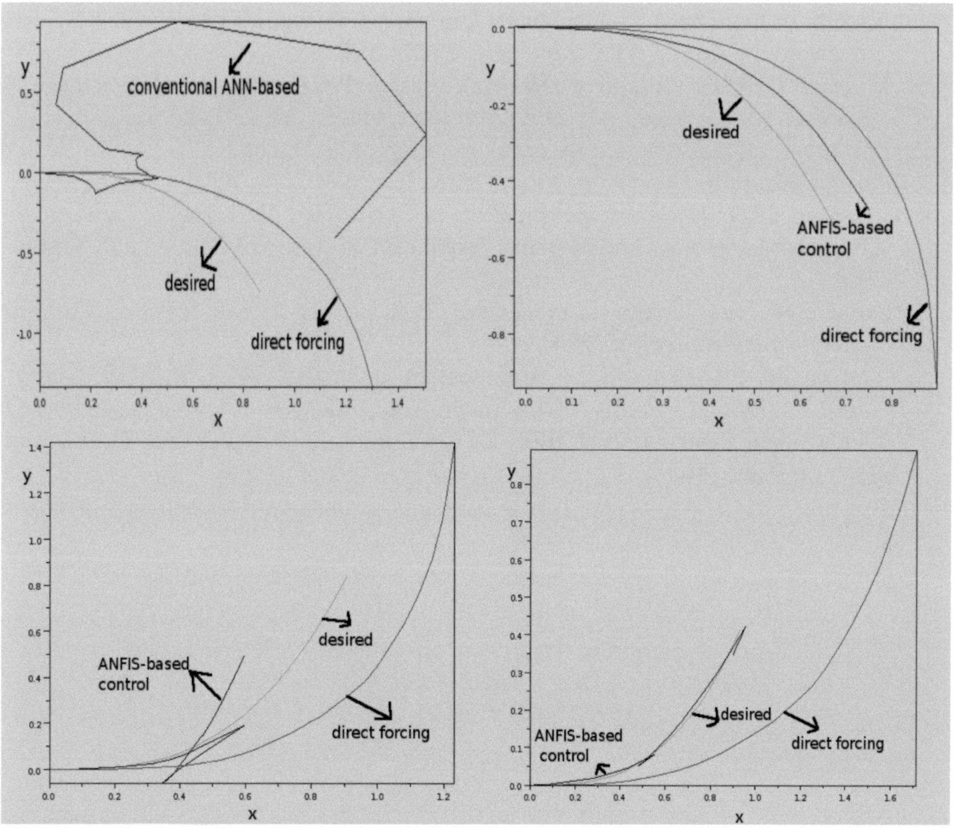

Fig. 15. Shows the results for using conventional ANNs and ANFIS instead of the proposed formulation for case B. By comparing these results with those in Fig. 7 , the superiority of the proposed approach-thanks to Allah- is clear.

8. References

[1] G J. Benitez, J. Castro, I. Requena, “Are Artificial ANNs Black Boxes?”, IEEE Trans. on ANNs, September, 1997.

[2] J. Espinosa, J. Vandewalle, V. Wertz, *Fuzzy Logic, Identification and Predictive Control (Advances in Industrial Control)*, Springer-Verlag, London, 2005.

[3] Simon Haykin, ANNs and Learning Machines, Prentice Hall, November 2008.

[4] R. Setiono, "Extracting M-of-N Rules from Trained ANNs", *IEEE Trans. on ANNs*, Vol. 11, No.2, January 2000. pp. 510-519.

[5] S. Mitra, S. Pal, "Fuzzy Multi-Layer Perceptron, Inferencing and Rule Generation" , *IEEE Trans. on ANNs*, Vol. 6, No.1, January 1995. pp. 51-63.

[6] H. Senousy, M. Abou-El Makarem, “New Reliable Neural-Based Automatic Diesel Fault Diagnosis Systems”, International Conference on Mechanical Engineering and Production MDP9, Cairo, Egypt, January 2008.

[7] I. Hamid, H. Senousy, M. Abou-Elmakarem, "An Improved Fuzzy Logic Controller For Ship Steering Based on Ior Operator and Neural Rule Extraction", ICCES08,

Faculty of Engineering - Ain Shams University, Computer Engineering & Systems Department Cairo, EGYPT, November 25-27, 2008.

[8] J.S. R. Jang "ANFIS: Adaptive Network based Fuzzy Inference Systems", *IEEE Transactions on Systems, Man, and. Cybernetics*, vol. 23, no. 3, (1993) 665–685.

[9] http://sourceforge.indices-masivos.com/projects/forallahfacon/

[10] S. Rao, Optimization, *Theory & Applications 2ed*, July 1984, John Wiley & Sons (Asia).

[11] R. Gonzalez, *ANNs for Variational Problems in Engineering,* PhD Thesis, Department of Computer Languages and Systems, Technical University of Catalonia,21 September 2008.

[12] G. Dudek, Michael Jenkin, *Computational Principles of Mobile Robotics,* Cambridge University Press; April 15, 2000.

[13] A. El-Bastawesy , A. El-sayed, M. Abdel-Salam, B. Salah, I. Adel, M. Alaa El-laffy, M. Tariq, B. Magdi, O. Fathi, A New Intelligent Strategy for Optimal Design of High Dimensional Systems, 2011 IEEE GCC Conference & Exhibition, Dubai, United Arab Emirates, 2011

3

Ranking Indices for Fuzzy Numbers

Tayebeh Hajjari
Department of Mathematics, Firoozkooh Branch, Islamic Azad University, Firoozkooh, Iran

1. Introduction

Fuzzy set theory has been studied extensively over the past 30 years. Most of the early interest in fuzzy set theory pertained to representing uncertainty in human cognitive processes (see for example Zadeh (1965)). Fuzzy set theory is now applied to problems in engineering, business, medical and related health sciences, and the natural sciences. In an effort to gain a better understanding of the use of fuzzy set theory in production management research and to provide a basis for future research, a literature review of fuzzy set theory in production management has been conducted. While similar survey efforts have been undertaken for other topical areas, there is a need in production management for the same. Over the years there have been successful applications and implementations of fuzzy set theory in production management. Fuzzy set theory is being recognized as an important problem modeling and solution technique.

Kaufmann and Gupta (1988) report that over 7,000 research papers, reports, monographs, and books on fuzzy set theory and applications have been published since 1965.

As evidenced by the large number of citations found, fuzzy set theory is an established and growing research discipline. The use of fuzzy set theory as a methodology for modeling and analyzing decision systems is of particular interest to researchers in production management due to fuzzy set theory's ability to quantitatively and qualitatively model problems which involve vagueness and imprecision. Karwowski and Evans (1986) identify the potential applications of fuzzy set theory to the following areas of production management: new product development, facilities location and layout, production scheduling and control, inventory management, quality and cost benefit analysis. Karwowski and Evans identify three key reasons why fuzzy set theory is relevant to production management research. First, imprecision and vagueness are inherent to the decision maker's mental model of the problem under study. Thus, the decision maker's experience and judgment may be used to complement established theories to foster a better understanding of the problem. Second, in the production management environment, the information required to formulate a model's objective, decision variables, constraints and parameters may be vague or not precisely measurable. Third, imprecision and vagueness as a result of personal bias and subjective opinion may further dampen the quality and quantity of available information. Hence, fuzzy set theory can be used to bridge modeling gaps in descriptive and prescriptive decision models in production management research.

2. Fuzzy ranking and neural network

Ordering fuzzy subsets is an important event in dealing with fuzzy decision problems in many areas. This issue has been of concern for many researchers over the years. Also, in the last several years, there has been a large and energetic upswing in neuroengineering research aimed at synthesizing fuzzy logic with computational neural networks. The two technologies often complement each other: neural networks supply the brute force necessary to accommodate and interpret large amounts of sensor data and fuzzy logic provides a structural framework that utilizes and exploits these low-level results. As a neural network is well known for its ability to represent functions, and the basis of every fuzzy model is the membership function, so the natural application of neural networks in fuzzy models has emerged to provide good approximations to the membership functions that are essential to the success of the fuzzy approach. Many researchers evaluate and analyze the performance of available methods of ranking fuzzy subsets on a set of selected examples that cover possible situations we might encounter as defining fuzzy subsets at each node of a neural network. Along with prosperity of computer and internet technology, more and more pepole used e-learning system to lecture and study. Therefore, how to evaluate the students' proficiency by arranging is the topic that deverses our attention. This chapter focus on fuzzy ranking approaches to evaluate fuzzy numbersas a tool in neural network.

3. Ranking fuzzy numbers

In many applications, ranking of fuzzy numbers is an important component of the decision process. Since fuzzy numbers do not form a natural linear order, like real numbers, a key issue in operationalzing fuzzy set theory is how to compare fuzzy numbers. Various approaches have been developed for ranking fuzzy numbers. In the existing research, the commonly used technique is to construct proper maps to transform fuzzy numbers into real numbers so called defuzzification. These real numbers are then compared. Herein, in approaches (; Abbasbandy & Asady, 2006; Abbasbandy & Hajjari, 2009, 2011; Asady, 2010; S. J. Chen & S. M. Chen, 2003, 2007, 2009; Deng & Liu, 2005; Deng et al., 2006; Hajjari, 2011a; Hajjari, 2011b; Z.-X. Wang et al. 2009) a fuzzy number is mapped to a real number based on the area measurement. In approaches (L. H. Chen & Lu, 2001, 2002; Liu & Han, 2005), $\alpha-$ cut set and decision-maker's preference are used to construct ranking function. On the other hand, another commonly used technique is the centroid-based fuzzy number ranking approach (Cheng, 1998; Chu, & Tsao, 2002; Y.J. Wang et al. 2008). It should be noted that with the development of intelligent technologies, some adaptive and parameterized defuzzification methods that can include human knowledge have been proposed. Halgamuge et al. (Halgamuge et al. 1996) used neural networks for defuzzification. Song and Leland (Song & Leland, 1996) proposed an adaptive learning defuzzification technique. Yager (1996) proposed knowledge based on defuzzification process, which becomes more intelligent. Similar to methods of Filve and Yager (Filev & Yager, 1991), Jiang and Li (Jiang & Li, 1996) also proposed a parameterized defuzzification method with Gaussian based distribution transformation and polynomial transformation, but in fact, no method gives a right effective defuzzification output. The computational results of these methods are often conflict.

We often face difficultly in selecting appropriate defuzzification, which is mainly based on intuition and there is no explicit decision making for these parameters. For more comparison details on most of these methods, in this chapter we review some of ranking methods.

4. Basic notations and definitions

4.1 Definition

First, In general, a generalized fuzzy number A is membership $\mu_A(x)$ can be defined as (Dubios & Prade, 1978)

$$\mu_A(x) = \begin{cases} L_A(x) & a \le x \le b \\ \omega & b \le x \le c \\ R_A(x) & c \le x \le d \\ 0 & otherwise, \end{cases} \tag{1}$$

where $0 \le \omega \le 1$ is a constant, and $L_A : [a,b] \to [0,\omega]$, $R_A : [c,d] \to [0,\omega]$ are two strictly monotonical and continuous mapping from R to closed interval $[0,\omega]$. If $\omega = 1$, then A is a normal fuzzy number; otherwise, it is a trapezoidal fuzzy number and is usually denoted by $A = (a,b,c,d,\omega)$ or $A = (a,b,c,d)$ if $\omega = 1$.

In particular, when $b = c$, the trapezoidal fuzzy number is reduced to a triangular fuzzy number denoted by $A = (a,b,d,\omega)$ or $A = (a,b,d)$ if $\omega = 1$ .Therefore, triangular fuzzy numbers are special cases of trapezoidal fuzzy numbers.

Since L_A and R_A are both strictly monotonical and continuous functions, their inverse functions exist and should be continuous and strictly monotonical. Let $L_A^{-1} : [a,b] \to [0,\omega]$ and $R_A^{-1} : [a,b] \to [0,\omega]$ be the inverse functions of $L_A(x)$ and $R_A(x)$, respectively. Then $L^{-1}{}_A(r)$ and $R^{-1}{}_A(r)$ should be integrable on the close interval $[0,\omega]$. In other words, both $\int_0^{\omega} L_A^{-1}(r)dr$ and $\int_0^{\omega} R_A^{-1}(r)dr$ should exist. In the case of trapezoidal fuzzy number, the inverse functions $L^{-1}{}_A(r)$ and $R^{-1}{}_A(r)$ can be analytically expressed as

$$\cdot L_A^{-1}(r) = a + (b-a)r / \omega \quad 0 \le \omega \le 1$$

$$R_A^{-1}(r) = d - (d-c)r / \omega \quad 0 \le \omega \le 1$$

The set of all elements that have a nonzero degree of membership in A, it is called the support of A, i.e.

$$S(A) = \{x \in X \mid \mu_A(x) \succ 0\} \tag{2}$$

The set of elements having the largest degree of membership in A, it is called the core of A, i.e.

$$C(A)=\left\{x \in X \mid \mu_A(x)=\sup_{x \in X} L_A(x)\right\} \quad (3)$$

In the following, we will always assume that A is continuous and bounded support $S(A)$. The strong support of A should be $S(A)=[a,d]$.

4.2 Definition

The addition and scalar multiplication of fuzzy numbers are defined by the extension principle and can be equivalent represented in (Zadeh, 1965; Ma et al., 1999; Dubois & Prade, 1980) as follows.

For arbitrary $A=\left(L_A^{-1}(r),R_A^{-1}(r)\right)$ and we define addition $B=\left(L_B^{-1}(r),R_B^{-1}(r)\right)$ $(A+B)$ and multiplication by scalar $k \succ 0$ as

$$\begin{gathered}(\underline{A+B})(r)=\underline{A}(r)+\underline{B}(r)\\ \left(\overline{A+B}(r)\right)=\overline{A}(r)+\overline{B}(r)\\ (\underline{kA})(r)=k\underline{A}(r),\left(\overline{kA}\right)(r)=k\overline{A}(r).\end{gathered}$$

To emphasis, the collection of all fuzzy numbers with addition and multiplication as defined by (8) is denoted by E, which is a convex cone. The image (opposite) of $A=(a,b,c,d)$ is $-A=(-d,-c,-b,-a)$ (Zadeh, L.A, 1965; Dubois, D. and H. Prade, 1980).

4.3 Definition

A function $f:[0,1]\rightarrow[0,1]$ is a reducing function if is s increasing and $f(0)=0$ and $f(1)=1$. We say that s is a regular function if $f(r)dr=1/2$.

4.4 Definition

If A is a fuzzy number with r-cut representation, $\left(L_A^{-1}(r),R_A^{-1}(r)\right)$ and s is a reducing function, then the value of A (with respect to s); it is defined by

$$Val(A)=\int_0^1 f(r)[L_A^{-1}(r)+R_A^{-1}(r)]dr \quad (4)$$

4.5 Definition

If A is a fuzzy number with r-cut representation $\left(L_A^{-1}(r),R_A^{-1}(r)\right)$, and s is a reducing function then the ambiguity of A (with respect to s) is defined by

$$Amb(A)=\int_0^1 f(r)[R_A^{-1}(r)-L_A^{-1}(r)]dr \quad (5)$$

Let also recall that the expected interval $EI(A)$ of a fuzzy number A is given by

$$EI(A)=\left[\int_0^1 L_A^{-1}(r)dr,\int_0^1 R_A^{-1}(r)dr\right]. \tag{6}$$

Another parameter is utilized for representing the typical value of the fuzzy number is the middle of the expected interval of a fuzzy number and it is called the expected value of a fuzzy number A i.e. number A is given by (Bodjanova, 2005)

$$EV(A)=\frac{1}{2}\left[\int_0^1 L_A^{-1}(r)dr+\int_0^1 R_A^{-1}(r)dr\right]. \tag{7}$$

4.6 Definition

The first of maxima (FOM) is the smallest element of $core(A)$. i.e.

$$FOM=\min core(A). \tag{8}$$

4.7 Definition

The last of maxima (LOM) is the greatest element of $core(A)$. i.e.

$$LOM=\max core(A). \tag{9}$$

4.8 Definition

For arbitrary fuzzy numbers $A=\left(L_A^{-1}(r),R_A^{-1}(r)\right)$ and $B=\left(L_B^{-1}(r),R_B^{-1}(r)\right)$ the equality

$$D(A,B)=\left[\int_0^1\left(L_A^{-1}(r)-L_B^{-1}(r)\right)^2 dr+\int_0^1\left(R_A^{-1}(r)-R_B^{-1}(r)\right)^2 dr\right]^{1/2} \tag{10}$$

is the distance between A and B. The function $D(A,B)$ is a metric in E and (E,D) is a complete metric space.

The ordering indices are organized into three categories by Wang and Kerre (Wang & Kerre, 2001) as follows:

- **Defuzzification method**: Each index is associated with a mapping from the set of fuzzy quantities to the real line. In this case, fuzzy quantities are compared according to the corresponding real numbers.
- **Reference set method**: in this case, a fuzzy set as a reference set is set up and all the fuzzy quantities to be ranked are compared with the reference set.
- **Fuzzy relation method**: In this case, a fuzzy relation is constructed to make pair wise comparisons between the fuzzy quantities involved.

Let M be an ordering method on E. The statement two elements A_1 and A_2 in E satisfy that A_1 has a higher ranking than A_2 when M is applied will be written as $A_1 \succ A_1$ by M. $A_1 \approx A_1$ and $A_1 \geq A_1$ are similarly interpreted. The following reasonable properties for the ordering approaches are introduced by Wang and Kerre (Wang & Kerre 2001).

1. For an arbitrary finite subset Γ of E and $A_1 \in \Gamma$, $A_1 \geq A_1$.
2. For an arbitrary finite subset Γ of E and $(A_1, A_2) \in \Gamma^2, A_1 \geq A_2$ and $A_2 \geq A_1$, we should have $A_1 \approx A_2$.
3. For an arbitrary finite subset Γ of E and $(A_1, A_2, A_3) \in \Gamma^3, A_1 \geq A_2$ and $A_2 \geq A_3$, we should have $A_1 \geq A_3$.
4. For an arbitrary finite subset Γ of E and $(A_1, A_2) \in \Gamma^2$, inf{supp(A_1)}> sup{supp(A_2), we should have $A_1 \geq A_2$.
5. For an arbitrary finite subset Γ of E and $(A_1, A_2) \in \Gamma^2$, inf{supp(A_1)}> sup{supp(A_2)}, we should have $A_1 \succ A_2$.
6. Let $A_1, A_2, A_1 + A_3$ and $A_2 + A_3$ be elements of E. If $A_1 \geq A_2$, then $A_1 + A_3 \geq A_2 + A_3$.

5. Ranking indices

a. Methods of centroid point

In order to determine the centroid points (x_0, y_0) of a fuzzy number A, Cheng (Cheng, 1998) provided a formula then Wang et al. (Y. M. Wang et al., 2006) found from the point of view of analytical geometry and showed the corrected centroid points as follows:

$$x_0 = \frac{\int_a^b x L_A(x)dx + \int_b^c x dx + \int_c^d x R_A(x)dx}{\int_a^b L_A(x)dx + \int_b^c dx + \int_c^d R_A(x)dx}$$

$$y_0 = \frac{\left[\int_0^\omega y R_A^{-1}(y)dy - \int_0^\omega y L_A^{-1}(y)dy\right]}{\int_0^\omega R_A^{-1}(y)dy - \int_0^\omega L_A^{-1}(y)dy}. \tag{11}$$

For non-normal trapezoidal fuzzy number $A = (a, b, c, d, \omega)$ formulas (11) lead to following results respectively.

$$x_0 = \frac{1}{3}\left[a + b + c + d - \frac{dc - ab}{(d + c) - (a + b)}\right]$$

$$y_0 = \frac{\omega}{3}\left[1 + \frac{c - d}{(d + c) - (a + b)}\right]. \tag{12}$$

Since non-normal triangular fuzzy numbers are, special cases of normal trapezoidal fuzzy numbers with $b = c$, formulas (12) can be simplified as

$$x_0 = \frac{1}{3}[a + b + d]$$

$$y_0 = \frac{\omega}{3}. \tag{13}$$

In this case, normal triangular fuzzy numbers could be compared or ranked directly in terms of their centroid coordinates on horizontal axis.

Cheng (Cheng, 1998) formulated his idea as follows:

$$R(A)=\sqrt{x_0(A)^2+y_0(A)^2}. \tag{14}$$

To overcome the drawback of Cheng's distance Chu and Tsao's (Chu & Tsao, 2002) computed the area between the centroid and original points to rank fuzzy numbers as:

$$S(A)=x_0(A).y_0(A). \tag{15}$$

Then Wang and Lee (Y. J. Wang, 2008) ranked the fuzzy numbers based on their x_0's values if they are different. In the case that they are equal, they further compare their y_0's values to form their ranks.

Further, for two fuzzy numbers A and B if $y_0(A)\geq y_0(B)$ based on $x_0(A)=x_0(B)$, then $A\geq B$.

By shortcoming of the mentioned methods finally, Abbasbandy and Hajjari (Abbasbandy & Hajjari 2010) improved Cheng's distance centroid as follows:

$$IR(A)=\gamma(A)\sqrt{x_0(A)^2+y_0(A)^2} \tag{16}$$

Where

$$\gamma(A)=\begin{cases} 1 & \int_0^1\left(L_A^{-1}(x)+R_A^{-1}(x)\right)dx\succ 0,\\ 0 & \int_0^1\left(L_A^{-1}(x)+R_A^{-1}(x)\right)dx=0,\\ -1 & \int_0^1\left(L_A^{-1}(x)+R_A^{-1}(x)\right)dx\prec 0.\end{cases} \tag{17}$$

However, there are some problems on the centroid point methods. In next section, we will present a new index for ranking fuzzy numbers. The proposed index will be constructed by fuzzy distance and centroid point.

b. Method of D-distance (Ma et al. 2000)

Let all of fuzzy numbers are positive or negative. Without less of generality, assume that all of them are positive. The membership function of $a\in R$ is $\mu_a(x)=1$, if $x=a$ and $\mu_a(x)=0$ if $x\neq a$. Hence if $a=0$ we have the following

$$\mu_0(0)=\begin{cases}1 & x=0\\ 0 & x\neq 0.\end{cases}$$

Since $\mu_0(x)\in E$, left fuzziness and right fuzziness are 0, so for each $\mu_A\in E$

$$D(A,\mu_0)=\left[\int_0^1\left(L_A^{-1}(r)^2+R_A^{-1}(r)_2\right)dr\right].^{1/2} \tag{18}$$

Thus, we have the following definition

5.1 Definition

For A and $B\in E$, define the ranking of A and B by saying

$$\begin{aligned}
A\succ B \quad &iff \quad d(A,\mu_0)\succ d(B,\mu_0),\\
A\prec B \quad &iff \quad d(A,\mu_0)\prec d(B,\mu_0),\\
A\approx B \quad &iff \quad d(A,\mu_0)=d(B,\mu_0).
\end{aligned}$$

5.2 Property

Suppose A and $B\in E$, are arbitrary, therefore

If $A=B$ then $A\approx B$.

If $B\subseteq A$ and $L_A^{-1}(r)^2+R_A^{-1}(r)^2\succ L_B^{-1}(r)^2+R_B^{-1}(r)^2$ for all $r\in[0,1]$ then $B\prec A$.

5.3 Remark

The distance triangular fuzzy number $A=(x_0,\sigma,\beta)$ of μ_0 is defined as following:

$$d(A,\mu_0)=\left[2x_0^2+\sigma^2/3+\beta^2/3+x_0(\beta-\sigma)\right].^{1/2} \tag{19}$$

The distance trapezoidal fuzzy number $A=(x_0,y_0,\sigma,\beta)$ of μ_0 is defined as following

$$d(A,\mu_0)=\left[2x_0^2+\sigma^2/3+\beta^2/3-x_0\sigma+y_0\beta)\right].^{1/2} \tag{20}$$

If $A\approx B$ it is not necessary that $A=B$.

If $A\neq B$ and $(L_A^{-1}(r)^2+R_A^{-1}(r)^2)^{1/2}=(L_B^{-1}(r)^2+R_B^{-1}(r)^2)^{1/2}$ then $A\approx B$.

c. Method of sign distance (Abbasbandy & Asady 2006)

5.4 Definition

For arbitrary fuzzy numbers $A=\left(L_A^{-1}(r),R_A^{-1}(r)\right)$ and $B=\left(L_B^{-1}(r),R_B^{-1}(r)\right)$ the function

$$D(A,A_0)=\left(\int_0^1(\left|L_A^{-1}(x)\right|^p+\left|R_A^{-1}(x)\right|^p)dx\right)^{\frac{1}{p}}. \tag{21}$$

is the distance between A and B.

5.5 Definition

Let $\gamma(A): E \longrightarrow \{-1,1\}$ be a function that is defined as follows:

$$\gamma(A) = sign\int_0^1 [L_A^{-1}(r) + R_A^{-1}(r)]dr$$

Where

$$\gamma(A) = \begin{cases} 1 & \int_0^1 (L_A^{-1}(r) + R_A^{-1}(r)) \succ 0 \\ -1 & \int (L_A^{-1}(r) + R_A^{-1}(r)) \prec 0 \end{cases}$$

5.6 Remark

1. If supp $(A) \geq 0$ or inf $L_A^{-1}(r) \geq 0$ then $\gamma(A) = 1$.
2. If supp $(A) \prec 0$ or sup $R_A^{-1}(r) \prec 0$ then $\gamma(A) = -1$.

5.7 Definition

For $A \in E$, $d_p(A, \mu_0) = \gamma(A)D(A, \mu_0)$ is called sign distance.

5.8 Definition

For A and $B \in E$ define the ranking order of A and B by d_p on E. i.e.

$$\begin{aligned} A_i \succ A_j \quad & iff \quad d_p(A_i, \mu_0) \succ d_p(A_j, \mu_0) \\ A_i \prec A_j \quad & iff \quad d_p(A_i, \mu_0) \prec d_p(A_j, \mu_0) \\ A_i \approx A_j \quad & iff \quad d_p(A_i, \mu_0) = d_p(A_j, \mu_0) \end{aligned}$$

5.9 Remark

1. The function d_p, sign distance has the Wang and Kerre's properties .
2. The function d_p, sign distance for $p = 1$ has the following properties

if

inf {supp (A), supp (B), supp $(A+C)$, supp $(B+C)$ } ≥ 0

or

sup {supp (A), supp (B), supp $(A+C)$, supp $(B+C)$ } ≤ 0

3. Suppose A and $B \in E$ are arbitrary then

a. If $A = B$ then $A \approx B$,

b. If $B \subseteq A$ and $\gamma(A)\left(\left|L_A^{-1}(r)\right|^p + \left|R_A^{-1}(r)^p\right|\right) \succ \gamma(B)\left(\left|L_B^{-1}(r)\right|^p + \left|R_B^{-1}(r)\right|^p\right)$, that for all $r \in [0,1]$ then $B \prec A.$,

4. If $A \approx B$ it is not necessary that $A = B$. Since if $A \neq B$ and $\gamma(A)\left(\left|L_A^{-1}(r)\right|^p + \left|R_A^{-1}(r)^p\right|\right) = \gamma(B)\left(\left|L_B^{-1}(r)\right|^p + \left|R_B^{-1}(r)\right|^p\right)$ that for all $r \in [0,1]$ then $B \approx A$.,
5. If $A \leq B$ then $-A \geq -B$.

Therefore, we can simply rank the fuzzy numbers by the defuzzification of $d_p(A, \mu_0)$. By Remark 3.12 part (5) we can logically infer ranking order of the image of the fuzzy numbers.

d. Method of H-distance

5.10 Definition

A continuous function $s:[0,1] \longrightarrow [0,1]$ with the following properties is a source function $s(0) = 0,\ s(1) = 1,\ s(r)$ is increasing, and $\int_0^1 s(r)dr = \frac{1}{2}$.

In fact, a reducing has the reflection of weighting the influence of the different r-cuts and diminishes the contribution of the lower r-levels. This is reasonable since these levels arise from values of membership function for which there is a considerable amount of uncertainty. For example, we can use $s(r) = r$.

5.11 Definition

For A and $B \in E$ we define H-distance of A and B by

$$D_H^*(A,B) = \frac{1}{2}\left\{\left|Val(A) - Val(B)\right| + \left|Amb(A) - Amb(B)\right| + d_H\left(\left|A\right|^1 + \left|B\right|^1\right)\right\} \tag{22}$$

where d_H is the Housdorf metric between intervals and $[.]^1$ is the 1-cut representation of a fuzzy number.

e. Method of source distance (Ma et al., 2000)

5.12 Definition

For A and $B \in E$ we define source distance of A and B by

$$D_s(A,B) = \frac{1}{2}\left\{\left|Val_s(A) - Val_s(B)\right| + \left|Amb_s(A) - Amb_s(B)\right| + \max\{|t_A - t_B|, |m_A - m_B|\}\right\},$$

where $[m_A, t_A]$ and $[m_B, t_B]$ are the cores of fuzzy numbers A and B respectively.

5.13 Property

The source distance metric D_s is a metric on E_{TR} and a pseudo-metric on E.

f. Method of magnitude (Abbasbandy & Hajjari 2009)

For an arbitrary trapezoidal fuzzy number $A=(x_0, y_0, \sigma, \beta)$ with parametric form $A=\left(L_A^{-1}(r), R_A^{-1}(r)\right)$, we define the magnitude of the trapezoidal fuzzy number A as

$$Mag(A)=\frac{1}{2}\left(\int_0^1 (L_A^{-1}(r)+R_A^{-1}(r)+x_0+y_0)f(r)dr\right). \quad f(r)=r \tag{23}$$

where the function $f(r)$ is a non-negative and increasing function on $[0,1]$ with $f(0)=0, f(1)=1$ and $\int_0^1 f(r)dr=\frac{1}{2}.$ for example, we can use. The resulting scalar value is used to rank the fuzzy numbers. The larger $Mag(A)$, the larger fuzzy number. Therefore for any two fuzzy number A and $B \in E$. We defined the ranking of A and B by the $Mag(A)$ on E as follows

$Mag(A) \succ Mag(B)$ if and only if $A \succ B$.

$Mag(A) \prec Mag(B)$ if and only if $A \prec B$.

$Mag(A) = Mag(B)$ if and only if $A \approx B$.

Then we formulate the order $\geq$ and $\leq$ as $A \geq B$ if and only if $A \succ B$ or $A \approx B$, $A \leq B$ if and only if $A \prec B$ or $A \approx B$. In other words, this method is placed in the first class of Kerre's categories(X. Wang & Kerre 2001).

g. Method of promoter operator (Hajjari & Abbasbandy 2011)

Let $A=(a,b,c,d)$ be a non-normal trapezoidal fuzzy number with $r-$cut representation $A=\left(L_A^{-1}(r), R_A^{-1}(r)\right)$.. Consequently, we have

$$Mag(A)=\frac{(3\omega^2+2)(b+c)}{12\omega}+\frac{(3\omega-2)(a+d)}{12\omega}. \tag{24}$$

It is clear that for normal trapezoidal fuzzy numbers the formula (24) reduces to

$$Mag(A)=\frac{5}{12}(b+c)+\frac{1}{12}(a+d). \tag{25}$$

In the following, we use an example to illustrate the ranking process of the proposed method.

Moreover, for normal fuzzy numbers we have

$$Mag(A)=\frac{1}{2}\left[\int_0^1 (L_A^{-1}(r)dr+R_A^{-1}(r)+L_A^{-1}(1)+R_A^{-1}(1))f(r)dr\right]. \tag{26}$$

h. Methods of deviation degree

Ranking L-R fuzzy numbers based on deviation degree (Z.X. Wang et al., 2009)

5.14 Definition

For any groups of fuzzy numbers $A_1, A_2, ..., A_n$ in E with support sets $S(A_i)$, $i = 1, . . ., n$. Let $S = \bigcap_{i=1}^{n} S(A_i)$ and $x_{\min} = \inf S$ and $x_{\max} = \sup S$. Then minimal and maximal reference sets $A_{\min}$ and $A_{\max}$ are defined as

$$\mu_{A_{\min}}(x) = \begin{cases} \dfrac{x_{\max} - x}{x_{\max} - x_{\min}}, & if \;\; x \in S \\ 0, & otherwise, \end{cases} \tag{27}$$

$$\mu_{A_{\max}}(x) = \begin{cases} \dfrac{x - x_{\min}}{x_{\max} - x_{\min}}, & if \;\; x \in S \\ 0, & otherwise. \end{cases} \tag{28}$$

5.15 Definition

For any groups of fuzzy numbers $A_1, A_2, ..., A_n$ in E, let $A_{\min}$ and $A_{\max}$ be minimal and maximal reference sets of these fuzzy numbers, respectively. Then left and right deviation degree of A_i, $i = 1, . . ., n$, are defined as follows:

$$d_i^L = \int_{x_{\min}}^{t_i} \left(\mu_{A_{\min}}(x) - L_A^{-1}(x) \right) dx$$

$$d_i^R = \int_{u_i}^{x_{\max}} \left(\mu_{A_{\max}}(x) - R_A^{-1}(x) \right) dx \tag{29}$$

where t_i and u_i, $i = 1,2,...,n$ are the abscissas of the crossover points of L_{A_i} and $\mu_{A_{\min}}$, and R_{A_i} and $\mu_{A_{\max}}$, respectively.

5.16 Definition

For any groups of fuzzy numbers $A_i = (a_i, b_i, c_i, d_i, \omega)$ in E, its expectation value of centroid is defined as follows:

$$M_i = \frac{\int_{a_i}^{d_i} x \mu_{A_i}(x) dx}{\int_{a_i}^{d_i} \mu_A(x) dx} \tag{30}$$

$$\lambda_i = \frac{M_i - M_{\min}}{M_{\max} - M_{\min}} \tag{31}$$

where $M_{\max} = \max\{M_1, M_2, ..., M_n\}$ and $M_{min} = min\{M_1, M_2, ..., M_n\}$

Based on mentioned formulae, the ranking index value of fuzzy numbers A_i, $i = 1, . . ., n$, is given by

$$d_i = \begin{cases} \dfrac{d_i^L \lambda_i}{1 + d_i^R (1 - \lambda_i)}, & M_{\max} \neq M_{\min}, \ i = 1, 2, ..., n, \\ \dfrac{d_i^L}{1 + d_i^R} & M_{\max} = M_{\min}, \ i = 1, 2, ..., n. \end{cases} \tag{32}$$

Now, by using (15), for any two fuzzy numbers A_i and Aj the ranking order is based on the following rules.

1. $A_i \succ A_j$ if and only if $d_i \succ d_j$,
2. $A_i \prec A_j$ if and only if $d_i \prec d_j$,
3. $A_i \approx A_j$ if and only if $d_i = d_j$.

- The revised method of ranking L-R fizzy number based on deviation degree (Asady, 2010)

Asady (Asady, 2010) revised Wang et al. (Z.X. Wang et al. 2009) method and suggested $D(.)$ operator for ranking of fuzzy numbers as follows:

Consider two fuzzy numbers A and B the ranking order is based on the following situations:

1. If $D(A) \prec D(B)$, then $A \prec B$.
2. If $D(A) \succ D(B)$, then $A \succ B$.
3. If $D(A) = D(B)$, then

if $\gamma_A \neq \gamma_B$, $D^*(A) \prec D^*(B)$ then $A \prec B$,

if $\gamma_A \neq \gamma_B$, $D^*(A) \succ D^*(B)$ then $A \succ B$,

else $A \approx B$.

where

$$D(A) = \frac{D_A^L}{1 + D_A^R} \tag{33}$$

$$D^*(A) = \frac{D_A^L \gamma}{1 + D_A^R \gamma} \tag{34}$$

where

$$D_A^L = \int_0^1 \left(R_A^{-1}(x) + L_A^{-1}(x) - 2x_{\min}\right)dx \quad (35)$$

$$D_A^R = \int_0^1 \left(2x_{\max} - R_A^{-1}(x) - L_A^{-1}(x)\right)dx \quad (36)$$

Ranking fuzzy numbers based on the left and the right sides of fuzzy numbers (Nejad & Mashinchi, 2011)

Recently Nejad and Mashinchi (Nejad & Mashinchi, 2011) pointed out the drawback of Wang et al. (Z.X. Wang et al. , 2009) hen they presented a novel ranking method as follows.

5.17 Definition

Let $A_i = (a_i, b_i, c_i, d_i, \omega)$, $i = 1,2,...,n$, are fuzzy numbers in E, $a_{\min} = \min\{a_1, a_2, ..., a_n\}$ and $d_{\max} = \max\{d_1, d_2, ..., d_n\}$. The areas s_i^L and s_i^R of the left and right sides of the fuzzy number A_i are defined as

$$s_i^L = \int_0^\omega \left(L_A^{-1}(r) - a_{\min}\right)dr \quad (37)$$

$$s_i^R = \int_0^\omega \left(d_{\max} - R_A^{-1}(r)\right)dr. \quad (38)$$

Based on above definitions, the proposed ranking index is

$$s_i = \frac{s_i^L \lambda_i}{1 + s_i^R (1 - \lambda_i)}, \quad i = 1,2,...,n. \quad (39)$$

Then the ranking order follows next rules.

1. $A_i \succ A_j$ if and only if $s_i \succ s_j$,
2. $A_i \prec A_j$ if and only if $s_i \prec s_j$,
3. $A_i \approx A_j$ if and only if $s_i = s_j$.

To obtain the reasonable they added two triangular fuzzy numbers A_0 and A_{n+1}, where

$$\begin{aligned} &A_0 = (a_0, b_0, d_0), \\ &a_0 = 2b_0 - d_0, \ b_0 = \min\{a_i, \ i = 1,2,...,n\}, \\ &d_0 = (d + b_0)/2, \ d = \min\{d_i, \ i = 1,2,...,n\} \end{aligned} \quad (40)$$

and

$$\begin{aligned} &A_{n+1} = (a_{n+1}, b_{n+1}, d_{n+1}), \\ &a_{n+1} = (b_{n+1} + a)/2, \ \ b_{n+1} = \max\{d_i, \ \ i = 1,2,...,n\}, \\ &d_{n+1} = 2b_{n+1} - a_{n+1}), \ \ a = \max\{a_i, \ \ i = 1,2,...,n\}. \end{aligned} \quad (41)$$

Then they ranked fuzzy numbers $A_1, A_2, ..., A_n$ based on the ranking area values $s_1, s_2, ..., s_n$.

Nevertheless, the new ranking method has drawback.

In the next section, we discuss on those methods that based on deviation degree by a number numerical counter examples.

6. Discussion and counter examples

6.1 Example

Let two fuzzy numbers *A= (3,6,9)* and *B= (5,6,7)* from (Z.-X. Wang et al., 2009) as shown in Fig. 1.

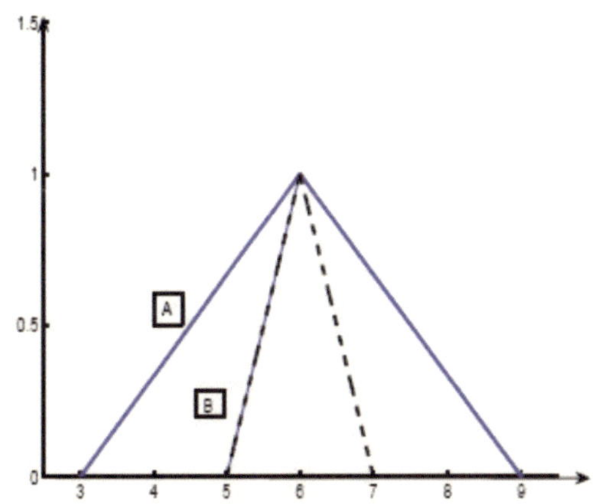

Fig. 1. Fuzzy numbers *A=(3,6,9)* and *B=(5,6,7)*

Through the approaches in this paper, the ranking index can be obtained as *Mag (A)=Mag(B)=12* and $EV(A) = EV(B) = 6$. Then the ranking order of fuzzy numbers is $A \approx B$. Because fuzzy numbers *A* and *B* have the same mode and symmetric spread, most of existing approaches have the identical results. For instance, by Abbasbandy and Asady's approach (Abbasbandy & Asady, 2006), different ranking orders are obtained when different index values p are taken. When $p = 1$ and $p = 2$ the ranking order is the same, i.e., $A \approx B$ Nevertheless, the same results produced when distance index, *CV* index of Cheng's approach and Chu and Tsao's area are respectively used, i.e., $x_A = x_B = 6$ and $y_A = y_B = \frac{1}{3}$ then from Cheng's distance and Chau and Tsao's area we get that $R(A) = R(B) = 2.2608$, $S(A) = S(B) = 1.4142$ respectively.

From the obtained results we have $A \approx B$, for two triangular fuzzy numbers *A=(3, 6, 9)* and *B=(5, 6, 7)*. Now we review the ranking approaches by promoter operator. Since *A* and *B* have the same ranking order and the same centroid points we then compute their ambiguities. Hence, from (Deng et al., 2006) it will be obtained $amb(A) = 1$ and $amb(B) = \frac{1}{3}$.

Consequently, by using promoter operator we have

$$P(A)=\left(Mag(A),\frac{1}{1+amb(A)}\right)=(12,\frac{1}{2}),\quad P(B)=\left(Mag(B),\frac{1}{1+amb(B)}\right)=(12,\frac{3}{4})$$

$$P(A)=\left(EV(A),\frac{1}{1+amb(A)}\right)=(6,\frac{1}{2}),\quad P(B)=\left(EV(B),\frac{1}{1+amb(B)}\right)=(6,\frac{3}{4})$$

$$P(A)=\left(R(A),\frac{1}{1+amb(A)}\right)=(2.2608,\frac{1}{2}),\quad P(B)=\left(R(B),\frac{1}{1+amb(B)}\right)=(2.2608,\frac{3}{4})$$

$$P(A)=\left(S(A),\frac{1}{1+amb(A)}\right)=(12,\frac{1}{2}),\quad P(B)=\left(S(B),\frac{1}{1+amb(B)}\right)=(12,\frac{3}{4}).$$

The ranking order is $A \prec B$ Through the proposed approach by Wang et al., the ranking index values can be obtained as d_1 = 0.1429 and d_2 = 0.1567. Then the ranking order of fuzzy numbers is also $A \prec B$.

In the following, we use the data sets shown in Chen and Chen (S. J. Chen et al. 2009) to compare the ranking results of the proposed approaches with Cheng method (Cheng, 1998), Chu and Tsao's method (Chu & Tsao 2002) and Chen and Chen (S. J. Chen et al. 2009). The comparing of ranking results for different methods will be explained in the following.

For the fuzzy numbers A and B shown in Set 1 of Fig. 4, Cheng's method (Cheng, C. H., 1998), Chu's method (Chu, T. and Tsao, C., 2002), Chen and Chen's method (Chen, S. J. and Chen, S. M., 2007; Chen, S.-M. and Chen, J.-H., 2009) and *Mag*- method (Abbasbandy, S. and Hajjari, T., 2009) get the same ranking order $A \prec B$.

4. For the fuzzy numbers A and B shown in Set 2 of Fig. 4, Cheng's method (Cheng, C. H., 1998), Chu 's method (Chu, T. and Tsao, C., 2002) and *Mag*- method (Abbasbandy, S. and Hajjari, T., 2009) get the same ranking order $A \approx B$, which is unreasonable. Whereas by applying the promoter operator the ranking order is the same as Chen and Chen's method (Chen, S. J. and Chen, S. M., 2007; Chen, S.-M. and Chen, J.-H., 2009), i.e. $A \prec B$.
5. For the fuzzy numbers A and B shown in Set 3 of Fig. 4, Cheng's method (Cheng, C. H., 1998), Chu and Tsao's method (Chu, T. and Tsao, C., 2002) and *Mag*- method (Abbasbandy, S. and Hajjari, T., 2009) get an inaccurate ranking order $A \approx B$ whereas by applying the promoter operator the ranking order is the same as Chen and Chen's method (Chen, S. J. and Chen, S. M., 2007; Chen, S.-M. and Chen, J.-H., 2009) i.e. $A \prec B$.
6. For the fuzzy numbers A and B shown in Set 4 of Fig. 4, Cheng's method (Cheng, C. H., 1998), Chu and Tsao's method (Chu, T. and Tsao, C., 2002), Chen and Chen's method (Chen, S. J. and Chen, S. M., 2007; Chen, S.-M. and Chen, J.-H., 2009) and *Mag*- method (Abbasbandy, S. and Hajjari, T., 2009) get the same ranking order: $A \prec B$.
7. For the fuzzy numbers A and B shown in Set 5 of Fig. 2, Cheng's method (Cheng, C. H., 1998), Chu and Tsao's method (Chu, T. and Tsao, C., 2002) cannot calculate the crisp-value fuzzy number, whereas Chen and Chen's method (S. J. Chen, 2009) and $Mag-$ *Mag*- method (Abbasbandy & Hajjari, 2009) get the same ranking order: $A \prec B$.

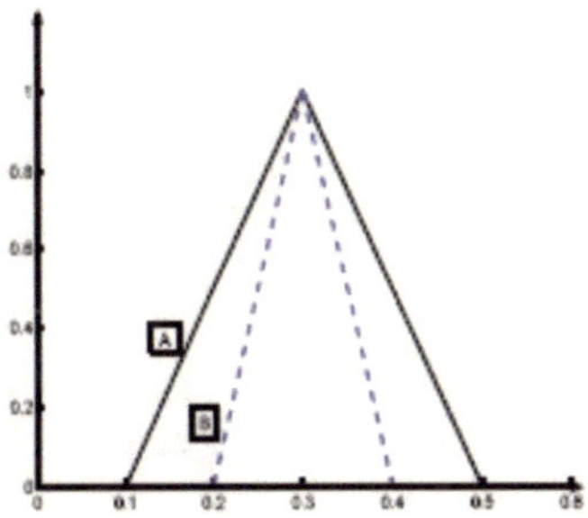

Set 3
A=(0.1, 0.3, 0.3, 0.5; 1)
B=(0.2, 0.3, 0.3, 0.4; 1)

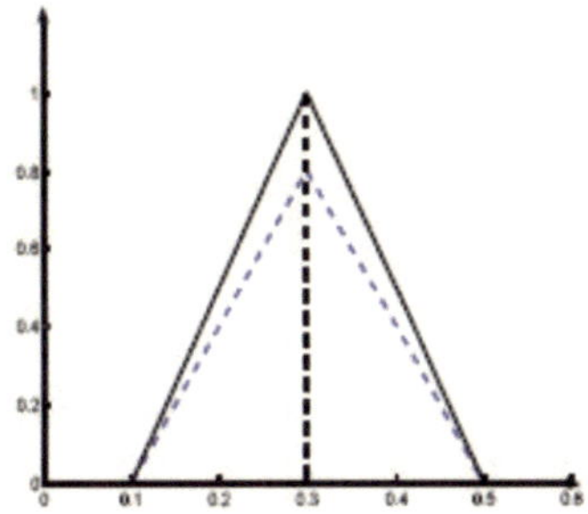

Set 4
A=(0.1, 0.3, 0.3, 0.5; 0.8)
B=(0.1, 0.3, 0.3, 0.5; 1)

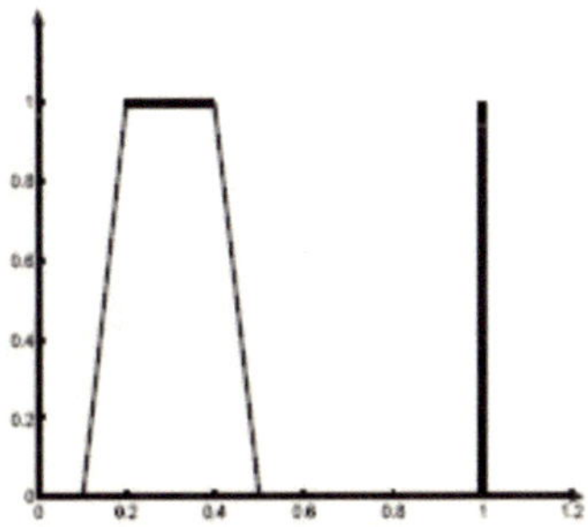

Set 5
A=(0.1, 0.2, 0.4, 0.5; 1)
B=(1.0, 1.0, 1.0, 1.0; 1)

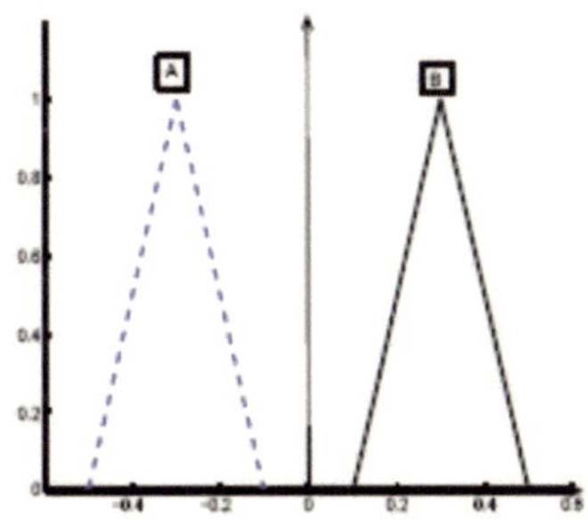

Set 6
A=(-0.5, -0.3, -0.3, -0.1; 1)
B=(0.1, 0.3, 0.3, 0.5; 1)

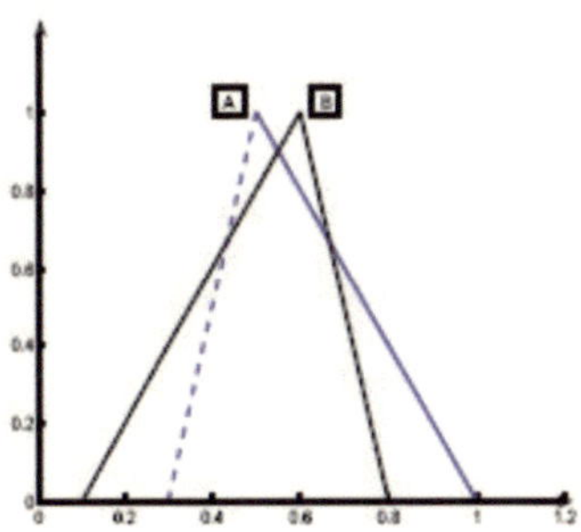

Set 7
A=(0.3, 0.5, 0.5, 1.0; 1)
B=(0.1, 0.6, 0.6, 0.8; 1)

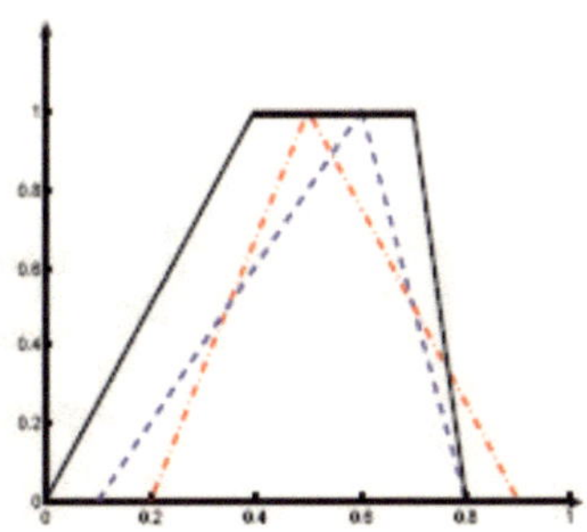

Set 8
A=(0.0, 0.4, 0.6, 0.8; 1)
B=(0.2, 0.5, 0.5, 0.9; 1)
C=(0.1, 0.6, 0.7, 0.8; 1)

Fig. 2.

Methods	F.n	set 1	set 2	set 3	set 4	set 5	set 6	set 7	set 8
Cheng's (1998)	A	.583	.583	.583	.461	.424	-.583	.767	.68
	B	.707	.583	.583	.583	*	.583	.724	.726
	C	*	*	*	*	*	*	*	.746
Results		$A \prec B$	$A \sim B$	$A \sim B$	$A \prec B$	*	$A \prec B$	$B \prec A$	$A \prec B \prec C$
P.O Results		*	$A \prec B$	$A \prec B$	*	*	*	*	*
Chau's (2002)	A	.15	.15	.15	.12	.15	-.15	.287	.228
	B	.25	.15	.15	.15	*	.15	.262	.262
	C	*	*	*	*	*	*	*	.278
Results		$A \prec B$	$A \sim B$	$A \sim B$	$A \prec B$	*	$A \prec B$	$B \prec A$	$A \prec B \prec C$
P.O Results		*	$A \prec B$	$A \prec B$	*	*	*	*	*
Chen's (2007)	A	.446	.424	.446	.357	.42	.446	.413	.372
	B	.489	.446	.473	.446	.860	.747	.401	.416
	C	*	*	*	*	*	*	*	.398
Results		$A \prec B$	$A \prec B$	$A \prec B$	$A \prec B$	$A \prec B$	$A \prec B$	$B \prec A$	$A \prec C \prec B$
P.O Results		*	*	*	*	*	*	*	*
Chen's (2009)	A	.258	.254	.258	.254	.206	-.258	.443	.335
	B	.430	.258	.278	.258	1	.258	.404	.408
	C	*	*	*	*	*	*	*	.420
Results		$A \prec B$	$A \prec B$	$A \prec B$	$A \prec B$	$A \prec B$	$A \prec B$	$B \prec A$	$A \prec B \prec C$
P.O Results		*	*	*	*	*	*	*	*
Mag (2009)	A	.3	.3	.3	.27	.3	-.3	.525	.483
	B	.5	.3	.3	.3	1	.3	.575	.508
	C	*	*	*	*	*	*	*	.617
Results		$A \prec B$	$A \sim B$	$A \sim B$	$A \prec B$	$A \prec B$	$A \prec B$	$A \prec B$	$A \prec B \prec C$
P.O Results		*	$A \prec B$	$A \prec B$	*	*	*	*	*

Table 1.

8. For the fuzzy numbers *A* and *B* shown in Set 6 of Fig. 2, Cheng's method (Cheng, C. H., 1998), Chu and Tsao's method (Chu & Tsao, 2002), Chen and Chen's method (S. J. Chen & S. M. Chen, 2007; S.-M. Chen & J.-H. Chen, 2009) and *Mag*- method (Abbasbandy & Hajjari, 2009) get the same ranking order: $A \prec B$.
9. For the fuzzy numbers *A* and *B* shown in Set 7 of Fig. 2, Cheng's method (Cheng, 1998), Chu and Tsao's method (Chu & Tsao, 2002), Chen and Chen's method (S. J. Chen et al. 2009) get the same ranking order: $B \prec A$, whereas the ranking order by *Mag*- method (Abbasbandy & Hajjari, 2009) is $A \prec B$. By comparing the ranking result of *Mag*- method with other methods with respect to Set 7 of Fig. 2, we can see that *Mag*- method considers the fact that defuzzified value of a fuzzy number is more important than the spread of a fuzzy number.
10. For the fuzzy numbers *A* and *B* shown in Set 8 of Fig. 2, Cheng's method (Cheng, 1998), Chu and Tsao's method (Chu & Tsao, 2002), Chen and Chen's method (S. J. Chen et al., 2009) and *Mag*- method (Abbasbandy & Hajjari, 2009) get the same ranking order: $A \prec B \prec C$, whereas the ranking order by Chen and Chen's method is $A \prec C \prec B$. By comparing the ranking result of mentioned method with other methods with respect to Set 8 of Fig. 4, we can see that Chen's method considers the fact that the spread of a fuzzy number is more important than defuzzified value of a fuzzy number.

The idea of ranking fuzzy numbers by deviation degree is useful, but a significant approaches should be reserved the important properties such that

- $A \leq B \Leftrightarrow -B \leq -A$
- $A \leq B \Leftrightarrow A+C \leq B+C$
- $A \leq B \wedge B \leq C \Rightarrow A \leq C$

Now we give some numerical example to show the drawback of the aforementioned methods.

6.2 Example

Given two triangular fuzzy number $A=(0.2,0.5,0.8)$ and $B=(0.4,0.5,0.6)$ (Nejad & Mashinchi, 2011), which are indicated in Fig. 3.

The ranking order by Nejad and Mashinchi is $A \prec B$. The images of two numbers A and B are *A=(-0.8, -0.5, -0.2)*, *B=(-0.6, -0.5, -0.4)* respectively, then the ranking order is $-B \prec -A$.

On the other hand, ranking order for A and B and their images by Wang et al.'s method and Asady's revised are $A \approx B$, $-A \approx -B$ respectively.

This example could be indicated that all methods are reasonable. However, we will show that functions of all three methods are not the same in different conditions.

6.3 Example

Consider the three triangular fuzzy numbers A=(1, 2, 6), B = (2.5, 2.75,3) and C = (2, 3, 4), which are taken from Asady's revised (Asady, 2010) (See Fig. 4).

Utilizing Nejad and Mashinchi's method the ranking order is $A \prec B \prec C$ and the ranking order of their images will be obtained $-C \prec -A \prec -B$, which is illogical.

By using Wang et al.'s method the ranking order is $B \prec A \prec C$ and for their images is $-A \approx -C \prec -B$, which is unreasonable too.

From point of revised deviation degree method (Asady, 2010) the ranking orders are $B \prec A \prec C$, $-C \prec -A \prec -B$, respectively.

From this example, it seems the revised method can rank correctly.

In the next example, we will indicate that none of the methods based on deviation degree can rank correctly in all situations.

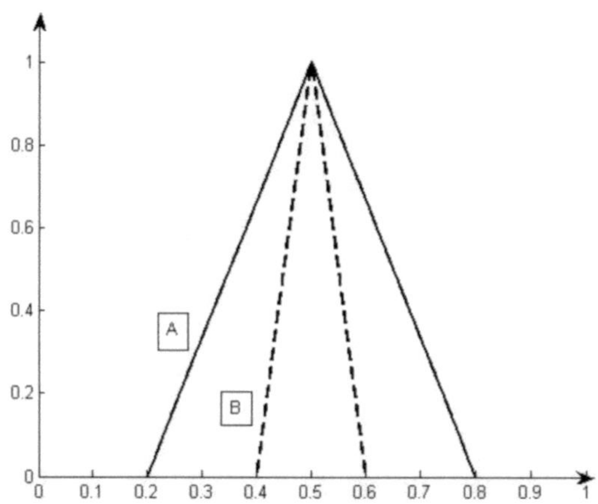

Fig. 3.

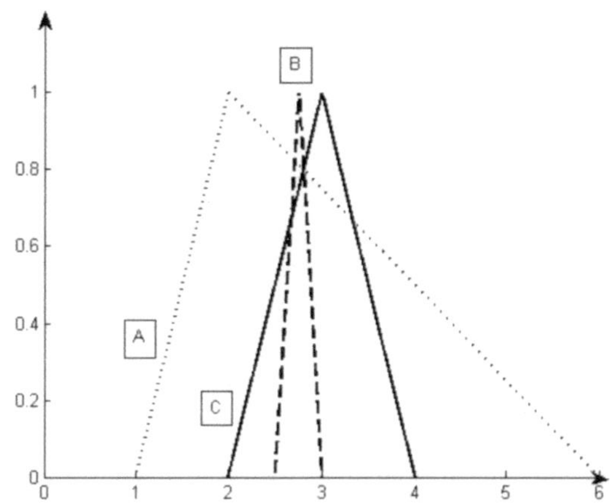

Fig. 4.

6.4 Example

Let the triangular fuzzy number $A=(1,2,3)$ and the fuzzy number $B=(1,2,4)$ with the membership function (See Fig. 5)

$$\mu_B(x)=\begin{cases}\left[1-(x-2)^2\right]^{1/2} & 1\leq x\leq 2,\\ \left[1-\frac{1}{4}(x-2)^2\right]^{1/2} & 2\leq x\leq 4,\\ 0 & otherwise.\end{cases}$$

Using Asady's method the ranking order is obtained $A\prec B$. However, the ranking order of their images is $-A\prec -B$, which is unreasonable.

From mentioned examples, we can theorize that ranking fuzzy numbers based on deviation degree cannot rank fuzzy numbers in all situations.

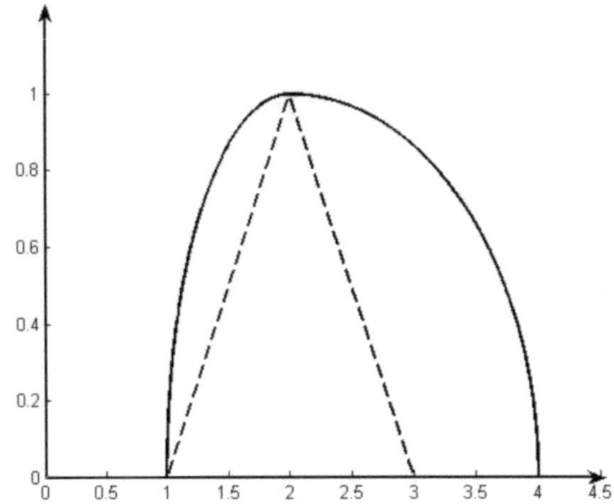

Fig. 5.

7. Conclusion

With the increasing development of fuzzy set theory in various scientific fields and the need to compare fuzzy numbers in different areas. Therefore, Ranking of fuzzy numbers plays a very important role in linguistic decision making, neural network and some other fuzzy application systems . Several strategies have been proposed for ranking of fuzzy numbers. Each of these techniques has been shown to produce non-intuitive results in certain case. In this chapter, we reviewed some recent ranking methods, which will be useful for the researchers who are interested in this area.

8. Acknowledgment

This work was partly supported by Islamic Azad University, FiroozKooh Branch.

9. References

Abbasbandy, S. and Asady, B. (2006). Ranking of fuzzy numbers by sign distance, Inform. Sci. 176: 2405-2416.

Abbasbandy, S. and Hajjari, T. (2009). A new approach for ranking of trapezoidal fuzzy numbers, Comput. Math. Appl. 57: 413-419.

Abbasbandy, S. and Hajjari, T. (2011). An improvement on centroid point method for ranking of fuzzy numbers, J. Sci. I.A.U. 78: 109-119.

Asady, B. (2010). The revised method of ranking LR fuzzy number based on deviation degree, Expert Systems with Applications, 37: 5056-5060.

Bodjanova, S. (2005). Median value and median interval of afuzzy number, Inform. Sci. 172: 73-89.

Chen, S. J. and Chen, S. M. (2003). A new method for handling multicriteria fuzzy decision-making problems using FN-IOWA operators, Cybernetic and Systems, 34: 109-137.

Chen, S. J. and Chen, S. M. (2007). Fuzzy risk analysis based on the ranking of generalized trapezoidal fuzzy numbers, Applied intelligence, 26: 1-11.

Chen, L. H. and Lu, H. W. (2001). An approximate approach for ranking fuzzy numbers based on left and right dominance, Comput. Math. Appl. 41: 1589-1602.

Chen, L. H. and Lu, H. W. (2002). The preference order of fuzzy numbers, Comput. Math. Appl. 44: 1455-1465.

Chen, S.-M. and Chen, J.-H. (2009). Fuzzy risk analysis based on the ranking of generalized fuzzy numbers with different heights and different spreads, Expert Systems with Applications, 36: 6833-6842.

Cheng, C. H., (1998). A new approach for ranking fuzzy numbers by distance method, Fuzzy Sets Syst. 95: 307-317.

Chu, T. and Tsao, C. (2002). Ranking fuzzy numbers with an area between the centroid point and orginal point, Comput. Math. Appl. 43: 111-117.

Deng, Y., Zhu, Z.F. and Liu, Q. (2006). Ranking fuzzy numbers with an area method using of gyration, Comput. Math. Appl. 51: 1127-1136

Deng, Y. and Liu, Q. (2005). A TOPSIS-based centroid index ranking method of fuzzy numbers and its application in decision-making, Cybernetic and Systems, 36: 581-595.

Dubios, D. and Prade, H. (1978). Operations on fuzzy numbers, Internat. J. System Sci. 9. 613-626.

Filev, D.P. and Yager, R.R. (1993). An adaptive approach to defuzzification based on level sets, Fuzzy Sets and Syst. 53: 353-360

Filev, D.P. and Yager, R.R. (1991). A generalized defuzzification method via BADD distributions, Int. J. Intell. Syst. 6: 687-697.

Halgamuge, S., Runkler, T. and Glesner, M. (1996). On the neural defuzzification methods, in: Proceeding of the 5th IEEE International Conference on Fuzzy Systems, 463-469.

Hajjari T. and Abbasbandy, S. (2011). A note on " The revised method of ranking LR fuzzy number based on deviation degree", Expert Syst with Applications, 38: 13491-134-92.

Hajjari, T. (2011a). Ranking of fuzzy numbers based on ambiguity degree, Australian Journal of Basic and Applied Sciences. 5 (1): 62-69.

Hajjari, T. (2011b). On deviation degree methods for ranking fuzzy numbers. Australian Journal of Basic and Applied Sciences, 5 (5): 750-758.

Hajjari, T., Abbasbandy, S. (2011). A Promoter Operator for Defuzzification Methods, Australian Journal of Basic and Applied Sciences, Inpress.

Jiang, T. and Li, Y. (1996). Generalized defuzzification strategies and their parameter learning procedure, IEEE Transactions on fuzzy systems, 4: 64-71.

Leekwijck, W.V. and Kerre, E. E. (2001). Continuity focused choice of maxima: Yet another defuzzification method, Fuzzy Sets and Syst. 122: 303-314.

Liu, X. W. and. Han, S. L. (2005). Ranking fuzzy numbers with preference weighting function expectationc, Comput. Math. Appl. 49: 1455-1465.

Ma, M., Friedman, M. and. Kandel. A (1999), A new fuzzy arithmetic. Fuzzy Sets and Systems, 108: 83-90.

Nejad, A.M. and Mashinchi, M. (2011). Ranking fuzzy numbers based on the areas on the left and the right sides of fuzzy number, Computers and Mathematics with Applications, 61: 431-442.

Roychowdhury, S. and Pedrycz, W. (2001). A survey of defuzzification strategies, Int. J. Intell. Syst. 16: 679-695.

Song, Q. and Leland, R. P. (1996). Adaptive learning defuzzificatin techniques and applications, Comput. Math. Appl. 81: 321-329.

Yager, R.R., (1996). Knowledge-based defuzzification, Fuzzy Sets and Syst 80: 177-185

Wang, Z.-X., Liu, Y.-J, Fan, Z.-P. and Feng, B., (2009). Ranking L-R fuzzy numbers based on deviation degree, Inform. Sci. 176: 2070-2077.

Wang, Y.J. and Lee, H. Sh. (2008). The revised method of ranking fuzzy numbers with an area between the centroid and original points, Comput. Math. Appl. 55: 2033-2042.

Wang, X., and Kerre, E. E. (2001). Reasonable properties for the ordering of fuzzy quantities (I), Fuzzy Sets and Syst. 118, 375.

4

Neuro-Fuzzy Digital Filter

José de Jesús Medel[1], Juan Carlos García[2] and Juan Carlos Sánchez[2]
[1]*Computing Research Centre, México D. F*
[2]*Superior School of Mechanical and Electrical Engineering,*
Department of Micro Electronics Research
Mexico

1. Introduction

1.1 Neural net

An artificial neural net is a computational model which imitates natural biological system actions, through neurons that adapt their gains as occurs in the brain, and these are interconnected constructing a neural net system (Nikola, 1996) (Medel, García y Sánchez, 2008), shown in figure 1.

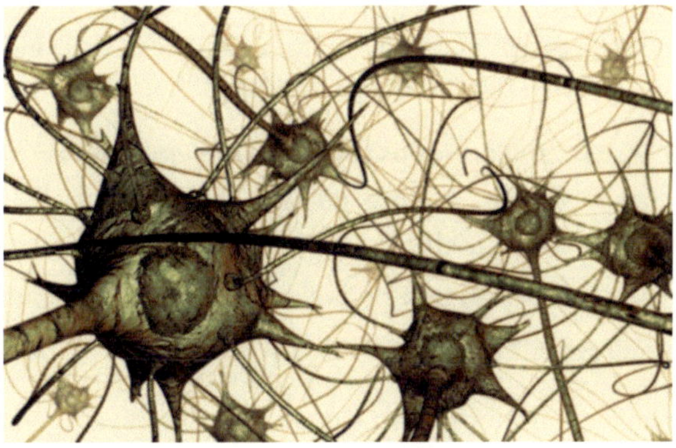

Fig. 1. Neural Network Interconnections (Source: Benedict Campbell 2008).

The Biological neuron is described illustratively in figure 2, taking into account a biological description.

In traditional concepts a neuron operates receiving signals from other neurons through bioelectrical connections, called *synapses*. The combination of these signals, in excess of a certain *threshold* or *activation* level, will result in the neuron *firing* that is sending a signal on to other interconnected neurons. Some signals act as *excitations* and others as *inhibitions* to a neuron firing.

These acts applied in a hundred billion interconnected neurons generate "thinking actions".

Each neuron has a body, called the *soma*. The soma is much like the body of any other cell, containing the cell nucleus, various bio-chemical factors and other components that support ongoing activity, and surround the soma *dendrites*. The dendrites have the receptor functions with respect to signals generated by other neurons. These signals combined may determine whether or not that neuron will fire.

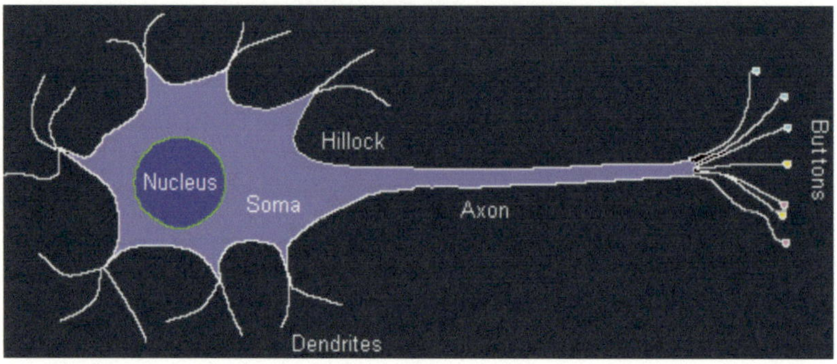

Fig. 2. Basic Biological Neuron with its elements.

If a neuron fires, an electrical impulse noise is generated. This impulse starts at the base, called the *hillock*, of a long cellular extension, called the *axon*, and proceeds down the axon to its ends. The end of the axon is split into multiple ends, called the *buttons*. The buttons are connected to the dendrites of other neurons and the resulting interconnections are the previously discussed synapses. (In figure 2, the buttons do not touch other dendrites having a small gap generating an electrical potential difference between them; i.e., if a neuron has fired, the electrical impulse noise that has been generated stimulates the buttons and results in electro-chemical activity which transmits the signal across the synapses dendrites actions).

Commonly, the neuron maintains an electrical interval potential $[35, 65]$ milli-volts; but when a neuron fires an electrical impulse noise it increases its chemical electric energy releasing an electrical potential $[90, 110]$ milli-volts. This impulse noise is transmitted with an interval velocity $[0.5, 100]$ in meters per second and is distributed on average in a 1 milli-second. The fast rate repetition on average corresponds to 10 milli-seconds per firing.

Considering an electronic computer whose signals travel on average at $2.0X10^9 \frac{m}{\text{sec}}$ (speed of electrical energy in a wire is 0.7 of that in air), whose impulse noises last for ten nanoseconds and may repeat such an impulse noise in each succeeding 10 nano-seconds. Therefore, an electronic computer has at least a two thousand times advantage in signal transmission speed considering the biological basic neuron, and a thousand times advantage in signal fire repetition. This difference in velocity manifests itself in at least one important way; the human brain is not as fast as an arithmetic electronic computer, which is many times faster and hugely more capable of patterns recognition and perception relationships. The main advantage of the brain in respect to other electronic devices is it is capable of "self-programming" with changing external stimuli, known as “adaptability”. In other words, it can learn dynamically and in all conditions.

Naturally, the brain has developed the neuron ways changing their response to new stimulus so that similar events may affect future neighborhood responses. The adaptability of a brain corresponds to survival actions.

1.2 Neural network structure

The computational Neural Network structures are based on biological neural configurations. The basic neural network is a model neuron, shown in figure 2, consisting of Multiple Inputs and a Single Output (MISO structure). Each input is modified by a *weight*, which multiplies the input value. The neuron combines these dendrite weight inputs and if the soma biological actions exceed a threshold value, then the nucleus in biological sense and activation function in computational actions, determines its output answer. In an electronic computational device as shown in Figure 3, a behavioral additional condition has the answer close to the real neuron actions.

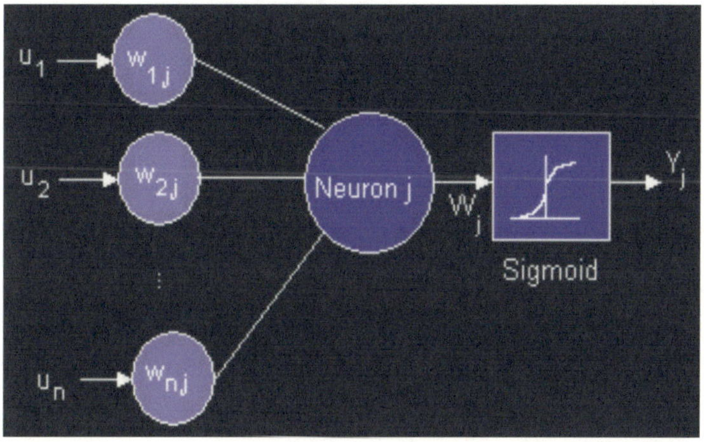

Fig. 3. Neuron device computational model

Meanwhile understanding how an individual neuron operates many researches generate the way neurons organize themselves and the mechanisms used by arrays of neurons to adapt their behavior to external bounded stimuli. There are a huge number of experimental neural network computational structures, and actually laboratories and researchers continue building new neural net configurations.

The common computational neural net used, is called *back-propagation network* and is characterized with a mathematical structure model, which knows its behavioral stability conditions (bounded inputs and bounded output, BIBO conditions).

Intuitively it is built taking a number of neurons and arrays them forming a *layer*. A layer is formed having all inputs and nodes interconnected with others nodes, but not both within the same node. A layer finishes with a node set connected with a succeeding layer or outputs giving the answer. The multiple layers are arrayed as an input layer, multiple intermediate layers and an output layer as shown in Figure 4; where the intermediate layers do not have inputs or outputs to the external world and are called *hidden layers*.

Back-propagation neural networks are usually *fully connected*. This means that each neuron is connected to every output from the preceding layer.

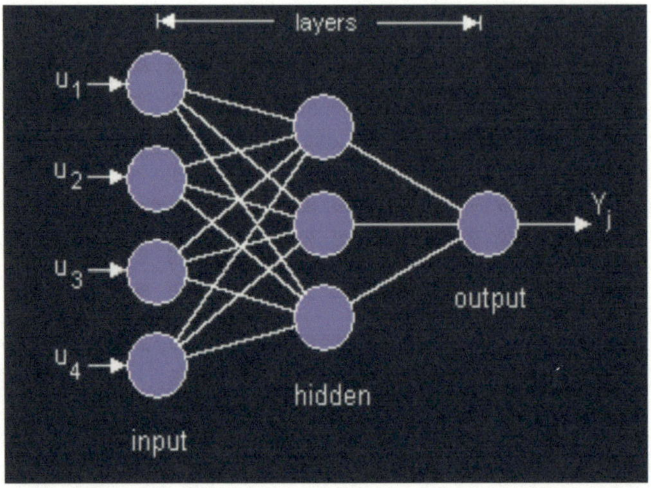

Fig. 4. MISO Back-propagation Network with three layers.

The layers are described as: input, distributing the signals from the external world; hidden, categorizing the signals; and the output collecting all features detected and producing a response. However the problem of the layers has many descriptions considering the set of optimal weights.

1.3 Neural network operation

The output of each neuron is a function of its inputs and weights, with a layer as described recursively in (1).

$$W_j(k) = u_n(k)w_{nj}(k) + W_{j-1}(k). \tag{1}$$

In where the basic function has the form $W_j(k) = \sum_{i=1}^{n} u_n(k)w_{ij}(k)$.

The output neural net answer is a convolution operation shown in (2).

$$y_j(k) = \left(F(k) \circ W(k)\right)_j. \tag{2}$$

The $W_j(k)$ value is convoluted with a threshold value giving an approximate biological neural net answer, but in a computational sense it is active considering a $t_j(k)$, known as an activation function. The activation function usually is the sigmoid function shown in Figure 5. The output answer $y_j(k)$, is the neural net response, observing that the threshold function corresponds to biological electrical potential [90, 110] mill-volts needed in synopsis operations.

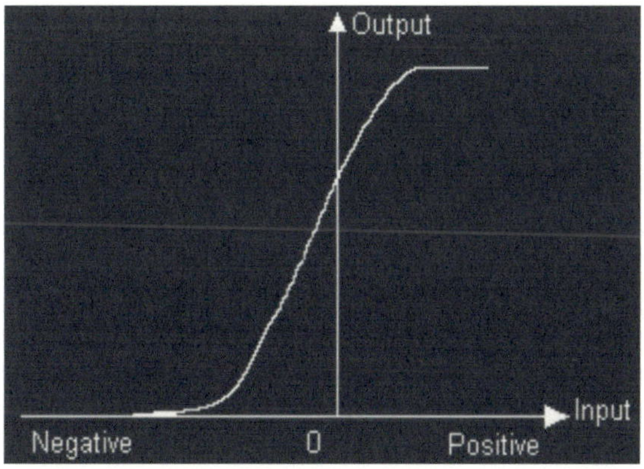

Fig. 5. Sigmoid Function as a neural net firing an electrical impulse noise.

The biological or computational fire answers correspond to threshold conditions that accomplish the excitation functions that permit generating an answer giving many inputs. Generally, the weights are selected intuitively in the first step; but with adaptive consideration can be adjusted to seek the desired answer.

2. Neural network adapting its weights usign fuzzy logic

The adaptation in a neural net means that it adapts its weights with a law action, seeking the convergence to the output desired answer. The difference between the desired ($d_j(k)$) and actual responses ($y_j(k)$) is known as convergence *error* ($e_j(k)$) and is defined as (3) and is shown in figure 6.

$$e_j(k) = d_j(k) - y_j(k). \tag{3}$$

The law action could be a sliding mode, proportional gain in its weight and other non-linear models that allows the neural net system converging to the desired answer with respect to the input set.

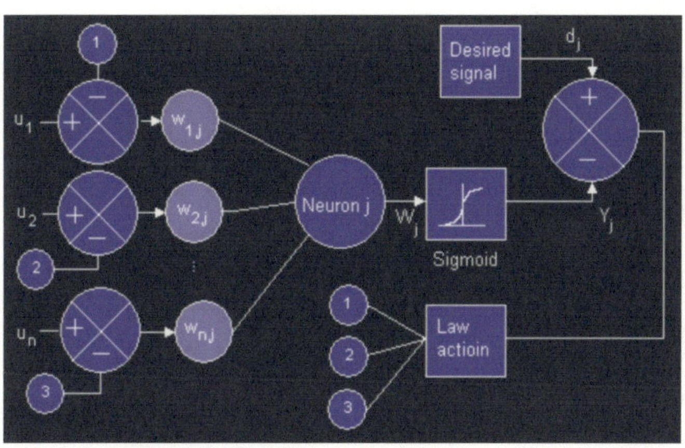

Fig. 6. Neuronal Weights Adjustment using a law action.

The adaptive back-*propagation* procedure is described in (4)

$$u'_{ij}(k) = u_{ij}(k) - L_j(k) \tag{4}$$

Where corresponds to law action considered by neural net designer.

Now applying the concept considered above with respect to neural net adjusting weights using fuzzy logic concepts gives a great advantage over traditional concepts such as the forgetting factor and sliding modes in other action laws.

The neural net that has adaptive weights is known as a digital identification filter, therefore, the neural net in where the adaptation process considered fuzzy inferences is known as a Neuro-Fuzzy Digital Filter.

A fuzzy neural net classifies, searches and associates information (Huang, Zhu and Siew, 2006) giving a specific answer value in accordance with a reference desired signal process, constructing a control volume described as $T_N = \{(y_j(k), \hat{y}_j(k))\} \subseteq R^2$ where a variant scheme has the form $T_N : \left(Y_N \times \hat{Y}_N\right) \times T \rightarrow \{(y_j(k), \hat{y}_j(k)), \tau(k)\}\Big|_{k=1}^{N} \subseteq R^2$ inside the membership intervals delimited by a Knowledge Base (KB) (Schneider y Kandel, 1996), with dynamical and bounded moments. The responses set into the KB represents all the possible correct filter responses (Gustafsson, 2000) (Margaliot and Langholz, 2000) (Zadeh, 1965) in accordance with an objective law, previously defined by the actual natural reference process in a distribution sense. The filtering mechanism adjusts the neural weights selecting the best answer from the KB when the state changes, to use fuzzy rules (*if-then*). The neuro-fuzzy filter is based on the back-propagation algorithm, because its weights have a dynamic actualization (Ali, 2003) (Amble, 1987) (Haykin, 1996) with different levels for each interval iteration (Huang, Zhu and Siew, 2006), using the error described as $e(k) \in R$ defined in (3) and considering its distribution function (García, Medel y Guevara, 2008) (Marcek, 2008)); this filter is shown in. Figure 7, integrating the fuzzy logic convenient actions into neural net structure using adaptive weights (Passino, 1998, and Medel 2008).

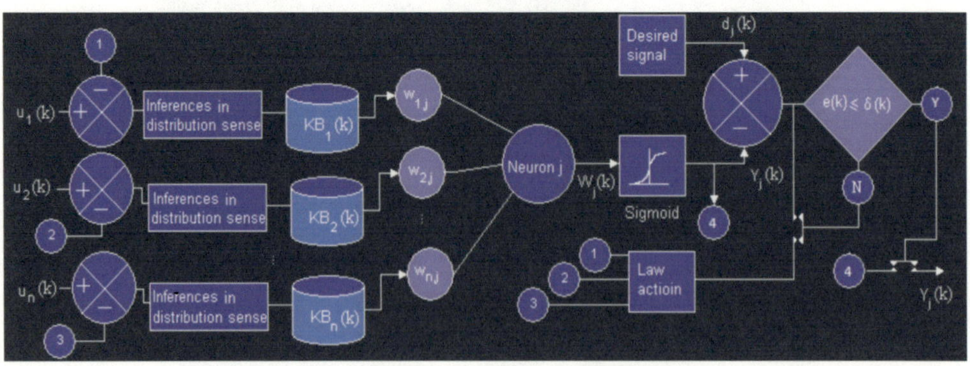

Fig. 7. Neuro-fuzzy Digital Filter Process

The error $\left(\left|e_j(k)\right|\right)$ has a interval limit $[0,\varepsilon]$ and ε is described as a positive value in accordance with $\inf\{\left|e_j(k)\right| \to \underline{\delta} > 0, \sup\{\left|e_j(k)\right|\} \to \bar{\delta} > \underline{\delta}$ in where $\varepsilon \in [\underline{\delta},\bar{\delta}]$ (k is index interval) (Margaliot and Langholz, 2000) (Morales, 2002).

The Neuro-Fuzzy Digital Filter considers the concepts described in (Ash, 1970) (Abraham, 1991) (Ali, 2003) (Gustafsson, 2000), (Mamdani, 1974) (Morales, 2002) (Medel et.al 2008), having the elements needed in its basic description:

a. Back propagation neural net scheme.
b. Adaptive weights considering the law action and Fuzzy Logic inferences
c. Convergence answer considering the stochastic error *e(k) and the its probability bounded moments*
d. In a metric sense, *weights distribution* is transformed in Fuzzy Inferences after the law action applied in the dendrites stage inputs.
e. *Rule Base allows the interpretation* of the stochastic weights bounded by distribution function accomplishing the actions using the logic *IF* connector.
f. *Inference Mechanism* as an expert consequence of the rule base, selects the membership function described as an adaptive weight $\left\{w_{ij}(k): i=\overline{1,n} \in Z_+\right\}_{j=\overline{1,m} \in Z_+}$ using logic *THEN connector selecting the dendrite value corresponding to the knowledge base (Yamakawa, 1989).*
g. *Activation Function is the stage where the* answer filter is transformed into a natural answer approximating to minimal convergence error region.
h. Neuro-Fuzzy Digital Filter process has a *Natural Actualization* obtaining the linguistic values and actualizes its weights dynamically based on a distribution error and observing the second probability moment basic law action (5).

$$J_j(k) = \frac{1}{k^2}\left[e_j(k)^2 + (k-1)^2 J_j(k-1)\right] \in R_{[0,1)} \ k \in Z_+. \tag{5}$$

The functional error $J(k)$ has an exponential convergence if the weights set into the Neuro-Fuzzy Filter allow that $\lim_{k\to\infty}\left|J_j(k)\right| \to m,\ m \in R_{[0,1)}$, if $0 < \left\{\left|e_j(k)\right|\right\} < 1$ and (6).

$$J_{\min} = \inf\left\{J_{\min,j} := \min J(d_j(k), \hat{y}_j(k)),\ j=\overline{1,s},\ s \in Z_+\right\} \tag{6}$$

The Neuro-Fuzzy Digital Filter needs the knowledge base in order to select the corresponding answer weights in accordance with the desired signal and law action. Firstly, the filtering process uses the neuronal net and requires the adaptation process for non-stationary answer conditions, and the fuzzy rules adjust to the adaptation process guarantying the convergence rate (Takagi and Sugeno, 1986). The filter mechanism makes a selection of the correct variable weights into its data form and selects the correct level into three fuzzy regions. Then, the rules mechanism selects the weights $\left\{w_{ij}(k): i=\overline{1,n}\right\}_{j=\overline{1,m}}$ adjusting the filter gain, giving the correct answer $\hat{y}_j(k)$ as the filter output (Rajem y Gopal, 2006) (Medel et.al 2008), with MISO (Multi Inputs Single Output) properties.

3. Weight properties

A neuto-fuzzy filter has a weight set $\{w_{ij}(k): i=\overline{1,n}\}_{j=\overline{1,m}}$, where the knowledge base in each layer accomplishes the condition $\sum_{i=1}^{n} w_{i,j}(k) \leq 1$ without losing the transition function basic properties (Medel, 2008):

i. Each weight has a dynamic transition function with natural restrictions:
   1. $\ln(\Phi_j(k)) < \infty$, 2) $\ln(\Phi_j(k)) > 0$, 3) $\ln(\Phi_j(k))k^{-1} < 1$.
ii. The weight is described using the transition function in (7).

$$w_j(k-k_0) = \ln \Phi_j(k)\left(\ln \phi_j(k_0)(k-k_0)\right)^{-1}, \tag{7}$$

iii. The velocity changes are limited inside the transition function (8).

$$\ln(\Phi_j(k)) \leq \ln \Phi_j(k_0)(k-k_0)^T,\ \ln \Phi_j(k_i) \leq \ln(\Phi_j(k_i-1)(k_i-(k_i-1))^T \tag{8}$$

The transition functions sum is bounded in each layer $0 \leq /\sum_{i=1}^{n} \Phi_{ij}(k)/ \leq 1$. In accordance with the value of $\ln \Phi_j(k_0)$, the weights are bounded considering (9).

$$w_j(k-k_0) \leq \ln \Phi_j(k_0) \tag{9}$$

The identifier described as (10) considered (6).

$$\hat{x}_j(k) = w_{ij}(k)(k-k_0)\hat{x}_j(k-1) + K_j(k)\hat{w}_j(k) \tag{10}$$

Where $K_j(k)$ is the function gain and is a functional identification error, defined by the second probability moment (5), $\hat{w}_j(k)$ represents generalized perturbations with $\{\hat{w}_j(k)\} \subseteq N(\mu, \sigma^2 < \infty)$.

4. Results

The MISO neuro-fuzzy filter, considers the digital filter structure (Hayking, 1996) with the transition matrix bounded by the knowledge base in accordance with the functional error criterion (Ash, 1970). The soft system (statistic in variance sense) considers the evolution times bounded by PC with AMD Sempron 3100+ processor performance at *k* intervals, with an average evolution time of 0.004 sec ± 0.0002 sec.

This chapter uses the first order difference discrete ARMA model (11) representing a reference system with *j=1*.

$$x(k+1) = a(k)x(k) + w(k) \tag{11}$$

And the output described as (12).

$$y(k) = x(k) + v(k) \tag{12}$$

$$x(k),\ y(k), w(k), v(k) \in R,\ a(k) \in R_{(-1,\,1)}$$

x(k) is the internal states vector, a(k) is the parameter, w(k) is the vector noise into the system, y(k) is the reference vector desired system signal and, v(k) is the output vector noise.

The different operational levels are described in order to operate the distribution function error. The filter process establishes in the fuzzy region the linguistic descriptors adjusted in its ranges. Figure 8 describes the reference signal and its identification without knowing the internal parameter model $\hat{a}(k) \in R_{(-1,\,1)}$.

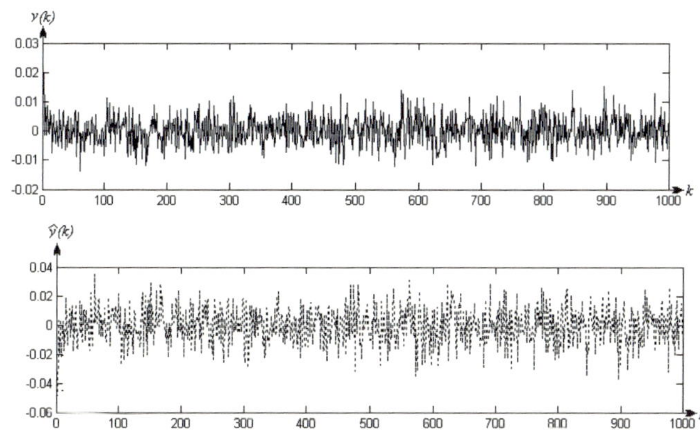

Fig. 8. Output signal $Y(k)$ and its identification $\hat{Y}(k)$ using the nero-fuzzy digital filter technique.

The fuzzy regions considered the distribution weights after applying the law action.

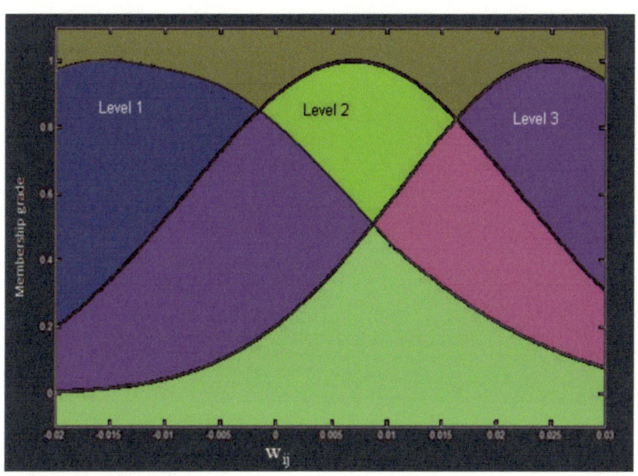

Fig. 9. A membership weights function.

The histogram identification evolution is shown illustratively in Figure 10, in where each weight is adjusted in neuro-fuzzy filter affecting the identification histogram convergence. The convergence in histogram is associated with the membership weights function, allowing that the identification system tends to the reference system.

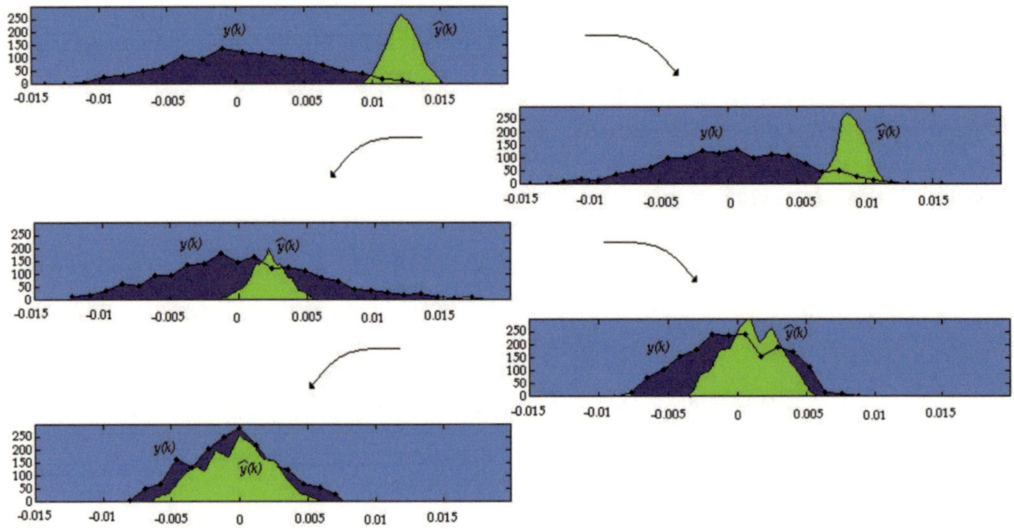

Fig. 10. The histogram convergence through the time evolution between the identification with respect to reference signal in base to adaptive weights.

Figures 11 and 12 show the $\hat{Y}(k)$ and desired signal *Y(k)* final *h*istograms, respectively.

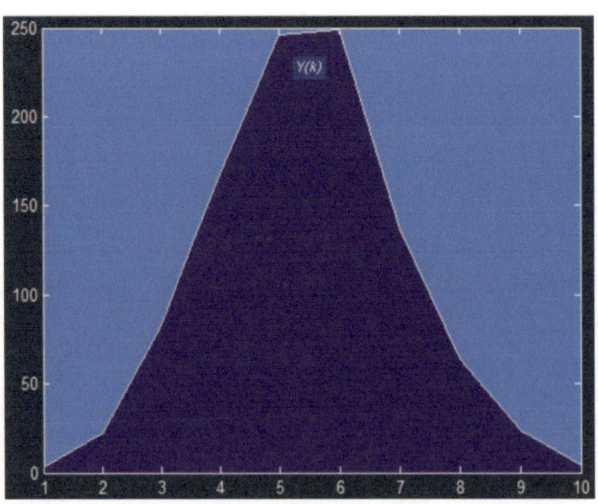

Fig. 11. Histogram of desired signal described as *Y(k)*

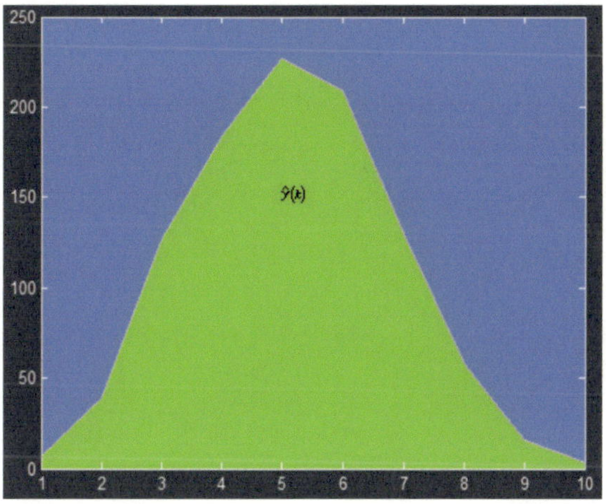

Fig. 12. Histogram of identification signal as $\hat{Y}(k)$

Figure 13, shows both overlapping final histogram considering the same time interval.

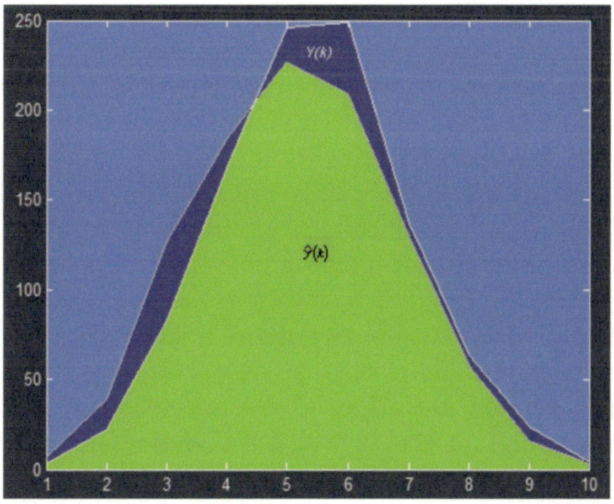

Fig. 13. Overlapping both final histograms with respect to $Y(k)$ and $\hat{Y}(k)$, respectively.

Figure 14, shows the evolution functional error described by (5).

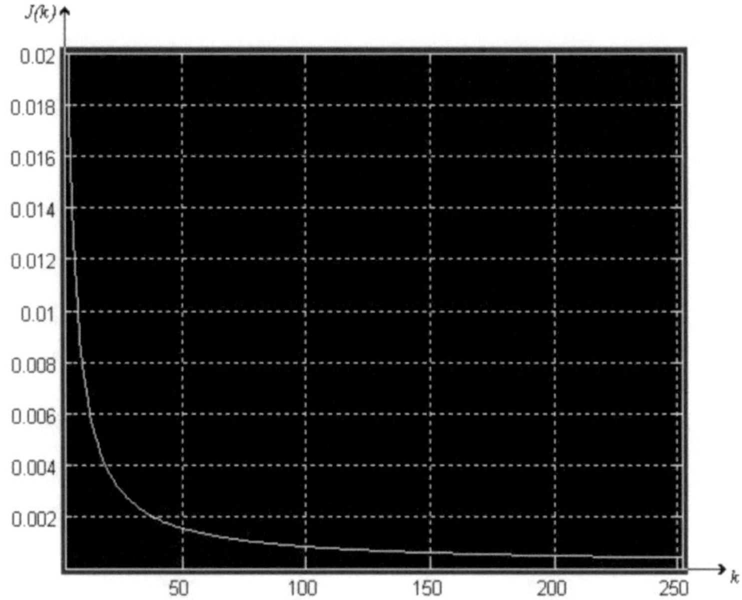

Fig. 14. Functional error considered in (5).

The Neuro-Fuzzy Digital Filter time evolution responses was less that the reference process time state change proposed with a value of 0.08 sec, and is delimited by the processor, considered in (10). The convergence time is 0.0862 sec, described in (Medel, 2008).

5. Conclusion

Neural net in identification sense, considered the adaptation process requiring adjust the weights dynamically using the common proportional condition. But in many cases, these applications generate convergence problems because the gain in all cases increase the neural net weights positive or negatively without converge to desired value. In the black box traditional scheme the internal weights are known, but in real conditions it is impossible and only has a desired or objective answer. But, the neural nets help jumping weights estimation adjusting dynamically their internal weights, needing adaptation process with smooth movements as a function of identification error (function generated by the difference between the filter answer with respect to desired answer.). An option considered was the fuzzy logic in where its natural actions based on distribution function error allowing built the adjustable membership functions and mobile inference limits. Therefore, the neural weights are adjusted dynamically considering the fussy logic adaptable properties applied in the law actions, shown in figure 7. Stable weights conditions were exposed in section 3, with movements bounded in (8). In the results section, the figure 13, illustrated the Neuro-Fuzzy Digital Filter advantages without lost the stability with respect to desired system answer observed in distribution sense, observing the Hausdorff condition approximating the filter to desired system answer in distribution sense.

6. References

Abraham K. (1991). *Fuzzy Expert Systems, Florida*, Ed. CRC Press, ISBN: 9780849342974

Ali H. S. (2003). *Fundamentals of Adaptive Filters*, Ed. John Wiley & Sons, New Jersey USA. ISBN.

Amble T. (1987). *Logic Programming and Knowledge Engineering*. Addison Wesley, USA,. ISBN.

Ash R. (1970). *Real Analysis and Probability*, Ed. Dover Publications. USA, ISBN: 0486472205

García J.C., Medel J.J., Guevara P. (2007), RTFDF Description for ARMA Systems, *WSEAS Journal: Transactions on Systems and Control*, Vol. 2, Issue 10, pp. 491-496.

García J.C., Medel J.J., Guevara P., (2008). Filtrado Digital Difuso en Tiempo Real, *Computación y Sistemas Journal*, Vol. 11, No. 4, pp. 390-401, ISSN: 1405-5546.

García J.C., Medel J.J., Guevara P., (2008). Real-time neuro-fuzzy digital filtering: Approach, *Computer and Simulation in Modern Science Journal, WSEAS press selected papers*, Vol. 1, pp. 122-125.

Haykin S. (1996). *Adaptive Filtering*, Prentice Hall, USA.

Huang G., Zhu K., Siew C. (2006). Real-Time Learning Capability of Neural Networks, *IEEE Transactions on Neural Networks*, Vol. 17, pp. 863-878.

Gustafsson F. (200). *Adaptive Filtering and Change Detection*, John Wiley and Sons, England.

Mamdani E. (1974). Applications of Fuzzy Algorithms for Control of Simple Dynamic Plant, *Proc. IEEE*, Vol. 121, pp. 1585-1588.

Manuel L. (2003). *Lebesgue Integral Measure Theory*, Ed. Del Rosario University, Buenos Aires.

Margaliot M., Langholz and G. (2000). *New Approaches to Fuzzy Modeling and Control Design and Analysis, Singapore*, Ed. World Scientific.

Medel J.J., Guevara P. (2004). Caracterización de Filtros Digitales en Tiempo-real para Computadoras Digitales, *Computación y Sistemas Journal*, Vol. VII, No. 3, ISSN:1405-5546

Medel J.J., García J.C., Guevara P. (2008). Real-time Fuzzy Digital Filters (RTFDF) Properties for SISO Systems, *Automatic Control and Computer Sciences*, AVT, Vol. 42, No. 1, pp. 26-34.

Medel J.J, García J.C., Sánchez J.C. (2008). Real-time Neuro-Fuzzy Digital Filtering: Basic Concepts, *WSEAS Transactions on Systems and Control*, 2008, Vol. 3, Issue 8, pp. 654-663.

Marcek D. (2004). *Statistical, Classical and Fuzzy Neural Networks, Modeling Decisions for Artificial Intelligence*, Ed. Springer Verlag, pp. 41-48.

Morales G. (2002), *Introducción a la Lógica Difusa*, Ed. Cinvestav, Mexico.

Nikola K. (1996). *Foundations of Neural Networks, Fuzzy Systems, and Knowledge Engineering*, Hong Kong, The MIT Press.

Passino K. M. (1998). *Fuzzy Control*, USA, Addison Wesley.

Rajen B., Gopal M. (2006), Neuro-Fuzzy Decision Trees. *International Journal of Neural Filters*, Vol. 16, pp. 63-68.

Shannon M. (1948). A Mathematical Theory of Communication, *Bell Systems Technical Journal*, Vol.27, pp.379-423 and pp. 623-656.

Schneider M., and Kandel A. (1996). *Fuzzy expert systems tools*, England, John Wiley & Sons.

Takagi T., Sugeno M. (1986). Fuzzy Identification of Systems and its Applications to Modelling and control, *IEEE Transactions and Systems, Man, and Cybernetics*, Vol. 15, pp. 116-132.

Yamakawa F. (1989). *Fuzzy Neurons and Fuzzy Neural Networks.*
Zadeh L. (1965). Fuzzy Sets, *Information and control,* Vol. 8, pp. 338-353.
National security. (2008). Intelligence on the Brain, A New Dialogue on Neuro- Research and National Security
http://www.scienceprogress.org/2008/11/intelligence-on-the-brain/

Part 2

Recurrent Neural Network

5

Recurrent Neural Network with Human Simulator Based Virtual Reality

Yousif I. Al Mashhadany
Al Anbar University, Engineering College, Electrical Dept., Iraq

1. Introduction

During almost three decades, the study on theory and applications of artificial neural network has increased considerably, due partly to a number of significant breakthroughs in research on network types and operational characteristics, but also because of some distinct advances in the power of computer hardware which is readily available for net implementation. In the last few years, recurrent neural networks (RNNs), which are neural network with feedback (closed-loop) connects, have been an important focus of research and development. Examples include bidirectional associative memory (BAM), Hopfield, cellular neural network (CNN), Boltzmann machine, and recurrent back propagation nets, etc.. RNN techniques have been applied to a wide variety of problems due to their dynamics and parallel distributed property, such as identifying and controlling the real-time system, neural computing, image processing and so on.

RNNs are widely acknowledged as an effective tool that can be employed by a wide range of applications that store and process temporal sequences. The ability of RNNs to capture complex, nonlinear system dynamics has served as a driving motivation for their study. RNNs have the potential to be effectively used in modeling, system identification, and adaptive control applications, to name a few, where other techniques may fall short. Most of the proposed RNN learning algorithms rely on the calculation of error gradients with respect to the network weights. What distinguishes recurrent neural networks from static, or feedforward networks, is the fact that the gradients are time dependent or dynamic. This implies that the current error gradient does not only depend on the current input, output, and targets, but rather on its possibly infinite past. How to effectively train RNNs remains a challenging and active research topic.

The learning problem consists of adjusting the parameters (weights) of the network, such that the trajectories have certain specified properties. Perhaps the most common online learning algorithm proposed for RNNs is the real-rime recurrent learning (RTRL), which calculates gradients at time (k) in terms of those at time instant (k-1). Once the gradients are evaluated, weight updates can be calculated in a straightf_Gorward manner. The RTRL algorithm is very attractive in that it is applicable to real-time systems. However, the two main drawbacks of RTRL are the large computational complexity of $O(N^4)$ and, even more critical, the storage requirements of $O(N^3)$, where N denotes the number of neurons in the network.

RNNS are mathematical abstractions of biological nervous systems that can perform complex mappings from input sequences to output sequences. In principle one can wire them up just like microprocessors, hence RNNs can compute anything a traditional computer can compute. In particular, they can approximate any dynamical system with arbitrary precision. However, unlike traditional, programmed computers, RNNs *learn* their behavior from a training set of correct example sequences. As training sequences are fed to the network, the error between the actual and desired network output is minimized using gradient descent, whereby the connection weights are gradually adjusted in the direction that reduces this error most rapidly. Potential applications include adaptive robotics, speech recognition, attentive vision, music composition, and innumerably many others where retaining information from arbitrarily far in the past can be critical to making optimal decisions. Recently, *Echo State Networks* ESNs and a very similar approach, *Liquid State Machines*, have attracted significant attention. Composed primarily of a large pool of hidden neurons (typically hundreds or thousands) with fixed random weights, ESNs are trained by computing a set of weights from the pool to the output units using fast, linear regression. The idea is that with so many random hidden units, the pool is capable of very rich dynamics that just need to be correctly "tapped" by setting the output weights appropriately. ESNs have the best known error rates on the Mackey-Glass time series prediction task.(Abraham, 2005)

Two main methods exist for providing a neural network with dynamic behavior: the insertion of a buffer somewhere in the network to provide an explicit memory of the past inputs, or the implementation of feedbacks. As for the first method, it builds on the structure of feed forward networks where all input signals flow in one direction, from input to output. Then, because a feed forward network does not have a dynamic memory, *tapped-delay-lines* (temporal buffers) of the inputs are used. The buffer can be applied at the network inputs only, keeping the network internally static as in the buffered multilayer perceptron (MLP) or at the input of each neuron as in the MLP with Finite Impulse Response (FIR) filter synapses (FIRMLP). The main disadvantage of the buffer approach is the limited past-history horizon, which needs to be used in order to keep the size of the network computationally manageable, thereby preventing modeling of arbitrary long time dependencies between inputs and outputs it is also difficult to set the length of the buffer given a certain application.

The second method, the most general example of implementation of feedbacks in a neural network is the fully recurrent neural network constituted by a single layer of neurons fully interconnected with each other or by several such layers. Because of the required large structural complexity of this network, in recent years growing efforts have been propounded in developing methods for implementing temporal dynamic feedback connections into the widely used multi-layered feed forward neural networks. Recurrent connections can be added by using two main types of recurrence or feedback: *external* or *internal*. *External recurrence* is obtained for example by feeding back the outputs to the input of the network as in NARX networks; *internal recurrence* is obtained by feeding back the outputs of neurons of a given layer in inputs to neurons of the same layer, giving rise to the so called *Locally Recurrent Neural Networks* (*LRNNs*) (Francesco et al., 2006)

The major advantages of LRNNs with respect to the buffered, tapped-delayed feedforward networks and to the fully recurrent networks are:

1. The hierarchic multilayer topology which they are based on is well known and efficient.
2. The use of dynamic neurons allows limiting the number of neurons required for modeling a given dynamic system, contrary to the tapped-delayed networks.
3. The training procedures for properly adjusting the network weights are significantly simpler and faster than those for the fully recurrent networks.

This chapter consists of the following items:

- Types of RNN.
- Some Special Recurrent Networks
- Training algorithms for recurrent neural networks
- Inverse kinematic For Humanied manipulator with 27-DOFs
- Solution of IKP by using RNN
- Simulation of the humaniod manipulator based upon Virtual Reality
- Conclusion

2. Types of RNN

The categories of RNN is very difficult where many parameters can be division according to consideration, therefore the division will explain by:

2.1 Types of RNN according to the performance of NN

There are many classes of RNN architectures. All architectures can be best described using the state-space model from systems theory. This state-space model is explain in many references (Cheron et al., 2007) (Cruse, 2006)(Dijk, 1999), the following architectures or classes of architectures are presented:

- Fully Recurrent Neural networks (FRNN).
- Subsets of FRNN: Recurrent Neural Networks (RNN).
- Partially Recurrent Networks (PRN).
- Simple Recurrent Networks (SRN).

These architectures emerge by applying constraints to the general state-space model. The architectures have been investigated and tested in applications by many researchers. In the following subsections, these specific constraints will be listed and the resulting architectures will be discussed. Each class is presented together with a quick look at some properties and examples of their application.

The architectures treated can be ordered hierarchically since some architecture is special cases of more general architectures. This hierarchy is visualized in Fig.1. The most general architectures are at the left, specific architectures are at the right. The accolades show what architectures are parts of a more general architecture description.

2.1.1 Fully recurrent neural networks (FRNN)

The Fully Recurrent Neural Network (FRNN) is first described here in terms of individual neurons and their connections, as was done in [Williams e.a., 1989]. Then the FRNN is considered as a special case of the general state-space model and a convenient matrix notation of the network is given.

The name Fully Recurrent Neural Network for this network type is proposed by [Kasper e.a., 1999]. Another name for this type of network is the .Real-Time Recurrent Network.. This name will not be used further, because the name strongly implies that training is accomplished using the Real-Time Recurrent Learning (RTRL) algorithm proposed for this network in [Williams e.a., 1989] which is not necessarily the case because other algorithms can be used. In general a FRNN has N neurons, M external inputs and L external outputs. In Fig.2 an example of a FRNN is given which has N=4 neurons, M=2 external inputs u 1(n), u2(n) and L=2 external outputs y1(n), y2(n).(Dijk, 1999).

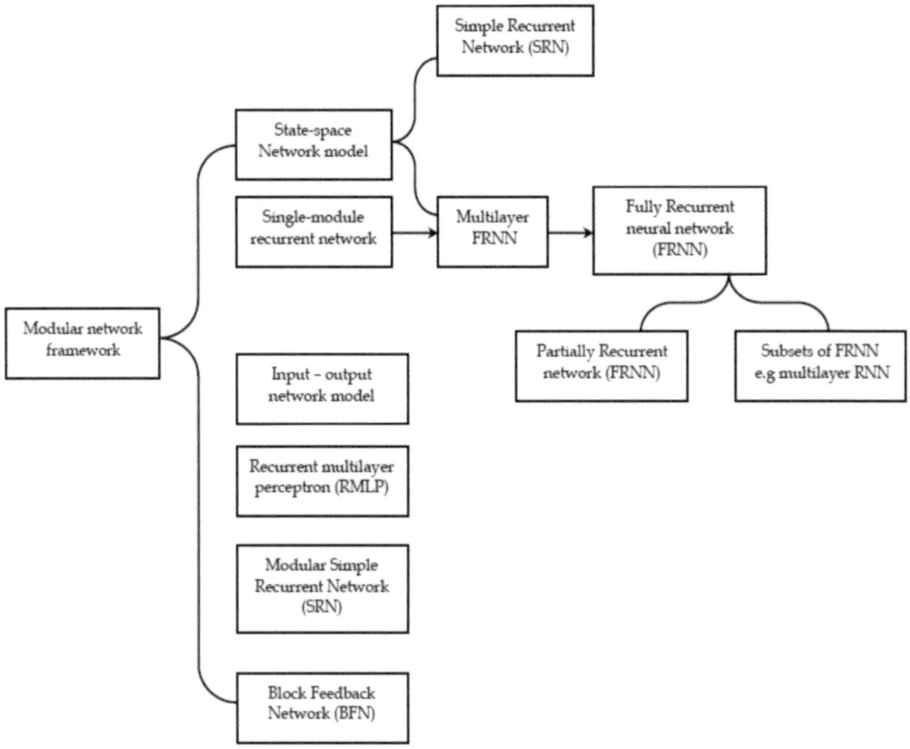

Fig. 1. Recurrent neural network architectures hierarchy (numbers indicate sections)

The network is called Fully Recurrent because the output of all neurons is recurrently connected (through N delay elements and N2 weighted feedback connections) to all neurons in the network. The external network inputs are connected to the neurons by N*M feed forward connections *without* delay element. A bias (also called threshold) can be introduced for every neuron by applying a constant external input u1(n) = 1 to the network.

For static neural networks, the number of layers in the neural network can be clearly defined as the number of neurons an input signal passes through before reaching the output. For the FRNN however the same definition is ambiguous, because signals applied at time n are fed back and reach the output at times n, n+1, and so on. The term layer therefore appears to be never used in literature in FRNN descriptions. By redefining the concept of layer to: the *minimum* number of neurons an input signal passes through before reaching the output, a workable definition is obtained for the FRNN.

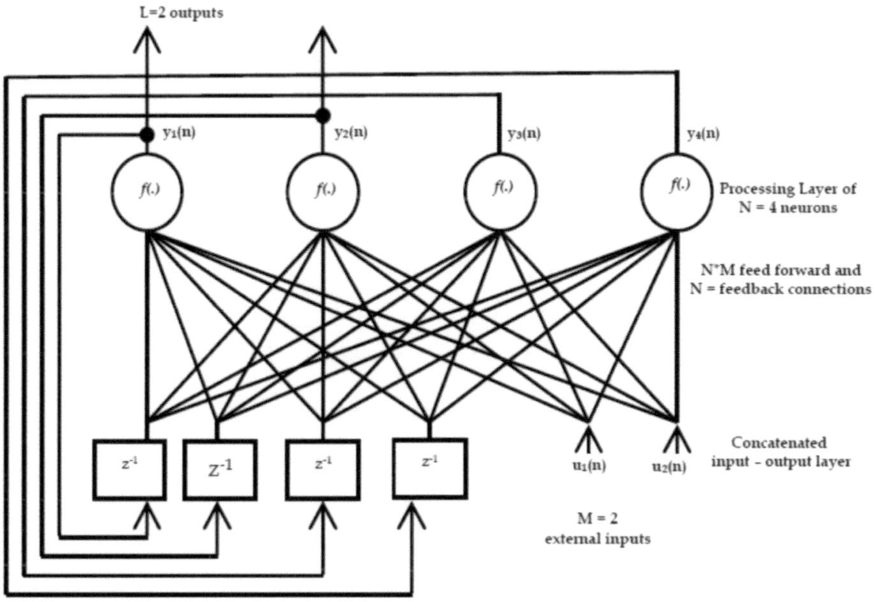

Fig. 2. Example of a fully recurrent neural network (of type 1) (Dijk, 1999).

2.1.2 Subsets of FRNN: Recurrent neural networks (RNN)

Additional restrictions can be imposed on the FRNN architecture described in the previous subsection to create other (restricted) Recurrent Neural Network (RNN) architectures. This subsection will describe some of these restricted architectures. Because the FRNN can be written as a state-space model, all .subsets. of FRNN are in many cases most conveniently written as state-space models.

The following categories of restrictions can be used (individually or in a combination):

1. forcing certain weights to zero (called removing or *pruning* the weight)
2. forcing weights to non-zero value (called *fixing* the weight or making the weight non-learnable)
3. forcing weights to be equal to other weights (called *sharing* of weights) or approximately equal to other weights (called *soft sharing* of weights)

These restrictions will be looked at in this subsection. Note that the three restrictions listed are fairly general and can be applied to other neural networks architecture than the FRNN, for example to the standard feedforward network.

All three restrictions have a property in common: the number of free parameters of the network is reduced when compared to a non-modified FRNN. Reasons for doing so will be given now. More reasons for applying restrictions will be given in the category descriptions. The training of a neural network is in fact a procedure that tries to estimate the parameters (weights) of the network such that an error measure is minimized. Reducing the number of parameters to be estimated may simplify training. Another good reason for reducing the number of free parameters is to reduce training algorithm overhead, which often grows quickly for an increasing number of weights NW.(Cruse, 2006).

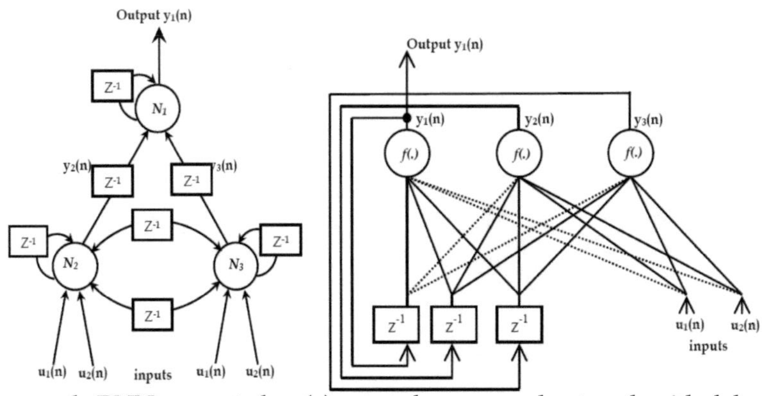

Fig. 3. One example RNN presented as (a). a two-layer neural network with delays and recurrent connections; and (b) as a FRNN with removed connections.

2.1.3 Partially recurrent networks (PRN)

The output vector (n) of the FRNN consists of the first L elements of the state vector [(n), as was shown in Fig. 2. So the output signals are a .subset. of state signals. In a general state space description this is certainly not the case, the output is determined by a separate calculation (the output equation) which is some function of the external input and the state. To obtain a network that effectively has separate state and output units (analogous to a state space system that has separate process and output equations), the feedback connections from all L output neurons yi(n) with i=1.L are removed. An example of the *partially recurrent neural network* (PRN) [Robinson e.a., 1991], also named the *simplified recurrent neural network* [Janssen, 1998], that results is shown in Fig. 4. The name partially recurrent neural network. will be used in this report to avoid confusion in the terms simple/simplified recurrent networks in the next subsection.

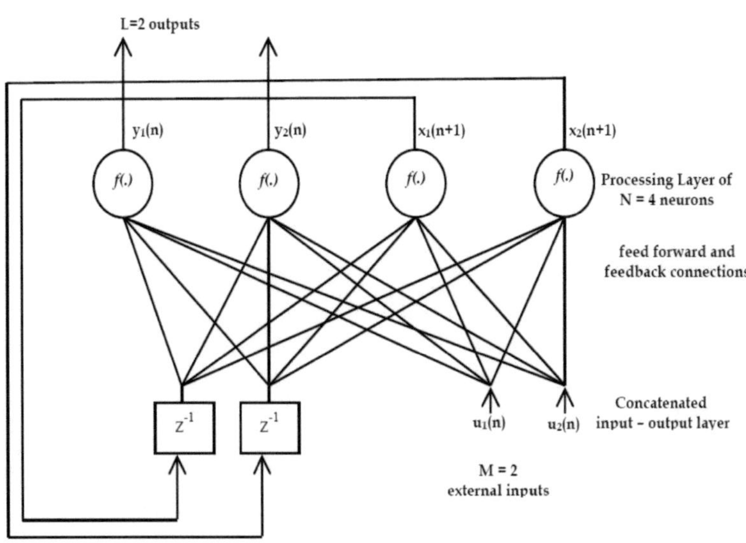

Fig. 4. Example of a partially recurrent neural network

2.2 Types of RNN according to NN structure

Some neural network architectures can be best described as modular architectures. The definition of a modular architecture as used in this report is: an architecture that consists of several static neural networks, that are interconnected in a specific way. There is, in most cases, not a clear boundary between a modular network and a single neural network because the total modular architecture can be looked at as a single neural network, and some existing single networks can also be described as modular networks. It is rather a convenient way of describing complex neural networks.(Paine W. Rainer & Tani Jun, 2004).

In this section the category of modular *recurrent* neural network architectures is looked at, modular architectures that all have one or more internal feedback connections. The modular recurrent neural network architectures were not introduced in previous sections, because they do not fit very well in the state-space system description or the NARX description.

Formally they can be described as a state-space system (like any dynamic system) but this could result in a very complicated and unnecessarily large state-space system description. In this section three classes of modular recurrent neural network architectures are presented:

- Recurrent Multi-layer Perceptron (RMLP).
- Block Feedback Networks (BFN) framework.
- General modular neural network framework.

2.2.1 Recurrent multi-layer perceptron (RMLP)

The first model (RMLP) is a rather specific one and it is included as an example of a modular architecture. Undoubtedly, many more such architectures are proposed in literature and they cannot all be listed here. Another example is the Pipelined Recurrent Neural Network found in [Haykin, 1998] and applied to speech prediction in [Baltersee e.a., 1998]. The second model is far more general and was meant to provide a structured way to describe a large class of recurrent neural networks and their training algorithms. The third model attempts to do the same and it turns out that this model is the most general one: it incorporates the first two as special cases, so in this section the attention will be mainly focussed on the third model, the general modular network framework. An extension of the regular MLP has been proposed by Puskorias e.a. (see [Haykin, 1998]) which adds self-feedback connections for each layer of the standard MLP. The resulting Recurrent Multilayer Perceptron (RMLP) structure with N layers is shown in Fig 5.

Each layer is a standard MLP layer. The layer outputs are fed forward to the inputs of the next layer and the delayed layer outputs are fed back into the layer itself. So the layer output of time n-1 for a certain layer acts as the state variable at time n for this layer. The global state of the network consists of all layer states [i(n) together. Effectively, this type of network can have both a very large total state vector and a relatively small number of parameters because the neurons in the network are not fully interconnected. There are no recurrent interconnections across layers. All recurrent connections are local (1-layer-to-itself).(Sit, 2005).

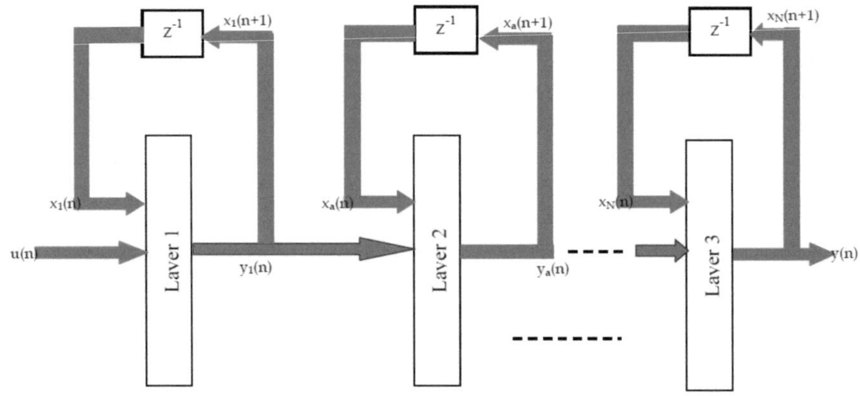

Fig. 5. Recurrent multi-layer perceptron (RMLP) architecture with N layers

2.2.2 Block feedback networks (BFN) framework

A framework for describing recurrent neural networks that has been introduced by [Santini e.a., 1995b] provides a systematic way for modular design of networks of high complexity. This class of networks is called Block Feedback Neural Networks (BFN), referring to the *blocks* that can be connected to each other using a number of elementary connections. The term *feedback* is used because one of the elementary connections is a feedback connection, thus enabling the construction of recurrent neural networks. The network that results from the construction can in turn be considered a .block. and it can be used again as a basic building block for further construction of progressively more complex networks.

So a recursive, modular way of designing networks is provided. The training algorithm for any BFN is based on backpropagation training for MLP and the backpropagation through time (BPTT) algorithm for recurrent networks. It is recursively constructed along with the network structure. So the BFN framework introduces a class of (infinitely many) recurrent networks, which can be trained using a correspondingly constructed backpropagation algorithm. The basic unit is a single neural network layer, an example of which is shown in Fig 6.a. The corresponding matrix notation is shown in Fig 6.b. $ is a 6-by-3 matrix and)(.) is a 6-by-6 diagonal mapping containing the neuron activation functions (of the form of equation 1). One such layer is defined as a *single layer block* N.(Zhenzhen Liu & Itamar Elhanany, 2008)

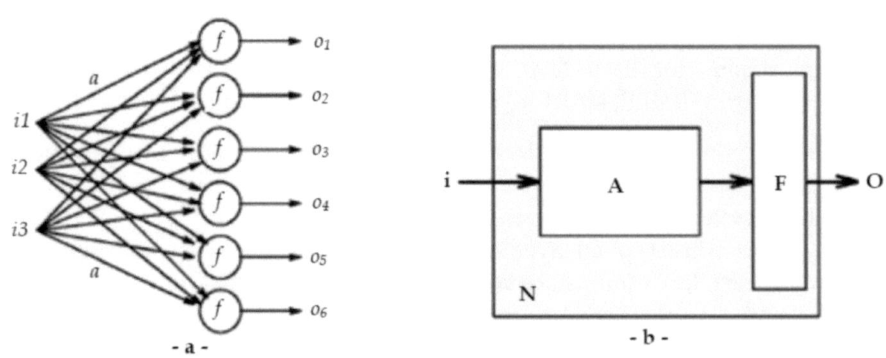

Fig. 6. a) example of a single network layer ; b) the layer in BFN block notation as a block N

This block computes the function:

$$o(n) = F(A.i(n)) \tag{1}$$

Single layer blocks can be connected together using the four elementary connections shown in Fig. 7. They are called the cascade, the sum, the split and the feedback connection. Each of these connections consists of one or two embedded BFN blocks (these are called N1 and N2 in the figure) and one connection layer (which has the structure of a single-layer block). This connection layer consists of the weight matrices $ and %, and the vector function)(.). Each of the four elementary connections itself is defined as a block and can therefore be used as the embedded block of yet another elementary connection.

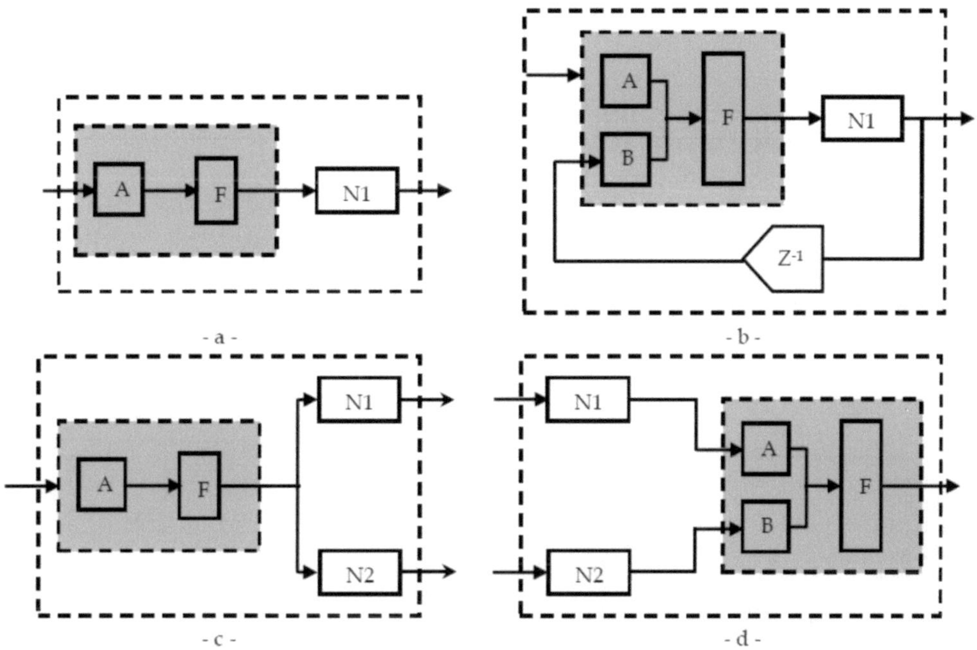

Fig. 7. The four elementary BFN connections: the cascade (a), feedback (b), split (c) and sum (d) connection.

2.2.3 General modular neural network framework

In [Bengio, 1996] a general modular network framework is introduced. This framework is similar to the BFN framework: it can be used to describe many different *modular networks* which are built of neural network modules linked together. Each module is a static feedforward neural network and the links between the modules can incorporate delay elements. The purpose of this framework is:

- to describe many types of recurrent neural networks as modular networks
- to derive a training algorithm for a network that is described as a modular network

The use of the framework for developing such a training algorithm, that can do *joint training* of the individual network modules.(Dijk O. Esko, 1999).

3. Some special recurrent networks

There are many special recurrent networks according to purpose of application or structure of networks. From these types can be explain the following:

3.1 Elman nets and Jordan nets

As was mentioned earlier, recurrent networks represent the most general format of a network. However, there is yet no general theoretical framework that describes the properties of recurrent nets. Therefore, several networks will be discussed below which have a specifically defined structure. In the first example, most layers have only feedforward connections, and only one contains specified recurrent connections. This example is given by Elman (1990) (Fig. 8.**a**). The system has an input layer, a hidden layer, and an output layer all of which are connected in a feedforward manner. The hidden layer, however, is not only connected to the output layer but also, in a simple 1 : 1 connection, to a further layer called the context layer. To form recurrent connections, the output of this context layer is also inputted to the hidden layer. Except for these 1 : 1 connections from hidden to context layer, the weights of which are fixed to 1, all other layers may be fully connected and all weights may be modifiable. The recurrent connections of the context layer provide the system with a short-term memory; the hidden units do not only observe the actual input but, via the context layer, also obtain information on their own state at the last time step. Since, at a given time step, hidden units have already been influenced by inputs at the earlier time steps, this recurrency comprises a memory which depends on earlier states (though their influence decays with time).(Cruse Holk, 2006).

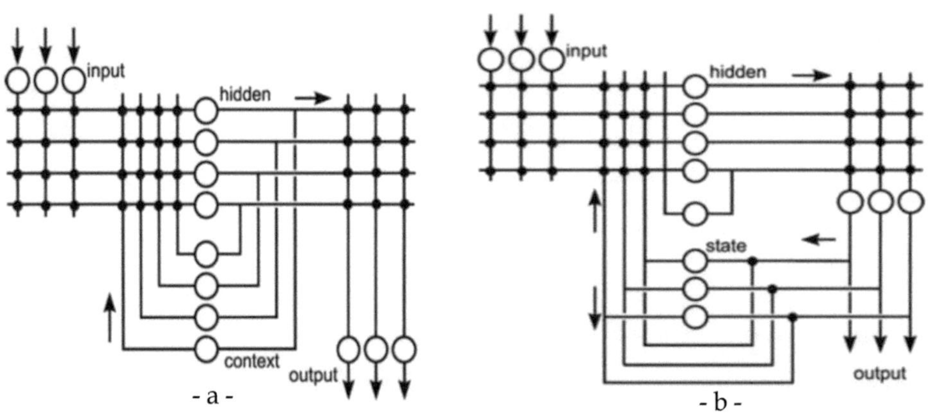

Fig. 8. Two networks with partial recurrent connections. (a) Elman net. (b) Jordan net. Only the weights in the feed forward channels can be modified.

Recurrent networks are particularly interesting in relation to motor control. For this purpose, Jordan (1986) proposed a very similar net (Fig. 8.**b**). A difference is that the recurrent connections start from the output, rather than the hidden layer. Furthermore, the layer corresponding to the context, here called state layer, comprises a recurrent net itself with 1:1 connections and fixed weights.

Another difference is that the network was used by Jordan so that a constant input vector is given to the net, and the output of the net performs a temporal sequence of vectors. The variation in time is produced by the two types of recurrent connections, namely those from the output layer to the state layer and those within the state layer. For each input vector, another temporal sequence can be produced. However, as the Elman net and the Jordan net are quite similar, each can be used for both purposes. Both types of networks have the advantage that only weights in the forward connections are modifiable and therefore no special training methods for recurrent nets have to be introduced.

3.2 Echo state networks

When we are interested to construct a recurrent neural network that shows a complex, but given dynamic behavior, back propagation through time can be applied as described above. A much simpler solution, however, is to use echo state networks (Jaeger and Haas 2004). An echo state network consists of two parts, a recurrent network with fixed weights, called dynamic reservoir, and output units that are connected to the neuroses of the dynamic reservoir. Only one output unit is depicted in Fig. 9 for simplicity.

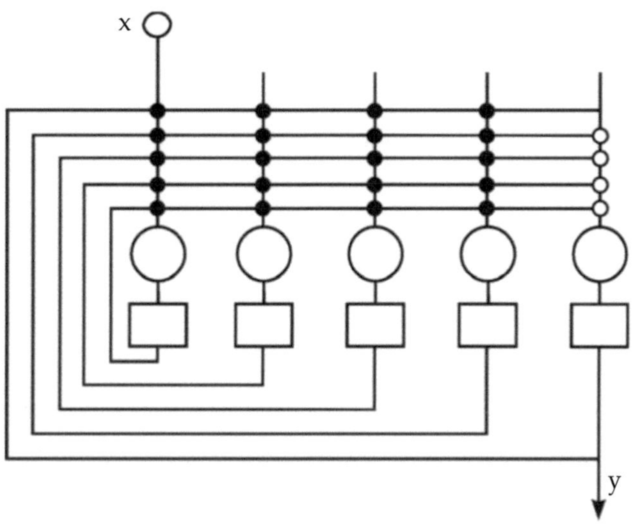

Fig. 9. Echo state network.

The dynamic reservoir consists of recurrently, usually sparsely connected units with logistic activation functions. The randomly selected strengths of the connections have to be small enough to avoid growing oscillations (this is guaranteed by using a weight matrix with the largest eigenvector smaller than 1). To test this property, the dynamic reservoir, after being excited by an impulse-like input to some of the units, may perform complex dynamics which however should decrease to zero with time. These dynamics are exploited by the output units. These output units are again randomly and recurrently connected to the units of the dynamic reservoir. Only those weights that determine the connections from the dynamic reservoir to the output units are learnt. All other weights are specified at the beginning and then held fixed (Hafizah et al., 2008).

3.3 Linear differential equations and recurrent neural networks

With respect to their dynamical properties, recurrent neural networks may be described as showing fixed point attractors. How is it possible to design a neural network with specific dynamics? Dynamical systems are often described by differential equations. In such cases the construction of a recurrent network is easily possible: Any system described by a linear differential equation of order n can be transformed into a recurrent neural network containing n units (Nauck et al., 2003). To this end, the differential equation has first to be transferred into a system of n coupled differential equations of the order one.

3.4 MMC nets

A specific type of recurrent neural networks that show fixed-point attractors and that are particularly suited to describe systems with redundant degrees of freedom are the so called MMC nets. The easiest way to construct such a net is to start with a simpler version. Given a linear equation with n variables

Each of these n equations represents the computation performed by one neuroid. So the complete network represents Multiple Solutions of the Basis Equation, and is therefore termed MSBE net. Different to Hopfield nets, the weights are in general asymmetric (apart from the special case that all parameters a are identical, i.e. a1 = a2 = a3), but follow the rule wij = 1/wji . The diagonal weights, by which each unit excites itself, could be zero, as in the example, or any positive value di, if all weights of this equation are further normalized by multiplication with 1/(di+1). Positive diagonal weights influence the dynamics to adopt low-pass filter-like properties, because the earlier state of this unit is transferred to the actual state with the factor d/(d+1). As di can arbitrarily be chosen (di $\leq$ 0), the weights may then not follow the rule wij = 1/wji anymore. Starting this net with any vector **a**, the net will stabilize at a vector fulfilling the basic equation. This means that the attractor points form a smooth, in this example two-dimensional, space. This is another difference to Hopfield nets which show discrete attractor points. Furthermore, there are no nonlinear characteristics necessary.

This network can be expanded to form an MMC net. MMC nets result from the combination of several MSBE nets (i.e. several basis equations) with shared units. Such MMC nets can be used to describe landmark navigation in insects and as a model describing place cells found in rodents (Cruse 2002). However, the principle can also be used to represent the kinematics of a body with complex geometry (Steinkühler and Cruse 1998). As a simple example, we will use a three-joint arm that moves in two dimensional space, therefore having one extra degree of freedom (Fig. 10.**a**)(Le Yang &Yanbo Xue, (2009).

The properties of this type of network can best be described by starting with a simple linear version (Fig. 10.**b**). As we have a two-dimensional case, the complete net consists of two identical networks. The output values correspond to the Cartesian coordinates of the six vectors shown in Fig.10.**a**, the x coordinates of the vectors given by the net shown with solid lines, the y coordinates by dashed lines. To obtain the weights, vector equations drawn from the geometrical arrangement shown in Fig. 10.**a** are used as basis equations. This means in this case there are several basis equations possible. For example, each three vectors forming a triangle can be used to provide a basis equation (e.g. **L1** + **L2** - **D1** = 0). As a given variable (e.g. **L1**) occurs in different basis equations, there are several equations to determine this variable.

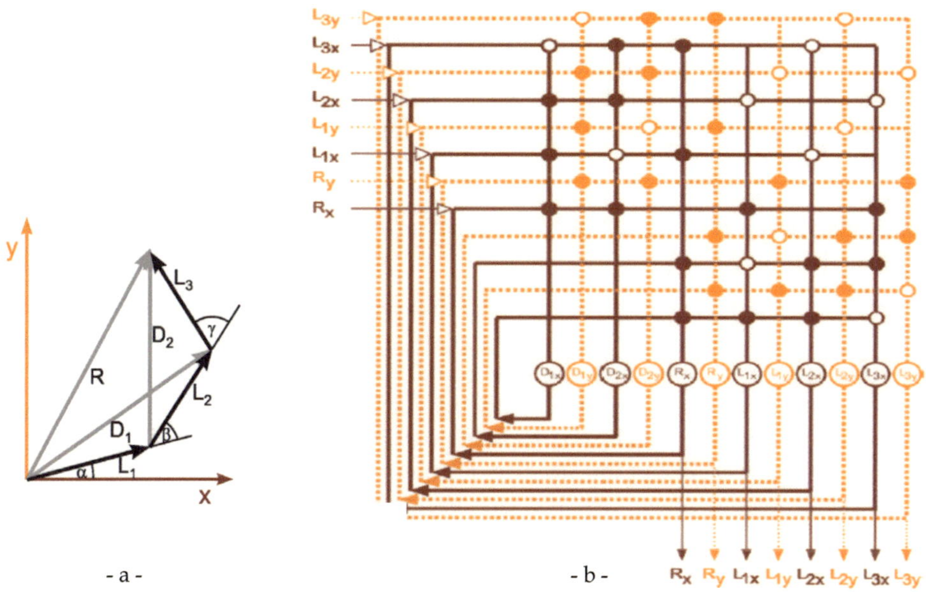

Fig. 10. An arm consisting of three segments described by the vectors L1 L2, and L3 which are connected by three planar joints.

3.5 Forward models and inverse models

Using recurrent neural networks like Jordan nets or MMC nets for the control of behavior, i.e. use their output for direct control of the actuators. Several models are proposed to control the movement of such a redundant (or non-redundant) arm. One model corresponds to a schema shown in Fig 11.**a**, where DK and IK may represent feedforward (e. g., three-layer) networks, computing the direct (DK) and inverse kinematics (IK) solutions, respectively. (In the redundant case, IK has to represent a particular solution)(Liu Meiqin, 2006).

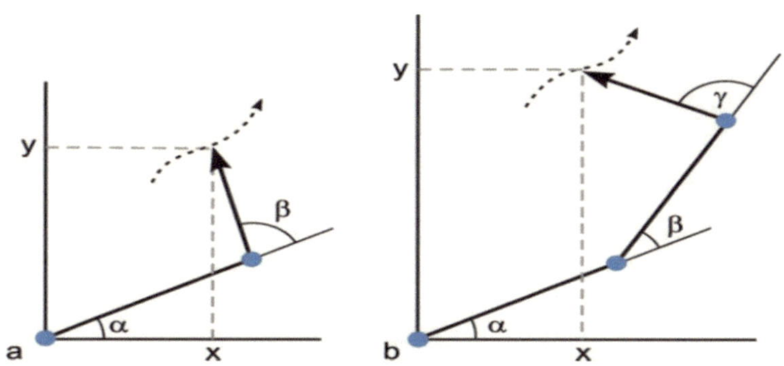

Fig. 11. A two-joint arm (a) and a three-joint arm (b) moving in a two dimensional (x-y) plane. When the tip of the arm has to follow a given trajectory (dotted arrow), in the redundant case (b) an infinite number of joint angle combinations can solve the problem for any given position of the tip.

Depending on the sensory system applied, the DK system might belong to the process, for example when the position of the tip of the arm is registered visually, or it might be part of the neuronal system, for example if joint angles are monitored. In principle, the process can be controlled with this feedback network. However, since in biological systems information transfer is slow, this solution is not appropriate for fast movements because long delays can lead to unstable behavior. A further complication of the control task occurs if there is a process with non negligible dynamic properties. This means that computation is more complex because not only the kinematics but also the forward and inverse dynamics have to be determined.

A simple solution of this problem would be to expand the system by introducing an internal (neuronal) model of the process (Fig. 12.b, FM). By this, the behavior of the process can be predicted in advance, e. g., inertia effects could be compensated for before they occur. This prediction system is called forward model (FM). Usually, although depicted separately in Figure 12.a, in this case the DK is considered part of the forward model. In other words, the FM predicts the next state of the arm (e.g. position, velocity) if the actual state and the motor command is known. Note that the network consists of serially connected IK and FM (including DK) forming a loop within the system and can therefore be represented by a recurrent neural network. The additional external feedback loop is omitted in Fig.12.b, but is still necessary if external disturbances occur. It should be mentioned that the output of the FM, i.e. the predicted sensory feedback, could also be compared with the real sensory feedback. This could be used to distinguish sensors effects produced by own actions from those produced by external activities.(Karaoglan D. Aslan, 2011).

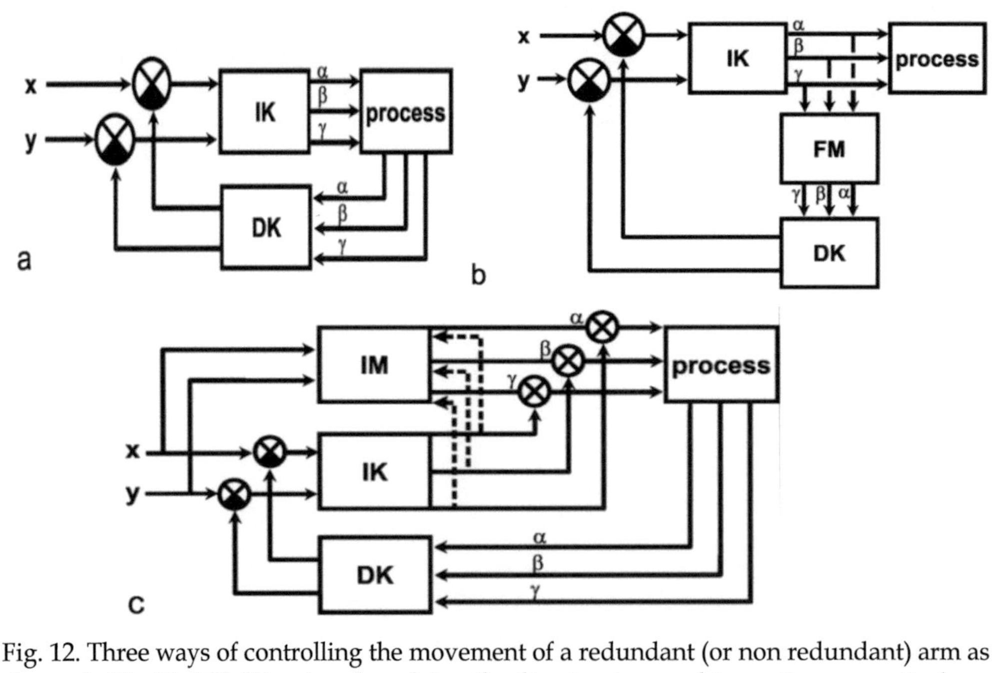

Fig. 12. Three ways of controlling the movement of a redundant (or non redundant) arm as shown in Fig. 11. DK, IK: networks solving the direct or inverse kinematics, respectively. FM: forward model of the process. IM: inverse model of the process. The dashed lines in (c) denote the error signals used to train the inverse model

An even faster way to solve this problem would be to introduce the inverse model (IM), which corresponds to the inverse kinematics, but may also incorporate the dynamic properties of the process (Fig. 11.c, upper part). Given the desired new state of the arm, the inverse model does provide the necessary motor command (**x** -> α) to reach this state. Using such an inverse model, the process could be controlled without the need of an internal feedback loop.

4. Training algorithms for recurrent neural networks

A training algorithm is a procedure that adapts the free parameters of a neural network in response to the behavior of the network embedded in its environment. The goal of the adaptations is to improve the neural network performance for the given task. Most training algorithms for neural networks adapt the network parameters in such a way that a certain error measure (also called cost function) is minimized. Alternatively, the *negative* error measure or a *performance measure* can be maximized.

Error measures can be postulated because they seem intuitively right for the task, because they lead to good performance of the neural network for the task, or because they lead to a convenient training algorithm. An example is the Sum Squared Error measure, which always has been a default choice of error measure in neural network research. Error measures can also be obtained by accepting some general.

Different error measures lead to different algorithms to minimize these error measures. Training algorithms can be classified into categories depending on certain distinguishing properties of those algorithms. Four main categories of algorithms that can be distinguished are:(Dijk, 1999)

1. *gradient-based algorithms.* The gradient of the equation of the error measure with respect to all network weights is calculated and the result is used to perform *gradient descent.* This means that the error measure is minimized in steps, by adapting the weight parameters proportional to the negative gradient vector.
2. *second-order gradient-based algorithms.* In second-order methods, not only the first derivatives of the error measure are used, but also the second-order derivatives of the error measure.
3. *stochastic algorithms.* Stochastic weight updates are made but the stochastic process is directed in such a way, that on average the error measure becomes smaller over time. A gradient of the error measure is not needed so an expression for the gradient doesn't have to exist.
4. *hybrid algorithms.* Gradient-based algorithms are sometimes combined with stochastic elements, which may capture the advantages of both approaches.

The following algorithms for the Fully Recurrent Neural Network and the subsets of the FRNN are investigated in this item:

4.1 Back propagation through time (BPTT) algorithm for FRNN

The Back propagation Through Time (BPTT) algorithm is an algorithm that performs an exact computation of the gradient of the error measure for use in the weight adaptation. In this section the BPTT algorithm will be derived for a (type 1) FRNN using a Sum Squared Error measure.(Omlin, 1996)

Methods of derivation of the algorithm

There are two different methods to develop the BPTT algorithm. Both are shown in this report:

- derivation by unfolding the network in time, which also gives intuitive insight in how the algorithm works.
- a formal derivation of the algorithm using the *ordered derivative* notation.

The BPTT algorithm can be summarized as follows:

1. set initial time n = n0
2. calculate the N neuron output values for time n using the network.
3. recursively calculate ei(m) then di(m) with backwards in time starting with m= n back to m = n0.
4. calculate for all i,j the weight updates .
5. update the weights wij
6. increase time n to n+1 and go back to step 2

4.2 Real-time recurrent learning (RTRL) algorithm for FRNN

A real-time training algorithm for recurrent networks known as Real-time Recurrent Learning (RTRL) was derived by several authors [Williams e.a., 1995]. This algorithm can be summarized by the explanation as:

In deriving a gradient-based update rule for recurrent networks, we now make network connectivity very very unconstrained. We simply suppose that we have a set of input units, $I = \{x_k(t),\ 0<k<m\}$, and a set of other units, $U = \{y_k(t),\ 0<k<n\}$, which can be hidden or output units. To index an arbitrary unit in the network we can use

$$z_k(t) = \begin{cases} x_k(t) & if \quad k \in I \\ y_k(t) & if \quad k \in U \end{cases} \tag{2}$$

Let **W** be the weight matrix with n rows and $n+m$ columns, where $w_{i,j}$ is the weight to unit i (which is in U) from unit j (which is in I or U). Units compute their activations in the now familiar way, by first computing the weighted sum of their inputs:

$$net_k(t) = \sum_{l \in U \cup I} w_{kl} z_l(t) \tag{3}$$

where the only new element in the formula is the introduction of the temporal index t. Units then compute some non-linear function of their net input

$$y_k(t+1) = f_k(net_k(t)) \tag{4}$$

Usually, both hidden and output units will have non-linear activation functions. Note that external input at time t does not influence the output of any unit until time $t+1$. The network is thus a discrete dynamical system. Some of the units in U are output units, for which a target is defined. A target may not be defined for every single input however. For example, if we are presenting a string to the network to be classified as either grammatical or ungrammatical, we may provide a target only for the last symbol in the string. In defining an error over the outputs, therefore, we need to make the error time dependent too, so that it can be undefined (or 0) for an output unit for which no target exists at present. Let *T(t)* be the set of indices *k* in *U* for which there exists a target value $d_k(t)$ at time *t*. We are forced to use the notation d_k instead of *t* here, as *t* now refers to time. Let the error at the output units be and define our error function for a single time step as

$$e_k(t) = \begin{cases} d_k(t) - y_k(t) & if \quad k \in T(t) \\ 0 & otherwise \end{cases} \tag{5}$$

The error function we wish to minimize is the sum of this error over all past steps of the network

$$E_{total}(t_o, t_1) = \sum_{\tau = to+1}^{t1} E(\tau) \tag{6}$$

Now, because the total error is the sum of all previous errors and the error at this time step, so also, the gradient of the total error is the sum of the gradient for this time step and the gradient for previous steps

$$\nabla_w E_{total}(t_o, t+1) = \nabla_w E_{total}(t_o, t) + \nabla_w E(t+1) \tag{7}$$

As a time series is presented to the network, we can accumulate the values of the gradient, or equivalently, of the weight changes. We thus keep track of the value

$$\Delta w_{ij}(t) = -\mu \frac{\partial E(t)}{\partial w_{ij}} \tag{8}$$

After the network has been presented with the whole series, we alter each weight w_{ij} by

$$\sum_{t=t_0+1}^{t1} \Delta w_{ij}(t) \tag{9}$$

We therefore need an algorithm that computes

$$-\frac{\partial E(t)}{\partial w_{ij}} = -\sum_{k \in U} \frac{\partial E(t)}{\partial y_k(t)} \frac{\partial y_k(t)}{\partial w_{ij}} = \sum_{k \in U} e_k(t) \frac{\partial y_k(t)}{\partial w_{ij}} \qquad (10$$

at each time step *t*. Since we know $e_k(t)$ at all times (the difference between our targets and outputs), we only need to find a way to compute the second factor

$$\frac{\partial y_k(t)}{\partial w_{ij}} \tag{11}$$

The key to understanding RTRL is to appreciate what this factor expresses. It is essentially a measure of the sensitivity of the value of the output of unit k at time t to a small change in the value of w_{ij}, taking into account the effect of such a change in the weight over the entire network trajectory from t_0 to t. Note that w_{ij} does not have to be connected to unit k. Thus this algorithm is non-local, in that we need to consider the effect of a change at one place in the network on the values computed at an entirely different place. Make sure you understand this before you dive into the derivation given next.(Baruch, 1999)

5. Inverse kinematic for humanied manipulator with 27-DOFs

Humanoid manipulators are the type of manipulator that practically suitable to coexist with human in builtfor-human environment because of its anthropomorphism, human friendly design and locomotion ability. Humanoid manipulator is different compare to other types of manipulators because the physical structure is designed to mimic as much as human's physical structure. Humanoid's shape shares many basic physical characteristics with actual humans, and for this reason, they are expected to coexist and collaborate with humans in environments where humans work and live. They may also be substituted for humans in hazardous environments or at disaster sites. These demands make it imperative for humanoid manipulators to attain many sophisticated motions such as walking, climbing stairs, avoiding obstacles, crawling, etc.

The *model* was designed in virtual reality to mimic as much as human characteristic, especially for contribution of its joints. The manipulator is consists of total of 27-DOFs: six for each leg, three for each arm, one for the waist, and two for the head. The high numbers of DOF's provide the ability to realize complex motions. Furthermore, the configuration of joints that closely resemble those of humans provides the advantages for the humanoid manipulator to attain human-like motion. Each joint feature a relatively wide range of rotation angles, shown in Table 1, particularly for the hip yaw of both legs, which permits the legs to rotate through wide angles when correcting the manipulator's orientation and avoiding obstacles. The specification of each joint rotation range is considered factors such as correlation with human's joint rotation range, manipulability of humanoid's manipulator, and safety during performing motions.(Nortman, 2001)

In this chapter, we propose and implement a simplified approach to solving inverse kinematics problems by classifying the robot's joints into several groups of joint coordinate frames at the robot's manipulator [11]. To describe translation and rotational relationship between adjacent joint links, we employ a matrix method proposed by Denavit-Hartenberg [12], which systematically establishes a coordinate system for each link of an articulated chain in the robot body.

Kinematical Solutions for 6-dof Arm

The humanoid manipulator design has 6-DOF on each arm: 3-DOF (yaw, roll and pitch) at the shoulder joint, one DOF (roll) at the elbow joint and 2-DOF ((pitch and yaw) at the wrist joint. Fig. 13 shows the arm structure and configuration of joints and links. The coordinate orientation follows the right-hand law, and a reference coordinate is fixed at the intersection point of two joints at the shoulder. Fig. 13 displays a model of the arm describing the configurations and orientation of each joint coordinates. To avoid confusion, only the x and z-axes appear in the figure. The arm's structure is divided into seven sets of joint coordinate's frames as listed below:

Σ*0:* Reference coordinate.
Σ*1:* shoulder yaw coordinate.
Σ*2:* shoulder roll coordinate.
Σ*3:* shoulder pitch coordinate.
Σ*4:* elbow pitch coordinate.
Σ*5:* wrist pitch coordinate.
Σ*6:* wrist roll coordinate.
Σ*h:* End-effector coordinate (at the end of middle fingerer).

Axis	Humanoid manipulator (deg)	Human (deg)
Neck (roll and pitch)	-90 ~ 90	-90 ~ 90
Shoulder (pitch) right & left	-180 ~ 120	-180 ~ 120
Shoulder (roll) right/left	-135 ~ 30/-30 ~ 135	-135 ~ 30/-30 ~ 135
Shoulder (yaw) right/left	-90 ~ 90/-90 ~ 90	-90 ~ 90/-90 ~ 90
Elbow (roll) right/left	0 ~ 135/0 ~ -135	0 ~ 135/0 ~ -135
Wrist (pitch) right/left	-30 ~ 60	-30 ~ 60
Wrist (yaw) right/left	-90 ~ 60	-90 ~ 60
Hip (pitch) right & left	-130 ~ 45	-130 ~ 45
Hip (roll) right/left	-90 ~ 22/-22 ~ 90 -	60 ~ 45/-45 ~ 60
Hip (yaw) right/left	-90 ~ 22/-22 ~ 90 -	60 ~ 45/-45 ~ 60
Knee (pitch) right &left	-20 ~150	0 ~150
Ankle (pitch) right & left	-90 ~ 60	-30 ~ 90
Ankle (roll) right/left	-20 ~ 90/-90 ~ 20	-20 ~ 30/-30 ~ 20
Waist (yaw)	-90 ~ 90	-45 ~ 45

Table 1. Comparison Joint rotation range between humanoid manipulator and Human

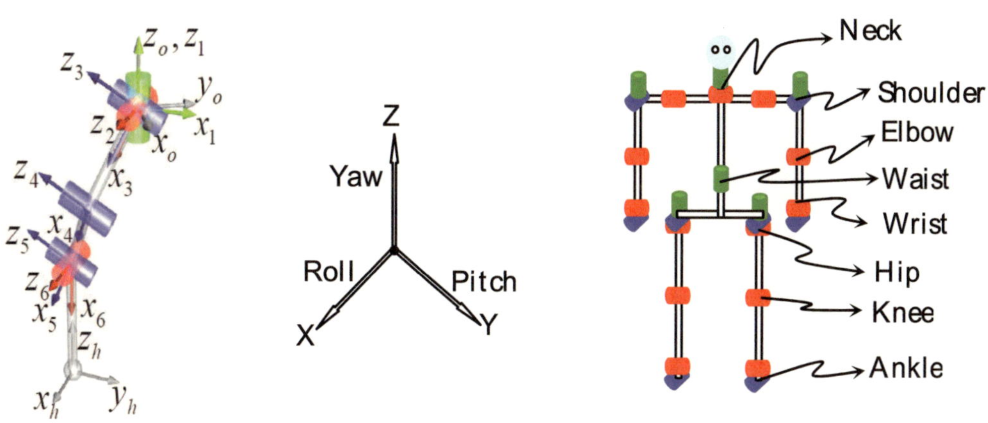

Fig. 13. a. Configurations of joint coordinates at the Manipulator arm with 6-DOF.
b. Structure of humanoid manipulator.

Consequently, corresponding link parameters of the arm can be defined as shown in Table 2. From the Denavit-Hartenberg convention mentioned above, definitions of the homogeneous transform matrix of the link parameters can be described as follows:

$$h_T^0 = Rot(z,\theta)Trans(0,0,d)Trans(l,0,0)Rot(x,\alpha) \tag{12}$$

Here, variable factor θ_i is the joint angle between the x_{i-1} and the x_i axes measured about the z_i axis; d_i is the distance from the x_{i-1} axis to the x_i axis measured along the z_i axis; α_i is the angle between the z_i axis to the z_{i-1} axis measured about the x_{i-1} axis, and l_i is the distance from the z_i axis to the z_{i-1} axis measured along the x_{i-1} axis. Here, link length for the upper and lower arm is described as l_1 and l_2, respectively. The following is used to obtain the forward kinematics solution for the robot arm. (Yussof, 2007)

Link	d_i	a_i	α_i	θ_i
1	d_1	0	π/2	θ^*
2	0	a_2	0	θ^*
3	0	a_3	0	θ^*
4	0	-π/2	0	θ^*
5	0	π/2	0	θ^*
6	d_6	0	0	θ^*

Table 2. DH parameters for the arm of humaniod manipulator.(* ≡ joint variable).

$$\begin{aligned}
A_1 &= \begin{bmatrix} c_1 & 0 & s_1 & 0 \\ s_1 & 0 & -c_1 & 0 \\ 0 & 1 & 0 & d_1 \\ 0 & 0 & 0 & 1 \end{bmatrix}; A_2 = \begin{bmatrix} c_2 & 0 & s_2 & a_2 \\ s_2 & 0 & -c_2 & 0 \\ 0 & 1 & 0 & 0 \\ 0 & 0 & 0 & 1 \end{bmatrix} \\
A_3 &= \begin{bmatrix} c_3 & 0 & -s_3 & a_3 \\ s_3 & 0 & c_3 & 0 \\ 0 & 1 & 0 & 0 \\ 0 & 0 & 0 & 1 \end{bmatrix}; A_4 = \begin{bmatrix} c_4 & 0 & -s_4 & 0 \\ s_4 & 0 & c_4 & 0 \\ 0 & 1 & 0 & 0 \\ 0 & 0 & 0 & 1 \end{bmatrix} \\
A_5 &= \begin{bmatrix} c_5 & 0 & s_5 & 0 \\ s_5 & 0 & -c_5 & 0 \\ 0 & 1 & 0 & 0 \\ 0 & 0 & 0 & 1 \end{bmatrix}; A_6 = \begin{bmatrix} c_6 & 0 & s_6 & 0 \\ s_6 & 0 & c_6 & 0 \\ 0 & 1 & 0 & d_6 \\ 0 & 0 & 0 & 1 \end{bmatrix}
\end{aligned} \tag{13}$$

The inverse kinematic is achieved by closed solution of above eqn's, and the general solution of angles of rotation can be summarized as follows:

$$\left.\begin{aligned}
&\theta_1 = a\tan 2(x_c, y_c)\\
&\theta_3 = a\tan(D, \pm\sqrt{1-D^2})\\
&where: D = \frac{x_c^2 + y_c^2 - d^2 + (z_c - d_1)^2 - a_2^2 - a_3^2}{2a_2a_3}\\
&\theta_2 = a\tan 2(\sqrt{x_c^2 + y_c^2 - d^2}, z_c - d_1)\\
&\theta_4 = a\tan 2(c_1c_{23}r_{13} + s_1c_{23}r_{23} + s_{23}r_{33},\\
&\qquad\qquad -c_1s_{23}r_{13} + s_1s_{23}r_{23} + c_{23}r_{33})\\
&\theta_5 = a\tan 2(s_1r_{13} - c_1r_{23}, \pm\sqrt{1-(s_1r_{13} - c_1r_{23})^2})\\
&\theta_6 = a\tan 2(-s_1r_{11} + c_1r_{21}, s_1r_{12} + c_1r_{22})\\
&where:\\
&c_i = \cos(\theta_i), and \quad s_i = \sin(\theta_i)
\end{aligned}\right\} \tag{14}$$

Kinematical Solutions for 6-dof Leg

Each of the legs has 6-DOFs: 3-DOFs (yaw, roll and pitch) at the hip joint, 1-DOF (pitch) at the knee joint and two DOF (pitch and roll) at the ankle joint. A reference coordinate is taken at the intersection point of the 3-DOF hip joint. In solving calculations of inverse kinematics for the leg, just as for arm, the joint coordinates are divided into eight separate coordinate frames as listed bellow.

$\Sigma 0$: Reference coordinate.
$\Sigma 1$: Hip yaw coordinate.
$\Sigma 2$: Hip roll coordinate.
$\Sigma 3$: Hip pitch coordinate.
$\Sigma 4$: Knee pitch coordinate.
$\Sigma 5$: Ankle pitch coordinate.
$\Sigma 6$: Ankle roll coordinate.
Σh: Foot bottom-center coordinate.

Furthermore, the leg's links are classified into three groups to short-cut the calculations, where each group of links is calculated separately as follows:

i. From link 0 to link 1 (Reference coordinate to coordinate joint number 1).
ii. From link 1 to link 4 (Coordinate joint number 2 to coordinate joint number 4).
iii. From link 4 to link 6 (Coordinate joint number 5 to coordinate at the bottom of the foot). Basically, i) is to control leg rotation at the *z*-axis,
iv. is to define the leg position, while iii) is to decide the leg's end-point orientation.

The solution in details is explain in the reference.(Youssof, 2007).

6. Solution of IKP by using RNN

This section introduces the basics of ANN architecture and its learning rule. Inspired by the idea of basing the feed forward and back propagation network structure. Fig.14 shows this structure , the Learning rule which is used in this paper is fast momentum back-propagation with delta rule structure of network with dimension (I-M-N). The inputs are the position of end-effector in (x,y,z) ,the network is single layer with dimension (33) neurons (this dimension limited by trial and error). The output dimensions are the angles of rotation and translation displacement in joints.

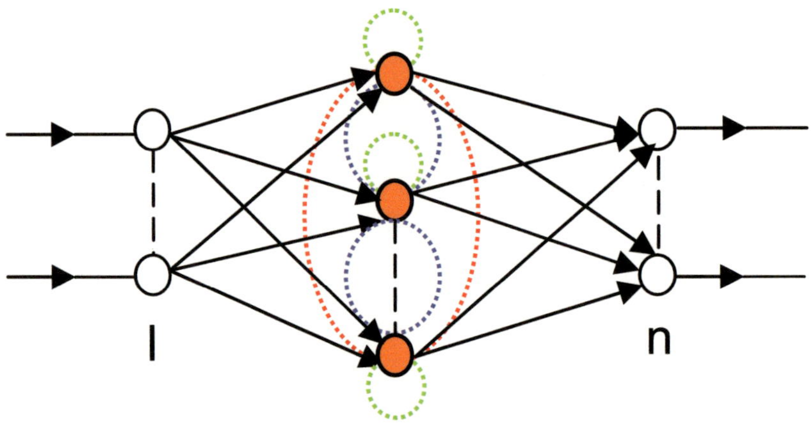

Fig. 14. FRBP Network with I inputs, one hidden layer of (M) unit and (N) outputs.(The dotted curve lines denote the finite recurrent connection)

The majority of adaptation learning algorithms are based on the fast momentum back propagation the mathematical characterization of a multilayer feed forward network is that of a composite application of functions each of these functions represents a particular layer and may be specific to individual units in the layer, e.g. all the units in the layer are required to have same activation function. The overall mapping is thus characterized by a composite function relating feed forward network inputs to output. That is $O=f_{composite}(x)$. Using (p) mapping layers in a (p+1) layer feed forward net yield:

$O=f^{Lp}(f^{Lp-1}(f^{L1}(x).))$. Thus the interconnection weights from unit (k) in L_1 to unit (I) in L_2 are w^{L1-L2} . If hidden units have a sigmoidal activation function, denoted f^{sig} .

$$O_i^{L2} = \sum_{k-1}^{Hi} w_{ik}^{L1\to L2} \left\{ f_k^{sig} \left[\sum_{j-1}^{I} w_{kj}^{Lo\to L1} i_j \right] \right\} \tag{15}$$

Above equation illustrates neural network with supervision and composition of non-linear function.The learning is a process by which the free parameters of a neural network are adapted through a continuing process of simulation by the environment in which the network is embedded. The type of learning is determined by the manner in which the parameters changes take place. A prescribed set of well defined rules for the solution of a learning problem is called learning algorithm. The Learning algorithms differ from each other in the way in which the adjustment kj, Δw to the synaptic weight w_{kj} is formulated. The basic approach in learning is to start with an untrained network.

The network outcomes are compared with target values that provide some error. Suppose that $\mathbf{t}_k(n)$ denote some desired outcome (response) for the Kth neuron at time n and let the actual response of the neuron is $O_k(n)$. Suppose the response $y_k(n)$ was produced when x(n) applied to the network. If the actual response $y_k(n)$ is not same as $\mathbf{t}_k(n)$, we may define an error signal as: $\mathbf{e}_k = \mathbf{t}_k(n) - \mathbf{y}_k(n)$. The purpose of error-correction learning is to minimize a cost function based on the error signal $\mathbf{e}_k(n)$. Once a cost function is selected, error-correction learning is strictly an optimization problem.

In case of non-linear neural network, the error surface may have troughs, valleys, canyons, and host of shapes, where as in low dimensional data, contains many minima and so many local minima plague the error landscapes, then it is unlikely that the network will find the global minimum. Another issue is the presence of plateaus regions where the error varies only slightly as a function of weights see and. Thus in presence of many plateaus, training will get slow. To overcome this situation momentum is introduced that forces the iterative process to cross saddle points and small landscapes.

7. Simulation of the humaniod manipulator based upon virtual reality

The humanoid manipulator 27-DOF model is built by using VR environment. It is shown in Fig. 15. The simulation of this model is achieved by solution the IKP with analytical model firstly. The data for analytical solution was using to learning FRNN that is shown in previous section with FRNN structure (15-33-27). The inputs are (I=27) six for each two arms and two lags (three position of end-effecter), one for waist and two for neck. The output of FRNN has dimension (N=27). The outputs are six angles of joint for each the limbs, one for waist and two for neck.

The initial posture form of humanoid manipulator is shown in Fig. 15. After solution of IKP by FRNN and get the joint angles. The values of joint angle were implemented by forward kinematic solution to get the posture of humanoid manipulator. The interaction between Matlab/Simulink and VR model will used the calculation of IKP by FRNN to implement the posture. The overall simulation design is shown in Fig. 16.

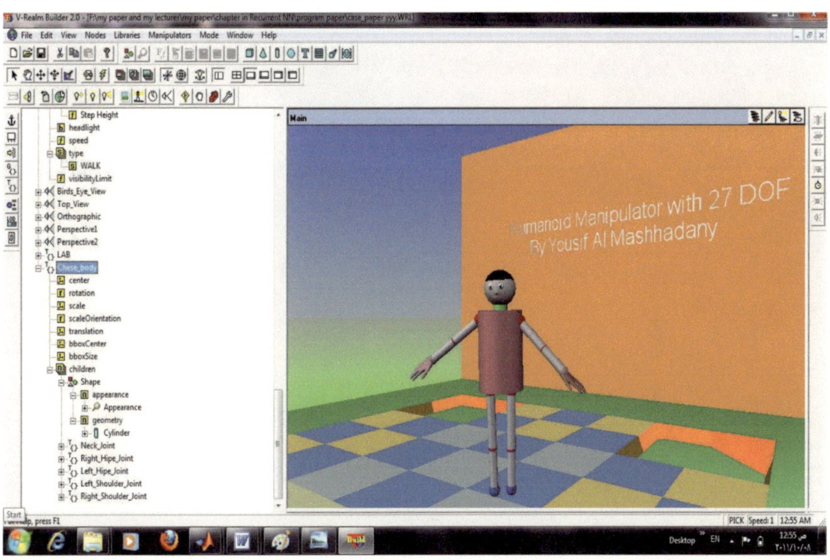

Fig. 15. Humanoid manipulator in VR.

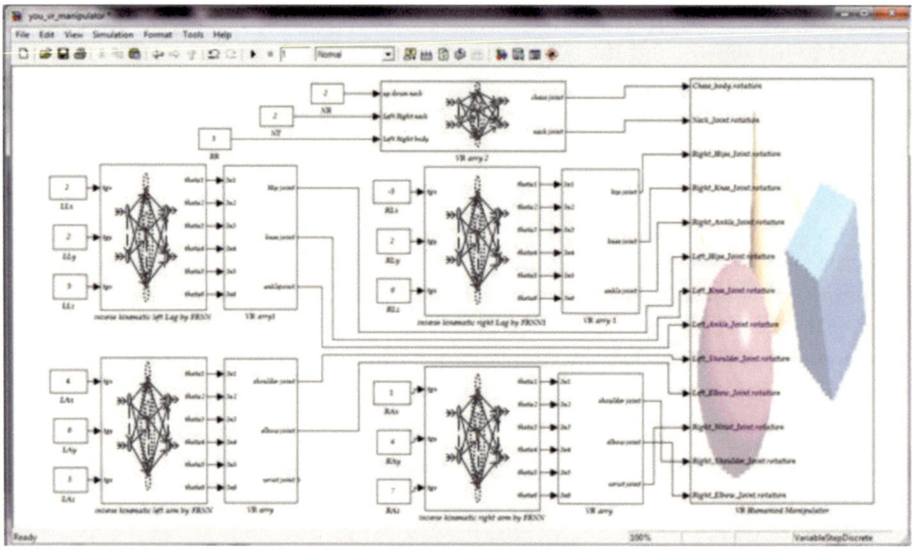

Fig. 16. The overall simulation of Humanoid Manipulator 27-DOF with Virtual Reality

The results of the simulation can be display by two methods. The first by running the design as one iteration by input one set of position and orientation of the limbs where the results is the posture form of humanoid manipulator in VR same as results shown in Fig. 17.a,b,c,d. The second method is achieved by enter many sets of coordinates to design. The results were movie of model in side the VR environment according to the path of inputs coordinate.

Fig. 17. a, b, c, d. The simulation results for posture of humanoid manipulator 27-DOF. Based upon FRNN with VR model.

8. Conclusion

From the description of the all types of RNN, some of special modified in the main types to get special RNN structure related to special application such as the calculation of system parameters by identification for the states system, recognition of fault with experience system and From the description of main types of training RNN can be seen that the RNN is very flexible structure to apply many mathematical algorithms and implement to solving system problem. The implement of feedback technique with memory in RNN gives the ability to dealing with many problems that needs high calculation with iteration to get the solution.

The solution of IKP is achieved by different method but the powerful method with practice application is the analytical solution. The calculation of posture for human body or manipulator which has the similar kinematic structure with human can be achieved by analytical solution, but this solution is very difficult because of high mathematic and very length calculation. This difficulty is increasing when we need calculated the posture with time to get the movie of manipulator. This problem is solving in this chapter by using FRNN with back propagation training algorithm.

The results of calculation are achieved for each limb separately at beginning such as for arm, lag and neck. After checking the accuracy of results by applying the forward kinematic to get the same coordinate of end- effecter for each part. The overall calculation of IKP is achieved to get the posture of manipulator. The data base for IKP is used to identify the FRNN for all point of envelop for movement where the internal memory and feedback in FRNN assistance this structure to overcame the problems of high calculation in the IKP solution.

The link between Matlab / Simulink and VR environment and the suitable of Matlab to execute any algorithm with high calculation are assistance to implement the posture of manipulator with high accuracy for two cases of running (movies and once posture). *The future* works for this design are:

- The calculation of IKP by RNN can be used as data base for implement the manipulator as practice system with human robot 27 DOF.
- The VR model for manipulator can be used as human - robot interactive system based on pc computer or microcomputer chip.
- Implement the algorithm of IKP solution based FRNN as microprocessor to able used with human robot manufacturing for many applications.

9. References

Abraham Ajith, (2005), 129: Artificial Neural Networks, *Handbook of Measuring System Design*, edited by Peter H. Sydenham and Richard Thorn. 2005 John Wiley & Sons, Ltd. ISBN: 0-470-02143-8. *Oklahoma State University, Stillwater, OK, USA*, From Web: http://www.softcomputing.net/ann_chapter.pdf

Baruch Ieroham, Gortcheva Elena, Thomas Federico & and Ruben Garrido, (1999), A neuro-fuzzy model for nonlinear plants identification, Proceedings of the IASTED International Conference Modeling and Simulation (MS '99), May 5-8, 1999, Philadelphia, Pennsylvania - USA, 291-021 - 326

Cheron G., etl, 2007, Toward an Integrative Dynamic Recurrent Neural Network for Sensorimotor Coordination Dynamics, Recurrent Neural Networks for Temporal Data Processing, 2007

Cruse Holk, 2006, Neural Networks as Cybernetic Systems - 2nd and revised edition, *Brains, Minds & Media,* ISSN 1861-1680, www.brains-minds-media.org

Dijk O. Esko, (1999), Analysis of Recurrent Neural Networks with Application to Speaker Independent Phoneme Recognition, *M.Sc. Thesis, University of Twente, department of Electrical Engineering,* June 1999, No. S&S 023N99

Francesco Cadini, Enrico Zio & Nicola Pedroni, (2008), Recurrent neural network for dynamic rellability analysis, *R&RATA # 2 (Vol.1)* 2008, June, pp 30 - 42

Hafizah Husain, Marzuki Khalid & Rubiyah Yusof, (2008), Direct Model Reference Adaptive Controller Based-On Neural-Fuzzy Techniques for Nonlinear Dynamical Systems, *American Journal of Applied Sciences* , Issue 7, Volume 5 ,2008, pp 769 – 776, ISSN 1546-9239

Huaien Gao, Rudolf Sollacher, (2008), Conditional Prediction of Time Series Using Spiral Recurrent Neural Network, (2008), *proceedings European Symposium on Artificial neural networks,* 23-25 April 2008, ISBN 2-930307-08-0

Le Yang &Yanbo Xue, (2009), Development of A New Recurrent Neural Network Toolbox (RNN-Tool) ,*A Course Project Report on Training Recurrent Multilayer Perceptron and Echo State Network,* McMaster university , 01 June 2006

Liu Meiqin, (2006), Delayed Standard Neural Network Models for the Stability Analysis of Recurrent Neural Networks, *International Journal of Computational Intelligence Research.* Vol.2, No. 1 (2006), pp. 10-16, ISSN 0973-1873, Research India Publications http://www.ijcir.info

Karaoglan D. Aslan, (2011), An integrated neural network structure for recognizing autocrrelated and trending processes , *Mathematical and Computational Applications,* Vol. 16, No. 2, 2011, pp. 514-523

Nortman Scott, Peach Jack, Nechyba Michael, Brown S. Louis & Arroyo A., (2001), Construction and Kinematic Analysis of an Anthropomorphic Mobile Robot, Machine Intelligence Laboratory, University of Florida, Gainesville, FL, FCRAR, May 10-11, 2001, FAMU

Omlin W. Christian & Giles C. Lee, (1996), Constructing Deterministic Finite-State Automata in Recurrent Neural Networks, Journal of the ACM, Vol. 43, No. 6, November 1996, pp. 937–972

Paine W. Rainer & Tani Jun, (2004), Adaptive Motor Primitive and Sequence Formation in a Hierarchical Recurrent Neural Network, Paine & Tani 2004: Accepted in SAB2004

Reza Jafari &Rached Dhaouadi, (Adaptive PID Control of a Nonlinear Servomechanism Using Recurrent Neural Networks, Advances in Reinforcement Learning, PP 275-296

Richards J, Holler P, Bockstahler B, Dale B, Mueller M, Burston J, Selfe J & Levine D, A comparison of human and canine kinematics during level walking, stair ascent, and stair descent, (2010*), Wien. Tierrztl. Mschr. - Vet. Med. Austria 97,* (2010), pp 92 - 100

Sit W.Chen, (2005),Application of artificial neural network-genetic algorithm in inferential estimation and control of a distillation column, Master of Engineering (Chemical) Faculty of Chemical and Natural Resources Engineering Universiti Teknologi Malaysia July 2005

Yussof Hanafiah, Yamano Mitsuhiro, Nasu Yasuo & Ohka Masahiro, (2007), Performance of a Research Prototype Humanoid Robot Bonten-Maru II to Attain Human-Like Motions, *WSEAS Transactions on Systems and Control,* Issue 9, Volume 2, September 2007, PP 458-467, ISSN: 1991-8763

Zhenzhen Liu & Itamar Elhanany, (2008), A Fast and Scalable Recurrent Neural Network Based on Stochastic Meta Descent, *IEEE Transactions on neural networks,* Vol. 19, No. 9, SEPTEMBER 2008, PP 1651 – 1657

6

Recurrent Neural Network-Based Adaptive Controller Design for Nonlinear Dynamical Systems

Hong Wei Ge and Guo Zhen Tan*

College of Computer Science and Technology, Dalian University Of Technology, Dalian, China

1. Introduction

The design goal of a control system is to influence the behavior of dynamic systems to achieve some pre-determinate objectives. A control system is usually designed on the premise that an accurate knowledge of a given object and environment cannot be obtained in advance. It usually requires suitable methods to address the problems related to uncertain and highly complicated dynamic system identification. As a matter of fact, system identification is an important branch of research in the automatic control domain. However, the majority of methods for system identification and parameters' adjustment are based on linear analysis: therefore it is difficult to extend them to complex non-linear systems. Normally, a large amount of approximations and simplifications have to be performed and, unavoidably, they have a negative impact on the desired accuracy. Fortunately the characteristics of the Artificial Neural Network (ANN) approach, namely non-linear transformation and support to highly parallel operation, provide effective techniques for system identification and control, especially for non-linear systems [1-9]. The ANN approach has a high potential for identification and control applications mainly because: (1) it can approximate the nonlinear input-output mapping of a dynamic system [10]; (2) it enables to model the complex systems' behavior and to achieve an accurate control through training, without a priori information about the structures or parameters of systems. Due to these characteristics, there has been a growing interest, in recent years, in the application of neural networks to dynamic system identification and control.

"Depth" and "resolution ratio" are the main characteristics to measure the dynamic memory performance of neural networks [11]. "Depth" denotes how far information can be memorized; "resolution ratio" denotes how much information in input sequences of neural networks can be retained. The memory of time-delay units is of lower depth and higher resolution ratio, while most recurrent neural networks, such as Elman neural networks, are higher depth and lower resolution ratio. The popular neural networks have much defect on dynamic memory performance. This chapter proposed a novel time-delay recurrent network model which has far more "depth" and "resolution ratio" in memory for

---

*Corresponding author

identifying and controlling dynamic systems. The proposed identification and control schemes are examined by the numerical experiments for identifying and controlling some typical nonlinear systems.

The rest of this chapter is organized as follows. Section 2 proposes a novel time-delay recurrent neural network (TDRNN) by introducing the time-delay and recurrent mechanism; moreover, a dynamic recurrent back propagation algorithm is developed according to the gradient descent method. Section 3 derives the optimal adaptive learning rates to guarantee the global convergence in the sense of discrete-type Lyapunov stability. Thereafter, the proposed identification and control schemes based on TDRNN models are examined by numerical experiments in Section 4. Finally, some conclusions are made in Section 5.

2. Time-delay recurrent neural network (TDRNN)

Figure 1 depicts the proposed time-delay recurrent neural network (TDRNN) by introducing the time-delay and recurrent mechanism. In the figure, Z^{-1} denotes a one-step time delay, the notation "□" represents the memory neurons in the input layer with self-feedback gain γ $(0 \le \gamma \le 1)$, which improves the resolution ratio of the inputs.

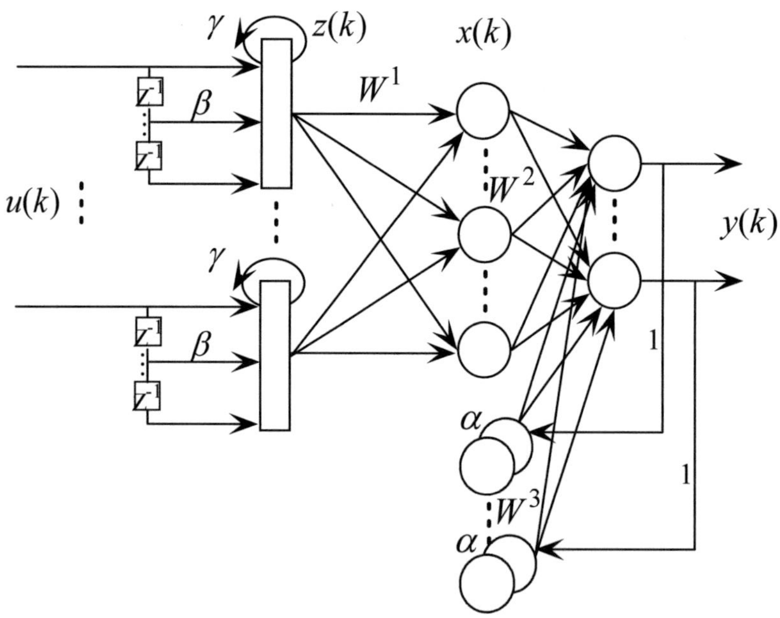

Fig. 1. Architecture of the modified Elman network

It is a type of recurrent neural network with different layers of neurons, namely: input nodes, hidden nodes, output nodes and, specific of the approach, context nodes. The input and output nodes interact with the outside environment, whereas the hidden and context nodes do not. The context nodes are used only to memorize previous activations of the output nodes. The feed-forward connections are modifiable, whereas the recurrent connections are fixed. More specifically, the proposed TDRNN possesses self-feedback links with fixed coefficient α in the context nodes. Thus the output of the context nodes can be described by

$$y_{Cl}(k) = \alpha y_{Cl}(k-1) + y_l(k-1) \quad (l = 1,2,\cdots,m). \tag{1}$$

where $y_{Cl}(k)$ and $y_l(k)$ are, respectively, the outputs of the lth context unit and the lth output unit and α ($0 \le \alpha < 1$) is the self-feedback coefficient. If we assume that there are r nodes in the input layer, n nodes in the hidden layer, and m nodes in the output layer and context layers respectively, then the input u is an r dimensional vector, the output x of the hidden layer is n dimensional vector, the output y of the output layer and the output y_C of the context nodes are m dimensional vectors, and the weights W^1, W^2 and W^3 are $n \times r$, $m \times n$ and $m \times m$ dimensional matrices, respectively.

The mathematical model of the proposed TDRNN can be described as follows.

$$y(k) = g(W^2 x(k) + W^3 y_C(k)), \tag{2}$$

$$y_C(k) = \alpha y_C(k-1) + y(k-1), \tag{3}$$

$$x(k) = f(W^1 z(k)), \tag{4}$$

$$z(k) = u(k) + \beta \sum_{i=1}^{\tau} u(k-i) + \gamma z(k-1). \tag{5}$$

where $0 \le \alpha, \beta, \gamma \le 1$, $\beta + \gamma = 1$, $z(0) = 0$, and τ is the step number of time delay. $f(x)$ is often taken as the sigmoidal function

$$f(x) = \frac{1}{1+e^{-x}}. \tag{6}$$

and $g(x)$ is often taken as a linear function, that is

$$y(k) = W^2 x(k) + W^3 y_C(k) \ . \tag{7}$$

Taking expansion for $z(k-1)$, $z(k-2)$,..., $z(1)$ by using Eq.(5), then we have

$$z(k) = \sum_{i=0}^{\tau} u(k-i) + \sum_{i=1}^{k-\tau} \gamma^i u(k-\tau-i) - \gamma^k u(0). \tag{8}$$

From Eq.(8) it can be seen that the memory neurons in the input layer include all the previous input information and the context nodes memorize previous activations of the output nodes, so the proposed TDRNN model has far higher memory depth than the popular neural networks. Furthermore, the neurons in the input layer can memory accurately the inputs from time $k-\tau$ to time k, and this is quite different from the memory performance of popular recurrent neural networks. If the delay step τ is moderate large, the TDRNN possesses higher memory resolution ratio.

Let the kth desired output of the system be $y_d(k)$. We can then define the error as

$$E = \frac{1}{2}(y_d(k) - y(k))^T (y_d(k) - y(k)). \tag{9}$$

Differentiating E with respect to W^3, W^2 and W^1 respectively, according to the gradient descent method, we obtain the following equations

$$\Delta w_{il}^3 = \eta_3 \delta_i^0 y_{C,l}(k) \qquad (i = 1,2,\cdots,m; l = 1,2,\cdots,m), \tag{10}$$

$$\Delta w_{ij}^2 = \eta_2 \delta_i^0 (x_j(k) + w_{ii}^3 \frac{\partial y_{C,i}(k)}{\partial w_{ij}^2}) \quad (i = 1,2,\cdots,m; j = 1,2,\cdots,n), \tag{11}$$

$$\Delta w_{jq}^1 = \eta_1 \sum_{t=1}^{n} \delta_t^0 w_{tj}^2 f_j'(\cdot) z_q(k) \quad (j = 1,2,\cdots,n; q = 1,2,\cdots,r). \tag{12}$$

which form the learning algorithm for the proposed TDRNN, where η_1, η_2 and η_3 are learning steps of W^1, W^2 and W^3, respectively, and

$$\delta_i^0 = (y_{d,i}(k) - y_i(k)) g_i'(\cdot), \tag{13}$$

$$\frac{\partial y_{C,i}(k)}{\partial w_{ij}^2} = \alpha \frac{\partial y_{C,i}(k-1)}{\partial w_{ij}^2} + \frac{\partial y_i(k-1)}{\partial w_{ij}^2}. \tag{14}$$

If $g(x)$ is taken as a linear function, then $g_i'(\cdot) = 1$. Clearly, Eqs. (11) and (14) possess recurrent characteristics.

3. Convergence of proposed time-delay recurrent neural network

In Section 2, we have proposed a TDRNN model and derived its dynamic recurrent back propagation algorithm according to the gradient descent method. But the learning rates in the update rules have a direct effect on the stability of dynamic systems. More specifically, a large learning rate can make the modification of weights over large in each update step, and this will induce non-stability and non-convergence. On the other hand, a small learning rate will induce a lower learning efficiency. In order to train neural networks more efficiently, we propose three criterions of selecting proper learning rates for the dynamic recurrent back propagation algorithm based on the discrete-type Lyapunov stability analysis. The following theorems give sufficient conditions for the convergence of the proposed TDRNN when the functions $f(\cdot)$ and $g(\cdot)$ in Eqs. (4) and (2) are taken as sigmoidal function and linear function respectively.

Suppose that the modification of the weights of the TDRNN is determined by Eqs. (10-14). For the convergence of the TDRNN we have the following theorems.

Theorem 1. The stable convergence of the update rule (12) on W^1 is guaranteed if the learning rate $\eta_1(k)$ satisfies that

$$0 < \eta_1(k) < \frac{8}{nr\left|\max_k z_k(k)\right|\left|\max_{ij}(W_{ij}^2(k))\right|}. \tag{15}$$

Proof. Define the Lyapunov energy function as follows.

$$E(k) = \frac{1}{2}\sum_{i=1}^{m} e_i^2(k). \tag{16}$$

Where

$$e_i(k) = y_{d,i}(k) - y_i(k). \tag{17}$$

And consequently, we can obtain the modification of the Lyapunov energy function

$$\Delta E(k) = E(k+1) - E(k) = \frac{1}{2}\sum_{i=1}^{m}\left[e_i^2(k+1) - e_i^2(k)\right]. \tag{18}$$

Then the error during the learning process can be expressed as

$$e_i(k+1) = e_i(k) + \sum_{j=1}^{n}\sum_{q=1}^{r}\frac{\partial e_i(k)}{\partial W_{jq}^1}\Delta W_{jq}^1 = e_i(k) - \sum_{j=1}^{n}\sum_{q=1}^{r}\frac{\partial y_i(k)}{\partial W_{jq}^1}\Delta W_{jq}^1. \tag{19}$$

Furthermore, the modification of weights associated with the input and hidden layers is

$$\Delta W_{jq}^1(k) = \eta_1(k)e_i(k)\frac{\partial e_i(k)}{\partial W_{jq}^1} = -\eta_1(k)e_i(k)\frac{\partial y_i(k)}{\partial W_{jq}^1}. \tag{20}$$

Hence, from Eqs.(18-20) we obtain

$$\begin{aligned}
\Delta E(k) &= \frac{1}{2}\sum_{i=1}^{m} e_i^2(k)\left[\left(1 - \eta_1(k)\left[\frac{\partial y_i(k)}{\partial W^1}\right]^T\left[\frac{\partial y_i(k)}{\partial W^1}\right]\right)^2 - 1\right] \\
&= \frac{1}{2}\sum_{i=1}^{m} e_i^2(k)\left[\left(1 - \eta_1(k)\left\|\frac{\partial y_i(k)}{\partial W^1}\right\|^2\right)^2 - 1\right] \\
&= -\sum_{i=1}^{m} e_i^2(k)\beta_i^1(k)
\end{aligned} \tag{21}$$

Where

$$\begin{aligned}
\beta_i^1(k) &= \frac{1}{2}\left[1 - \left(1 - \eta_1(k)\left\|\frac{\partial y_i(k)}{\partial W^1}\right\|^2\right)^2\right] \\
&= \frac{1}{2}\eta_1(k)\left\|\frac{\partial y_i(k)}{\partial W^1}\right\|^2\left(2 - \eta_1(k)\left\|\frac{\partial y_i(k)}{\partial W^1}\right\|^2\right)
\end{aligned}. \tag{22}$$

W^1 represents an $n \times r$ dimensional vector and $\|\cdot\|$ denotes the Euclidean norm.

Notice that the activation function of the hidden neurons in the TDRNN is the sigmoidal type, we have $0 < f'(x) \le 1/4$. Thus,

$$\left|\frac{\partial y_i(k)}{\partial W_{jq}^1}\right| = \left|W_{ij}^2(k) f_j^{'}(\cdot) z_q(k)\right| \le \frac{1}{4}\left|\max_q z_q(k)\right|\left|\max_{ij}(W_{ij}^2(k))\right| . \quad (23)$$
$$(i = 1,2,\cdots,m; j = 1,2,\cdots,n; q = 1,2,\cdots,r)$$

According to the definition of the Euclidean norm we have

$$\left\|\frac{\partial y(k)}{\partial \boldsymbol{W}^1}\right\| \le \sqrt{\frac{nr}{4}\left|\max_q z_q(k)\right|\left|\max_{ij}(W_{ij}^2(k))\right|} . \quad (24)$$

Therefore, while $0 < \eta_1(k) < \dfrac{8}{nr\left|\max_q z_q(k)\right|\left|\max_{ij}(W_{ij}^2(k))\right|}$, we have $\beta_i^1(k) > 0$, then from Eq.(21) we obtain $\Delta E(k) < 0$. According to the Lyapunov stability theory, this shows that the training error will converges to zero as $t \to \infty$. This completes the proof.

Theorem 2. The stable convergence of the update rule (11) on W^2 is guaranteed if the learning rate $\eta_2(k)$ satisfies that

$$0 < \eta_2(k) < \frac{2}{n} . \quad (25)$$

Proof. Similarly, the error during the learning process can be expressed as

$$e_i(k+1) = e_i(k) + \sum_{j=1}^{n} \frac{\partial e_i(k)}{\partial W_{ij}^2} \Delta W_{ij}^2 = e_i(k) - \sum_{j=1}^{n} \frac{\partial y_i(k)}{\partial W_{ij}^2} \Delta W_{ij}^2 . \quad (26)$$

Therefore,

$$\begin{aligned}\Delta E(k) &= \frac{1}{2}\sum_{i=1}^{m} e_i^2(k)\left[\left(1 - \eta_2(k)\left[\frac{\partial y_i(k)}{\partial W_i^2}\right]^T \left[\frac{\partial y_i(k)}{\partial W_i^2}\right]\right)^2 - 1\right] \\ &= \frac{1}{2}\sum_{i=1}^{m} e_i^2(k)\left[\left(1 - \eta_2(k)\left\|\frac{\partial y_i(k)}{\partial W_i^2}\right\|^2\right)^2 - 1\right] \\ &= -\sum_{i=1}^{m} e_i^2(k)\beta_i^2(k)\end{aligned} . \quad (27)$$

Where

$$\beta_i^2(k) = \frac{1}{2}\left[1 - \left(1 - \eta_2(k)\left\|\frac{\partial y_i(k)}{\partial W_i^2}\right\|^2\right)^2\right]. \tag{28}$$

Notice that the activation function of the hidden neurons in the TDRNN is the sigmoidal type, and neglect the dependence relation between $y_C(k)$ and the weights w_{ij}^2, we obtain

$$\frac{\partial E}{\partial w_{ij}^2} = -\delta_i^0 x_j(k). \tag{29}$$

Hence,

$$\left|\frac{\partial y_i(k)}{\partial W_{ij}^2}\right| = \left|x_j(k)\right| < 1 \quad (i = 1,2,\cdots,m; j = 1,2,\cdots,n). \tag{30}$$

According to the definition of the Euclidean norm we have

$$\left\|\frac{\partial y_i(k)}{\partial W_i^2}\right\| < \sqrt{n}. \tag{31}$$

Therefore, while $0 < \eta_2(k) < \frac{2}{n}$, we have $\beta_i^2(k) > 0$, then from Eq.(27) we obtain $\Delta E(k) < 0$. According to the Lyapunov stability theory, this shows that the training error will converges to zero as $t \to \infty$. This completes the proof.

Theorem 3. The stable convergence of the update rule (10) on W^3 is guaranteed if the learning rate $\eta_3(k)$ satisfies that

$$0 < \eta_3(k) < \frac{2}{m\left|\max_l (y_{C,l}(k))\right|^2}. \tag{32}$$

Proof. Similarly, as the above proof, we have

$$\begin{aligned}\Delta E(k) &= \frac{1}{2}\sum_{i=1}^{m} e_i^2(k)\left[\left(1 - \eta_3(k)\left[\frac{\partial y_i(k)}{\partial W^3}\right]^T\left[\frac{\partial y_i(k)}{\partial W^3}\right]\right)^2 - 1\right] \\ &= \frac{1}{2}\sum_{i=1}^{m} e_i^2(k)\left[\left(1 - \eta_3(k)\left\|\frac{\partial y_i(k)}{\partial W^3}\right\|^2\right)^2 - 1\right] \\ &= -\sum_{i=1}^{m} e_i^2(k)\beta_i^3(k)\end{aligned} \tag{33}$$

Where

$$\beta_i^3(k) = \frac{1}{2}\left[1 - \left(1 - \eta_3(k)\left\|\frac{\partial y_i(k)}{\partial W^3}\right\|^2\right)^2\right]. \tag{34}$$

Furthermore, according to the learning algorithm we have

$$\left|\frac{\partial y_s(k)}{\partial W_{il}^3}\right| = \left|\delta_{is} y_{C,h}(k)\right| = \delta_{is}\left|y_{C,l}(k)\right| \le \delta_{is}\left|\max_l(y_{C,l}(k))\right|. \tag{35}$$
$$(i = 1,2,\cdots,m;\ s = 1,2,\cdots,m; l = 1,2,\cdots,m)$$

Where

$$\delta_{is} = \begin{cases} 1 & i = s \\ 0 & i \ne s \end{cases}. \tag{36}$$

According to the definition of the Euclidean norm we have

$$\left\|\frac{\partial y(k)}{\partial W^3}\right\| \le \sqrt{m}\left|\max_l(y_{C,l}(k))\right|. \tag{37}$$

Therefore, from Eq.(34), we have $\beta_i^3(k) > 0$, while $0 < \eta_3(k) < \dfrac{2}{m\left|\max_l(y_{C,l}(k))\right|^2}$. Then from Eq.(33) we obtain $\Delta E(k) < 0$. According to the Lyapunov stability theory, this shows that the training error will converges to zero as $t \to \infty$. This completes the proof.

4. Numerical results and discussion

The performance of the proposed time-delay recurrent neural network for identifying and controlling dynamic systems is examined by some typical test problems. We provide four examples to illustrate the effectiveness of the proposed model and algorithm.

4.1 Nonlinear time-varying system identification

We have carried out the identification for the following nonlinear time-varying system using the TDRNN model as an identifier.

$$y(k+1) = \frac{y(k)}{1 + 0.68\sin(0.0005\pi k)y^2(k)} + 0.78u^3(k) + v(k). \tag{38}$$

Where $v(k)$ is Gauss white noise with zero mean and constant variance 0.1. The input of system is taken as $u(k) = \sin(0.01\pi k)$.

To evaluate the performance of the proposed algorithm, the numerical results are compared with those obtained by using Elman neural network (ENN). The Elman network is a typical recurrent network proposed by Elman [12]. Some parameters on the TDRNN in our experiments are taken as follows. The number of hidden nodes is taken as 6, the weights are initialized in the interval [-2, 2] randomly, besides, α, β and γ are set as 0.4, 0.6, 0.4 respectively. The number of hidden nodes in the ENN is also taken as 6.

Figure 2 shows the identification result, where the "Actual curve" is the real output curve of the dynamic system, represented by the solid line; the "Elman curve" is the output curve identified using the ENN model, and represented by the dash line; the "TDRNN curve" is the output curve identified by the proposed TDRNN model, and represented by the dash dot line. Figure 3 shows the identification error curves obtained with the TDRNN and ENN respectively, in which the error is the absolute value of the difference between identification result and the actual output. From the two figures it can be seen that the proposed method is superior to the ENN method. These results demonstrate the power and potential of the proposed TDRNN model for identifying nonlinear systems.

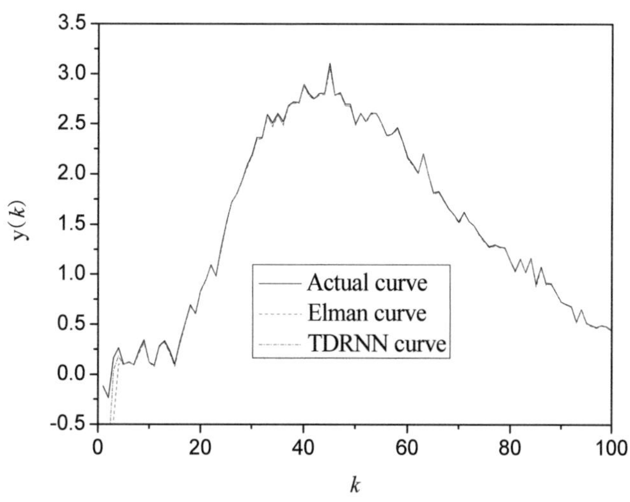

Fig. 2. Identification curves with different methods

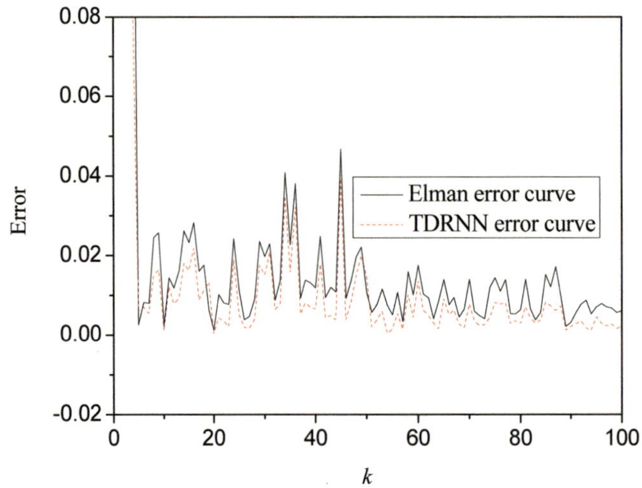

Fig. 3. Comparison of error curves obtained by different methods

4.2 Bilinear DGP system control

In this section, we control the following bilinear DGP system using the TDRNN model as a controller.

$$z(t) = 0.5 - 0.4z(t-1) + 0.4z(t-1)u(t-1) + u(t). \tag{39}$$

The system output at an arbitrary time is influenced by all the past information. The control reference curves are respectively taken as:

1. Line type:

$$z(t) = 1.0\,; \tag{40}$$

2. Quadrate wave:

$$z(t) = \begin{cases} 0.0 & (2k \cdot 5 \le t < (2k+1) \cdot 5, (k = 0,1,2,\cdots)) \\ 1.0 & ((2k-1) \cdot 5 \le t < 2k \cdot 5, (k = 1,2,3,\cdots)) \end{cases} \tag{41}$$

The parameters on the TDRNN in the experiments are taken as follows. The number of hidden nodes is taken as 6, the weights are initialized in the interval [-2, 2] randomly, besides, α, β and γ are set as 0.3, 0.6, 0.4 respectively. Figures 4 and 5 show the control results. Figure 4 shows the control curve using the proposed TDRNN model when the control reference is taken as a line type. Figure 5 shows the control curve when the reference is taken as a quadrate wave type. From these results it can be seen that the proposed control model and algorithm possess a satisfactory control precision.

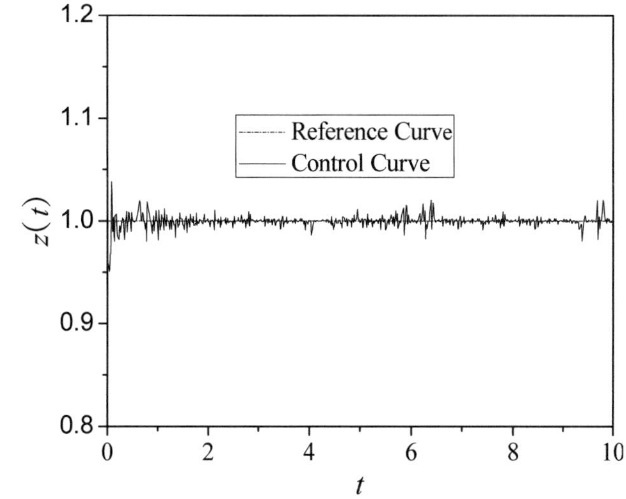

Fig. 4. Control curves with line type reference

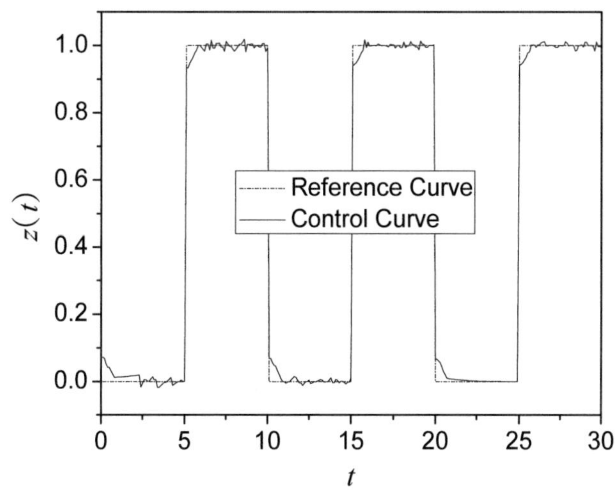

Fig. 5. Control curves with quadrate wave reference

4.3 Inverted pendulum control

The inverted pendulum system is one of the classical examples used in many experiments dealing with classical as well as modern control, and it is often used to test the effectiveness of different controlling schemes [13-16]. So in this chapter, to examine the effectiveness of the proposed TDRNN model, we investigate the application of the TDRNN to the control of inverted pendulums.

The inverted pendulum system used here is shown in Fig.6, which is formed from a cart, a pendulum and a rail for defining position of cart. The Pendulum is hinged on the center of the top surface of the cart and can rotate around the pivot in the same vertical plane with the rail. The cart can move right or left on the rail freely.

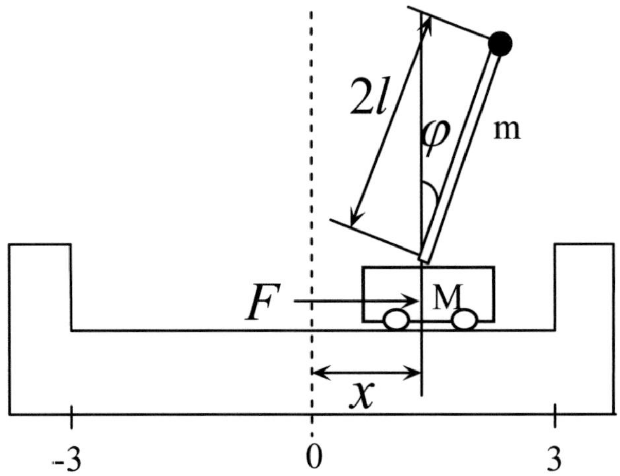

Fig. 6. Schematic diagram of inverted pendulum system

The dynamic equation of the inverted pendulum system can be expressed as the following two nonlinear differential equations.

$$\ddot{\varphi} = \frac{g\sin\varphi + \cos\varphi[-F - ml\dot{\varphi}^2 \sin\varphi + \mu_c \operatorname{sgn}(\dot{x})\cdot(m+M)^{-1}] - \dfrac{\mu_p \dot{\varphi}}{ml}}{\dfrac{4}{3}l - \dfrac{m\cos^2\varphi}{m+M}\cdot l}, \tag{42}$$

$$\ddot{x} = \frac{F + ml(\dot{\varphi}^2 \sin\varphi - \ddot{\varphi}\cos\varphi) - \mu_c \operatorname{sgn}(\dot{x})}{m+M}. \tag{43}$$

Where the parameters, M and m are respectively the mass of the cart and the mass of the pendulum in unit (kg), $g = 9.81 m/s^2$ is the gravity acceleration, l is the half length of the pendulum in unit (m), F is the control force in the unit (N) applied horizontally to the cart, u_c is the friction coefficient between the cart and the rail, u_p is the friction coefficient between the pendulum pole and the cart. The variables φ, $\dot{\varphi}$, $\ddot{\varphi}$ represent the angle between the pendulum and upright position, the angular velocity and the angular acceleration of the pendulum, respectively. Moreover, given that clockwise direction is positive. The variables x, $\dot{x}$, $\ddot{x}$ denote the displacement of the cart from the rail origin, its velocity, its acceleration, and right direction is positive.

We use the variables φ and x to control inverted pendulum system. The control goal is to make φ approach to zero by adjusting F, with the constraint condition that x is in a given interval. The control block diagram of the inverted pendulum system is shown in Figure 7. The TDRNN controller adopts variables φ and x as two input items.

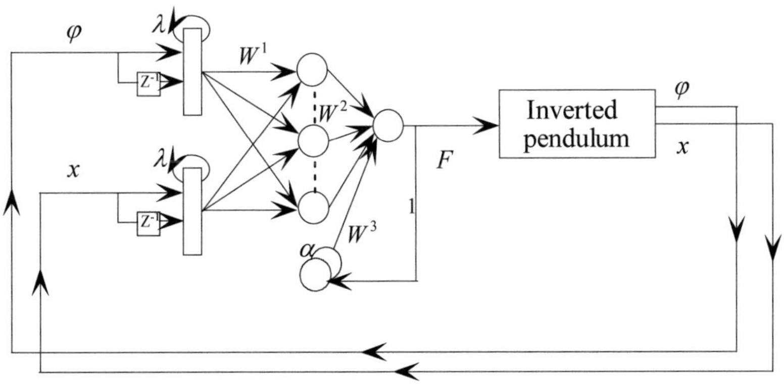

Fig. 7. Control block diagram of inverted pendulum system

In the numerical experiments, the motion of the inverted pendulum system is simulated by numerical integral. The parameter setting is listed in the Table 1.

parameter	g	M	m	l	μ_c	μ_p	φ	$\dot{\varphi}$	x	$\dot{x}$
value	9.81	1.0	0.1	0.6	0.002	0.00002	5°	0	0	0

Table 1. Parameter Setting of Inverted Pendulum

Besides, the number of hidden nodes is taken as 6, the weights are initialized in the interval [-3, 3] randomly, the parameters α, β and γ on the TDRNN are set as 0.3, 0.6, 0.4 respectively. The control goals are to control the absolute value of φ within 10° and make it approximate to zero as closely as possible, with the constraint condition of the absolute value of x within 3.0m.

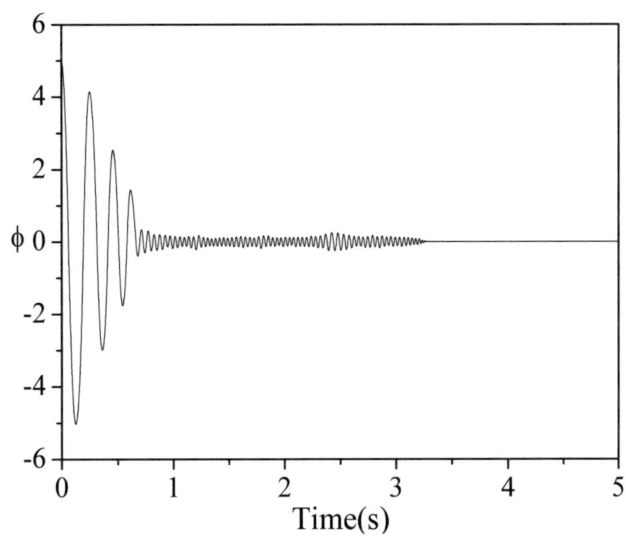

Fig. 8. Control curve of the angle φ

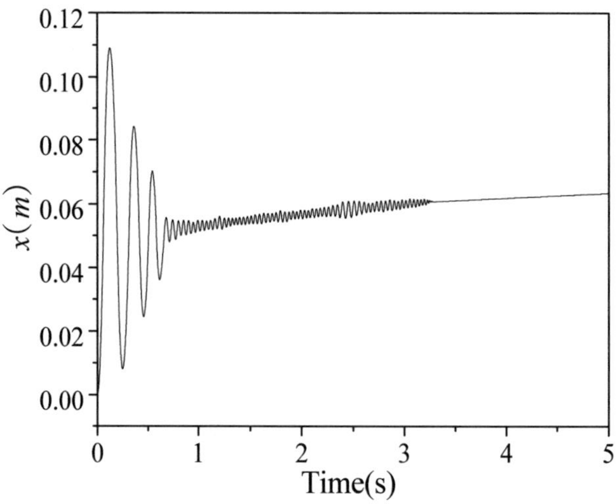

Fig. 9. Control curve of the displacement x

The control results are shown in Figures 8 and 9, and the sampling interval is taken as $T = 1ms$. Figures 8 and 9 respectively show the control curve of the angle φ and the control curve of the displacement x. From Figure 8, it can be seen that the fluctuation degree of φ is large at the initial stage, as time goes on, the fluctuation degree becomes smaller and smaller, and it almost reduces to zero after 3 seconds. Figure 9 shows that the change trend of x is similar to that of φ except that it has a small slope. These results demonstrate the proposed control scheme based on the TDRNN can effectively perform the control for inverted pendulum system.

4.4 Ultrasonic motor control

In this section, a dynamic system of the ultrasonic motor (USM) is considered as an example of a highly nonlinear system. The simulation and control of the USM are important problems in the applications of the USM. According to the conventional control theory, an accurate mathematical model should be set up. But the USM has strongly nonlinear speed characteristics that vary with the driving conditions and its operational characteristics depend on many factors. Therefore, it is difficult to perform effective control to the USM using traditional methods based on mathematical models of systems. Our numerical experiments are performed using the model of TDRNN for the speed control of a longitudinal oscillation USM [17] shown in Figure 10.

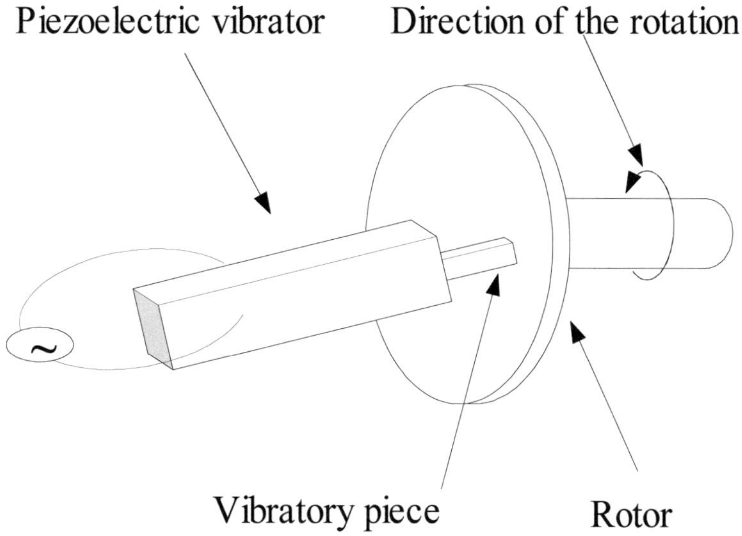

Fig. 10. Schematic diagram of the motor

Some parameters on the USM model are taken as: driving frequency 27.8 kHZ, amplitude of driving voltage 300 V, allowed output moment 2.5 $kg \cdot cm$, rotation speed 3.8 m/s. Besides, the number of hidden nodes of the TDRNN is taken as 5, the weights are initialized in the interval [-3, 3] randomly, the parameters α, β and γ on the TDRNN are taken as 0.4, 0.6, 0.4 respectively. The input of the TDRNN is the system control error in the last time, and the output of the TDRNN, namely the control parameter of the USM is taken as the frequency of the driving voltage.

Figure 11 shows the speed control curves of the USM using the three different control strategies when the control speed is taken as 3.6 m/s. In the figure the dotted line a represents the speed control curve based on the method presented by Senjyu et al.[18], the solid line b represents the speed control curve using the method presented by Shi et al.[19] and the solid line c represents the speed curve using the method proposed in this paper. Simulation results show the stable speed control curves and the fluctuation amplitudes obtained by using the three methods. The fluctuation degree is defined as

$$\zeta = (V_{\max} - V_{\min}) / V_{ave} \times 100\% \tag{44}$$

where $V_{\max}$, $V_{\min}$ and V_{ave} represent the maximum, minimum and average values of the speeds. From Figure 11 it can be seen that the fluctuation degrees when using the methods proposed by Senjyu and Shi are 5.7% and 1.9% respectively, whereas, it is just 1.1% when using the method in this paper. Figure 12 shows the speed control curves of the reference speeds vary as step types. From the figures it can be seen that this method possesses good control precision.

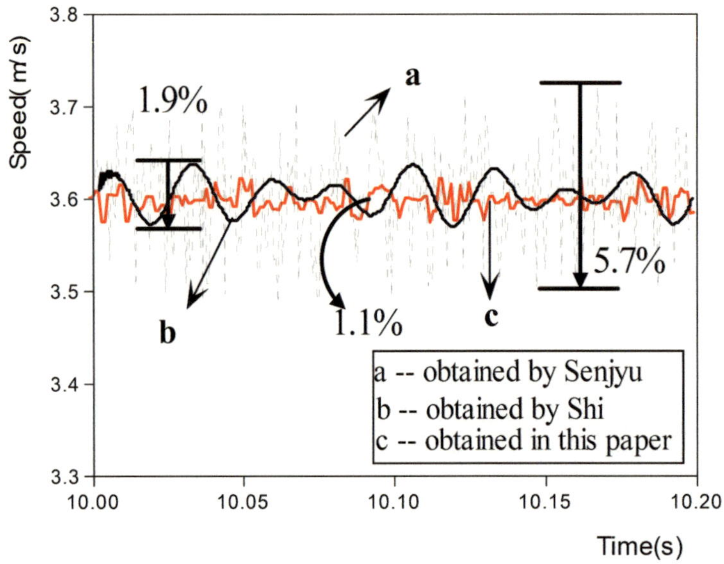

Fig. 11. Comparison of speed control curves using different schemes

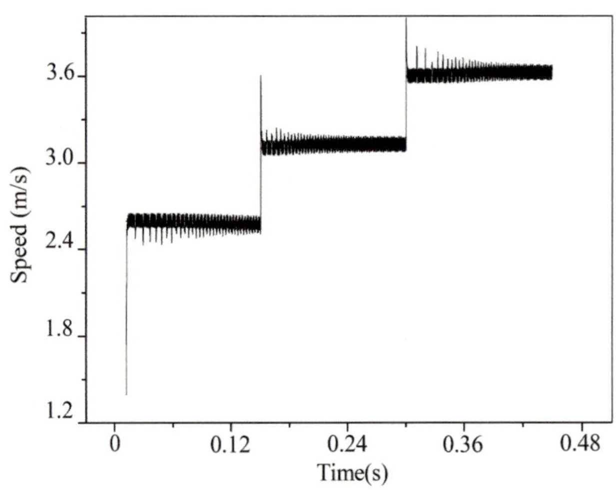

Fig. 12. Speed control curve for step type

5. Conclusions

This chapter proposes a time-delay recurrent neural network (TDRNN) with better performance in memory than popular neural networks by employing the time-delay and recurrent mechanism. Subsequently, the dynamic recurrent back propagation algorithm for the TDRNN is developed according to the gradient descent method. Furthermore, to train neural networks more efficiently, we propose three criterions of selecting proper learning rates for the dynamic recurrent back propagation algorithm based on the discrete-type Lyapunov stability analysis. Besides, based on the TDRNN model, we have described, analyzed and discussed an identifier and an adaptive controller designed to identify and control nonlinear systems. Our numerical experiments show that the TDRNN has good effectiveness in the identification and control for nonlinear systems. It indicates that the methods described in this chapter can provide effective approaches for nonlinear dynamic systems identification and control.

6. Acknowledgment

The authors are grateful to the support of the National Natural Science Foundation of China (61103146) and (60873256), the Fundamental Research Funds for the Central Universities (DUT11SX03).

7. References

[1] M. Han, J.C. Fan and J. Wang, A Dynamic Feed-forward Neural Network Based on Gaussian Particle Swarm Optimization and its Application for Predictive Control, IEEE Transactions on Neural Networks, 22 (2011) 1457-1468.

[2] G. Puscasu and B. Codres, Nonlinear System Identification and Control Based on Modular Neural Networks, International Journal of Neural Systems, 21(2011), 319-334.

[3] L.Li, G. Song, and J.Ou, Nonlinear Structural Vibration Suppression Using Dynamic Neural Network Observer and Adaptive Fuzzy Sliding Mode Control. Journal of Vibration and Control, 16 (2010), 1503-1526.

[4] T. Hayakawa, W.M. Haddad, J.M. Bailey and N. Hovakimyan, Passivity-based Neural Network Adaptive Output Feedback Control for Nonlinear Nonnegative Dynamical Systems, IEEE Transactions on Neural Networks, 16 (2005) 387-398.

[5] M. Sunar, A.M.A. Gurain and M. Mohandes, Substructural Neural Network Controller, Computers & Structures, 78 (2000) 575-581.

[6] D. Wang and J. Huang, Neural Network-based Adaptive Dynamic Surface Control for a Class of Uncertain Nonlinear Systems in Strict-feedback Form, IEEE Transactions on Neural Networks, 16 (2005) 195-202.

[7] Y.M. Li, Y.G. Liu and X.P. Liu, Active Vibration Control of a Modular Robot Combining a Back-propagation Neural Network with a Genetic Algorithm, Journal of Vibration and Control, 11 (2005) 3-17.

[8] J.C. Patra and A.C. Kot, Nonlinear Dynamic System Identification Using Chebyshev Functional Link Artificial Neural Networks, IEEE Transactions on Systems, Man, and Cybernetics, Part B: Cybernetics, 32 (2002) 505-511.

[9] R.J. Wai, Hybrid Fuzzy Neural-network Control for Nonlinear Motor-toggle Servomechanism, IEEE Transactions on Control Systems Technology, 10 (2002) 519-532.

[10] G. Cybenko, Approximation by superpositions of a sigmoidal function, Math. Control Signals and System, 2 (1989) 303–314.

[11] S. Haykin, Neural Networks: A Comprehensive Foundation (Englewood Cliffs, NJ: Prentice Hall, 1999).

[12] J.L. Elman, Finding Structure in Time, Cognitive Science, 14 (1990) 179-211.

[13] C.H. Chiu, Y.F. Peng, and Y.W. Lin, Intelligent backstepping control for wheeled inverted pendulum, Expert Systems With Applications, 38 (2011) 3364-3371.

[14] M.I. El-Hawwary, A.L. Elshafei and H.M. Emara, Adaptive Fuzzy Control of the Inverted Pendulum Problem, IEEE Transactions on Control Systems Technology, 14 (2006) 1135-1144.

[15] P.J. Gawthrop and L.P. Wang, Intermittent Predictive Control of An Inverted Pendulum, Control Engineering Practice, 14 (2006) 1347-1356.

[16] R.J. Wai and L.J. Chang, Stabilizing and Tracking Control of Nonlinear Dual-axis Inverted-pendulum System Using Fuzzy Neural Network, IEEE Transactions on Fuzzy systems, 14 (2006) 145-168.

[17] X. Xu, Y.C. Liang, H.P. Lee, W.Z. Lin, S.P. Lim and K.H. Lee, Mechanical modeling of a longitudinal oscillation ultrasonic motor and temperature effect analysis, Smart Materials and Structures, 12 (2003) 514-523.

[18] T. Senjyu, H. Miyazato, S. Yokoda, and K. Uezato, Speed control of ultrasonic motors using neural network, IEEE Transactions on Power Electronics, 13 (1998) 381-387.

[19] X.H. Shi, Y.C. Liang, H.P. Lee, W.Z. Lin, X.Xu and S.P. Lim, Improved Elman networks and applications for controlling ultrasonic motors, Applied Artificial Intelligence 18 (2004) 603-629.

7

BRNN-SVM: Increasing the Strength of Domain Signal to Improve Protein Domain Prediction Accuracy

Kalsum U. Hassan[1], Razib M. Othman[2], Rohayanti Hassan[2], Hishammuddin Asmuni[3], Jumail Taliba[2] and Shahreen Kasim[4]

[1]*Department of Information Technology, Kolej Poly-Tech MARA Batu Pahat, Tingkat 3, Bangunan Tabung Haji, Batu Pahat,*

[2]*Laboratory of Computational Intelligence and Biotechnology, Faculty of Computer Science and Information Systems Universiti Teknologi Malaysia, UTM Skudai,*

[3]*Department of Software Engineering Faculty of Computer Science and Information Systems Universiti Teknologi Malaysia, UTM Skudai,*

[4]*Department of Web Technology, Faculty of Computer Science and Information Technology Universiti Tun Hussien Onn, UTHM Parit Raja, Malaysia*

1. Introduction

A protein domain is the basic unit of protein structure that can develop itself by using its own shapes and functions, and exists independently from the rest of the protein sequence. Protein domains can be seen as distinct functional or structural units of a protein. Protein domains provide one of the most valuable information for the prediction of protein structure, function, evolution, and design. Protein domain is detected from protein structure that is predicted from protein sequence of amino acid. The protein sequence may be contained of single-domain, two-domain, or multiple-domain with different or matching copies of protein domain. A protein domain comprises of protein domain boundary that relates to a part in amino acid residue where each residue in the protein chain is defined as domain position. Each shape of protein domain is a compacted and folded structure that is independently stable. It exists independently since the protein domain is a part of the protein sequence. The independent modular nature of protein domain means that it can often be found in proteins with the same domain content, but in different orders or in different proteins. The knowledge of protein domain boundaries is useful in analysing the different functions of protein sequences.

Several methods have been developed to detect the protein domain, which can be categorized as follows: (1) Methods based on similarity and used multiple sequence alignments to represent domain boundaries, e.g. KemaDom (Lusheng et al., 2006) and Biozon (Nagaranjan and Yona, 2004); (2) Methods that depend on known protein structure to identify the protein domain, e.g. AutoSCOP (Gewehr et al., 2007) and DOMpro (Cheng et al., 2006); (3) Methods that used dimensional structure to assume protein domain boundaries, e.g. GlobPlot (Linding et al., 2003), Mateo (Lexa and Valle, 2003), and Dompred-DPS (Marsden et al., 2002); (4) Methods that used comparative model such as Hidden Markov Models (HMM) to identify other member of protein domain family, e.g. HMMPfam (Bateman et al., 2004) and HMMSMART (Ponting et al., 1999); and (5) Methods that are solely based on protein sequence information, e.g. Armadillo (Dumontier et al., 2005) and SBASE (Kristian et al., 2005). However, these methods only produce good results in the case of single-domain proteins.

There is no sign to indicate when a protein domain starts and ends. Protein sequence with closely related homologues can reveal conserved regions which are functionally important (Elhefnawi et al., 2010). Nowadays, it is not only important to detect a protein domain accurately from large numbers of protein sequences with unknown structure, but it is also essential to detect protein domain boundaries of the protein sequence (Chen et al., 2010). Protein domain boundaries are important to understand and analyse the different functions of protein (Paul et al., 2008) as shown in Fig. 1. The difficulty in protein domain prediction lies in the detection of the protein domain boundaries in the protein sequences, since the protein sequences alone contain the structural information but it is only available in small portion along the protein space. The secondary structure provides the sequence information used in protein domain prediction such as the similarity of protein chain, the potential of protein domain region and boundaries. Methods that used secondary structure information in protein domain prediction, such as DOMpro and KemaDom has shown improvement in predicting the protein domain compared to other protein domain predictors.

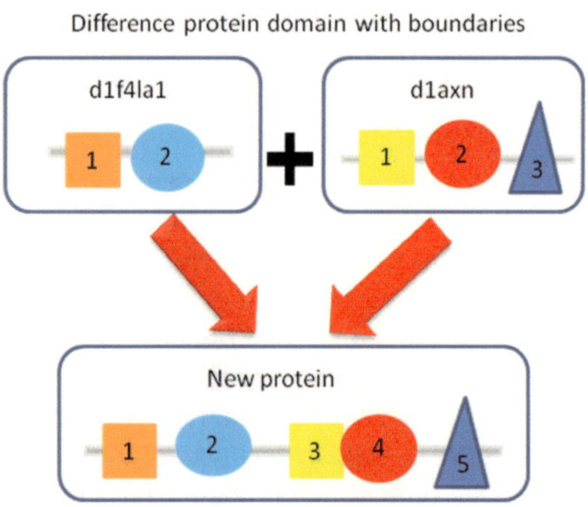

Fig. 1. An example of constructing a new protein from different protein domain boundaries.

Previously, Neural Network (NN) is used as a classifier to detect protein domain such as in the work of Armadillo, Biozon, Dompred-DPS, and DOMpro. Of late, Support Vector Machines (SVM) is perceived as a strong contender to NN in protein domain classification. Unlike NN, SVM is much less affected by the dimension of the input space and employs structural risk minimization rather than empirical risk minimization. SBASE (Kristian et al., 2005) and KemaDom are examples that apply SVM in protein domain prediction. The results from these methods are more accurate compared to NN.

2. BRNN-SVM algorithm

The BRNN-SVM begins with seeking the seed protein sequences using BLAST (Altschul et al., 1997) in order to generate a dataset. The dataset is split into training and testing sets. Multiple-alignment is performed using ClustalW (Larkin et al., 2007), where the alignments are represented as a protein sequence of alignment column that is associated to one position in the seed protein sequence. Bidirectional Recurrent Neural Network (BRNN) is used to generate secondary structure from alignment of protein sequence in order to highlight the signal of protein domain boundaries. The protein secondary structure is predicted into three types: alpha-helices, beta-sheet, and coil. The information of secondary structure are extracted using six measures (which are entropy, protein sequence termination, correlation, contact profile, physio-chemical properties, intron-exon information, and score of secondary structure) to increase the domain signal. This extracted information will be used for SVM input for the protein domain prediction. SVM processes the information and classify the protein domain into single-domain, two-domain, and multiple-domain. The BRNN-SVM is evaluated by comparing it with other existing methods either based on similarity and multiple sequence alignment (Biozon and KemaDOM), known protein structure (AutoSCOP and DOMpro), dimensional structure (GlobPlot, Mateo, and Dompred-DPS), comparative model (HMMPfam and HMMSMART), and sequence alone (Armadillo and SBASE). An analysis of the results has demonstrated that the BRNN-SVM shows outstanding performance on single-domain, two-domain, and multiple-domain. The steps involved in BRNN-SVM can be simplified as follows: (1) Generate training and testing sets using BLAST; (2) Perform multiple sequence alignment using ClustalW; (3) Predict secondary structure by BRNN; (4) Extract information from protein secondary structure; (5) Classify the protein domain by SVM; and (6) Evaluate the performance using sensitivity and specificity, and accuracy.

3. Secondary structure prediction by BRNN

For each protein sequence, the secondary structure information is predicted based on an ensemble of BRNNs. The input for predicting secondary structure is a single protein sequence from a multiple sequence alignment. Then, BRNN derives protein sequence information from PSI-BLAST (Altschul et al., 1997) to include homology structure that is used in the protein secondary structure information prediction. Subsequently, the protein secondary structure information is divided into three classes: alpha-helices, beta-sheets, and coils.

The BRNN is described in Fig. 2–3. This BRNN involves a set of *i* protein sequences as input X_i variable, a forward F_i, and backward B_i, a chain of hidden variables, and a set of O_i as an output variable. The relationship between these variables is implemented using feed-forward NN. Three NNs N_o, N_f, and N_b are used to implement BRNN. The output O_i (Chen and Chaudhari, 2007) is as follows:

$$O_i = N_o(X_i, F_i, B_i) . \tag{1}$$

The output O_i depends on input X_i at the position *i*, the forward F_i (Chen and Chaudhari, 2007) is the hidden context in the vector $F_i \in \mathbb{Z}^n$ and the backward B_i (Chen and Chaudhari, 2007) is the hidden context in the vector $B_i \in \mathbb{Z}^m$ where $m = n$. To obtain the composite the F_i and B_i, the BRNN equation is applied as follows:

$$F_i = N_f(X_i, F_{i-1}), \tag{2}$$

$$B_i = N_b(X_i, B_{i+1}), \tag{3}$$

where $N_f(X_i, F_{i-1})$ and $N_b(X_i, B_{i+1})$ are learnable non-linear state transition function. The boundary condition for F_i and B_i can be set to 0, for example $F_i = F_{n+1} = 0$ where n is length of the protein sequence being processed.

The N_f and N_b are assigned to be a "tool" that can be shifted along the protein sequence. For the prediction class at the position *i*, the "tool" is shifted in the opposite direction starting from the *N*, and *C* terminus, up to position *i*. Then, the "tool" output at position *i* is combined with the input X_i to compute the output O_i using N_o. From the output O_i, the membership probability of the residue at the position *i* is computed to predict the domain boundary.

BRNN is used to predict protein secondary structure into alpha-helices, beta-sheet, or coils. The BRNN consists of an input layer, hidden layer, and output layer. The protein sequences are fed into the input layer. The protein secondary structure is encoded into the output layer as follows:

(1, 0) = Alpha-Helices
(0, 1) = Beta-Sheets
(0, 0) = Coil

The input layer (John et al., 2006) is defined as follows:

$$I_k = \sum_i W_{ik} Y_i + b_k, \tag{4}$$

where W_{ik} is the sum of all the input to the unit, Y_i is the connection strength, b_k is the bias from the protein sequence, *i* is the number of protein sequence, and *k* is the number of output from the protein sequence. The output layer (John et al., 2006) is defined as follows:

$$O_k = \frac{1}{1+e^{-X_k}}, \tag{5}$$

where X is a real number between -8 and 8. This has been experimentally determined as the best range. *k* represents the number of outputs from the protein sequence.

The alpha-helices measure is divided into two types: amphipathic helices and hydrophobic helices. To predict an amphipathic helices region, Helical Wheel Representation (HWR: Renaund and McConkey, 2005) is applied. The HWR predicts the residues from the solvent and side chains interaction of protein sequence with amphipathic helices. Then, the score of amphipathic helices and hydrophobic helices are merged to predict the alpha-helices region for the protein sequence. The beta-sheets are assigned using Kabsch and Sander's program (Kabsch and Sander, 1983). The extension of beta-sheets is situated and connected to form theatre-backbone H-bonds according to the Pauling pairing rules (Pauling and Corey, 1951). When two H-bond is formed or surrounded by two H-bond in the sheet, this formation is defined as beta-sheet (E). If only one amino acid fulfils the criteria, the sheet will be called beta-bridge (B). The residues that are neither alpha-helices nor beta-sheets are classified as coils.

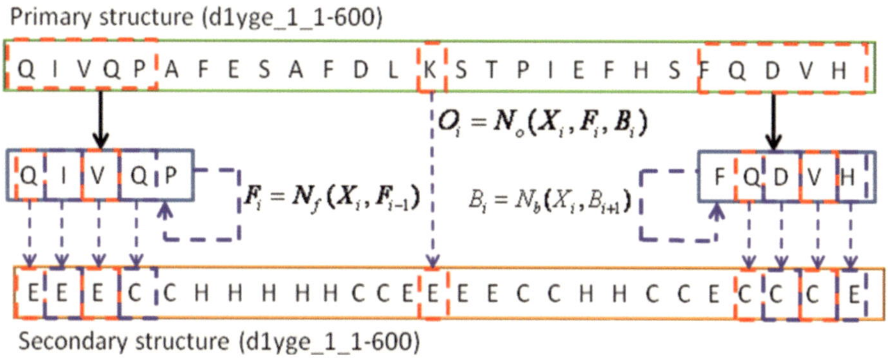

Fig. 2. BRNN architecture with left (forward) and right (backward) context associated with two recurrent networks ("tool"). The left and right contexts are produced by two similar recurrent networks which intuitively can be thought in term of two "tools" that are shifted along the protein chain.

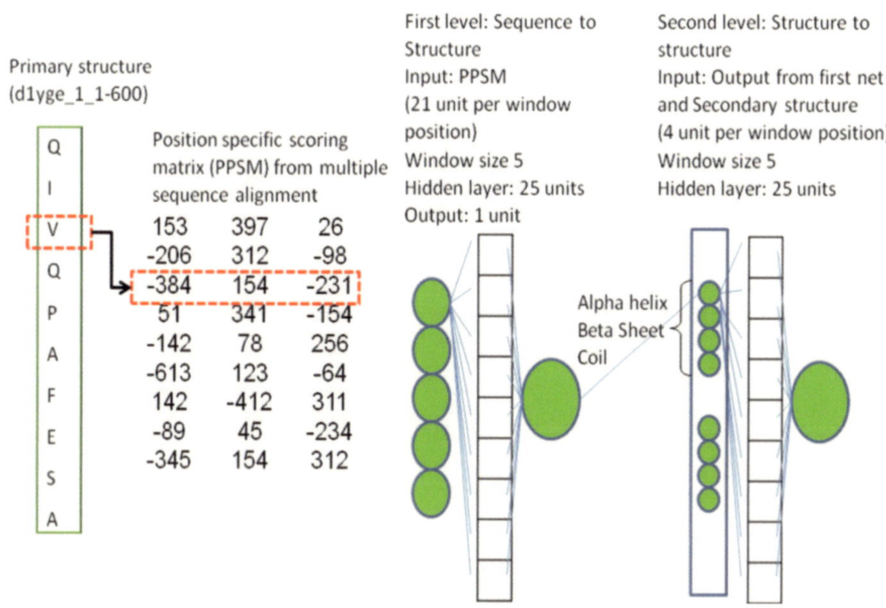

Fig. 3. An example of secondary structure prediction using BRNN.

4. Features extraction

Features extraction in BRNN-SVM is important to obtain the protein domain information from the predicted secondary structure. The secondary structure information is used to compute the change of the protein sequence position that constitutes a part of the protein domain boundary. This information is believed to reflect the protein structural properties that have informative protein domain structure and is used to detect the protein domain boundaries. The information as shown in Fig. 4–9 is entropy, protein sequence termination, correlation, contact profile, physio-chemical properties and intron-exon information.

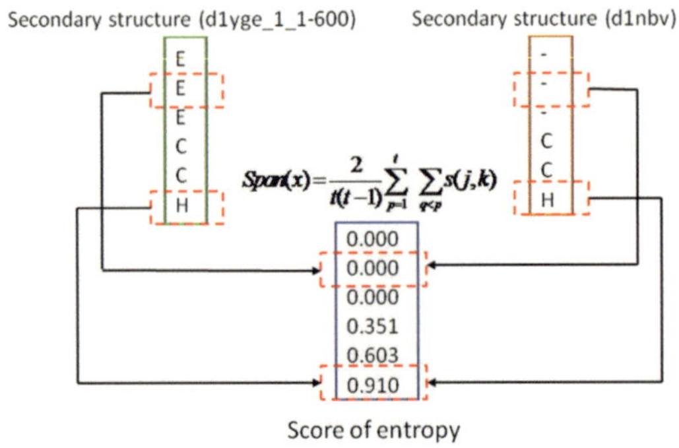

Fig. 4. An example of entropy calculation.

The effective entropy measure takes into account the similarity of amino acids. An evolutionary pressure is used to calculate the evolutionary span (Nagaranjan and Yona, 2004) defined as:

$$Span(x) = \frac{2}{t(t-1)} \sum_{p=1}^{t} \sum_{q<p} s(j,k), \tag{6}$$

where $s(j,k)$ is $s(\alpha_{px},\alpha_{qx})$. $Span()$ is used to compare the sum of pairwise similarity of amino acids. The x is an alignment from the multiple sequence alignment and t is the number of protein sequences that has participated in x. α_{px} and α_{qx} represent the amino acids in position x. $s(j,k)$ is the similarity score of amino acids where j and k refer to the scoring matrix BLOSUM50 (Henikoff and Henikoff, 1992).

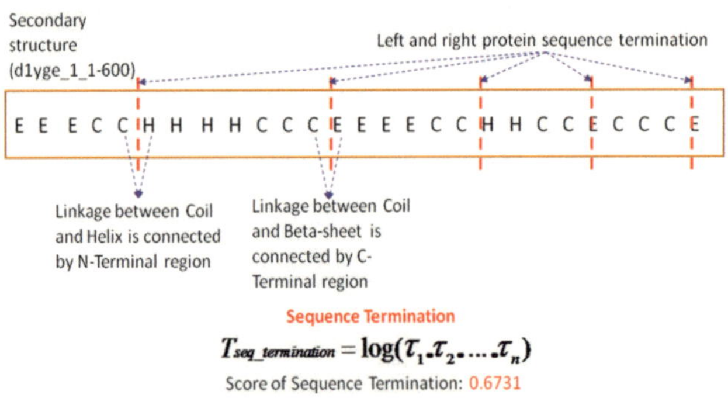

Fig. 5. An example of protein sequence termination calculation.

In a multiple sequence alignment, the protein sequence termination is not necessarily displayed. The left and right protein sequence termination score is calculated for each protein sequence with an e-value that is larger than 0. The scores of protein sequence termination are then used to identify the strong signal of the protein domain boundary. Left and right protein sequence terminations score (Menachem and Chen, 2008) are defined as:

$$T_{seq\_termination} = \log(\tau_1 \bullet \tau_2 \bullet \ldots \bullet \tau_n), \tag{7}$$

where τ_n is the e-value of the n protein sequence.

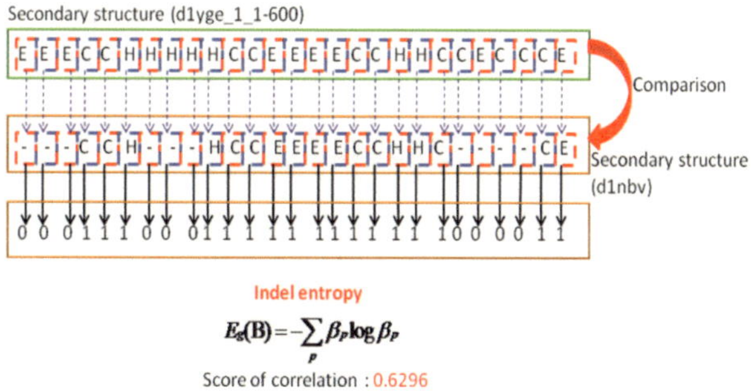

Fig. 6. An example of correlation calculation.

Correlation is two random protein sequences that are positively correlated if high values of one are likely to be associated with high values of the other. Possible correlations range is 1 or 0. A zero correlation indicates that there is no relationship between the sequences. A correlation of 1 indicates a perfect positive correlation, meaning that both sequence move in the same direction together. The correlation of amino acids with protein secondary structure information is used to predict the protein structure. It is also important to understand the force that causes the flexibility of a protein structure. Every protein sequence in a multiple sequence alignment contains information of structural flexibility. To find a position that is more flexible in a protein sequence, indel entropy (Zou et al., 2008) based on the distribution of protein sequence lengths is used:

$$E_g(\mathrm{B}) = -\sum_{p} \beta_p \log \beta_p , \tag{8}$$

where β_p is the various indel lengths seen at a position.

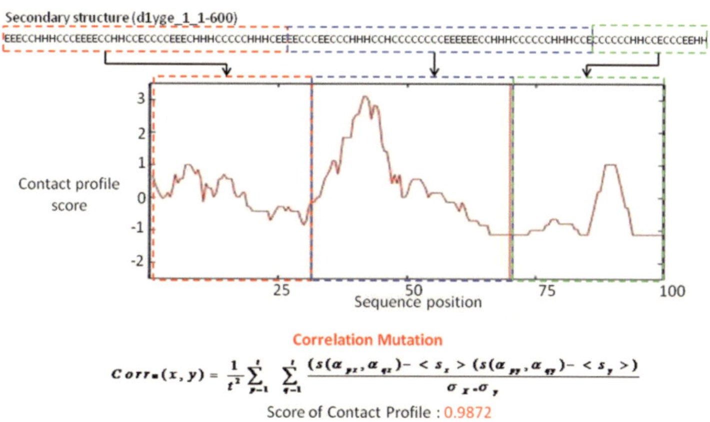

Fig. 7. An example of contact profile calculation.

The predicted contact profile of a protein sequence is obtained by getting the structural flexibility information. Then, the number of pairwise contact profile is counted for each protein sequence. The contact profile between residues in a protein sequence is predicted based on correlated mutations. Correlated mutations (Pazos et al., 1997) between two columns x and y are defined as:

$$Corrm(x,y)=\frac{1}{t^2}\sum_{p=1}^{t}\sum_{q=1}^{t}\frac{(s(\alpha_{px},\alpha_{qx})-<s_x>(s(\alpha_{py},\alpha_{qy})-<s_y>)}{\sigma_X \bullet \sigma_y}, \quad (9)$$

where α_{px} and α_{qx} represent the amino acids in position x and the α_{py} and α_{qy} represent the amino acids in position y. The $s(\alpha_{px},\alpha_{qx})$ and $s(\alpha_{py},\alpha_{qy})$ are the similarity score of amino acids and α_{px}, α_{qx}, α_{py}, and α_{qy} refer to the scoring matrix BLOSUM50. The $<s_x>$ and $<s_y>$ are the average similarity of amino acids in position x and y. The σ_X and σ_y are standard deviations and t is the number of protein sequences that are indicated in the columns.

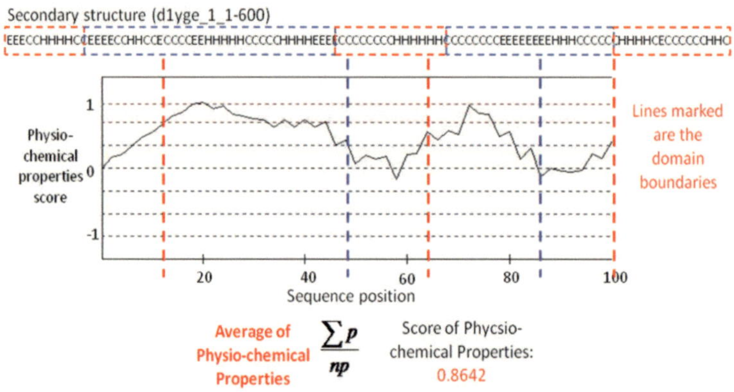

Fig. 8. An example of physio-chemical properties calculation.

Physio-chemical properties are information that is used to predict protein domain boundaries. Hydrophobicity is used to display the distribution of protein sequence residue that in turn, used for the detection of physio-chemical properties. In BRNN-SVM, the score of hydrophobicity and molecular weight (Black and Mould, 1991) is used to predict physio-chemical properties in protein sequence. The average hydropobicity and molecular weight for each measure of protein sequence is calculated to determine the physio-chemical properties that are affecting the protein domain boundary detection.

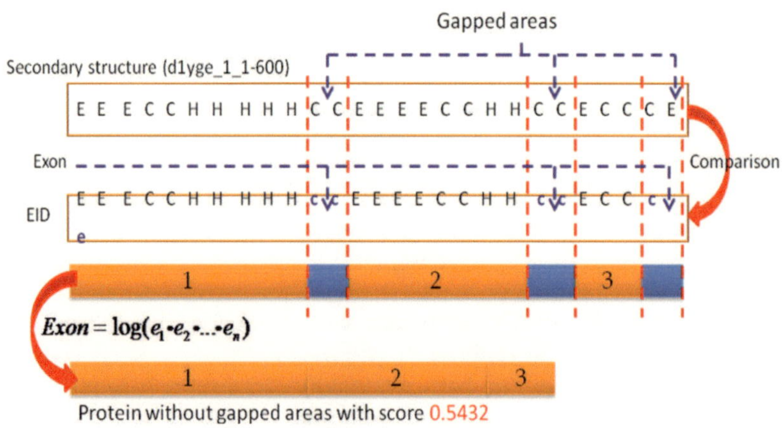

Fig. 9. An example of intron-exon calculation.

The intron-exon data contains intron-exon structure at Deoxyribonucleic Acid (DNA) level that is related to protein domain boundaries in which folded protein domain boundaries exist independently. Each protein domain defines the intron-exon position. The intron-exon data is taken from the EID database (Saxonov et al., 2000). Then, each protein sequence is compared with the database and the gapless matching protein sequence is kept. The similarity of the protein sequence is calculated in order to define the exon boundary using an equation defined as the sequence termination. Finally, the exon termination score (Saxonov et al., 2000) is calculated as follows:

$$E_{\text{exon\_termination}} = \log(\varepsilon_1 \bullet \varepsilon_2 \bullet \ldots \bullet \varepsilon_n)\,, \tag{10}$$

where ε_n is the e-value of the n protein sequence. After that, the average of measures score from features extraction's phase is calculated in order to generate the features vector and used as input to SVM as follows:

$$\sum \frac{(Score\_of\_measures)}{n}, \tag{11}$$

where $Score\_of\_measures$ is obtain from features extraction (entropy, protein sequence termination, correlation, contact profile, physio-chemical properties and intron-exon information) score and n refer to quantity of features extraction measurements where it could be seven. Fig. 10 has shown the example of features vector calculation.

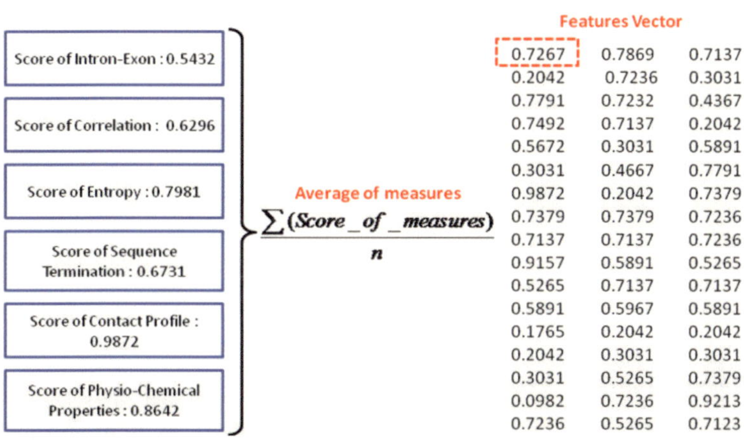

Fig. 10. An example of features vector calculation.

5. Domain detection by SVM

SVM is a machine learning technique based on statistical learning theory that trains multiple functions such as polynomial functions, radial basic functions and spines to form a single classifier. The SVM is applied to identify the protein domain boundaries position. The SVM works by: (1) Mapping the input vector into a feature space which is relevant to the kernel function; and (2) Seeking an optimized linear division from multiple n-separated hyperplane, where n is classes of protein sequence in the dataset. The input (Dong et al., 2003) vector is defined as follows:

$$l_s \in \{+1,-1\}, \tag{12}$$

where I_s is the input space with corresponding predefined labels (Dong et al., 2003):

$$y_i \in I_s(i=1,...,n), \tag{13}$$

where +1 and -1 are used to stand, respectively, for the two classes. The SVM is trained with Radial Basic Function (RBF) kernel, a function that is often used in pattern recognition. The parameters of SVM training are σ^2, the RBF kernel smoothing parameter and C, the learning variable to trade-off between under- and over-generalization. The RBF (Zou et al., 2008) is defined as follows:

$$K(\vec{y}_i,\vec{y}_j) = \exp(\frac{-r\,|\,|\vec{y}_i - \vec{y}_j\,|\,|^2}{2\sigma^2}), \tag{14}$$

where $\vec{y}_i$ is labels and $\vec{y}_j$ is input vector. The input vector will be the centre of the RBF and σ will determine the area of influence this input vector has over the feature space. A larger value of σ will give a smoother decision surface and a more regular decision boundary since the RBF with large σ will allow an input vector to have a strong influence over a larger area.

The best pair of parameter of C and σ is search via k-fold cross-validation scheme to safeguard unbiased tweaking. In this study, k = 10 is applied where the protein sequence is split into k subsets of approximately equal size portions. The best combinations of C and σ obtained from the optimization process were used for training the final SVM classifier using the entire training set. The SVM classifier is subsequently used to predict the testing datasets. The SVM training detects the protein domain boundaries based on scores that corresponds to the domain information or different domain information. The SVM classified the protein domain into single-domain, two-domain, and multiple-domain. Various quantitative metrics were obtained to measure the effectiveness of the BRNN-SVM: true positives (TP) for the number of correctly classified protein domain; false positives (FP) for the number of incorrectly classified protein domain; true negatives (TN) for the number of correctly classified non protein domain; and false negatives (FN) for the number of incorrectly classified non protein domain.

6. Dataset and evaluation measure

To test the BRNN-SVM, seed protein sequences obtained from the PDB database (Berman et al., 2000) are selected with their corresponding domain structure that exists in SCOP database (Andreeva et al., 2008) version 1.73. The SCOP 1.73 with 40% less identity in PDB contains 9,536 protein sequences. The protein sequences are reconstructed from which short protein sequences that are less than 40 amino acids are removed. Then, the protein sequences are searched from the NR database (Henikoff et al., 1999) using BLAST and protein sequences that have more than 20 hits are kept. Hence, the number of protein data retained is 6,242. The dataset is divided into training and testing sets. Training set is used for optimizing the SVM parameters and for training the SVM classifier to predict unseen protein domain boundaries. Testing set is used for evaluating the performance of the SVM. The dataset are randomly split into training and testing sets in the same ratio which is 3,121 protein sequences respectively. The process of generating the dataset is shown in Fig. 10.

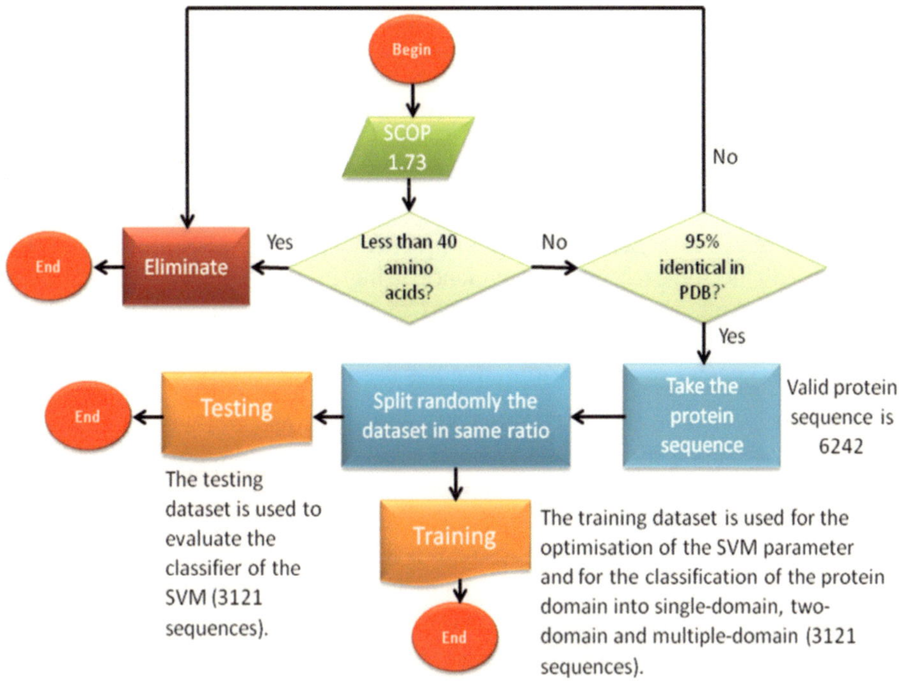

Fig. 11. Dataset generation process.

Based on the classification output of SVM, a series of statistical metrics were computed to measure the effectiveness of the BRNN-SVM. Sensitivity (SN: Zaki et al., 2006) and specificity (SP: Zaki et al., 2006), which indicates the ability of the prediction system to correctly classify the protein domain and not protein domain respectively; the SN and SP are defined as follows:

$$SN = \frac{TP}{TP + FN} \times 100\,, \tag{15}$$

$$SP = \frac{TP}{TP + FP} \times 100\,. \tag{16}$$

To provide an indication of the overall performance of the system, we computed accuracy (AC: Zaki et al., 2006), for the percentage of the correctly predicted protein domain. The AC is defined as follows:

$$AC = \frac{TP - TN}{TP + FN + TN + FP} \times 100\,. \tag{17}$$

7. Computational results

The BRNN-SVM is tested and compared its performance with other methods such as based on similarity and multiple sequence alignment (Biozon and KemaDOM), known protein structure (AutoSCOP and DOMpro), dimensional structure (GlobPlot, Mateo, and

Dompred-DPS), comparative model (HMMPfam and HMMSMART), and sequence alone (Armadillo and SBASE). The properties of protein sequence are derived from a protein secondary structure using several measures such as entropy, correlation, protein sequence termination, contact profile, physio-chemical properties and intron-exon boundaries measures. The protein secondary structure generates a strong signal of protein domain boundaries and is used to locate the protein domain regions using the following procedures. Firstly, the BRNN-SVM starts by searching large protein sequences and comparing them with the NR database to generate multiple sequence alignments. Secondly, the secondary structure is predicted for each protein sequence using BRNN. Thirdly, some of the scores from several measures are calculated as input in the SVM training. Finally, the results generated by SVM are evaluated. This evaluation provides a clear understanding of strengths and weaknesses of an algorithm that has been designed.

The datasets obtained from SCOP 1.73 that have been defined in the previous section are used to test and evaluate the BRNN-SVM and other protein domain prediction methods. The results of the prediction accuracy compared with other protein domain prediction methods including sensitivity and specificity for single-domain, two-domain and multiple-domain are presented in Table 1 and Fig. 11-14. It is easy to see that predicting two-domain or multiple-domain is more difficult than predicting single-domain. The results depict the higher sensitivity and specificity represent better achievement and the priority is given to sensitivity in order to determine the achievement of protein domain prediction since sensitivity measures the proportion of actual positives which are correctly identified for protein domain prediction. The BRNN-SVM achieved a higher sensitivity of 87% for single-domain, 73% for the two-domain and 81% for the multiple-domain compared to other methods. The BRNN-SVM achieved a higher specificity of 76% for the two-domain and 79% for the multiple-domain compared to other methods. The BRNN-SVM increases of 83% for accuracy as compared to KemaDom method with 79% and SBase method with 80%.

The properties of protein sequence have given a strong signal to assign protein boundaries because the protein secondary structure predicted is based on interaction between long-range interactions of the amino acid. The use of protein secondary structure prediction based on BRNN involves informative communion between an input and an output sequence of variable length. The BRNN is based on the forward, backward and hidden Markov chains that transmit information in both directions along the sequence between the input and output. This shows that interaction exists in protein folding and plays an important role in the formation of protein secondary structure. The information does have an effect on the protein domain boundaries prediction. The BRNN-SVM relies on scores of measures to detect the protein domain region in order to classify a domain for the protein sequence.

However, the prediction of specificity for a single-domain prediction is 79% which is 14% lower compared to the Biozon and 10% lower compared to Armadilo. The reason is that the BRNN-SVM classifies the protein sequence with no predicted protein domain boundaries as a single-domain. Therefore, the number of protein domain for the protein sequence is from the start until the end. The situation is aggravated when the protein sequence is too long. To solve this problem, the protein sequence can be split into protein sub-sequences before predicting the protein domain (Kalsum et al., 2009).

Method	Single-Domain SN	Single-Domain SP	Two-Domain SN	Two-Domain SP	Multiple-Domain SN	Multiple-Domain SP	AC
BRNN-SVM	0.87	0.79	0.73	0.76	0.81	0.79	0.83
Similarity and multiple sequence alignment							
Biozon	0.27	0.93	0.33	0.23	0.21	0.35	0.38
KemaDom	0.82	0.76	0.70	0.73	0.78	0.76	0.79
Known protein structure							
AutoSCOP	0.80	0.65	0.62	0.57	0.73	0.72	0.69
DOMpro	0.85	0.80	0.43	0.55	0.79	0.73	0.71
Dimensional structure							
GlobPlot	0.78	0.74	0.32	0.58	0.59	0.67	0.69
Mateo	0.57	0.74	0.21	0.25	0.47	0.53	0.45
Dompred-DPS	0.55	0.73	0.52	0.43	0.67	0.66	0.62
Comparative model							
HMMPfam	0.65	0.60	0.53	0.59	0.35	0.33	0.62
HMMSmart	0.77	0.69	0.66	0.63	0.23	0.20	0.71
Sequence alone							
SBASE	0.86	0.77	0.69	0.74	0.76	0.76	0.80
Armadillo	0.31	0.89	0.29	0.21	0.17	0.35	0.27

Table 1. Performance comparison between BRNN-SVM and other protein domain prediction methods.

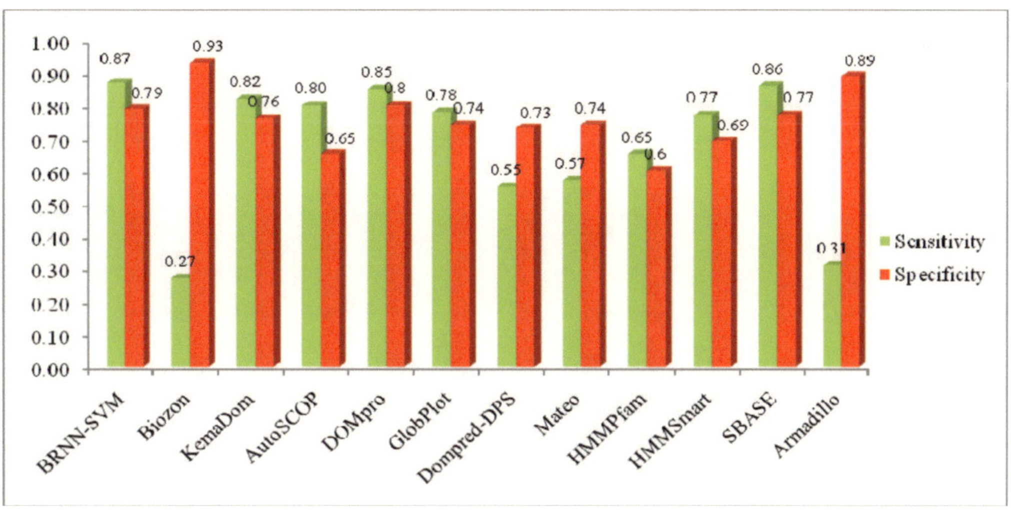

Fig. 12. Performance comparison between BRNN-SVM and other protein domain prediction methods on single-domain. The best sensitivity is BRNN-SVM with 87% and the best specificity is Armadillo with 89% since the BRNN-SVM classifies the protein sequence with no predicted protein domain boundaries as a single-domain.

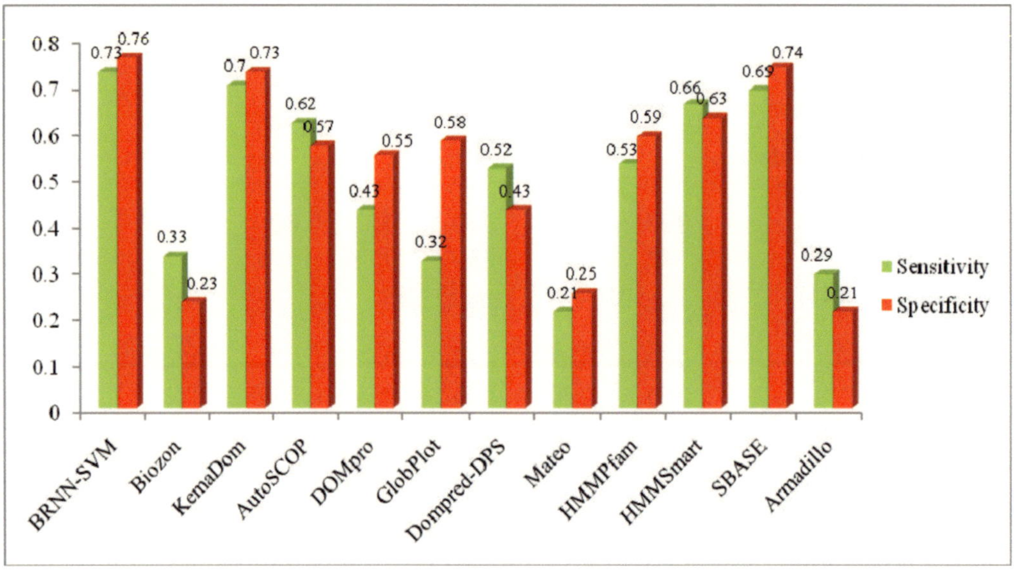

Fig. 13. Performance comparison between BRNN-SVM and other protein domain prediction methods on two-domain. The best performance for two-domain prediction is BRNN-SVM with 73% for sensitivity and 76% for specificity since the secondary structure information has given a strong signal to assign protein boundaries because the protein secondary structure predicted is based on interaction between long-range interactions of the amino acid.

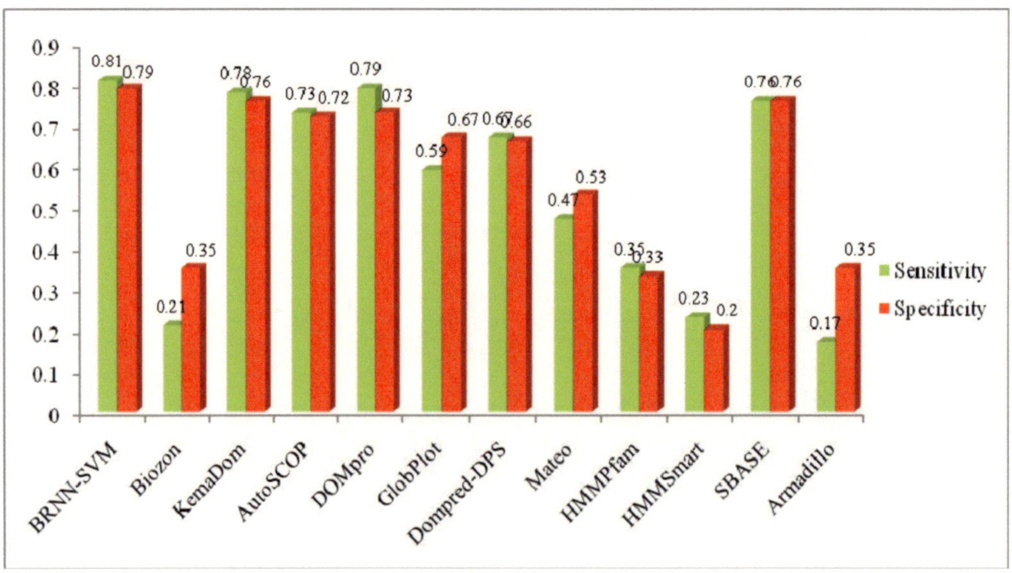

Fig. 14. Performance comparison between BRNN-SVM and other protein domain prediction methods on multiple-domain. The best performance of multiple-domain prediction is BRNN-SVM with 81% sensitivity and 79% specificity since the BRNN is a transaction between an input and an output sequence of variable length. This shows that interaction exists in protein folding and plays an important role in the formation of protein secondary structure.

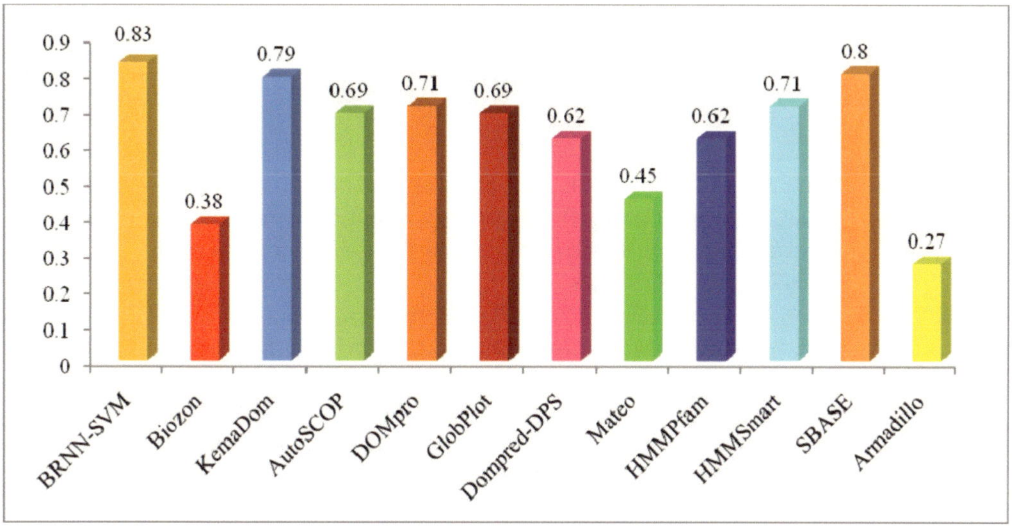

Fig. 15. Performance comparison between BRNN-SVM and other protein domain prediction methods on accuracy. The best accuracy of protein domain prediction is BRNN-SVM with 83% since the protein secondary structure is predicted using BRNN and the information of secondary structure is extracted from features extraction which increases the protein domain signal.

8. Conclusion

An algorithm named BRNN-SVM has been developed in order to solve the problem of weak domain signal. The algorithm begins with searching the seed protein sequences as dataset from SCOP 1.73. The dataset is split into training and testing sets. Then, multiple sequence alignment is performed prior to the prediction of protein secondary structure using BRNN. Several measures such as entropy, protein sequence termination, correlation, contact profile, physio-chemical properties and intron-exon data are used to increase the strength of domain signal from protein secondary structure. SVM classified the prediction into single-domain, two-domain and multiple-domain. Lastly, the results from SVM are evaluated in term of sensitivity and specificity. BRNN is based on forward, backward and hidden Markov chains that transmit information in both directions along the sequence between the input and output. Therefore, it increases accuracy of protein secondary prediction and well as providing strong domain signal from this protein secondary structure based on the generated measures. This is believed to be the reason why BRNN-SVM is a good method for protein domain predictors especially in two-domain and multiple-domain

9. Acknowledgements

We would like to express our appreciation to the reviewers of this paper for their valuable suggestions. This work is supported by the Malaysian Ministry of Science, Technology and Innovation (MOSTI) under Grant No. 02-01-06-SF0230.

10. References

Altschul, S.F.; Madden, T.L.; Schaffer, A.A.; Zhang, J.; Zhang, Z.; Miller, W. & Lipman, D.J. (1997). Gapped BLAST and PSI-BLAST: a new generation of protein database search programs. *Nucleic Acids Research*, Vol.25, No.17, (July 1997), pp.3389-3402, ISSN 0305-1048

Andreeva, A.; Howorth, D.; Chandonia, J.M.; Brenner, S.E.; Hubbard, T.J.P.; Chothia, C. & Murzin, A.G. (2008). Data growth and its impact on the SCOP database: new developments. *Nucleic Acids Research*, Vol.36, No.Database Issue, (November 2007), pp.D419-D425, ISSN 0305-1048

Bateman, A.; Birney, E.; Cerruti, L.; Durbin, R.; Etwiller, L.; Eddy, S.R.; Griffiths-Jones, S.; Howe, K.L.; Marshall, M.; Sonnhammer, E.L.; David, J.; Studholme, C.Y. & Sean, R.E. (2004). The Pfam protein families database. *Nucleic Acids Research*, Vol.32, No.Database Issue, (January 2004), pp.D138-D141, ISSN 0305-1048

Berman, H.M.; Westbrook, J.; Feng, Z.; Gilliand, G.; Bhat, T.N.; Weissing, H.; Ilya, N.S. & Bourne, P.E. (2000). The protein data bank. *Nucleic Acids Research*, Vol.28, No.1, (January 2000), pp.235-242, ISSN 0305-1048

Black, S.D. & Mould, D.R. (1991). Development of hydrophobicity parameters to analyze proteins which bear post or contranslation modification. *Analytical Biochemistry*, Vol.193, No.1, (February 1991), pp.72-82, ISSN 0003-2697

Chen, J. & Chaudhari, N. (2007). Cascaded bidirectional recurrent neural networks for protein secondary structure prediction. *IEEE/ACM Transactions on Computational Biology and Bioinformatics*, Vol.4, No.4, (October 2007), pp.572-582, ISSN 1545-5963

Chen, P.; Liu, C.; Burge, L.; Li, J.; Mohammad, M.; Southerland, W.; Gloster, C. & Wang, B. (2010). DomSVR: domain boundary prediction with support vector regression from sequence information alone. *Amino Acids*, Vol.39, No.3, (February 2010), pp.713-726, ISSN 0939-4451

Cheng, J.; Sweredoski, M.J. & Baldi, P. (2006). DOMpro: protein domain prediction using profiles, secondary structure, relative solvent accessibility, and recursive neural networks. *Data Mining and Knowledge Discovery*, Vol.13, No.1, (July 2006) pp.1-10, ISSN 1384-5810

Dong, L.; Yuan, Y. & Cai, T. (2006). Using bagging classifier to predict protein domain structural class. *Journal of Biomolecular Structure and Dynamics*, Vol.24, No.3, (December 2006), pp.239-242, ISSN 0739-110

Dumontier, M.; Yao, R.; Feldman, H.J. & Hogue, C.W. (2005). Armadillo: domain boundary prediction by amino acid composition. *Journal of Molecular Biology*, Vol.350, No.5, (July 2005), pp.1061-1073, ISSN 0305-1048

Elhefnawi, M.M; Youssif, A.A; Ghalwash, A.Z & El Behaidy, W.H. (1 January 2010). *An Integrated Methodology for Mining Promiscuous Proteins: A Case Study of an Integrative Bioinformatics Approach for Hepatitis C Virus Non-structural 5a Protein*, Springer, Retrieved from http://www.springerlink.com/content/ l067380601040028/

Gewehr, J. E.; Hintermair, V. & Zimmer, R. (2007). AutoSCOP: automated prediction of SCOP classification using unique pattern-class mapping. *Bioinformatics*, Vol.23, No.10, (March 2007), pp.1203-1210, ISSN 1367-4803

Henikoff, S. & Henikoff, J. G. (1992). Amino acid substitution matrices from protein blocks, *PNAS*, Vol.89, No.22, (November 1992), pp.10915-10919, ISSN 0027-8424

Henikoff, S.; Henikoff, J.G. & Pietrokovski. S. (1999). Block+: a non-redundant database of protein alignment blocks derived from multiple compilations. *Bioinformatics*, Vol.15, No.6, (June 1999), pp.471-479, ISSN 1471-2105

John, B.; Ryan, M. & Fernando, P. (2006). Domain adaptation with structural correspondence learning, *Proceedings of the Empirical Methods in Natural Language*, pp. 120-128, ISBN 1-932432-73-6, Sydney, Australia, (July 22-23), 2006

Kabsch, W. & Sander, C. (1983). Dictionary of protein secondary structure: pattern recognition of hydrogen-bonded and geometrical features. *Biopolymers*, Vol.22, No.12, (December 1983), pp.2577-2637, ISSN 0305-1048

Kalsum, H.U.; Shah, Z.A.; Othman, R.M.; Hassan, R.; Rahim S.M.; Asmuni, H.; Taliba, J. & Zakaria, Z. (2009). SPlitSSI-SVM: an algorithm to reduce the misleading and increase the strength of domain signal. *Computer in Biology and Medicine*, Vol.39, No.11, (November 2009), pp.1013-1019, ISSN 0010-4825

Kristian, V.; Laszlo, K.; Vilmos, A. & Sandor, P. (2005). The SBASE domain sequence resource, release 12: prediction of protein domain-architecture using support vector machines. *Nucleic Acids Research*, Vol.33, No.Database Issue, (January 2005), pp.D223-D225, ISSN 0305-1048

Larkin, M.A.; Blackshields, G.; Brown, N.P.; Chenna, R.; McGettigan, P.A.; McWilliam, H.; Valentin, F.; Wallace, I.M.; Wilm, A.; Lopez, R.; Thompson, J.D.; Gibson, T.J. & Higgins, D.G. (2007). ClustalW and ClustalX version 2.0. *Bioinformatics*, Vol.23, No.21, (November 2007), pp.2947-2948, ISSN 1367-4803

Lexa, M. & Valle, G. (2003). Pimex: rapid identification of oligonucleotide matches in whole genomes. *Bioinformatics*, Vol.19, No.18, (May 2003), pp.2486-2488, ISSN 1367-4803

Linding, R.; Russell, R.B.; Neduva, V. & Gibson, T.J. (2003). GlobPlot: exploring protein sequences for globularity and disorder. *Nucleic Acids Research*, Vol.31, No.13, (July 2003), pp.3701-3708, ISSN 0305-1048

Lusheng, C.; Wei, W.; Shaoping, L.; Caiyan, J. & Fei, W. (2006). KemaDom: a web server for domain prediction using kernel machine with local context. *Nucleic Acids Research*, Vol.34, No.Web Server Issue, (July 2006), pp.W158-W163, ISSN 1362-4962

Marsden, R.L.; McGuffin, L.J. & Jones, D.T. (2002). Rapid protein domain assignment from amino acid sequence using predicted secondary structure. *Protein Science*, Vol.11, No.12, (December 2002), pp.2814-2824, ISSN 0961-8368

Menachem, F. & Chen, Y. (2008). A computational framework to empower probabilistic protein design. *Bioinformatics*, Vol.24, No.13, (July 2008), pp.I214-222, ISSN 1367-4803

Nagaranjan, N. & Yona, G. (2004). Automatic prediction of protein domain from sequence information using a hybrid learning system. *Bioinformatics*, Vol.20, No.1, (February 2004), pp.1335-1360, ISSN 1367-4803

Paul, D.Y.; Abdur R.S.; Bing B.Z. & Albert Y.Z. (2008). Improving general regression network for protein domain boundary prediction. *BMC Bioinformatic*, Vol.9, No.1, (February 2008), pp.S12, ISSN 14712105

Pauling, L. & Corey, R. B. (1951). Configurations of polypeptide chains with favored orientations around single bonds: two new pleated sheets, *PNAS*, Vol.37, No.11, (November 1951), pp.729-740, ISSN 0027-8424

Pazos, F.; Helmer-Citterich, M.; Ausiello, G. & Valencia, A. (1997). Correlated mutation contain information about protein-protein interaction. *Journal of Molecular Biology*, Vol.271, No.4, (June 1997), pp.511-523, ISSN 00222836

Ponting, P.; Schultz, J.; Milpetz, F. & Bork, P. (1999). SMART: identification and annotation of domains from signaling and extracellular protein sequences. *Nucleic Acids Research*, Vol.27, No.1, (January 1999), pp.229-232, ISSN 0305-1048

Renaund, G. & McConkey, B.J. (2005). Ab initio secondary structure prediction using inter-residue contacts, *Proceedings of the Research in Computational Molecular Biology*, pp.1-2, ISBN 3-540-25866-3, Cambridge, USA, (May 14-18), 2005

Saxonov, S.; Daizadeh, I.; Fedorov, A. & Gilbert, W. (2000). EID: the Exon-Intron Database - an exhaustive database of protein-coding intron-containing genes. *Nucleic Acids Research*, Vol.28, No.1, (January 2000), pp.185-190, ISSN 0305-1048

Zaki, N.; Deris, S. & Alashwal, H. (2006). Protein-protein interaction detection dased on substring sensitivity measure. *International Journal of Biomedical Science*, Vo.1, No. 1, (January 2006), pp.1216-1306, ISSN 2010-3832

Zou, S.; Huang, Y.; Wang, Y. & Zhou, C. (2008). A novel method for predicition of protein domain using distance-based maximal entropy. *Journal of Bionic Engineering*, Vol.5, No.3, (April 2008), pp. 215-223, ISSN 1672-6529

8

Recurrent Self-Organizing Map for Severe Weather Patterns Recognition

José Alberto Sá, Brígida Rocha, Arthur Almeida and José Ricardo Souza
Federal University of Pará (UFPA)
Brazil

1. Introduction

Weather patterns recognition is very important to improve forecasting skills regarding severe storm conditions over a given area of the Earth. Severe weather can damage electric and telecommunication systems, besides generating material losses and even losses of life (Cooray et al., 2007; Lo Piparo, 2010; Santos et al., 2011). In especial for the electrical sector, is strategic to recognize weather patterns that may help predict weather caused damages. Severe weather forecast is crucial to reduce permanent damage to the systems equipments and outages in transmission or distribution lines.

This study aimed to evaluate the temporal extensions applicability of Self-Organizing Map (Kohonen, 1990, 2001) for severe weather patterns recognition over the eastern Amazon region, which may be used in improving weather forecasting and mitigation of the risks and damages associated.

A large part of this region is located at low latitudes, where severe weather is usually associated with the formation of peculiar meteorological systems that generate a large amount of local rainfall and a high number of lightning occurrences. These systems are noted for their intense convective activity (Jayaratne, 2008; Williams, 2008).

Convective indices pattern recognition has been studied by means of neural network to determine the best predictors among the sounding-based indices, for thunderstorm prediction and intensity classification (Manzato, 2007). The model was tested for the Northern Italy conditions (Manzato, 2008). Statistical regression methods have also been used for radiosonde and lightning observations data obtained over areas of Florida Peninsula in the U. S. A. (Shafer & Fuelberg, 2006).

These important contributions to this area of study have shown that the applications should be pursued to find out the best predicting statistical tools. Moreover, the achieved skills are largely dependent on the hour of the sounding and the local climatic conditions. So far few studies have been carried out for the extremely moist tropical conditions, prevailing over the Amazon region, where the data for the case studies analyzed in this chapter were obtained.

In this context, the convective patterns recognition for the Amazon region may be used in local weather forecast. These forecasts are subsidiary elements in decision-making regarding preventive actions to avoid further damage to the electrical system. These outages lead to productivity and information losses in the industrial production processes, which contribute negatively to the composition of the electric power quality indices (Rakov & Uman, 2005).

This study sought to recognize severe weather indices patterns, starting from an atmospheric sounding database. It is known that the atmospheric instability may be inferred from available radiosondes atmospheric profiling data. The stability indices drawn from observed atmospheric conditions have been used to warn people of potential losses (Peppier, 1988). Thus, this work analyzed the capacity of the Self-Organizing Map (SOM) and two of its temporal extensions: Temporal Kohonen Map and Recurrent Self-Organizing Map (Chappell & Taylor, 1993; Koskela et al., 1998a, 1998b; Varsta et al., 2000; Varsta et al., 2001) for clustering and classification of atmospheric sounding patterns in order to contribute with the weather studies over the Brazilian Amazon. The option of using this type of neural network was due to the fact that it uses only the input parameters, making it ideal for problems where the patterns are unknown.

Although there are other temporal extensions of SOM, such as recursive SOM - RecSOM (Hammer et al., 2004; Voegtlin, 2002), Self-Organizing Map for Structured Data - SOMSD (Hagenbuchner et al., 2003) and Merge Self-Organizing Map – MSOM (Strickert & Hammer, 2005), all these of global context, the option in this work was to apply local context algorithms, leaving to future studies the application of global context algorithms in this knowledge area. It is also important to refer the existence of the recent studies on the TKM and RSOM networks (Cherif et al., 2011; Huang & Wu, 2010; Ni & Yin, 2009).

In summary, with the original SOM algorithm and its extensions TKM and RSOM; stability indices data (Peppier, 1988); multivariate statistical techniques (principal component analysis and k-means); confusion matrix (Han & Kamber, 2006) and receiver operating characteristics (ROC) analysis (Fawcett, 2006); it was possible to evaluate the usefulness of these recurrent neural networks for the severe weather patterns recognition.

2. SOM and temporal extensions (TKM and RSOM)

This section discusses the fundamental concepts of Self-Organizing Map (SOM) and the proposed changes to introduce temporal sequence processing by the SOM: Temporal Kohonen Map (TKM) and Recurrent Self-Organizing Map (RSOM).

2.1 Self-organizing map (SOM)

The SOM is a nonlinear algorithm used for data clustering and classification. This algorithm is characterized by the processing of static data, i.e., not considering the data timelines, with the output of this neural network dependent only on present input data (Kohonen, 1990, 2001). The SOM is a single-layer neural network, in which it is recorded the learning by algorithm. This layer usually has low dimension structure (1D or 2D).

The training of the SOM is based on unsupervised learning, by adjusting of prototypes, according to the distribution of the input data, performed as follows:

The weight vector of each unit in the map space V_O is compared to an input vector. A metric-based criterion is chosen to determine the unit that has the minimum distance (Best Matching Unit), i.e., the neuron with the most similar prototype is selected as winner or winning unit, according to equation 1:

$$b(t) = \arg\min_{i \in Vo} \{ \| \mathbf{x}(t) - \mathbf{w}_i(t) \| \} \quad (1)$$

Where:

- $\mathbf{x}(t)$ is an input vector, at time t, from the input space V_I;
- $\mathbf{w}_i(t)$ is a prototype, at time t, from the map space V_O;
- $b(t)$ is the index (position) of the winner neuron, at time t.

The neurons of the SOM cooperate to receive future incoming stimuli in an organized manner around the winner neuron. The winner neuron will be the center of a topological neighbourhood where neurons help each other to receive input signals along the iterations of network training. Thus, after obtaining the winning neuron, its weights are adjusted to increase the similarity with the input vector, the same being done for the weights of its neighbours, by an update rule, according to equation 2:

$$\mathbf{w}_i(t+1) = \mathbf{w}_i(t) + \gamma(t) h_{ib}(t)(\mathbf{x}(t) - \mathbf{w}_i(t)) \quad (2)$$

Where:

- $\gamma(t)$ is a learning rate;
- $h_{ib}(t)$ is a neighbourhood function.

Usually, the learning rate $\gamma(t)$ is defined by equation 3:

$$\gamma(t) = \gamma_0 \exp\left(-\frac{t}{\tau_1} \right) \quad (3)$$

Where:

- t is the number of iterations;
- γ_0 is the initial value of the learning rate (value between 0 and 1);
- τ_1 is the time constant.

The neural network decreases its ability to learn, gradually over time, in order to prevent the drastic change by new data, in the sedimented knowledge through several iterations. The time constant influences the network learning as follows: high τ_1 value generates long period of intensive learning.

The neighbourhood function in a SOM is a similar way to reproduce the interactions of biological neurons, which stimulate their neighbours, in decreasing order, by increasing the lateral distance between them. So, for the SOM, this feature is reproduced by the parameter $h_{ib}(t)$ that determines how each neuron will receive readjustment to gain the future input stimuli. The largest adjustments are applied to the winner neuron and its neighbours, and minors to the neurons further from the winner neuron, because this parameter decreases with increasing lateral distance. Normally it is used the Gaussian function to represent the rate of cooperation between the neurons, by equation 4:

$$h_{ib}(t) = \exp\left(-\frac{l_{ib}^2}{2\sigma(t)^2} \right) \quad (4)$$

Where:

- l_{ib} is the lateral distance between neurons *i* and *b*;
- $\sigma(t)$ is the effective width of the topological neighbourhood.

Considering that the effective width of the topological neighbourhood will diminish with time increasingly specialized network regions will be built for certain input patterns. Over the course of iterations the radius of a neighbourhood should be smaller, which implies lower $h_{ib}(t)$ values, over time, thereby resulting in a restricted and specialized neighbourhood. For this, the exponential function is usually used, according to equation 5:

$$\sigma(t) = \sigma_0 \exp\left(-\frac{t}{\tau_1}\right) \quad (5)$$

Where:

- σ_0 is the initial value of effective width;
- τ_1 is a time constant.

2.2 Temporal Kohonen Map (TKM)

The SOM was originally designed for the static data processing, but for the dynamic data patterns recognition, it becomes necessary to include the temporal dimension in this algorithm. A pioneer algorithm in this adaptation was the Temporal Kohonen Map - TKM (Chappell & Taylor, 1993). It introduces the temporal processing using the same update rule of the original SOM, just changing the way of choosing the winner neuron. It uses the neurons activation history, by equation 6:

$$V_i(t) = dV_i(t\text{-}1)\text{-}\frac{1}{2}\left\|\mathbf{x}(t) - \mathbf{w}_i(t)\right\|^2 \quad (6)$$

Where:

- $Vi(t)$ is the neuron activation, at time t;
- *d* is a time constant (value between 0 and 1);
- $\mathbf{x}(t)$ is a input vector, at time *t;*
- $\mathbf{w}_i(t)$ is a prototype, at time *t.*

A TKM algorithm flow diagram is displayed in Figure 1. The current activation of the neuron is dependent on previous activation.

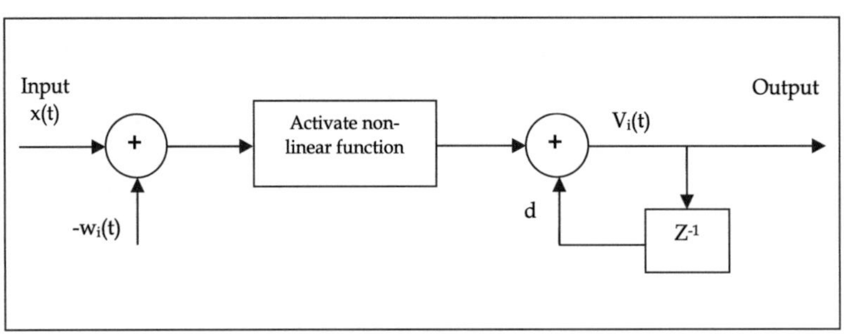

Fig. 1. TKM algorithm flow diagram

In the original SOM, for each new iteration, the value *1* is applied to the winner neuron and the value *0* to the other neurons. This creates an abrupt change in the neuron activation. In the TKM occurs a smooth change in the activation value (leaky integrator), because it uses the previous activation value, as shown in equation 6. In the TKM algorithm, the neuron that has the highest activation will be considered the winner neuron, according to the equation 7:

$$b(t) = \arg\max_{i \in Vo} \{V_i(t)\} \tag{7}$$

After choosing the winner neuron, the TKM network performs operations identical to the original SOM.

The basic differences between TKM and SOM networks are:

- For the determination of the winner neurons in TKM is necessary to calculate and record the activation $V_i(t)$, while in SOM is necessary to calculate the quantization error $\mathbf{x}(t)$-$\mathbf{w}_i(t)$;
- The winner neuron in TKM is one with greater activation $V_i(t)$, while in SOM is one with smallest quantization error $\mathbf{x}(t)$-$\mathbf{w}_i(t)$.

Interestingly, for d=0 the TKM network becomes equivalent to SOM network used for static data (Salhi et al., 2009).

2.3 Recurrent self-organizing map (RSOM)

Another algorithm that introduced the temporal processing to the SOM was the Recurrent Self-Organizing Map - RSOM using a new form of selection of the winner neuron and weights update rule (Koskela et al., 1998a, 1998b; Varsta et al., 2000; Varsta et al., 2001). This algorithm moved the leaky integrator from the unit outputs into the inputs. The RSOM allows storing information in the map units (difference vectors), considering the past input vectors, by equation 8:

$$\mathbf{y}_i(t) = (1-\alpha)\mathbf{y}_i(t-1) + \alpha(\mathbf{x}(t) - \mathbf{w}_i(t)) \tag{8}$$

Where:

- $\mathbf{y}_i(t)$ is called recursive difference of the neuron i, at time t;
- α is the leaking coefficient (value between 0 and 1).

Considering the term $\mathbf{x}(t)$ - $\mathbf{w}_i(t)$ with the quantization error, the winner neuron will be one that has the least recursive difference, i.e., the smallest sum of the present and past quantization errors, according to the equation 9:

$$b(t) = \arg\min_{i \in Vo} \{\|\mathbf{y}_i(t)\|\} \tag{9}$$

In the RSOM the weights update occur according to the equation 10:

$$\mathbf{w}_i(t+1) = \mathbf{w}_i(t) + \gamma(t) h_{ib}(t) \mathbf{y}_i(t) \tag{10}$$

Where:

- $\gamma(t)$ is a learning rate, at time t;
- $h_{ib}(t)$ is a neighbourhood function, at time t;
- $\mathbf{y}_i(t)$ is the recursive difference of the neuron i, at time t.

Thus, the RSOM takes into account the past inputs and also starts to remember explicitly the space-time patterns.

A RSOM algorithm flow diagram is exhibited in Figure 2.

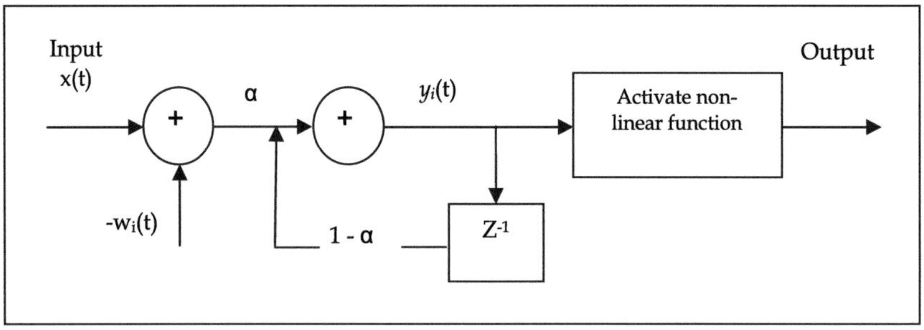

Fig. 2. RSOM algorithm flow diagram

The basic differences between RSOM and SOM networks are:

- For the determination of the winner neurons in RSOM is necessary to calculate and record the recursive difference $\mathbf{y}_i(t)$, while in SOM the choice criterion of the winner neurons is the quantization error;
- The winner neuron in RSOM is one with smallest recursive difference $\mathbf{y}_i(t)$, while in SOM is one with smallest quantization error.

To note that if α=1 the RSOM network becomes identical to a SOM network (Salhi et al., 2009).

Angelovič (2005) discribes several advantages of the use RSOM for prediction systems. First, the small computing complexity, opposite to the global models. Then, the unsupervised learning. It allows building models from the data with only a little a priori knowledge.

3. Materials and methods

This section discusses the study area, data pre-processing and models training.

3.1 Study area and data pre-processing

The study used sounding data from weather station denominated SBBE, number 82193 (Belem airport), in the interval 2003 to 2010. The data were collected at the University of Wyoming website. The Figure 3 shows the station location, in the eastern Amazon Region, with their geographic coordinates (latitude: 1.38 S and longitude: 48.48 W).

3.1.1 Data characteristics

The sounding data are obtained by radiosondes transported by meteorological balloons. A radiosonde may determine various atmospheric parameters, such as atmospheric pressure, temperature, dewpoint temperature, relative humidity, among others, in various atmospheric levels. These parameters are used to calculate sounding indices that seek to analyze the state of the atmosphere at a given time. Figure 4 shows an example of sounding indices collected from a radiosonde launched on January 1, 2010 at 12 h UTC.

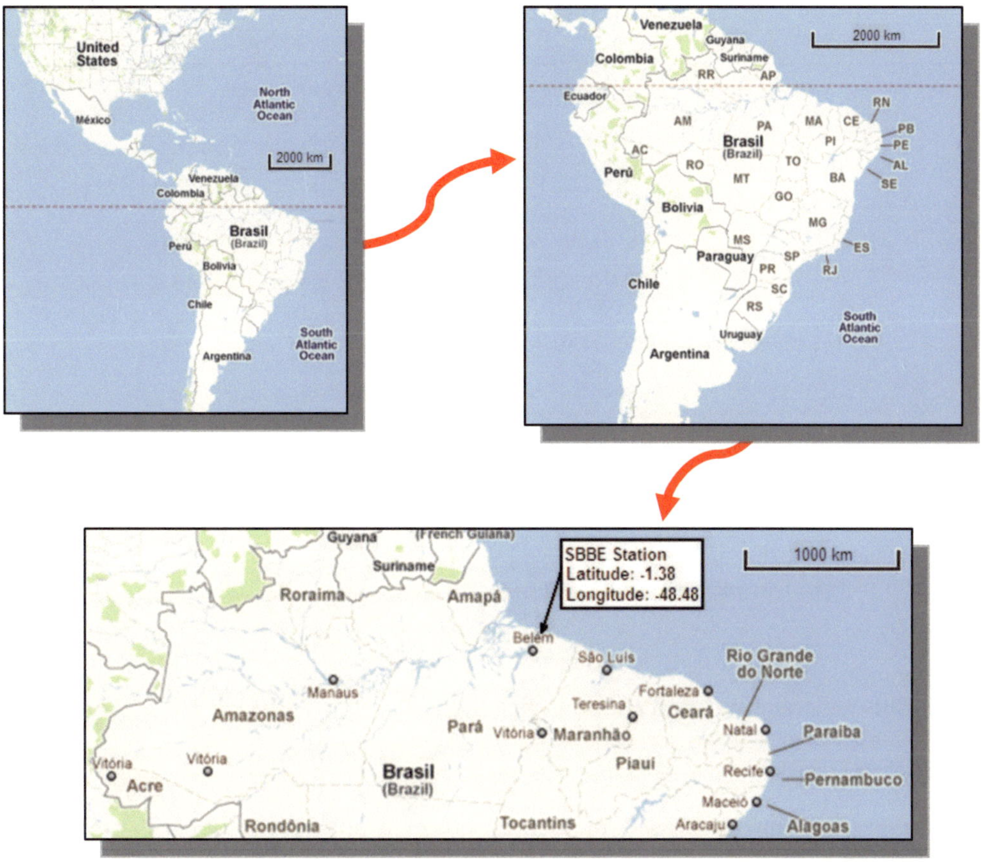

Fig. 3. SBBE station localization (Belem airport).

For the evaluation of the atmospheric static stability, used for thunderstorms forecasting, several indicators have been developed (Peppier, 1988). Some indicators admit as instability factors the temperature difference and humidity difference between two pressure levels; while others, besides these factors, add the characteristics of the wind (speed and direction) at the same pressure levels. There are also indices based on the energy requirements for the occurrence of convective phenomena. Some indices and parameters used for the thunderstorms forecasting are: Showalter Index, K Index, Lifted Index, Cross Totals Index, Vertical Totals Index, Total Totals Index, SWEAT Index, Convective Inhibition, Convective Available Potential Energy, Level of Free Convection, Precipitable Water, among others.

Station identifier:	SBBE
Station number:	82193
Observation time:	100101/1200
Station latitude:	-1.38
Station longitude:	-48.48
Station elevation:	16.0
Showalter index:	0.50
Lifted index:	-1.41
LIFT computed using virtual temperature:	-1.75
SWEAT index:	208.81
K index:	32.50
Cross totals index:	21.00
Vertical totals index:	22.10
Totals totals index:	43.10
Convective Available Potential Energy:	198.35
CAPE using virtual temperature:	266.66
Convective Inhibition:	-13.84
CINS using virtual temperature:	-10.40
Equilibrum Level:	367.16
Equilibrum Level using virtual temperature:	359.12
Level of Free Convection:	884.68
LFCT using virtual temperature:	893.44
Bulk Richardson Number:	20.60
Bulk Richardson Number using CAPV:	27.70
Temp [K] of the Lifted Condensation Level:	293.91
Pres [hPa] of the Lifted Condensation Level:	955.56
Mean mixed layer potential temperature:	297.76
Mean mixed layer mixing ratio:	16.44
1000 hPa to 500 hPa thickness:	5756.00
Precipitable water [mm] for entire sounding:	56.66

Fig. 4. SBBE station information and sounding indices

3.1.2 Data selection

A selection algorithm was used to identify all 24 available atmospheric indices from radiosoundings performed at 12h UTC (9h Local Time) in the period analyzed. Subsequently, the indices calculated with virtual temperature were eliminated, leaving only 18 indices.

After normalization of these 18 indices by the standard deviation, the principal component analysis was used to reduce the number of variables. It was found that among the 18 principal components, the first three represented about 70% (seventy percent) of the total variance. Four variables related to severe weather conditions had considerable numerical values of the respective coefficients in the linear combinations of these principal components. Namely: SWEAT index (SWET), Convective Available Potential Energy (CAPE), Level of Free Convection (LFCT) and Precipitable Water (PWAT). Therefore, these elements were defined as the input vectors variables of the SOM, TKM and RSOM networks. Figure 5 shows a variance explained for principal components, until the ninth principal component.

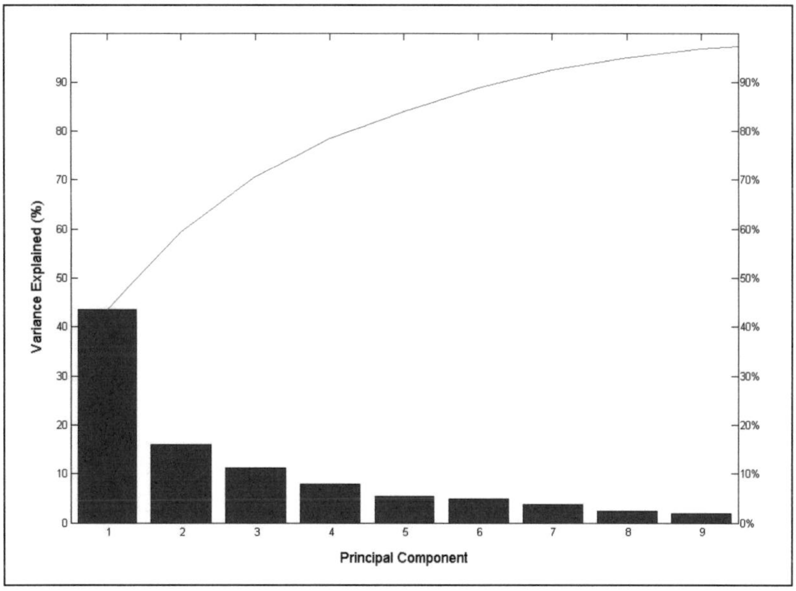

Fig. 5. Variance explained for principal components

The SWEAT index (or Severe Weather Threat Index) uses several variables (dewpoint, wind speed and direction, among others) to determine the likeliness of severe weather. The Convective Available Potential Energy (CAPE) is the integration of the positive area on a Skew-T sounding diagram. It exists when the difference between the equivalent potential temperature of the air parcel and the saturated equivalent potential temperature of the environment is positive. This means that the pseudo-adiabatic of the displaced air parcel is warmer than the environment (unstable condition). The Level of Free Convection (LFCT) is the CAPE region lower boundary. At this level a lifted air parcel will become equal in temperature to that of the environmental temperature. Once an air parcel is lifted to the LFCT it will rise all the way to the CAPE region top. The Precipitable Water (or Precipitable Water Vapor) is a parameter which gives the amount of moisture in the troposphere.

3.1.3 Data cleansing

The input vectors contained four variables: SWEAT index (SWET), Convective Available Potential Energy (CAPE), Level of Free Convection (LFCT) and Precipitable Water (PWAT). The vectors containing missing data from one or more variables were discarded. At the end of the cleansing process, a total of 1774 examples were obtained.

3.1.4 Data normalization

To reduce the discrepancies magnitude in the input vectors values, the min-max normalization was applied according to the equation 11. This transformed the original values of these input variables in normalized values within the range [0, 1].

$$value_{normalized} = \frac{value_{original} - \min A}{\max A - \min A} \tag{11}$$

Where:

- min A is the minimum value of the variable A;
- max A is the maximum value of the variable A.

3.1.5 Clusters formation for evaluation of the models

For the evaluation of the applicability of SOM and two of its temporal extensions: Temporal Kohonen Map (TKM) and Recurrent Self-Organizing Map (RSOM) for the weather patterns recognition related to atmospheric instability factors, clusters were built using the K-means technique, which generated three clusters, containing 697, 484 and 593 examples, for the cluster 1, 2 and 3, respectively. Figure 6 shows the characteristics of the three clusters according to the four variables analyzed.

In describing some of the differential characteristics between the clusters, it is noticed that in cluster 1 CAPE and PWAT have their concentrations at low values, while in cluster 2 the concentration of the CAPE is in low values, however for PWAT the values are high. In cluster 3 both CAPE and PWAT have their concentrations at high values. Another distinctive feature among clusters is the gradual rise of the LFCT median value for the clusters 1, 2 and 3, respectively. It is also noticed that the cluster 1 has a SWET median value lower when compared with clusters 2 and 3.

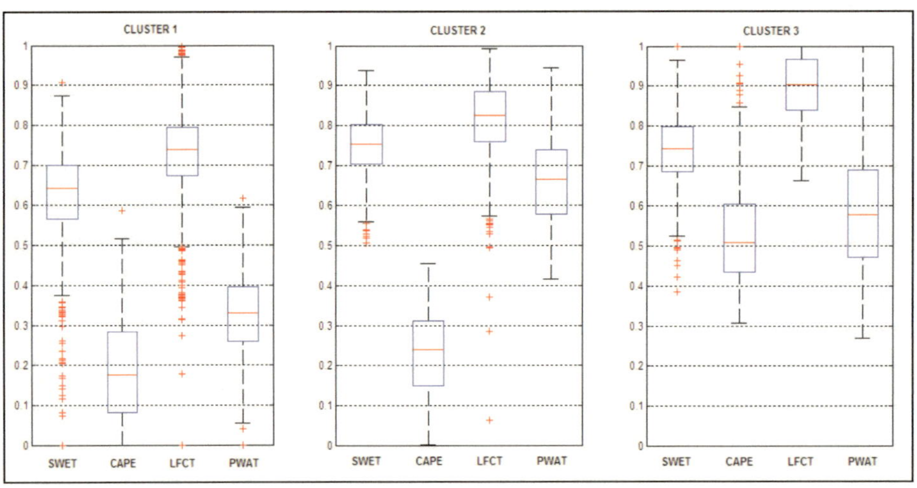

Fig. 6. Characteristics of the clusters

3.2 Training and evaluation of the models

For the performance analysis of the networks (SOM, TKM and RSOM) 3 maps were constructed, for each network type, in the grids: 5 x 5 units, 7 x 7 units and 9 x 9 units, therefore 9 maps in total.

Each network was trained with 600 examples extracted of the data set, with 200 examples of each cluster, randomly chosen. After training, the units of the maps were labeled according to their winning histories during training. This allowed that the networks were used as classifiers to evaluate their discrimination power.

The parameters used in the training of the SOM, TKM and RSOM networks were:

- Random weight initialization;
- Initial learning rate equal to 0.8;
- Final learning rate equal to 0.001;
- Number of epochs equal to 50.

Specifically for the TKM network was used the time constant d equal to 0.65 and for the RSOM network was used the leaking coefficient α equal to 0.35.

Subsequently it was evaluated the performance of the TKM and RSOM classifiers for different values of the constants α and d.

The results were presented in confusion matrices. In the confusion matrix each column represents the expected results, while each row corresponds to the actual results. During the simulation 1174 remaining examples of the data set were used.

After, a ROC analysis was done. The ROC graph is a technique for visualizing and evaluating classifiers based on their performance (Fawcett, 2006). A ROC graph allows identifying relative tradeoffs of a discrete classifier (one that your output is only a class label). In ROC graph the true positive rate (tp rate) of a classifier is plotted on the Y axis, while the false positive rate (fp rate) is plotted on the X axis. Fig. 7 shows a ROC graph with three classifiers labeled A through C.

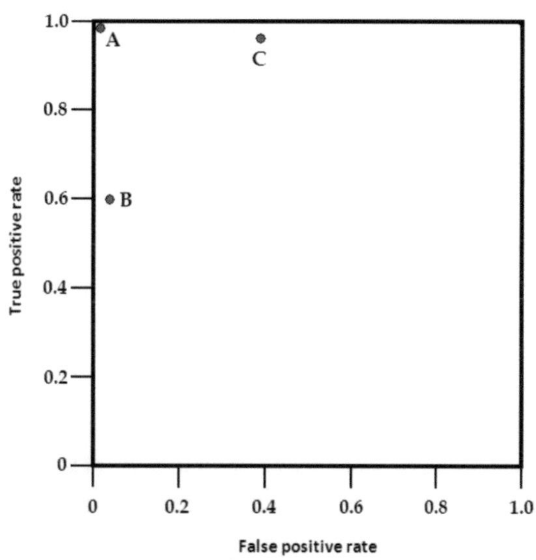

Fig. 7. ROC graph showing three discrete classifiers

Some points in ROC graph are very important. The lower left point (0, 0) represents a classifier that commits no false positive errors but also gains no true positives. The opposite situation is represented by the upper right point (1, 1). The upper left point (0, 1) represents a perfect classification (tp rate = 1 and fp rate = 0). In Fig 7, the point A is the ideal classifier; the point B represents a conservative classifier; and the point C represents a liberal classifier. Conservative classifiers make positive classifications only with strong evidence, i.e., their false positive rates are low but they also have low true positive rates. Liberal classifiers have high true positive rates but they also have high false positive rates.

4. Results

This section presents the results of the assessment among the studied networks: Self-Organizing Map (SOM), Temporal Kohonen Map (TKM) and Recurrent Self-Organizing Map (RSOM) for the severe weather pattern classification.

4.1 Evaluation of the SOM, TKM and RSOM classifiers

Table 1 shows the confusion matrices and the global accuracy of the neural networks studied. It is noticed that with the TKM and RSOM classifiers were provided superior performances to the original SOM, and between the recurrent networks, the RSOM network showed the best results.

Fig. 8 exhibits the ROC graph for the SOM, TKM and RSOM when the grids of the neural networks are 5 x 5. One may notice that the RSOM presents a larger tp rate and a smaller fp rate for the labels 2 and 3. For the label 1, the SOM network presented itself as the most liberal, and the RSOM as the most conservative network. Therefore, for this grid, the results have indicated that the RSOM classifier has a better performance than the other networks analyzed in this work.

Grids	SOM classifier			TKM classifier			RSOM classifier		
5 x 5	447	39	11	415	67	15	441	53	3
	16	267	1	1	275	8	1	282	1
	28	51	314	8	24	361	2	22	369
	Global accuracy (87.6%)			Global accuracy (89.5%)			Global accuracy (93.0%)		
7 x 7	422	53	22	454	27	16	470	22	5
	4	272	8	21	245	18	3	280	1
	12	10	371	1	21	371	13	22	358
	Global accuracy (90.7%)			Global accuracy (91.1%)			Global accuracy (94.4%)		
9 x 9	434	42	21	464	21	12	473	19	5
	9	254	21	32	231	21	3	280	1
	11	15	367	12	27	354	7	17	369
	Global accuracy (89.9%)			Global accuracy (89.4%)			Global accuracy (95.6%)		

Legend:

confusion matrix		Predicted cluster 1	2	3
True cluster	1	$n_{1,1}$	$n_{1,2}$	$n_{1,3}$
	2	$n_{2,1}$	$n_{2,2}$	$n_{2,3}$
	3	$n_{3,1}$	$n_{3,2}$	$n_{3,3}$

Table 1. Evaluation of the SOM, TKM and RSOM classifiers in different grids

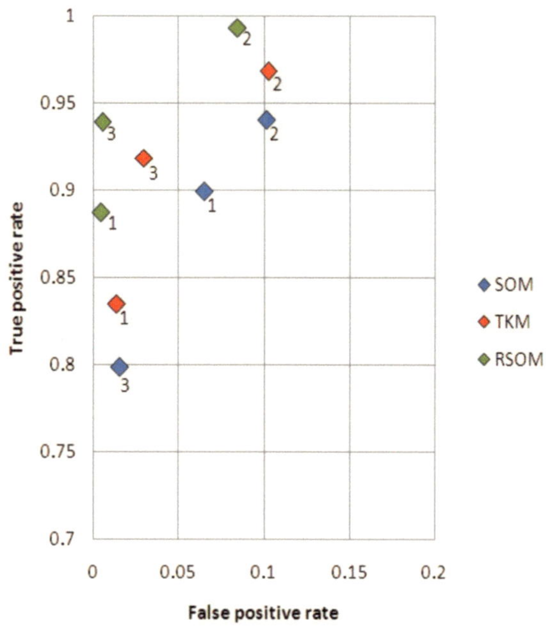

Fig. 8. ROC graph for the SOM, TKM and RSOM in 5x5 grid

Fig. 9 displays the ROC graph of the analyzed models for the 7x7 grid. It is evident that the RSOM network has a larger tp rate and a smaller fp rate for labels 1 and 2. For the label 3 the SOM and TKM networks presented similar liberal characteristics, while the RSOM network showed a more conservative behavior. For these dimensions the results also indicated a better performance of the RSOM classifier when compared to the SOM and TKM network options.

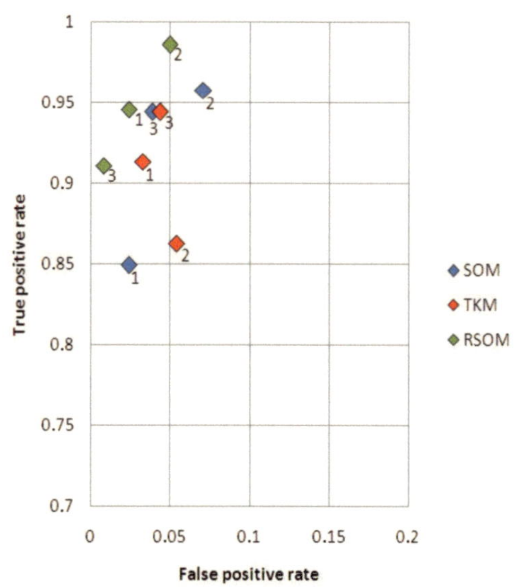

Fig. 9. ROC graph for the SOM, TKM and RSOM in 7x7 grid

The ROC graph for the SOM, TKM and RSOM in 9x9 grid is presented in Figure 10. One notices that for this grid, the RSOM network has a larger tp rate and smaller fp rate for all three labels considered. This fact confirms even more the best performance observed for the RSOM classifier, among all networks analyzed.

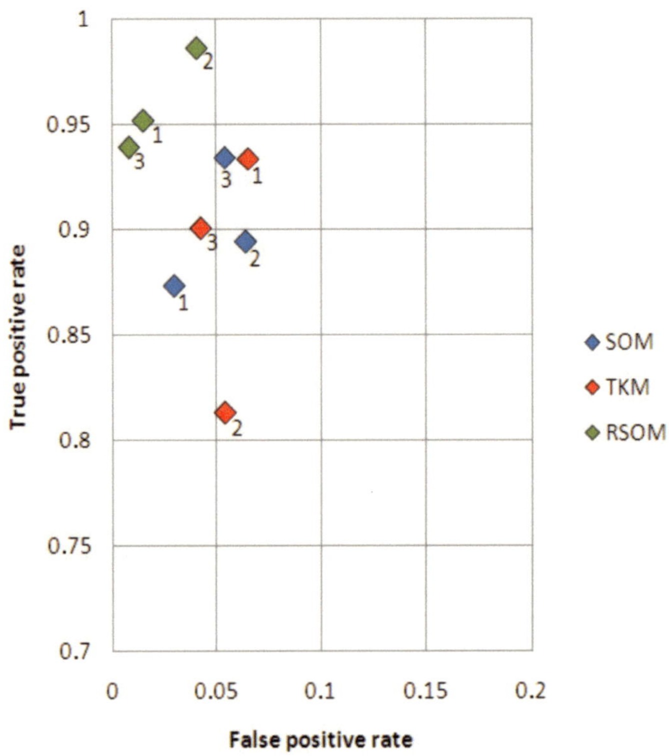

Fig. 10. ROC graph for the SOM, TKM and RSOM in 9x9 grid

4.2 U-matrix of the SOM, TKM and RSOM networks

Table 2 shows a comparison among the U-Matrices of the networks studied. The U-Matrices are representations of the self-organizing networks where the Euclidean distance between the codebook vector of the neighbouring neurons is represented in a two-dimensional color scale image.

It is observed that the RSOM network presented the best view among the networks studied, distinguishing clearly the existence of three clusters in the data set used for training this neural network.

Grids	SOM network	TKM network	RSOM network
5 x 5	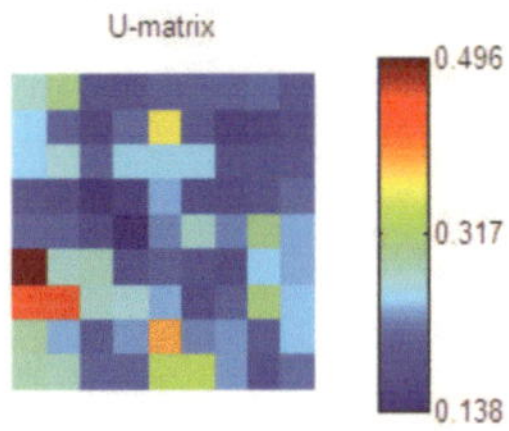	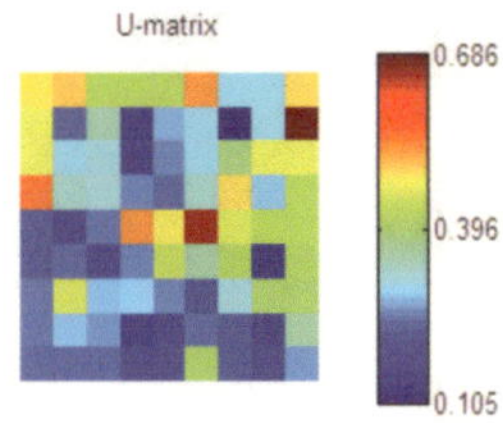	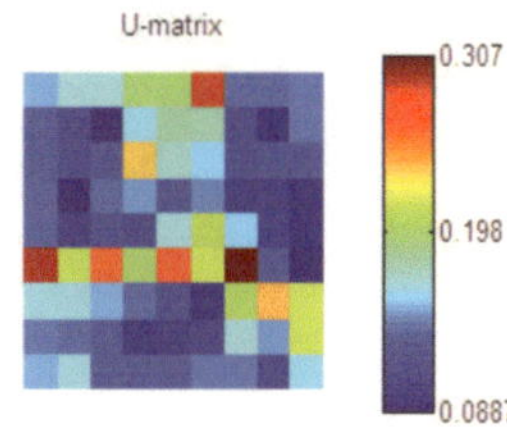
7 x 7	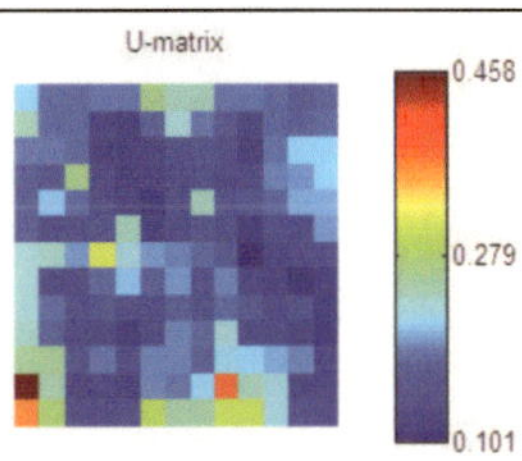	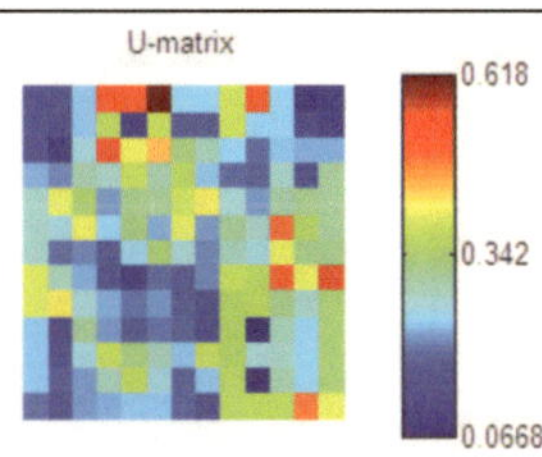	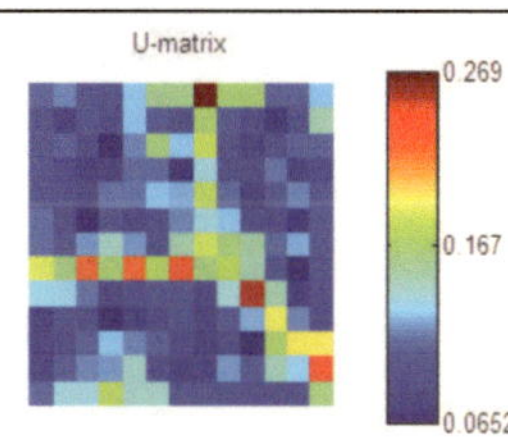
9 x 9	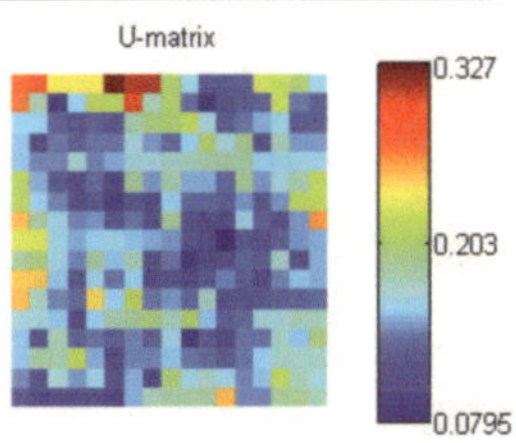	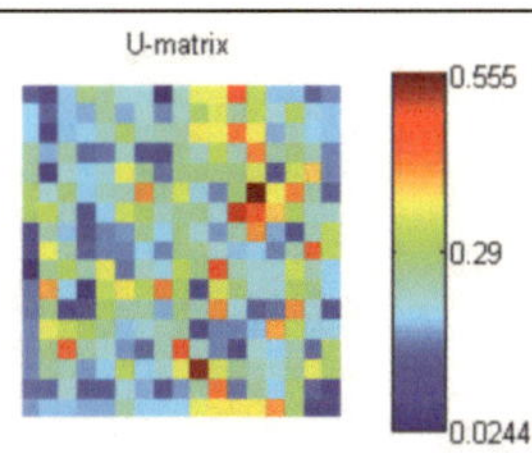	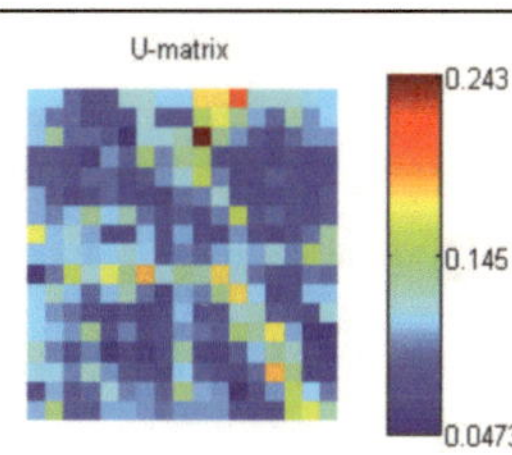

Legend: Color scale represent the Euclidean distance between the codebook vector of the neighbouring neurons

Table 2. U-matrix of the SOM, TKM and RSOM networks

4.3 Labeling of the neurons after the training of the SOM, TKM and RSOM networks

Table 3 shows a comparison between the labeling of the neurons after the training process, using as criteria the activation frequency. It is noticed that RSOM network has a higher organization when compared with the other networks. The labels: blue for the cluster 1, green for the cluster 2, and red for the cluster 3, were used.

Grids	SOM network	TKM network	RSOM network
5 x 5	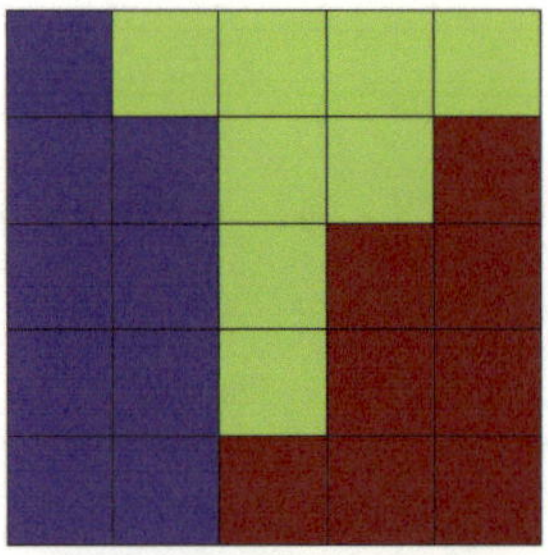		
7 x 7			
9 x 9	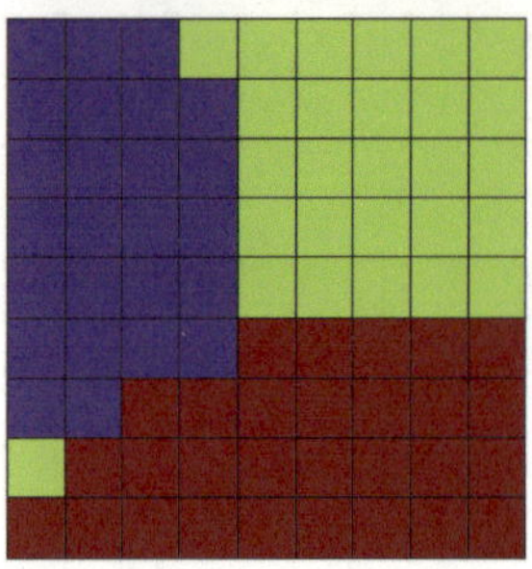	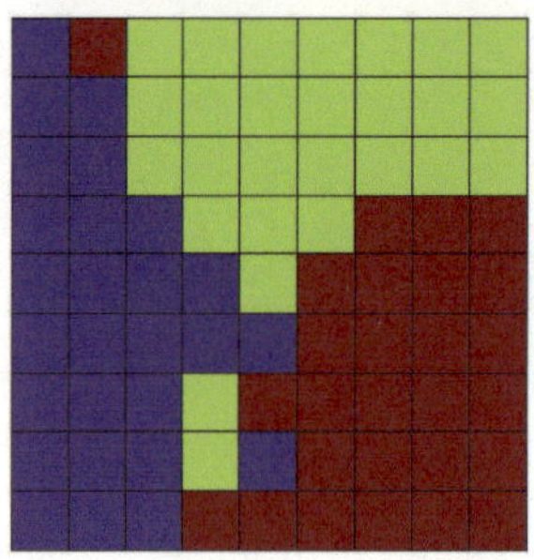	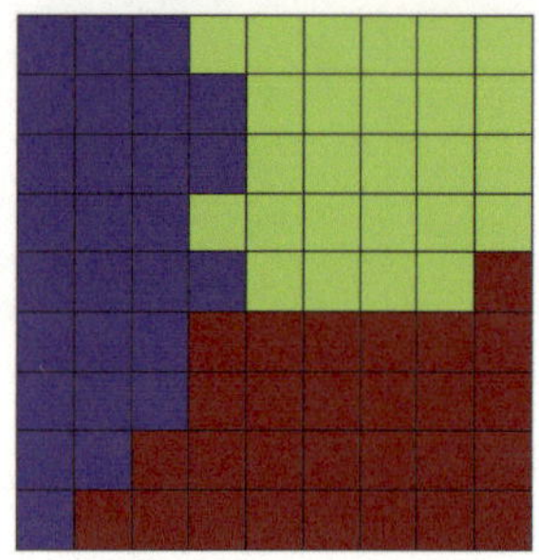

Legend: Blue for the cluster 1. Green for the cluster 2. Red for the cluster 3

Table 3. Labeling of the SOM, TKM and RSOM networks neurons in different grids

4.4 Time constants variation of the TKM and RSOM classifiers

One difference between the SOM network and its temporal extensions TKM and RSOM is the change in the performance when occur variation in the time constants. In the section 4.4.1 and 4.4.2 are shown the results when the time coefficients (d and α) vary in the range 0 to 1.

4.4.1 *d* variation

For different *d* values the TKM network presented different global accuracies, reducing their values in the range limits of 0 to 1. The table 4 shows the confusion matrices and Figure 11 shows the superposition of the global accuracies due to the *d* variation. For each TKM dimension studied the points were spaced at 0.25 intervals.

Grid: 5 x 5 units											
d = 0.10			d = 0.35			d = 0.60			d = 0.85		
433	47	17	446	35	16	440	48	9	387	39	71
0	276	8	15	266	3	55	218	11	50	233	1
4	57	332	2	43	348	20	22	351	0	81	312
Global accuracy (88.7%)			Global accuracy (90.3%)			Global accuracy (85.9%)			Global accuracy (79.4%)		

Grid: 7 x 7 units											
d = 0.10			d = 0.35			d = 0.60			d = 0.85		
448	38	11	455	33	9	412	70	15	372	23	102
5	251	28	10	262	12	0	280	4	62	215	7
16	15	362	4	13	376	1	51	341	18	83	292
Global accuracy (90.4%)			Global accuracy (93.1%)			Global accuracy (88.0%)			Global accuracy (74.9%)		

Grid: 9 x 9 units											
d = 0.10			d = 0.35			d = 0.60			d = 0.85		
455	29	13	448	37	12	456	37	4	406	31	60
11	258	15	21	251	12	7	276	1	23	249	12
17	34	342	12	15	366	10	24	359	16	54	323
Global accuracy (89.9%)			Global accuracy (90.7%)			Global accuracy (92.9%)			Global accuracy (83.3%)		

Legend:

confusion matrix		Predicted cluster		
		1	2	3
True cluster	1	$n_{1,1}$	$n_{1,2}$	$n_{1,3}$
	2	$n_{2,1}$	$n_{2,2}$	$n_{2,3}$
	3	$n_{3,1}$	$n_{3,2}$	$n_{3,3}$

Table 4. *d* variation and global accuracy of the TKM network in different grids

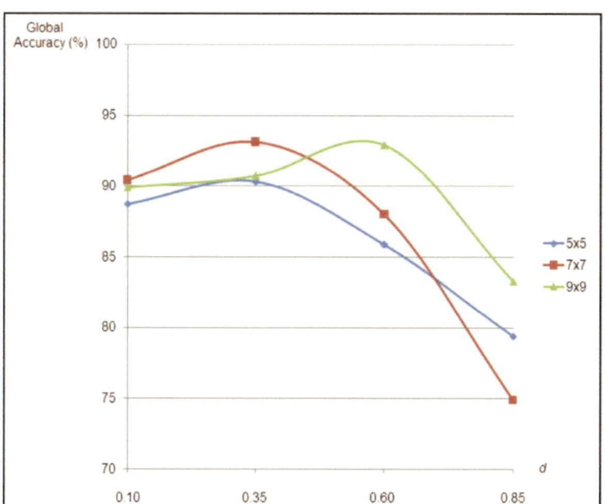

Fig. 11. Superposition of the TKM networks global accuracies due to the *d* variation

Figure 12 shows the ROC graph of the TKM model with 5x5 map units and *d* variations. It indicates that for lower values of *d* (*d*=0.10 and *d*=0.35) this classifier presented more conservative characteristics for labels 1 and 3, and the most liberal behaviour for the label 2. On the other hand, for higher values of *d* (*d*=0.60 and *d*=0.85), in general one notices a decrease of the tp rate values and an increment of the fp rate for all labels. One may conclude therefore, that the TKM better performances were observed for the lower values of *d*.

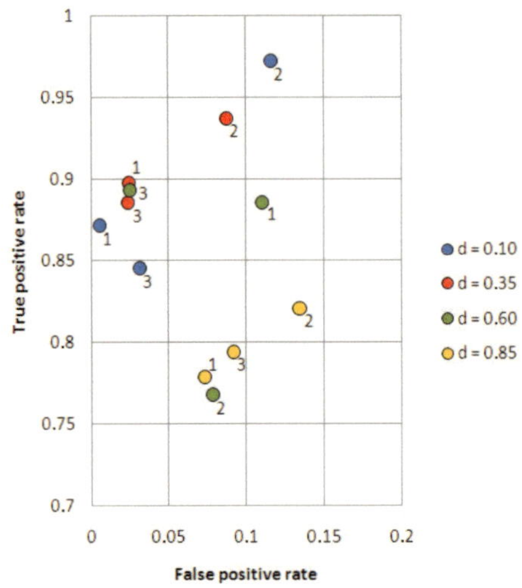

Fig. 12. ROC graph for the TKM model in 5x5 grid with *d* variation

Figure 13 displays a ROC graph for the TKM model with 7x7 grid and *d* variation. In this particular case, it is even more evident the superior performance of this classifier when one uses the lower values of d. Indeed, its best performance was found for *d*=0.35 and the worst corresponded to *d*=0.85.

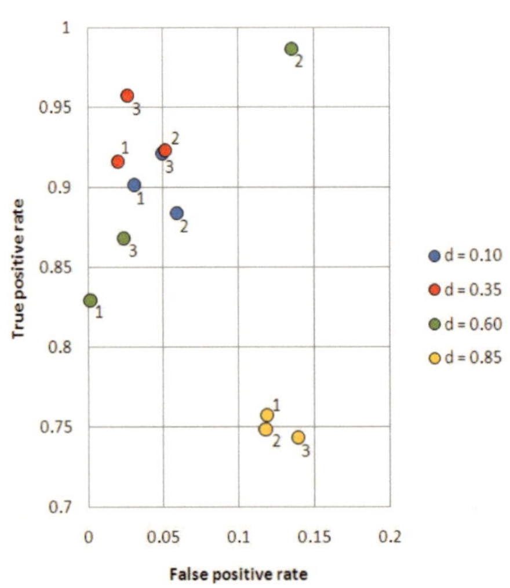

Fig. 13. ROC graph for the TKM model in 7x7 grid with *d* variation

The results relative to the TKM model with 9x9 grid and *d* variation are graphically displayed in Figure 14. For this case, one may notice an approximation among the performances of the model for *d*=0.60 and the results obtained for lower values of d, such as the cases for *d*=0.10 and *d*=0.35. This togetherness was also observed for the *d*=0.85 case, even though it remains as the worst performance case for the TKM model. Therefore, the conclusion was that the smaller values of d provided the best performances for the clusters classification by this network type.

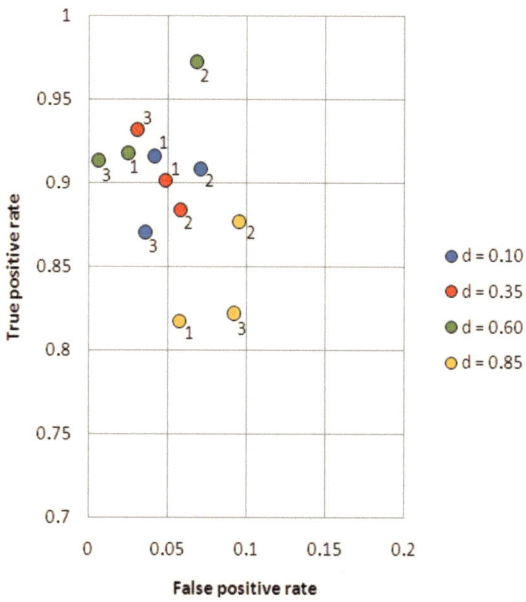

Fig. 14. ROC graph for the TKM model in 9x9 grid with *d* variation

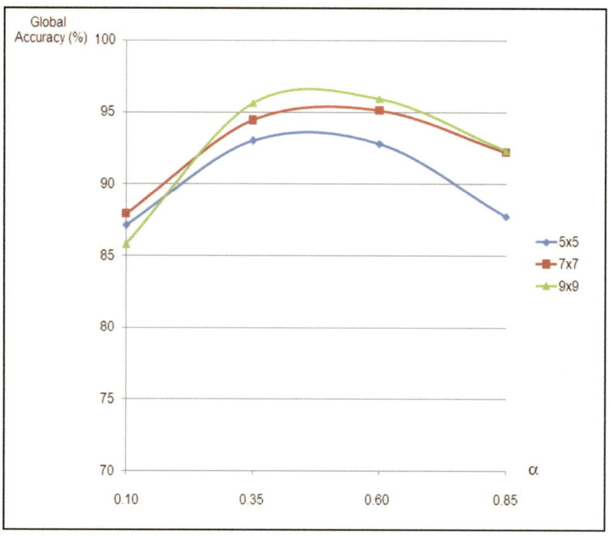

Fig. 15. Superposition of the RSOM networks global accuracies due to the α variation

4.4.2 α variation

For different α values the RSOM network presented a global accuracy significant variation. Table 5 shows the confusion matrices and figure 15 shows the superposition of the global accuracies due to the α variation, for each RSOM dimension studied.

Figure 16 shows a ROC graph for the RSOM model with 5x5 grid and α variation. One notices that with intermediate values of α (α=0.35 and α=0.60) the classifier presented the greatest performances (larger tp rate and smaller fp rate).

Figure 17 shows a ROC graph for the RSOM model with 7x7 grid and α variation. There is an approximation of the performances in this network, between the extreme values (α=0.10 and α=0.85) and the intermediate values of α (α=0.35 and α=0.60). Despite this fact, the intermediate α values still presented a general tendency to be the best performers, with larger tp rate and smaller fp rate.

Grid: 5 x 5 units											
α = 0.10			α = 0.35			α = 0.60			α = 0.85		
437	20	40	441	53	3	455	37	5	445	42	10
0	244	40	1	282	1	1	283	0	35	248	1
45	7	341	2	22	369	6	36	351	4	52	337
Global accuracy (87.1%)			Global accuracy (93.0%)			Global accuracy (92.8%)			Global accuracy (87.7%)		

Grid: 7 x 7 units											
α = 0.10			α = 0.35			α = 0.60			α = 0.85		
425	72	0	470	22	5	458	28	11	457	35	5
1	260	23	3	280	1	4	279	1	4	280	0
43	3	347	13	22	358	1	12	380	13	35	345
Global accuracy (87.9%)			Global accuracy (94.4%)			Global accuracy (95.1%)			Global accuracy (92.2%)		

Grid: 9 x 9 units											
α = 0.10			α = 0.35			α = 0.60			α = 0.85		
440	57	0	473	19	5	465	24	8	458	29	10
4	259	21	3	280	1	6	277	1	15	260	9
49	36	308	7	17	369	0	9	384	11	16	366
Global accuracy (85.8%)			Global accuracy (95.6%)			Global accuracy (95.9%)			Global accuracy (92.3%)		

Legend:

confusion matrix		Predicted cluster		
		1	2	3
True cluster	1	$n_{1,1}$	$n_{1,2}$	$n_{1,3}$
	2	$n_{2,1}$	$n_{2,2}$	$n_{2,3}$
	3	$n_{3,1}$	$n_{3,2}$	$n_{3,3}$

Table 5. α variation and global accuracy of the RSOM network in different grids

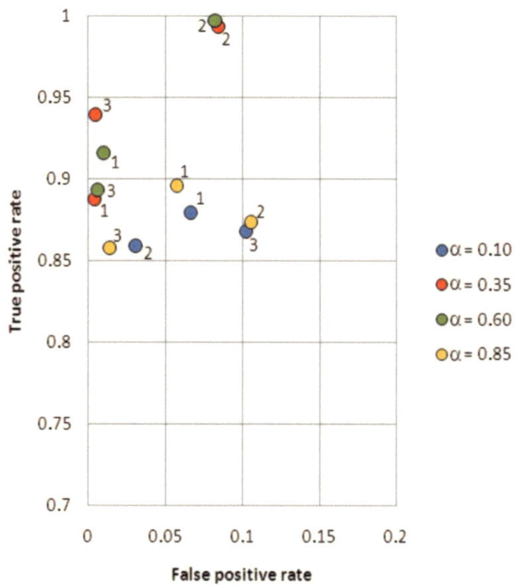

Fig. 16. ROC graph for the RSOM model in 5x5 grid with α variation

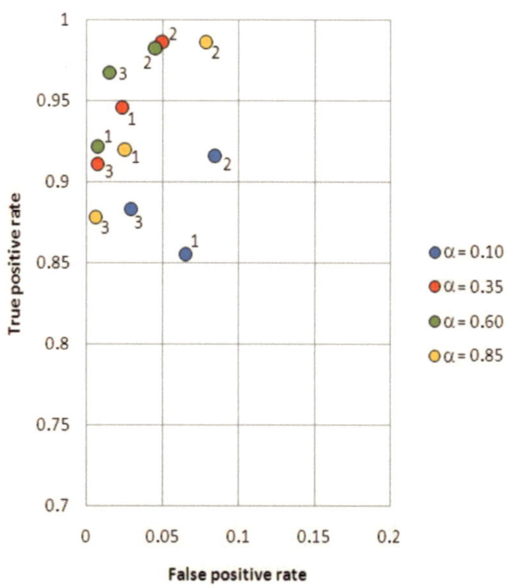

Fig. 17. ROC graph for the RSOM model in 7x7 grid with α variation

Figure 18 shows a ROC graph for the RSOM model with 9x9 grid and α variation. This figure indicates a superior performance of this classifier, when one uses intermediate values of α (α=0.35 and α=0.60). In such cases the classifier becomes nearly ideal, with tp rate approaching 100% and fp rate near 0%. On the other hand, this classifier performance becomes very poor for the lowest extreme (α=0.10) when compared to the other α parameters.

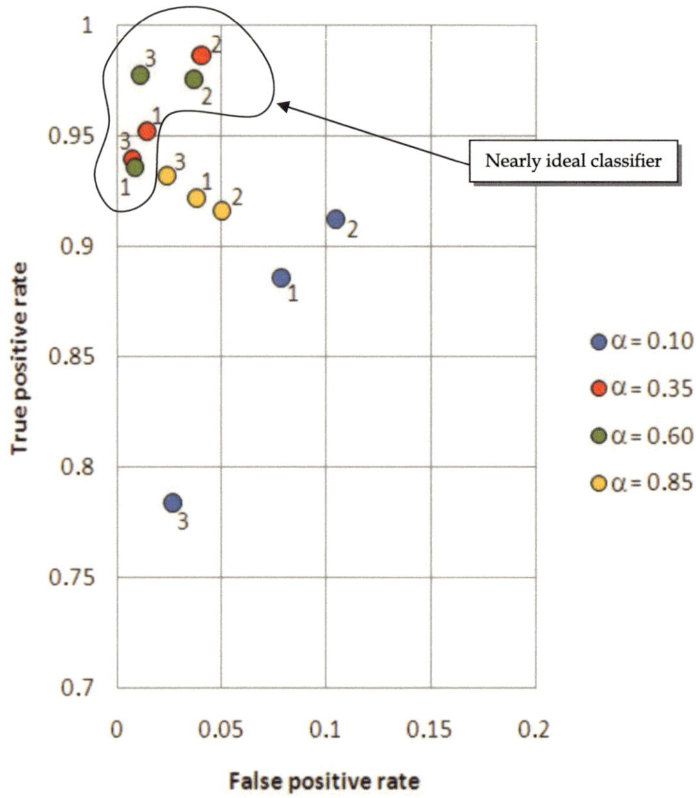

Fig. 18. ROC graph for the RSOM model in 9x9 grid with α variation

In summary, we can say that the RSOM network was the one which offered the best clusters classification performance, as long as, using intermediate α values.

5. Conclusion

This work aimed to evaluate the applicability of the self-organizing map local temporal extensions (Temporal Kohonen Map and Recurrent Self-Organizing Map) in the severe weather patterns recognition. The study area was the eastern Amazon region, one of the areas of the Earth with higher frequency and intensity of extreme weather events, especially in terms of the lightning occurrences.

Its purpose was to contribute in the identification of a useful tool for the weather studies, to reduce the damages associated with this natural phenomenon. The performance analysis of the recurrent neural networks (TKM and RSOM) with relation to the original SOM resulted in the following main conclusions:

- There is significant change in the global accuracy of the TKM and RSOM classifiers depending on the choice of the time coefficients (d and α), respectively;
- The recurrent neural networks (TKM and RSOM), used as classifiers, presented improved performance over the original SOM when adjusted its time coefficients with core values within the range of 0 to 1;

- The U-matrix of the RSOM network presented a better cluster visualization (in terms of separation) when compared with other networks studied, allowing a clear differentiation among the three clusters;
- The labeling of the neurons in the maps, after the training, was better defined for the RSOM network when compared with the other networks studied;
- Finally, after the ROC analysis, it was concluded that among the neural networks studied, the RSOM had the best performance as classifier, confirming its usefulness as a potential tool for studies related to the severe weather patterns recognition.

6. References

Angelovič, P. (2005). Time series prediction using RSOM and local models, *Proceedings of IIT. SRC 2005*, pp. 27–34, April 27, 2005

Chappell, G. & Taylor, J. (1993). The temporal Kohonen map. *Neural Networks*, Vol.6, No.3, pp. 441-445, ISSN: 0893-6080

Cherif, A.;Cardot, H. & Bone, R. (2011). SOM time series clustering and prediction with recurrent neural networks. *Neurocomputing*, Vol.74, Issue 11, (May 2011), pp. 1936-1944, ISSN 0925-2312, doi: 10.1016/j.neucom.2010.11.026

Cooray, V.; Cooray, C. & Andrews, C. (2007). Lightning caused injuries in humans. *Journal of Electrostatics*, Vol.65, Issues 5-6, (May 2007), pp. 386-394, ISSN 0304-3886, doi:10.1016/j.elstat.2006.09.016

Fawcett, T. (2006). An introduction to ROC analysis. *Pattern Recognition Letters*, Vol.27, Issue 8, (June 2006), pp. 861-874, ISSN 0167-8655, doi:10.1016/j.patrec.2005.10.010

Hagenbuchner, M.; Sperduti, A. & Tsoi, A. (2003). A self-organizing map for adaptive processing of structured data. *IEEE Transactions on Neural Networks*, Vol.14, No.3, pp.491–505, ISSN: 1045-9227

Hammer, B. ; Micheli, A. ; Sperduti, A. & Strickert, M. (2004). Recursive self-organizing network models. *Neural Networks*, Vol. 17, Issues 8-9, New Developments in Self-Organizing Systems (October-November 2004), pp. 1061-1085, ISSN 0893-6080, doi: 10.1016/j.neunet.2004.06.009

Han, J. & Kamber, M. (2006). *Data Mining: Concepts and Techniques*, 2nd ed., Morgan Kaufmann Publishers, San Francisco, USA, ISBN: 978-1-55860-901-3

Huang, S.-C. & Wu, T.-K. (2010). Integrating recurrent SOM with wavelet-based kernel partial least square regressions for financial forecasting. *Expert Systems with Applications*, Vol.37, Issue 8, (August 2010), pp. 5698-5705, ISSN 0957-4174, doi: 10.1016/j.eswa.2010.02.040

Jayaratne, R. (2008). Thunderstorm electrification mechanisms, In: *The Lightning Flash*, V. Cooray, (Ed.), pp. 17-44, Institution of Engineering and Technology,ISBN 978-0-85296-780-5, London, United Kingdom

Kohonen, T. (1990). The self-organizing map. *Proceedings of the IEEE*, Vol.78, No.9, (September 1990), pp. 1464-1480, ISSN 0018-9219

Kohonen, T. (2001). *Self-organizing maps*, Springer Series in Information Sciences, ISBN 3-540-67921-9, Berlin, Germany

Koskela, T. ; Varsta, M. ; Heikkonen, J. & Kaski, K. (1998a). Recurrent SOM with local linear models in time series prediction, *Proceedings of Sixth European Symposium on Artificial Neural Networks*, pp. 167–172

Koskela, T.; Varsta, M.; Heikkonen, J. & Kaski, K. (1998b). Time series prediction using recurrent SOM with local linear models, *International Journal of Knowledge-based and Intelligent Engineering Systems*, Vol.2, pp. 60–68, ISSN: 1327-2314

Lo Piparo, G. (2010). Lightning protection of telecommunication towers, In: *Lightning Protection,* V. Cooray, (Ed.), pp. 723-787, Institution of Engineering and Technology, ISBN 978-0-86341-744-3, London, United Kingdom

Manzato, A. (2007). Sounding-derived indices for neural network based short-term thunderstorm and rainfall forecasts. *Atmospheric Research,* Vol.83, Issues 2-4, (February 2007), pp. 349-365, ISSN 0169-8095, doi:10.1016/j.atmosres.2005.10.021

Manzato, A. (2008). A verification of numerical model forecasts for sounding-derived indices above Udine, Northeast Italy. *Weather and Forecasting - American Meteorological Society,* Vol.23, (June 2008), pp. 477-495, doi: 10.1175/2007WAF2007018.1

Ni, H. & Yin, H. (2009). Exchange rate prediction using hybrid neural networks and trading indicators. *Neurocomputing,* Vol.72, Issues 13-15, (August 2009), pp. 2815-2823, ISSN 0925-2312, doi: 10.1016/j.neucom.2008.09.023

Peppier, R. (1988). *A Review of Static Stability Indices and Related Thermodynamic Parameters.* Illinois State Water Survey Climate and Meteorology Section, USA

Rakov, V. & Uman, M. (2005). *Lightning: Physics and Effects,* Cambridge University Press, ISBN 978-0-521-58327-5, New York, USA

Salhi, M. S.; Arous, N. & Ellouze, N. (2009). Principal temporal extensions of SOM: Overview. *International Journal of Signal Processing, Image Processing and Pattern Recognition* , Vol.2, (December 2009), pp. 61-84, ISSN 2005-4270

Santos, A. ; Souza, J. ; Souza, E. ; Carmo, A. ; Ribeiro, W. & Oliveira, R. (2011). The climatic context of lightning storms, associated to electric systems power outages in eastern Amazonia, *Proceedings of XIV International Conference on Atmospheric Electricity-ICAE,* Rio de Janeiro, Brazil, August 7-12, 2011

Shafer, P. E. & Fuelberg, H. E. (2006). A statistical procedure to forecast warm season lightning over portions of the Florida peninsula. *Weather and Forecasting - American Meteorological Society,* Vol.21, (October 2006), pp. 851-868, ISSN 0882-8156, doi: 10.1175/WAF954.1

Strickert, M. & Hammer, B. (2005). Merge SOM for temporal data. *Neurocomputing,* Vol.64, (March 2005), pp. 39-71, ISSN 0925-2312, doi: 10.1016/j.neucom.2004.11.014

Varsta, M.; Heikkonen, J. & Lampinen, J. (2000). Analytical comparison of the temporal Kohonen map and the recurrent self organizing map. In: M. Verleysen (Ed.),273–280, ESANN'2000

Varsta, M. ; Heikkonen, J. ; Lampinen, J. & Millan, J. (2001). Temporal Kohonen map and the recurrent self-organizing map: Analytical and experimental comparison. *Neural Processing Letters,* Vol.13, No.3, pp. 237 - 251, ISSN 1370-4621

Voegtlin, T. (2002). Recursive self-organizing maps. *Neural Networks,* Vol.15, Issues 8–9,(October 2002), pp. 979–991, doi :10.1016/S0893-6080(02)00072-2

Williams, E. (2008). Charge structure and geographical variation of thunderclouds, In: *The Lightning Flash,* V. Cooray, (Ed.), pp. 1-15, Institution of Engineering and Technology, ISBN 978-0-85296-780-5, London, United Kingdom

9

Centralized Distributed Parameter Bioprocess Identification and I-Term Control Using Recurrent Neural Network Model

Ieroham Baruch[1], Eloy Echeverria-Saldierna[1] and Rosalba Galvan-Guerra[2]
[1]*CINVESTAV-IPN, Mexico City, Department of Automatic Control,*
[2]*ESIMEZ-IPN, Mexico City, Department of Control and Automation Engineering,*
Mexico

1. Introduction

In the last two decades new identification and control tools, like Neural Networks (NN), have been used for biotechnological plants (Boskovic & Narendra, 1995). Among several possible network architectures the ones most widely used are the Feedforward NN (FFNN) and the Recurrent NN (RNN), (Haykin, 1999). The main NN property namely the ability to approximate complex non-linear relationships without prior knowledge of the model structure makes them a very attractive alternative to the classical modeling and control techniques. This property has been proved for both types of NNs by the universal approximation theorem (Haykin, 1999). The preference given to NN identification with respect to the classical methods of process identification is clearly demonstrated in the solution of the "bias-variance dilemma" (Haykin, 1999). The FFNN and the RNN have been applied for Distributed Parameter Systems (DPS) identification and control too. In (Deng & Li, 2003; Deng et al. 2005; Gonzalez et al, 1998), an intelligent modeling approach is proposed for Distributed Parameter Systems (DPS). In (Gonzalez et al, 1998), it is presented a new methodology for the identification of DPS, based on NN architectures, motivated by standard numerical discretization techniques used for the solution of Partial Differential Equations (PDE). In (Padhi et al, 2001), an attempt is made to use the philosophy of the NN adaptive-critic design to the optimal control of distributed parameter systems. In (Padhi & Balakrishnan, 2003) the concept of proper orthogonal decomposition is used for the model reduction of DPS to form a reduced order lumped parameter problem. In (Pietil & Koivo, 1996), measurement data of an industrial process are generated by solving the PDE numerically using the finite differences method. Both centralized and decentralized NN models are introduced and constructed based on this data. The multilayer feedforward NN realizing a NARMA model for systems identification has the inconvenience that it is sequential in nature and require input and feedback tap-delays for its realization. In (Baruch et al, 2002; Baruch et al, 2004; Baruch et al, 2005a; Baruch et al, 2005b; Baruch et al, 2007a; Baruch et al, 2007b; Baruch et al, 2008; Baruch & Mariaca-Gaspar, 2009; Baruch & Mariaca-Gaspar, 2010), a new completelly parallel canonical Recurrent Trainable NN (RTNN) architecture, and a dynamic BP learning algorithm has been applied for systems identification and control of nonlinear plants with equal input/output dimensions, obtaining good results. The RTNN do not need the use of tap delays and has a minimum number of weights due to its Jordan canonical structure. In the present paper, this RTNN model will be used for identification, and direct control, of a digestion anaerobic DPS of wastewater treatment, (Aguilar-Garnica, 2006), modeled by PDE/ODE (Ordinary Differential Equations), and simplified using the Orthogonal Collocation Method (OCM) in four collocation points of the fixed bed and one more- for the recirculation tank. We needs to use this simplified ODE mathematical model as an input/output data generator for RTNN BP learning instead of the real plant. Furthermore the mathematical model description of the plant help us to understand the work and the meaning of all process variables of this complex biotechnological plant. Here the plant identification by means of RTNN BP learning will be changed by the RTNN Levenberg Marquardt (L-M) second order learning, (Baruch et al, 2009). This distributed nonlinear parameter plant, described by ODE, has excessive high-dimensional measurements which means that the plant output dimension is greater than the plant control input one (rectangular system), requiring to use learning by data fusion technique and special reference choice. Furthermore the used control laws are extended with an integral term, (Baruch et al.2005b; Baruch et al, 2007b), so to form an integral plus state control action, capable to speed up the reaction of the control system and to augment its resistance to noise.

2. Mathematical description of the anaerobic digestion bioprocess plant

The development of the anaerobic digestion process PDE model is based on the two-step (acidogenesis-methanization) mass-balance and bacterial kinetics involving the Monod equations of the specific growth rates (eq. 1-4). The model incorporates electrochemical equilibria in order to include the alkalinity which has to play a central role in the related monitoring and control strategy of a wastewater treatment plant. The dynamics of the species in the recirculation tank is described by ODE (eq. 7). The parameters of this model are obtained by parameter identification and validation (see Bernard et al., 2001). The biochemical nature of the processes of waste degradation is described in (Schoefs et al., 2003, and Bernard et al., 2001) and in cited bibliography. The physical meaning of all variables and constants (also its values), are summarized in Table 1. The complete analytical model of wastewater treatment anaerobic bioprocess (see Fig. 1), taken from (Schoefs et al. 2003 and Aguilar-Garnica et al., 2006), could be described by the following system of PDE:

$$\frac{\partial X_1}{\partial t} = (\mu_1 - \varepsilon D) X_1, \quad \mu_1 = \mu_{1\max} \frac{S_1}{K_{S1} X_1 + S_1}, \tag{1}$$

$$\frac{\partial X_2}{\partial t} = (\mu_2 - \varepsilon D) X_2, \quad \mu_2 = \mu_{2s} \frac{S_1}{K_{S2} X_2 + \frac{S_2^2}{K_{I2}}}, \tag{2}$$

$$\frac{\partial S_1}{\partial t} = \frac{E_z}{H^2} \frac{\partial^2 S_1}{\partial z^2} - D \frac{\partial S_1}{\partial t} - k_1 \mu_1 X_1, \tag{3}$$

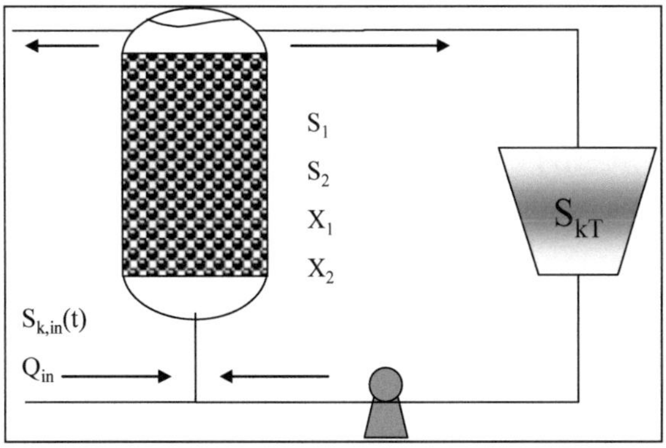

Fig. 1. Block-diagram of anaerobic digestion bioreactor

Variable	*Units*	*Name*	*Value*
z	$z \in [0,1]$	*Space variable*	
t	D	*Time variable*	
E_z	m^2/d	*Axial dispersion coefficient*	1
D	1/d	*Dilution rate*	0.55
H	m	*Fixed bed length*	3.5
X_1	g/L	*Concentration of acidogenic bacteria*	
X_2	g/L	*Concentration of methanogenic bacteria*	
S_1	g/L	*Chemical Oxygen Demand*	
S_2	mmol/L	*Volatile Fatty Acids*	
ε		*Bacteria fraction in the liquid phase*	0.5
k_1	g/g	*Yield coefficients*	42.14
k_2	mmol/g	*Yield coefficients*	250
k_3	mmol/g	*Yield coefficients*	134
μ_1	1/d	*Acidogenesis growth rate*	
μ_2	1/d	*Methanogenesis growth rate*	
μ_{1max}	1/d	*Maximum acidogenesis growth rate*	1.2
μ_{2s}	1/d	*Maximum methanogenesis growth rate*	0.74
K_{1s}'	g/g	*Kinetic parameter*	50.5
K_{2s}'	mmol/g	*Kinetic parameter*	16.6
K_{I2}'	mmol/g	*Kinetic parameter*	256
Q_T	m^3/d	*Recycle flow rate*	0.24
V_T	m^3	*Volume of the recirculation tank*	0.2
S_{1T}	g/L	*Concentration of Chemical Oxygen Demand in the recirculation tank*	
S_{2T}	mmol/L	*Concentration of Volatile Fatty Acids in the recirculation tank*	
Q_{in}	m^3/d	*Inlet flow rate*	0.31
V_B	m^3	*Volume of the fixed bed*	1
V_{eff}	m^3	*Effective volume tank*	0.95
$S_{1,in}$	g/L	*Inlet substr. Concentration*	
$S_{2,in}$	mmol/L	*Inlet substr. Concentration*	

Table 1. Summary of the variables in the plant model

$$\frac{\partial S_2}{\partial t} = \frac{E_z}{H^2}\frac{\partial^2 S_2}{\partial z^2} - D\frac{\partial S_2}{\partial t} - k_2\mu_1 X_1, \tag{4}$$

$$S_1(0,t) = \frac{S_{1,in}(t) + RS_{1T}}{R+1}, \quad S_2(0,t) = \frac{S_{2,in}(t) + RS_{2T}}{R+1}, \quad R = \frac{Q_T}{DV_{eff}}, \tag{5}$$

$$\frac{\partial S_1}{\partial z}(1,t) = 0, \quad \frac{\partial S_2}{\partial z}(1,t) = 0, \tag{6}$$

$$\frac{dS_{1T}}{dt} = \frac{Q_T}{V_T}\left(S_1(1,t) - S_{1T}\right), \quad \frac{dS_{2T}}{dt} = \frac{Q_T}{V_T}\left(S_2(1,t) - S_{2T}\right). \tag{7}$$

For practical purpose, the full PDE bioprocess model is reduced to an ordinary differential equations system using the OCM (Bialecki & Fairweather, 2001). The precision of the orthogonal collocation method of approximation of the PDE model depended on the number of measurement (collocation) points, but the approximation is always exact in that points. If the number of points is very high and the point positions are chosen inappropriately, the ODE model could loose identifiability.

Here, the ODE plant model is used as a plant data generator, illustrating the centralized neural identification and control of the DPS, so, the point number not need to be too high. Our reduced order model have only four points, (0.2H, 0.4 H, 0.6H, 0.8H), but it generated 18 measured variables as: X_1 (acidogenic bacteria), X_2 (methanogenic bacteria), S_1 (chemical oxygen demand) and S_2 (volatile fatty acids), and the following variables in the recirculation tank: S_{1T} (chemical oxygen demand) and S_{2T} (volatile fatty acids). So the plant input/output dimensions are M=2, L=18. The reference set points generated for all that variables keep the form but differ in amplification due to its position. The plant ODE system model, obtained by OCM is described by the following system of ODE:

$$\frac{dX_{1,i}}{dt} = \left(\mu_{1,i} - \varepsilon D\right)X_{1,i}, \quad \frac{dX_{2,i}}{dt} = \left(\mu_{2,i} - \varepsilon D\right)X_{2,i}, \tag{8}$$

$$\frac{dS_{1,i}}{dt} = \frac{E_z}{H^2}\sum_{j=1}^{N+2} B_{i,j}S_{1,j} - D\sum_{j=1}^{N+2} A_{i,j}S_{1,j} - k_1\mu_{1,i}X_{1,i}, \tag{9}$$

$$\frac{dS_{2,i}}{dt} = \frac{E_z}{H^2}\sum_{j=1}^{N+2} B_{i,j}S_{1,j} - D\sum_{j=1}^{N+2} A_{i,j}S_{2,j} - k_2\mu_{1,i}X_{2,i} - k_3\mu_{2,i}X_{2,i}, \tag{10}$$

$$\frac{dS_{1T}}{dt} = \frac{Q_T}{V_T}\left(S_{1,N+2} - S_{1T}\right), \quad \frac{dS_{2T}}{dt} = \frac{Q_T}{V_T}\left(S_{2,N+2} - S_{2T}\right), \tag{11}$$

$$S_{k,1} = \frac{1}{R+1}S_{k,in}(t) + \frac{R}{R+1}S_{kT}, \quad S_{k,N+2} = \frac{K_1}{R+1}S_{k,in}(t) + \frac{K_1 R}{R+1}S_{kT} + \sum_{i=1}^{N+1} K_i S_{k,i}, \tag{12}$$

$$K_1 = \frac{A_{N+2,1}}{A_{N+2,N+2}}, \quad K_i = \frac{A_{N+2,i}}{A_{N+2,N+2}}, \tag{13}$$

$$A = \Lambda\phi^{-1}, \quad \Lambda = \left[\omega_{m,l}\right] = (l-1)z_m^{l-2}, \tag{14}$$

$$B = \Gamma\phi^{-1}, \quad \Gamma = \left[\tau_{m,l}\right], \quad \tau_{m,l} = (l-1)(l-2)z_m^{l-3}, \quad \phi_{m,l} = z_m^{l-1}, \tag{15}$$

$$i = 2,\ldots N+2, \quad m,l = 1,\ldots N+2. \tag{16}$$

The reduced plant model (8)-(16), could be used as unknown plant model which generate input/output process data for centralized adaptive neural identification and control system design, based on the concepts, given in (Baruch et al., 2008; Baruch & Mariaca-Gaspar, 2009).

3. Description of the RTNN topology and learning

The more general BP rule for single neuron learning is the delta rule of Widrow and Hoff, given in Haykin, 1999. If we define the cost function of learning as:

$$\xi(k) = (1/2)e^2(k), e(k) = t(k) - y(k)$$

where $\xi(k)$ is the cost function, e(k) is the neuron output error, y(k) is the neuron output signal, t(k) is the neuron output target signal, w(k) is the neuron weight, x(k) is the neuron input, we could write the following delta rule of neuron learning as:

$$w(k+1) = w(k) + \Delta w(k), \Delta w(k) = \eta e(k)x(k)$$

We could generalise this delta rule and applied it for learning of multilayer feedforward, recurrent or mixed neural networks if we design and draw its topology in block form. Then using the diagrammatic method (see Wan & Beaufays, 1996) we could design the adjoint NN topology. The NN topology is used to execute the forward pass of the BP learning so to compute predictions of the input signals of NN weight blocks. The adjoint NN topology is used to execute the backward pass of the BP learning so to compute predictions of the error signals of the outputs of that NN weight blocks. So having both predictions we could execute the delta learning rule layer by layer and weight by weight. In the following part we will apply this simple methodology for the two layered RTNN topology and learning given in vector matrix form where the delta rule is generalized as vector product of the local error and local input RTNN vectors.

3.1 RTNN topology and recursive BP learning

The block-diagrams of the RTNN topology and its adjoint, obtained by means of the diagrammatic method of (Wan & Beaufays, 1996), are given on Fig. 2, and Fig. 3. Following Fig. 2, and Fig. 3, we could derive the dynamic BP algorithm of its learning based on the RTNN topology and its adjoined using the generalized delta rule, given above. The RTNN topology is described in vector-matrix form as:

$$X(k+1) = AX(k) + BU(k), B^T = \left|B_1 \quad B_2\right|, U^T = \left|U_1 \quad U_2\right| \tag{17}$$

$$V(k) = CZ(k), C = |C_1 \quad C_0|, Z^T = |Z_1 \quad Z_2|, Z_1(k) = G[X(k)], Y(k) = F[V(k)] \tag{18}$$

$$A = block - diag(A_i), |A_i| < 1 \tag{19}$$

The BP learning is described in the following general form:

$$W(k+1) = W(k) + \eta \Delta W(k) + \alpha \Delta W(k-1) \tag{20}$$

Using the adjoint RTNN we could derive the BP learning for the RTNN weights applying the generalized delta rule as vectorial products of input and error predictions, as:

$$\Delta C(k) = E_1(k)Z^T(k), \Delta B(k) = E_3(k)U^T(k), \Delta A(k) = E_3(k)X^T(k) \tag{21}$$

$$Vec(\Delta A(k)) = E_3(k) \otimes X(k) \tag{22}$$

Where the error predictions are obtained from the adjoint RTNN as follows:

$$E(k) = T(k) - Y(k), E_1(k) = F'[Y(k)]E(k), F'[Y(k)] = [1 - Y^2(k)] \tag{23}$$

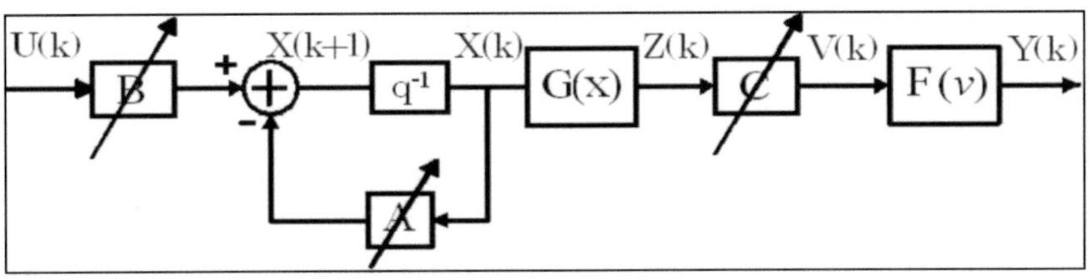

Fig. 2. Block diagram of the RTNN model

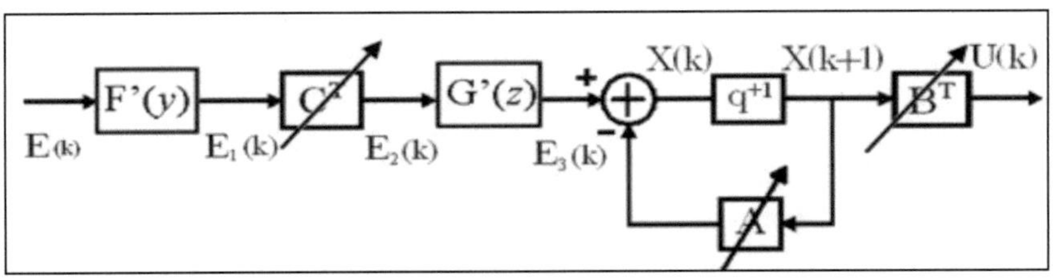

Fig. 3. Block diagram of the adjoint RTNN model

$$E_2(k) = C^T(k)E_1(k), E_3(k) = G'[Z(k)]E_2(k), G'[Z(k)] = [1 - Z^2(k)] \tag{24}$$

Here: X, Y, U are state, augmented output, and input vectors with dimensions N, (L+1), (M+1), respectively, where Z_1 and U_1 are the (Nx1) output and (Mx1) input of the hidden layer; the constant scalar threshold entries are $Z_2 = -1$, $U_2 = -1$, respectively; V is a (Lx1) pre-synaptic activity of the output layer; T is the (Lx1) plant output vector, considered as a RTNN reference; A is (NxN) block-diagonal weight matrix; B and C are [Nx(M+1)] and [Lx(N+1)]- augmented weight matrices; B_0 and C_0 are (Nx1) and (Lx1) threshold weights of the hidden and output layers; F[·], G[·] are vector-valued tanh(·)-activation functions with corresponding dimensions; F'[·], G'[·] are the derivatives of these tanh(·) functions, computed by (23), (24); W is a general weight, denoting each weight matrix (C, A, B) in the

RTNN model, to be updated; ΔW (ΔC, ΔA, ΔB), is the weight correction of W; η, α are learning rate parameters; ΔC is a weight correction of the learned matrix C; ΔB is a weight correction of the learned matrix B; ΔA is a weight correction of the learned matrix A; the diagonal of the matrix A is denoted by Vec($\cdot$) and equation (22) represents its learning as an element-by-element vector products; E, E_1, E_2, E_3, are error vectors with appropriate dimensions, predicted by the adjoint RTNN model, given on Fig.3. The stability of the RTNN model is assured by the activation functions (-1, 1) bounds and by the local stability weight bound condition, given by (19). Below it is given a theorem of RTNN stability which represented an extended version of Nava's theorem, (Baruch et al., 2008; Baruch & Mariaca-Gaspar, 2009; Baruch & Mariaca-Gaspar, 2010).

Theorem of stability of the BP RTNN. Let the RTNN with Jordan Canonical Structure is given by equations (17)-(19) (see Fig.2) and the nonlinear plant model, is as follows:

$$X_p(k+1) = G[X_p(k), U(k)], Y_p(k) = F[X_p(k)] \tag{25}$$

where: {Y_p ($\cdot$), X_p ($\cdot$), U($\cdot$)} are output, state and input variables with dimensions L, N_p, M, respectively; F($\cdot$), G($\cdot$) are vector valued nonlinear functions with respective dimensions. Under the assumption of RTNN identifiability made, the application of the BP learning algorithm for A($\cdot$), B($\cdot$), C($\cdot$), in general matricial form, described by equation (20)-(24), and the learning rates η (k), α (k) (here they are considered as time-dependent and normalized with respect to the error) are derived using the following Lyapunov function:

$$L(k) = L_1(k) + L_2(k), \tag{26}$$

Where: $L_1(k)$ and $L_2(k)$ are given by:

$$L_1(k) = \frac{1}{2} e^2(k),$$

$$L_2(k) = tr\left(\widetilde{W}_A(k)\widetilde{W}_A^T(k)\right) + tr\left(\widetilde{W}_B(k)\widetilde{W}_B^T(k)\right) + tr\left(\widetilde{W}_C(k)\widetilde{W}_C^T(k)\right);$$

Here: $\widetilde{W}_A(k) = \hat{A}(k) - A^*$, $\widetilde{W}_B(k) = \hat{B}(k) - B^*$, $\widetilde{W}_C(k) = \hat{C}(k) - C^*$, are vectors of the weight estimation error; (A^*, B^*, C^*), $(\hat{A}(k), \hat{B}(k), \hat{C}(k))$ denote the ideal neural weight and the estimate of the neural weight at the k-th step, respectively, for each case. Then the identification error is bounded, i.e.:

$$L(k+1) = L_1(k+1) + L_2(k+1) < 0,$$
$$\Delta L(k+1) = L(k+1) - L(k);$$

where the condition for $L_1(k+1) < 0$ is that:

$$\frac{\left(1 - \frac{1}{\sqrt{2}}\right)}{\psi_{\max}} < \eta_{\max} < \frac{\left(1 + \frac{1}{\sqrt{2}}\right)}{\psi_{\max}};$$

and for $L_2(k+1)<0$ we have:

$$\Delta L_2(k+1) < -\eta_{max}\left|e(k+1)\right|^2 \alpha_{max}\left|e(k)\right|^2 + d(k+1).$$

Note that η_{max} changes adaptively during the RTNN learning and:

$$\eta_{max} = \max_{i=1}^{3}\{\eta_i\};$$

where all: the unmodelled dynamics, the approximation errors and the perturbations, are represented by the d-term. The rate of convergence lemma used, is given below. The complete proof of that Theorem of stability is given in (Baruch et al., 2008).

Rate of convergence lemma (Baruch & Mariaca-Gaspar, 2009). Let ΔL_k is defined. Then, applying the limit's definition, the identification error bound condition is obtained as:

$$\overline{\lim_{k\to\infty}}\frac{1}{k}\sum_{t=1}^{k}\left(\left|E(t)\right|^2 + \left|E(t-1)\right|^2\right) \le d.$$

Proof. Starting from the final result of the theorem of RTNN stability:

$$\Delta L(k) \le -\eta(k)\left|E(k)\right|^2 - \alpha(k)\left|E(k-1)\right|^2 + d$$

and iterating from k=0, we get:

$$L(k+1) - L(0) \le -\sum_{t=1}^{k}\left|E(t)\right|^2 - \sum_{t=1}^{k}\left|E(t-1)\right|^2 + dk,$$

$$\sum_{t=1}^{k}\left(\left|E(t)\right|^2 + \left|E(t-1)\right|^2\right) \le dk - L(k+1) + L(0) \le dk + L(0).$$

From here, we could see that d must be bounded by weight matrices and learning parameters, in order to obtain: $\Delta L(k) \in \mathbb{L}(\infty)$.

As a consequence: $A(k) \in \mathbb{L}(\infty), B(k) \in \mathbb{L}(\infty), C(k) \in \mathbb{L}(\infty)$

3.2 Recursive Levenberg-Marquardt RTNN learning

The general recursive L-M algorithm of learning, (Baruch & Mariaca-Gaspar, 2009; Baruch & Mariaca-Gaspar, 2010) is given by the following equations:

$$W(k+1) = W(k) + P(k)\nabla Y\left[W(k)\right]E\left[W(k)\right], \tag{27}$$

$$Y\left[W(k)\right] = g\left[W(k), U(k)\right], \tag{28}$$

$$E^2\left[W(k)\right]=\left\{Y_p(k)-g\left[W(k),U(k)\right]\right\}^2, \tag{29}$$

$$DY\left[W(k)\right]=\left.\frac{\partial g\left[W(k),U(k)\right]}{\partial W}\right|_{W=W(k)}; \tag{30}$$

Where: W is a general weight matrix (A, B, C) under modification; P is a symmetric matrix updated by (37); DY[·] is an Nw-dimensional gradient vector; Y is the RTNN output vector which depends of the updated weights and the input; E is an error vector; Yp is the plant output vector, which is in fact the target vector. Using the same RTNN adjoint block diagram (see Fig.3), it was possible to obtain the values of the gradients DY[·] for each updated weight, propagating the value D(k) = I through it. Applying equation (30) and using the RTNN adjoint (see Fig. 3) we could compute each weight matrix (A, B, C) in order to be updated. The corresponding gradient components are found as follows:

$$DY\left[C_{ij}(k)\right]=D_{1,i}(k)Z_j(k), \tag{31}$$

$$D_{1,i}(k)=F_j^{'}\left[Y_i(k)\right], \tag{32}$$

$$DY\left[A_{ij}(k)\right]=D_{2,i}(k)X_j(k), \tag{33}$$

$$DY\left[B_{ij}(k)\right]=D_{2,i}(k)U_j(k), \tag{34}$$

$$D_{2,i}(k)=G_i^{'}\left[Z_j(k)\right]C_iD_{1,i}(k). \tag{35}$$

Therefore the Jacobean matrix could be formed as:

$$DY\left[W(k)\right]=\left[DY\left(C_{ij}(k)\right),DY\left(A_{ij}(k)\right),DY\left(B_{ij}(k)\right)\right]. \tag{36}$$

The P(k) matrix was computed recursively by the equation:

$$P(k)=\alpha^{-1}(k)\left\{P(k-1)-P(k-1)\Omega\left[W(k)\right]S^{-1}\left[W(k)\right]\Omega^T\left[W(k)\right]P(k-1)\right\}; \tag{37}$$

where the S(·), and Ω(·) matrices were given as follows:

$$S\left[W(k)\right]=\alpha(k)\Lambda(k)+\Omega^T\left[W(k)\right]P(k-1)\Omega\left[W(k)\right], \tag{38}$$

$$\Omega^T\left[W(k)\right]=\begin{bmatrix} & & \nabla Y^T\left[W(k)\right] & & \\ 0 & \cdots & 1 & \cdots & 0\end{bmatrix};$$

$$\Lambda(k)^{-1}=\begin{bmatrix}1 & 0\\ 0 & \rho\end{bmatrix};\quad 10^{-4}\le\rho\le10^{-6}; \tag{39}$$

$$0.97\le\alpha(k)\le1;\quad 10^3\le P(0)\le10^6.$$

The matrix $\Omega(\cdot)$ had a dimension (Nwx2), whereas the second row had only one unity element (the others were zero). The position of that element was computed by:

$$i = k\text{mod}\left(Nw\right) + 1; \quad k > Nw \tag{40}$$

After this, the given up topology and learning are applied for an anaerobic wastewater distributed parameter centralized system identification and control.

4. Description of the direct centralized recurrent neural control with I-term

The block-diagram of the closed loop control system is given on Fig.4.

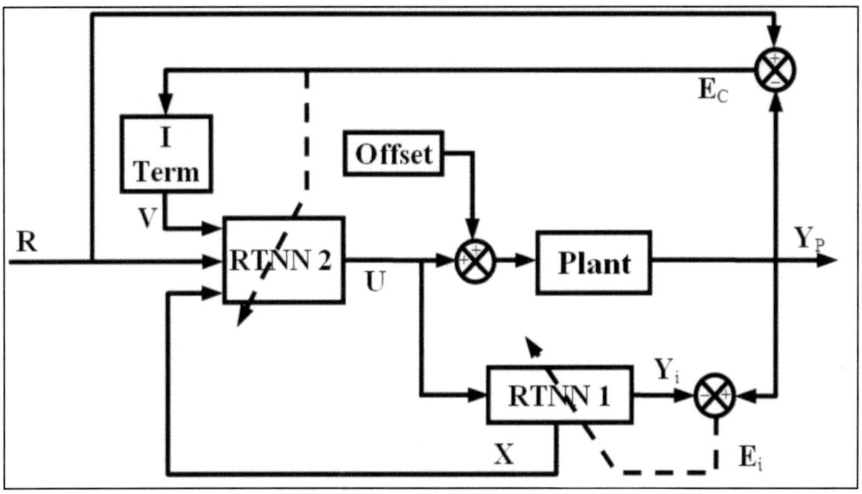

Fig. 4. Block diagram of the direct adaptive I-term control containing RTNN identifier and RTNN controller

It contained a recurrent neural identifier RTNN 1, and a RTNN-2 controller with entries – the reference signal R, the I-term signal V, and the state vector X estimated by the RTNN-1. The input of the plant is perturbed by a constant load perturbation Offset which took into account also the imperfect identification of the plant model. The RTNN-1, 2 topologies are given by (17)-(19), and the nonlinear plant model is given by equations (8)-(16). Let us to linearize the equations of the plant and the RTNN-2 controller and to introduce the equation of the I-term as:

$$V(k+1) = V(k) + T_0 E_c(k) \tag{41}$$

where the dimension of the I-term vector V(k) is equal of the dimension of the error vector, equal of the dimension L of the plant output Yp(k). Now we could write the following z-transfer functions with respect to V, X, R, corresponding to Fig.4:

$$W_p(z) = C_p(zI - A_p)^{-1} B_p \tag{42}$$

$$P_i(z) = (zI - A_i)^{-1} B_i \tag{43}$$

$$Q_1(z) = C_c(zI - A_c)^{-1} B_{cv} \tag{44}$$

$$Q_2(z) = C_c(zI - A_c)^{-1} B_{cx} \tag{45}$$

$$Q_3(z) = C_c(zI - A_c)^{-1} B_{cr} \tag{46}$$

$$I(z) = T_0(zI - I)^{-1} \tag{47}$$

The RTNN topology is controllable and observable, and the BP/L-M algorithms of learning are convergent, (see Baruch & Mariaca-Gaspar, 2009; Baruch & Mariaca-Gaspar, 2010). Then the identification and control errors tend to zero ($E_i(k) = Y_p(k) - Y(k) \rightarrow 0$ and $E_c(k) = R(k) - Y_p(k) \rightarrow 0$; $k \rightarrow \infty$). This means that each transfer function given by equations (42)-(46) is stable with minimum phase. The z-transfer functions (42)-(47) are connected by the next equation, derived following the block-diagram of the Fig. 4:

$$\begin{aligned} &\{I + W_p(z)[I - Q_2(z)P_i(z)]^{-1} Q_1(z) I(z)\} Y_p(z) = \\ &= W_p(z)[I - Q_2(z)P_i(z)]^{-1}[Q_1(z)I(z) + Q_3(z)]R(z) + W_p(z)Of(z) \end{aligned} \tag{48}$$

Substituting (47) in (48), finally we obtained:

$$\begin{aligned} &\{(z-1)I + W_p(z)[I - Q_2(z)P_i(z)]^{-1} Q_1(z) T_0\} Y_p(z) = \\ &= W_p(z)[I - Q_2(z)P_i(z)]^{-1}[Q_1(z)T_0 + (z-1)Q_3(z)]R(z) + W_p(z)(z-1)Of(z) \end{aligned} \tag{49}$$

The equation (49) showed that the closed-loop system is stable ($Y_p(k) \rightarrow R(k)$; $k \rightarrow \infty$) and that the I-term eliminated the constant perturbation Of(z) because the last term tended to zero when z tended to 1.

The centralized DPS could be considered as a system with excessive measurements (L>M), where the Direct Adaptive Neural Control (DANC) performed a data fusion so to elaborate the control action. So we need to compute the plant input error for the learning of the RTNN-2 controller. An approximated way to obtain the input error from the output error is pre-multiplying it by the $(CB)^+$ using the estimated C,B-matrices as follows:

$$E_u(k) = (CB)^+ E_c(k), (CB)^+ = [(CB)^T (CB)]^{-1} (CB)^T \tag{50}$$

5. Description of the indirect (sliding mode) centralized recurrent neural control with I-term

The block-diagram of the control system is given on Fig.5. It contained a recurrent neural identifier RTNN 1, and a Sliding Mode (SM) controller with entries - the reference signal R, the output error Ec, and the states X and parameters A, B, C, estimated by the neural identifier RTNN-1. The total control is a sum of the SM control and the I-term control, computed using (41).

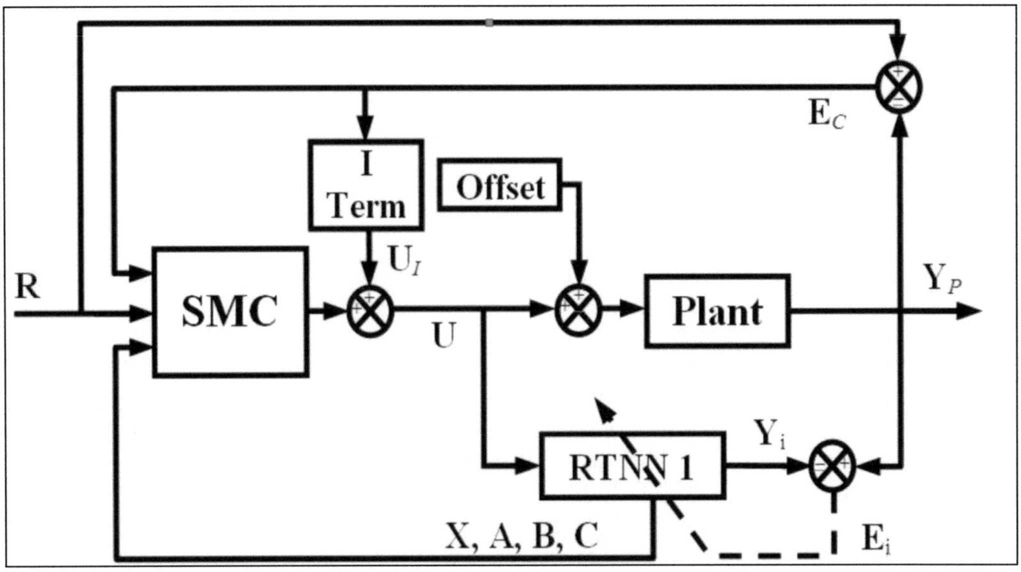

Fig. 5. Block diagram of the indirect adaptive SM control with I-term containing RTNN identifier and SM controller

The linearization of the activation functions of the local learned identification RTNN-1 model, which approximated the plant, leads to the following linear local plant model:

$$X(k+1) = AX(k) + BU(k), Y(k) = CX(k) \tag{51}$$

where L > M (rectangular system), is supposed. Let us define the following sliding surface with respect to the output tracking error:

$$S(k+1) = E(k+1) + \sum_{i=1}^{P} \gamma_i E(k-i+1)\,; \quad |\gamma_i| < 1; \tag{52}$$

where: S(·) is the sliding surface error function; E(·) is the systems local output tracking error; γ_i are parameters of the local desired error function; P is the order of the error function. The additional inequality in (52) is a stability condition, required for the sliding surface error function. The local tracking error is defined as:

$$E(k) = R(k) - Y(k); \tag{53}$$

where R(k) is a L-dimensional local reference vector and Y(k) is an local output vector with the same dimension. The objective of the sliding mode control systems design is to find a control action which maintains the systems error on the sliding surface assuring that the output tracking error reached zero in P steps, where P<N, which is fulfilled if:

$$S(k+1) = 0. \tag{54}$$

As the local approximation plant model (51), is controllable, observable and stable, (Baruch et al., 2004; Baruch et al., 2008), the matrix A is block-diagonal, and L>M (rectangular system is supposed), the matrix product (CB) is nonsingular with rank M, and the plant states X(k) are smooth non- increasing functions. Now, from (51)-(54), it is easy to obtain the equivalent control capable to lead the system to the sliding surface which yields:

$$U_{eq}(k) = (CB)^{+}\left[-CAX(k) + R(k+1) + \sum_{i=1}^{P}\gamma_i E(k-i+1)\right] + Of, \tag{55}$$

$$(CB)^{+} = \left[(CB)^{T}(CB)\right]^{-1}(CB)^{T}. \tag{56}$$

Here the added offset Of is a learnable M-dimensional constant vector which is learnt using a simple delta rule (see Haykin, 1999, for more details), where the error of the plant input is obtained backpropagating the output error through the adjoint RTNN model. An easy way for learning the offset is using the following delta rule where the input error is obtaned from the output error multiplying it by the same pseudoinverse matrix, as it is:

$$Of(k+1) = Of(k+1) = Of(k) + \eta(CB)^{+}E(k). \tag{57}$$

If we compare the I-term expression (41) with the Offset learning (57) we could see that they are equal which signifyed that the I-term generate a compensation offset capable to eliminate steady state errors caused by constant perturbations and discrepances in the reference tracking caused by non equal input/output variable dimensions (rectangular case systems). So introducing an I-term control it is not necessary to use an compensation offset in the SM control law (55).

The SMC avoiding chattering is taken using a saturation function inside a bounded control level Uo, taking into account plant uncertainties. So the SMC has the form:

$$U(k) = \begin{cases} U_{eq}(k), & \text{if } \|U_{eq}(k)\| < U_0 \\ \dfrac{-U_0 U_{eq}(k)}{\|U_{eq}(k)\|}, & \text{if } \|U_{eq}(k)\| \geq U_0. \end{cases}; \tag{58}$$

The proposed SMC cope with the characteristics of the wide class of plant model reduction neural control with reference model, and represents an indirect adaptive neural control, given by (Baruch et al., 2007a; Baruch et al., 2007b).

6. Description of the centralized optimal control with I-term

The block-diagram of the optimal control system is given on Fig.6. It contained a recurrent neural identifier RTNN 1, and an optimal controller with entries – the reference signal R, the output of the I-term block, and the states X and parameters A, B, C, estimated by the neural identifier RTNN-1. The optimal control algorithm with I-term could be obtained extending the linearized model (51) with the model of the I-term (41). The extended model is:

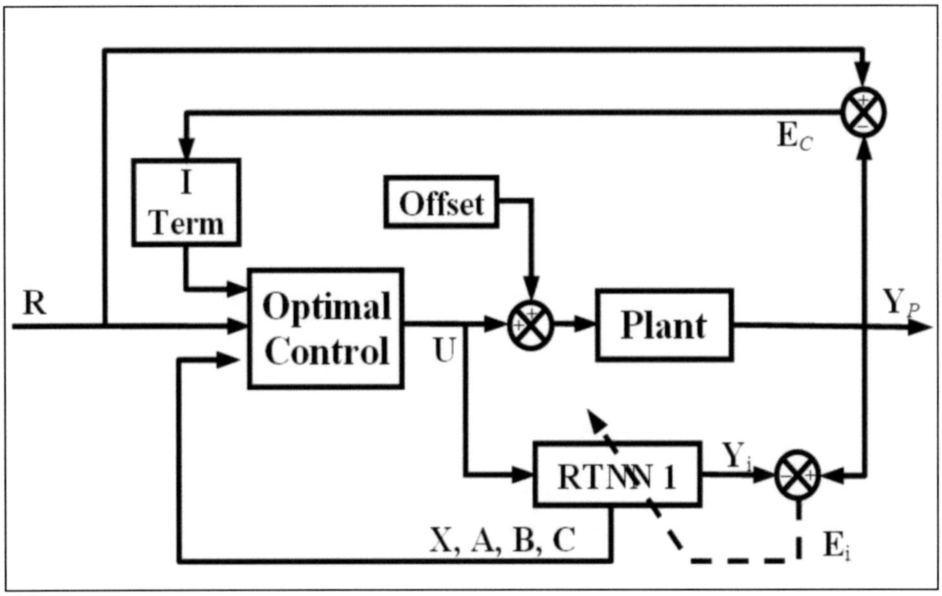

Fig. 6. Block diagram of the real-time optimal control with I-term containing RTNN identifier and optimal controller

$$X_e(k+1) = A_e X_e(k) + B_e U(k) \tag{59}$$

Where: $X_e = [X \mid V]^T$ is a state vector with dimension (L + N) and:

$$A_e = \begin{vmatrix} A & 0 \\ -(CB)^{+}CA & I \end{vmatrix}, B_e = \begin{vmatrix} B \\ -I \end{vmatrix} \tag{60}$$

The optimal I-term control is given by:

$$U(k) = -[B_e^{\ T} P_e B_e + R]^{-1} [B_e^{\ T} P_e B_e] X_e(k) \tag{61}$$

Where the P_e is solution of the discrete Riccati equation:

$$P_e(k+1) = A_e^{\ T} [P_e(k) - P_e(k) B_e (B_e^{\ T} P_e(k) B_e + R)^{-1} B_e^{\ T} P_e(k)] A_e + Q \tag{62}$$

The given up optimal control is rather complicated and here it is used for purpose of comparison.

7. Simulation results

In this paragraph, graphical and numerical simulation results of system identification, direct, indirect (SM), and optimal control, with and without I-term, will be given. For lack of space we will give graphical results only for the X_1 variable. Furthermore the graphical results for the other variables possessed similar behavior. The identification results are obtained from an RTNN identifier by a BP or L-M learning. For sake of comparison we give results of systems identification using both algorithms of learning.

7.1 Simulation results of the system identification

The RTNN-1 performed real-time neural system identification (parameters and states estimation) of 18 output plant variables, which are: 4 variables for each collocation point z=0.2H, z=0.4H, z=0.6H, z=0.8H of the fixed bed as: X_1 (acidogenic bacteria), X_2 (methanogenic bacteria), S_1 (chemical oxygen demand) and S_2 (volatile fatty acids), and the following variables in the recirculation tank: S_{1T} (chemical oxygen demand) and S_{2T} (volatile fatty acids). For lake of space we shall show some graphical results (see Fig. 7-9) only for the X_1 variable. The topology of the RTNN-1 is (2, 20, 18), the activation functions are tanh(.) for both layers. The learning rate parameters for the L-M learning are as follows: the forgetting factor is $\alpha=1$, the regularization constant is $\rho=0.001$, and the initial value of the P matrix is an identity matrix with dimension 420x420. For the BP algorithm of learning the learning constants are chosen as $\alpha=0$, $\eta=0.4$. The simulation results of RTNN-1 system identification are obtained on-line during 400 days with a step of 0.5 day in four measurement points using BP and L-M learning. The identification inputs used are combination of three sinusoids as:

$$S_{1,in} = 0.5 + 0.02\sin\left(\frac{\pi}{100}t\right) + 0.1\sin\left(\frac{3\pi}{100}t\right) + 0.04\cos\left(\frac{\pi}{100}t\right) \tag{63}$$

$$S_{2,in} = 0.5 + 0.1\sin\left(\frac{\pi}{100}t\right) + 0.1\sin\left(\frac{5\pi}{100}t\right) + 0.1\cos\left(\frac{8\pi}{100}t\right) \tag{64}$$

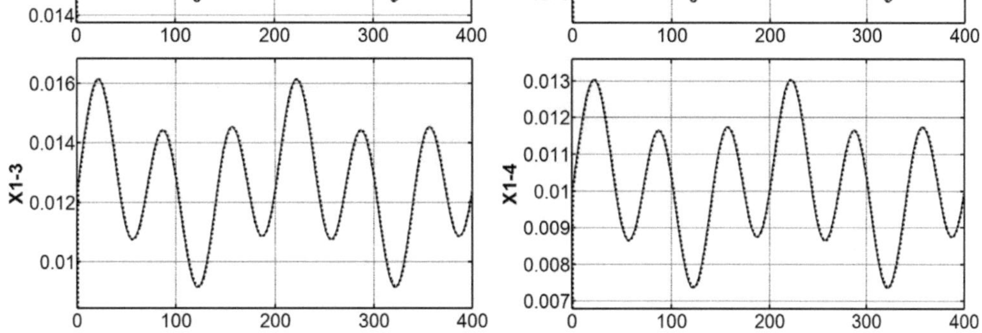

Fig. 7. Graphical simulation results of the neural identification of the plant output X_1 vs. RTNN output in four measurement points for the total time of L-M learning : a) z=0.2H, b) z=0.4H, c) z=0.6H, d) z=0.8H

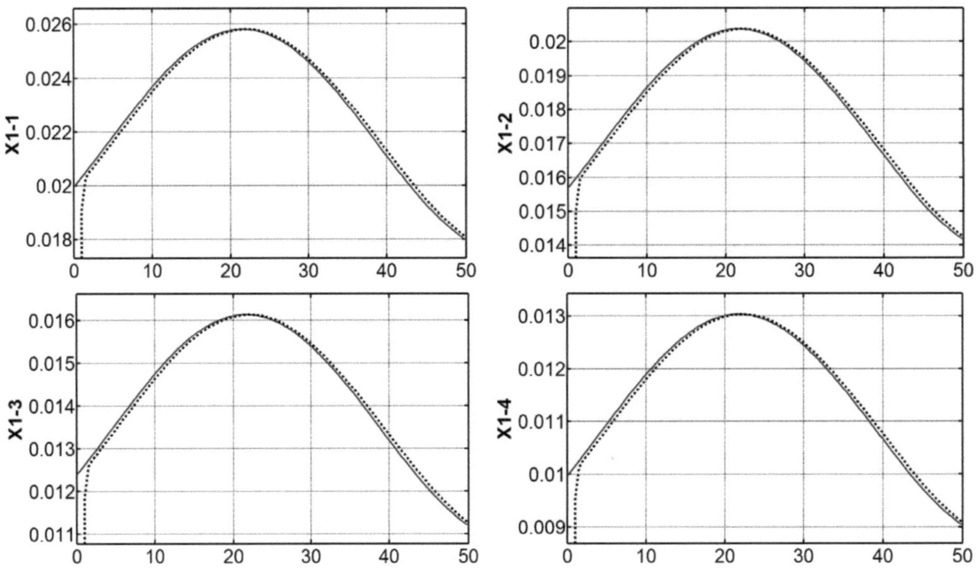

Fig. 8. Graphical simulation results of the neural identification of the plant output X_1 vs. RTNN output in four measurement points for the beginning of L-M learning : a) z=0.2H, b) z=0.4H, c) z=0.6H, d) z=0.8H

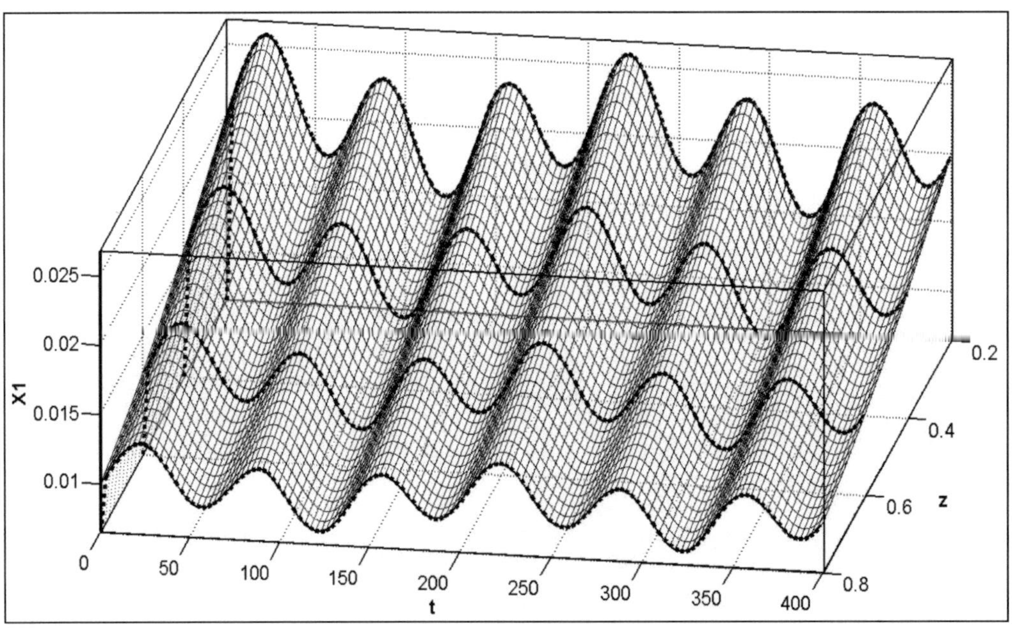

Fig. 9. Three dimensional plot of the neural identification results of the plant output X_1 in four measurement points of L-M learning : z=0.2H, z=0.4H, z=0.6H, z=0.8H

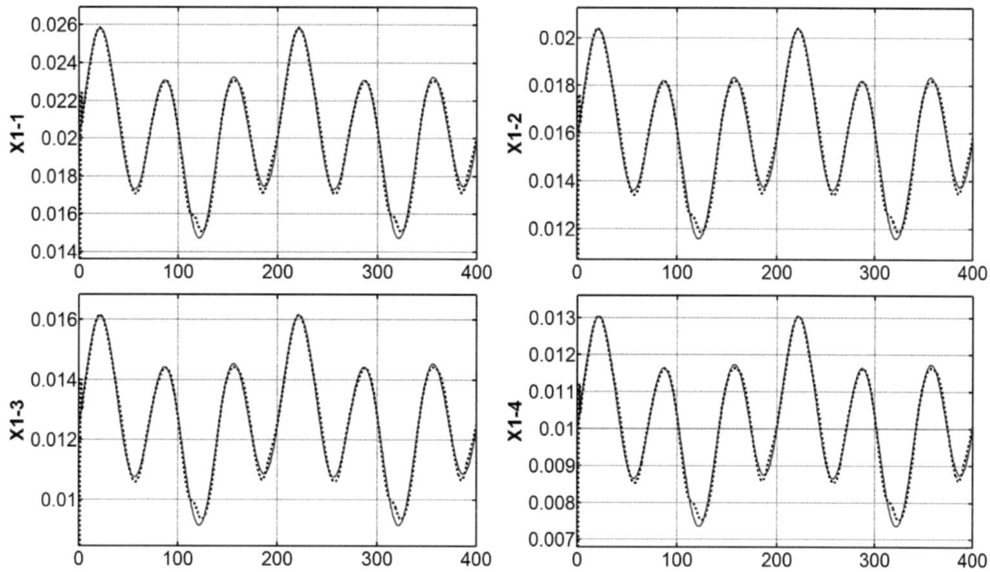

Fig. 10. Graphical simulation results of the neural identification of the plant output X_1 vs. RTNN output in four measurement points for the total time of BP learning : a) z=0.2H, b) z=0.4H, c) z=0.6H, d) z=0.8H

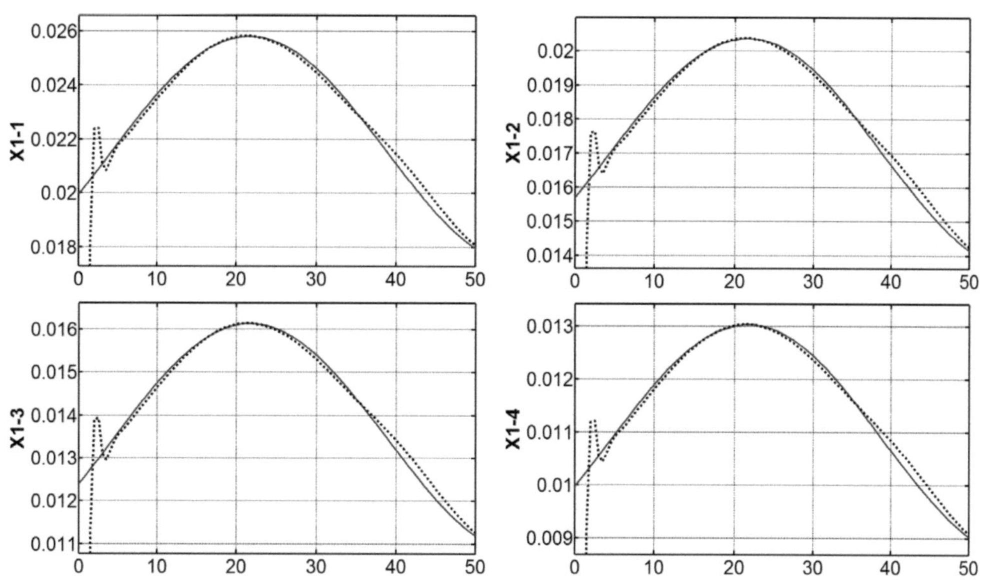

Fig. 11. Graphical simulation results of the neural identification of the plant output X_1 vs. RTNN output in four measurement points for the beginning of BP learning: a) z=0.2H, b) z=0.4H, c) z=0.6H, d) z=0.8H

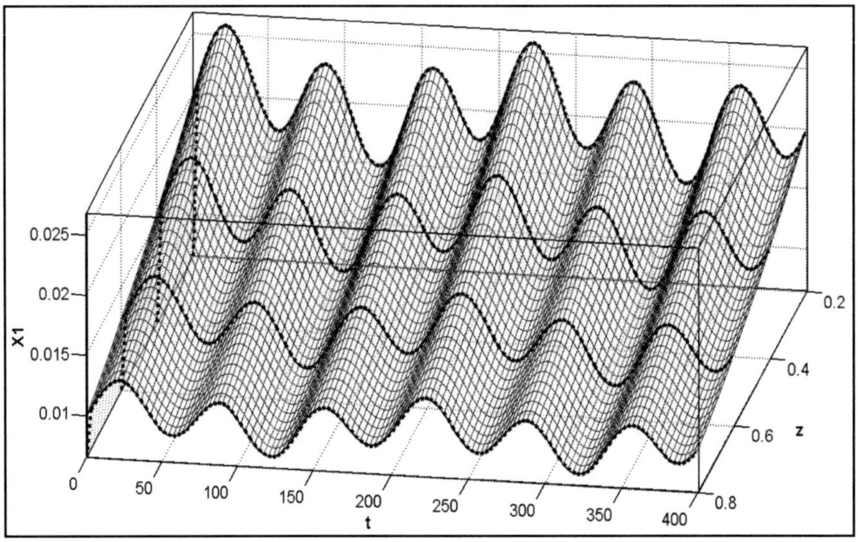

Fig. 12. Three dimensional plot of the neural identification results of the plant output X_1 in four measurement points of BP learning : z=0.2H, z=0.4H, z=0.6H, z=0.8H

Table 2 and Table 3 compared the final Means Squared Error (MSE%) results of the L-M and BP neural identification of plant variables for the fixed bed and the recirculation tank. Note that the form of the plant process variables in the different measurement points is equal but the amplitude is different depending on the point position.

Collocation point	X_1	X_2	S_1/S_{1T}	S_2/S_{2T}
z=0.2	5.0843E-7	1.8141E-6	1.3510E-4	2.5476E-4
z=0.4	3.1428E-7	1.3934E-6	8.3839E-5	1.8217E-4
z=0.6	1.9617E-7	9.6976E-7	5.2303E-5	1.2200E-4
z=0.8	1.2669E-7	6.6515E-7	3.3940E-5	8.1905E-5
Recirculation tank			2.6318E-5	6.3791E-5

Table 2. MSE of the centralized RTNN approximation of the bioprocess output variables in the collocation points, using the L-M RTNN learning

Collocation point	X_1	X_2	S_1/S_{1T}	S_2/S_{2T}
z=0.2	5.9981E-7	2.1006E-6	1.5901E-4	2.8282E-4
z=0.4	3.7111E-7	1.6192E-6	9.8240E-5	2.0506E-4
z=0.6	2.3145E-7	1.1308E-6	6.1119E-5	1.3908E-4
z=0.8	1.4997E-7	7.7771E-7	3.9595E-5	9.4061E-5
Recirculation tank			3.0694E-5	7.3404E-5

Table 3. MSE of the centralized RTNN approximation of the bioprocess output variables in the collocation points, using the BP RTNN learning

The graphical and numerical results of the centralized RTNN identification (see Fig. 7-12, and Tables 2, 3) showed a good RTNN convergence and precise plant output tracking (MSE is 2.5476E-4 for the L-M, and 2.8282E-4 for the BP RTNN learning in the worst case).

7.2 Simulation results of the centralized direct adaptive neural control with I-term using L-M learning

The real-time DANC (see Fig. 4) contained a neural identifier RTNN-1 and a neural controller RTNN-2 with topology (40, 10, 2). Both RTNNs-1, 2 are learnt by the L-M algorithm with parameters: RTNN-1 (α=1, ρ=0.0001, Po=10 I with dimension 420x420); RTNN-2 (α=1, ρ=0.01, Po=0.8 I with dimension 430x430). The simulation results of DANC are obtained on-line during 1000 days with a step of 0.1 day. The control signals are shown on Fig. 13. The Fig. 14-16 compared the plant output X_1 with the reference signal in different measurement points. The form of the set points (train of pulses with random amplitude) of the variable X_1 in the different measurement points is equal but the amplitude is different depending on the point position. This means that the plant has different signal amplification in each measurement point which needs to be taken in consideration.

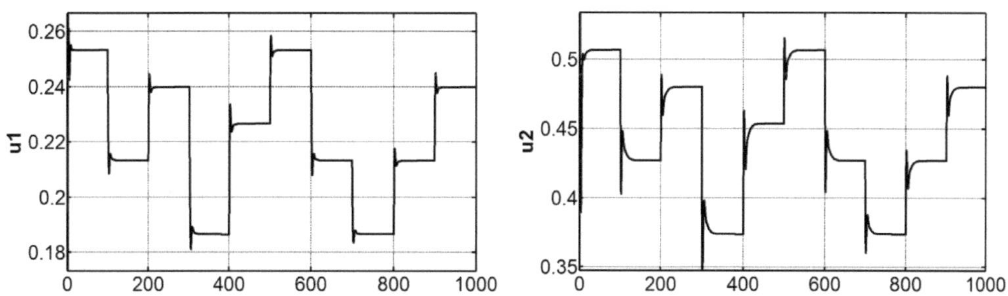

Fig. 13. Plant input control signals generated by I-term DANC: a) Sin1, and b) Sin2

Collocation point	X_1	X_2	S_1/S_{1T}	S_2/S_{2T}
z=0.2	2.2920E-8	1.3366E-7	5.9740E-6	1.7568E-5
z=0.4	1.4517E-8	8.0704E-8	3.4003E-6	9.3272E-6
z=0.6	8.5061E-9	4.3891E-8	1.9213E-6	4.9682E-6
z=0.8	4.4770E-9	2.1242E-8	1.2789E-6	3.1322E-6
Recirculation tank			1.0067E-6	2.2073E-6

Table 4. MSE of the centralized I-term DANC of the bioprocess output variables in the collocation points, using the L-M RTNN learning

The given on Fig. 14-16 graphical results of I-term DANC showed smooth exponential behavior. It could be seen also that the L-M learning converge fast and the I-term remove the constant noise Of, and the plant uncertainties. The obtained numerical results (see Table 4) of final MSE of L-M learning possessed small values (1.7568E-5 in the worse case).

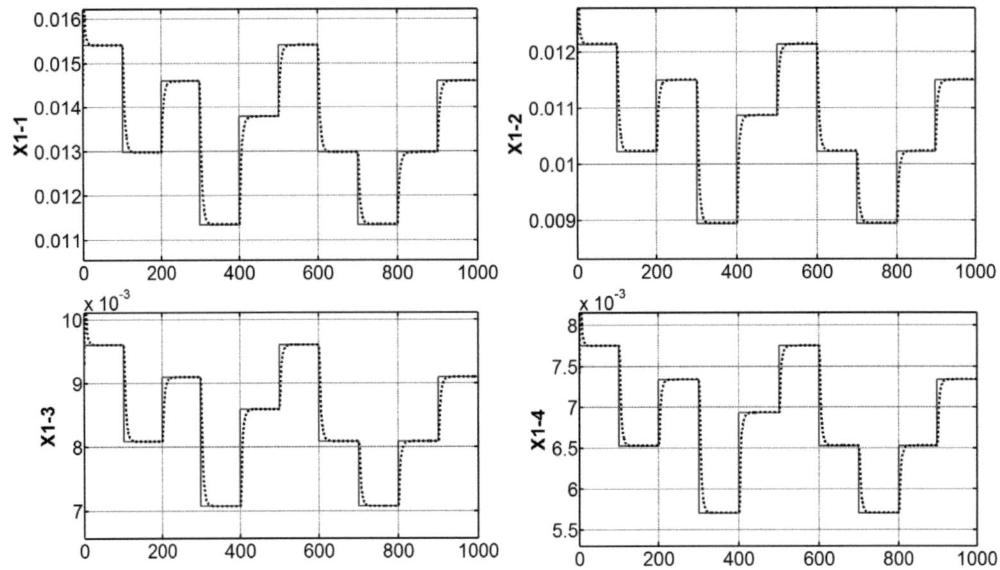

Fig. 14. Graphical simulation results of the I-term DANC of the plant output X_1 vs. system reference in 4 measurement points for the total time of L-M learning: a)z=0.2H, b) z=0.4H, c) z=0.6H, d)z=0.8H

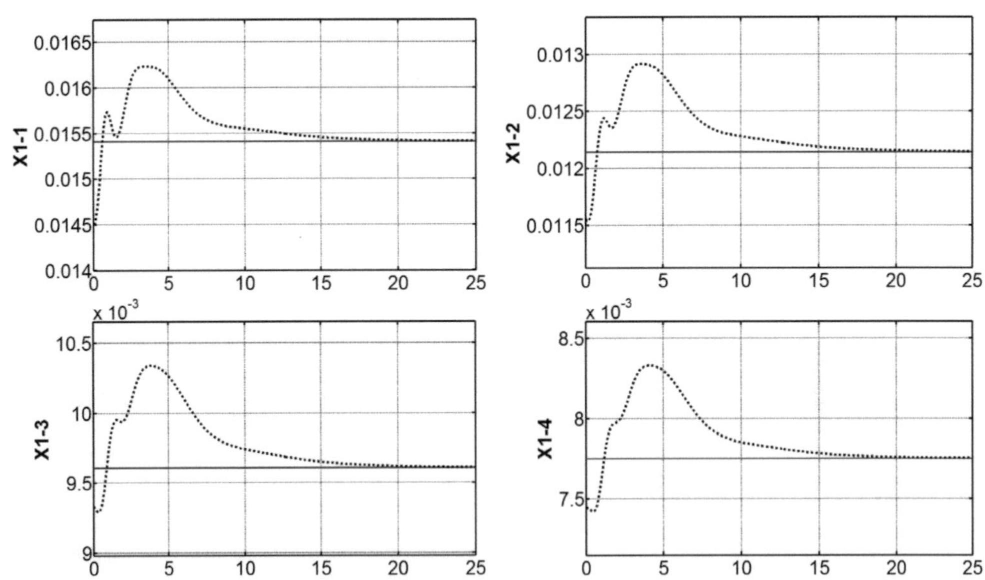

Fig. 15. Graphical simulation results of the I-term DANC of the output X_1 vs. system reference in four measurement points for the beginning of L-M learning: a) z=0.2H, b) z=0.4H, c) z=0.6H,d) z=0.8H

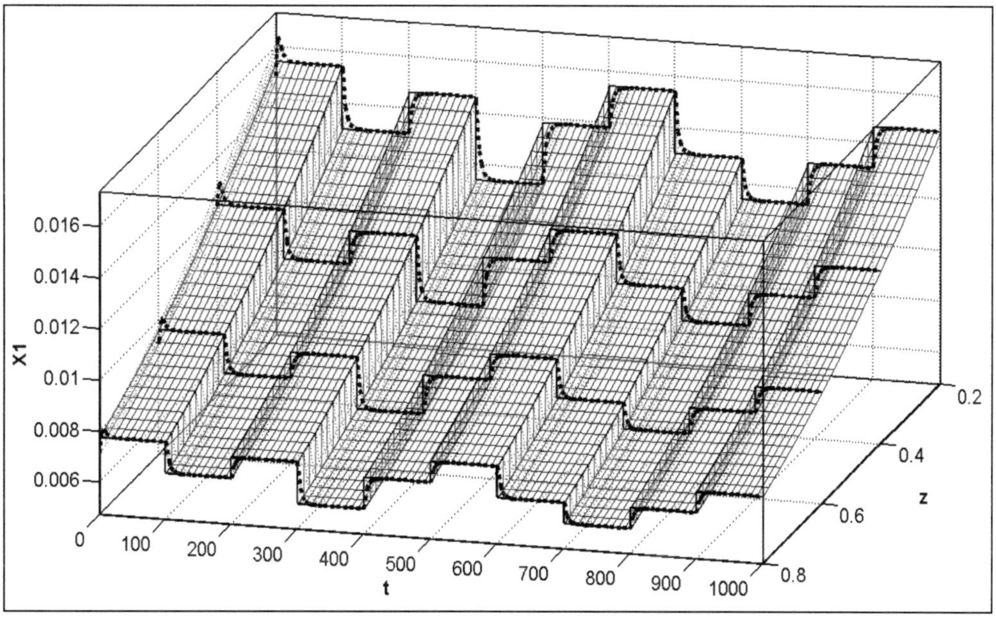

Fig. 16. Three dimensional plot of the I-term DANC of the plant output X_1 in four measurement points of L-M learning : z=0.2H, z=0.4H, z=0.6H, z=0.8H

7.3 Simulation results of the centralized indirect (SM) adaptive neural control with I-term using L-M learning

In this case the indirect adaptive I-term control is a sum of the I-term control signal and the SM control, computed using the state and parameter information issued from the RTNN-1 neural identifier. The control signals are shown on Fig. 17. The X_1 control simulation results are given on Fig. 18-20. The simulation results of SMC are obtained on-line during 1000 days with a step of 0.1 day. The given on Fig. 18-20 graphical results of I-term SMC demonstrated smooth behavior. It could be seen also that the L-M learning converge fast and the I-term remove the constant noise Of, and the plant uncertainties.

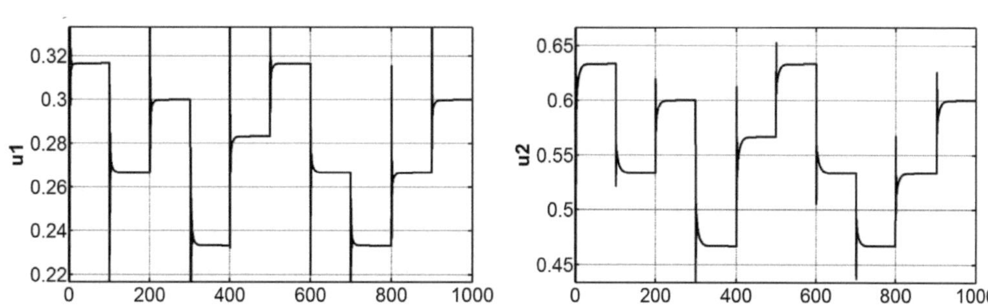

Fig. 17. Plant input control signals generated by the I-term centralized indirect SMC: a) Sin1, and b) Sin2

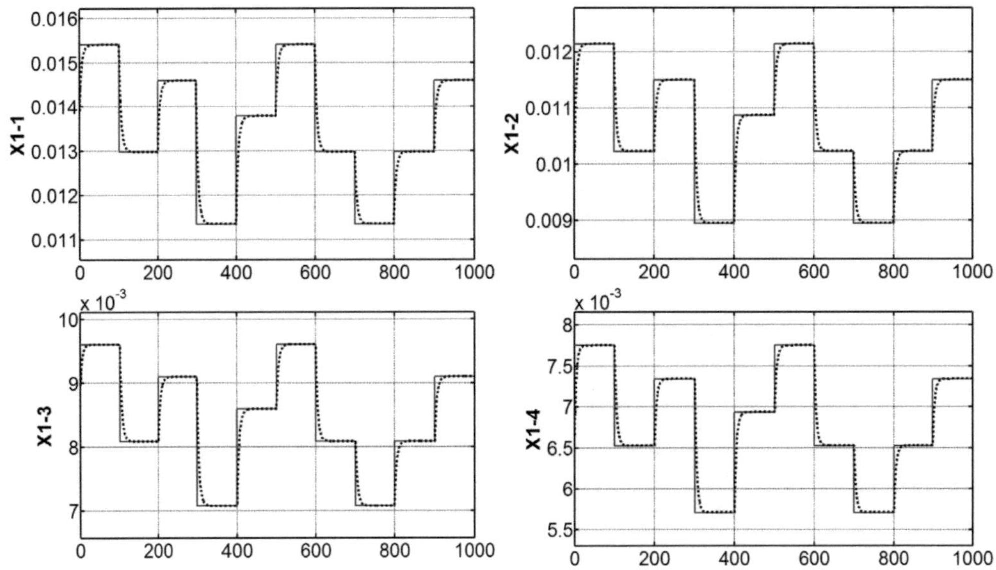

Fig. 18. Graphical simulation results of the I-term indirect SM control of the plant output X_1 vs. system reference in four measurement points for the total time of L-M learning: a) z=0.2H, b) z=0.4H, c) z=0.6H, d) z=0.8H

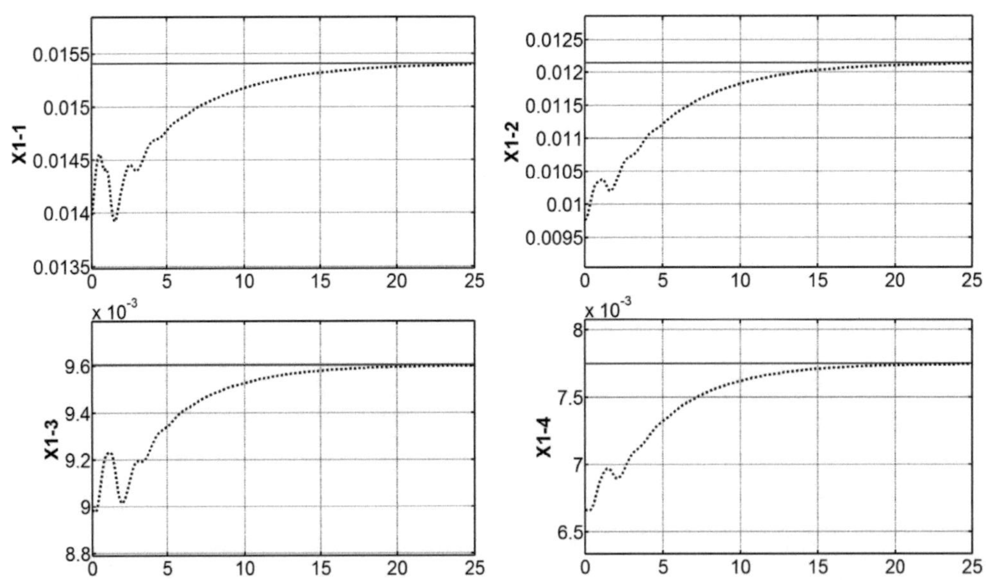

Fig. 19. Graphical simulation results of the I-term indirect SM control of the plant output X_1 vs. system reference in four measurement points for the beginning of L-M learning: a) z=0.2H, b) z=0.4H, c) z=0.6H, d) z=0.8H

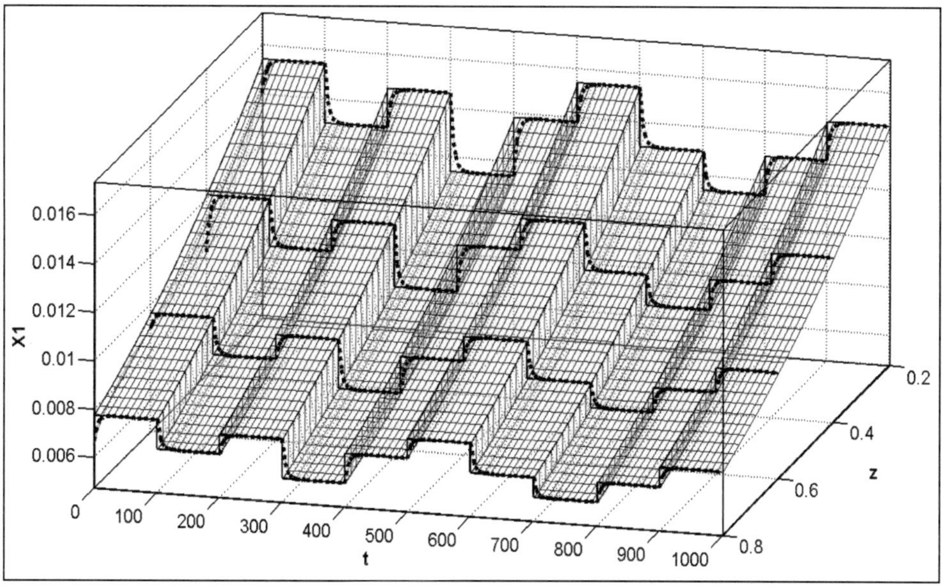

Fig. 20. Three dimensional plot of the I-term indirect SM control results of the plant output X_1 in four measurement points of L-M learning : z=0.2H, z=0.4H, z=0.6H, z=0.8H

The Fig. 21 illustrated the behavior of the SMC system without I-term perturbed by a constant noise Of, causing a big error of reference tracking.

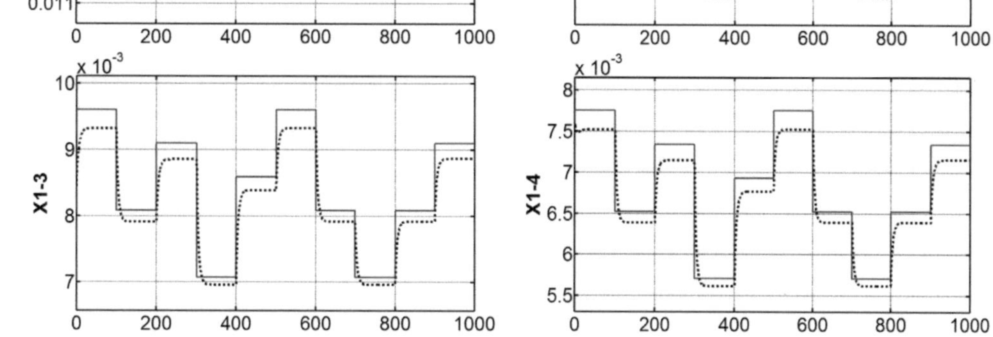

Fig. 21. Graphical simulation results of the indirect SM control without I-term of the plant output X_1 vs. system reference in four measurement points for the total time of L-M learning: a) z=0.2H, b) z=0.4H, c) z=0.6H, d) z=0.8H

The given on Fig. 18-20 graphical results of I-term SMC showed smooth exponential behavior, fast convergence and the removal of the constant noise terms. The Fig. 21 showed that the constant perturbation in the input of the plant caused a deviation of the plant output X_1 with respect of the set point R_1 and this occurred for all other plant output signals and measurement points. The final MSE for all point output variables are given in Table 5.

Collocation point	X_1	X_2	S_1/S_{1T}	S_2/S_{2T}
z=0.2	2.6969E-8	1.7122E-7	9.9526E-6	2.1347E-5
z=0.4	1.3226E-8	1.2511E-7	5.2323E-6	1.2903E-5
z=0.6	1.0873E-8	6.5339E-8	3.2234E-6	7.0511E-6
z=0.8	5.9589E-9	4.4750E-8	1.6759E-6	4.4548E-6
Recirculation tank			1.1842E-6	2.5147E-6

Table 5. MSE of the I-term indirect (SM) centralized control of the bioprocess plant variables in all measurement points

The final MSE given on Table 5 possessed small values (2.1345E-5 in the worse case).

7.4 Simulation results of the centralized I-term optimal control using neural identifier and L-M RTNN learning

The integral term extended the identified local linear plant model so it is part of the indirect optimal control algorithm. The generated by the optimal control plant input signals are given on Fig. 22. The Fig. 23-25 illustrated the X_1 I-term optimal control results. The MSE numerical results for all final process variable and measurement points control results, given on Table 6 possessed small values (1.4949E-5 in the worse case).

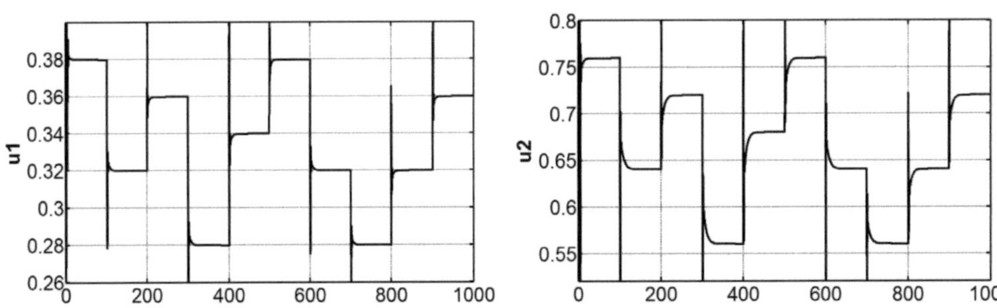

Fig. 22. Plant input control signals generated by the I-term centralized optimal control: a) Sin1, and b) Sin2

Collocation point	X_1	X_2	S_1/S_{1T}	S_2/S_{2T}
z=0.2	2.06772E-8	1.5262E-7	9.3626E-6	1.4949E-5
z=0.4	1.3819E-8	7.5575E-8	5.6917E-6	1.0197E-5
z=0.6	1.8115E-8	4.7505E-8	2.8872E-6	6.1763E-6
z=0.8	1.5273E-8	5.9744E-8	1.6295E-6	4.2868E-6
Recirculation tank			1.3042E-6	2.5136E-6

Table 6. MSE of the I-term opt. control of the bioprocess plant variables in all meas. points

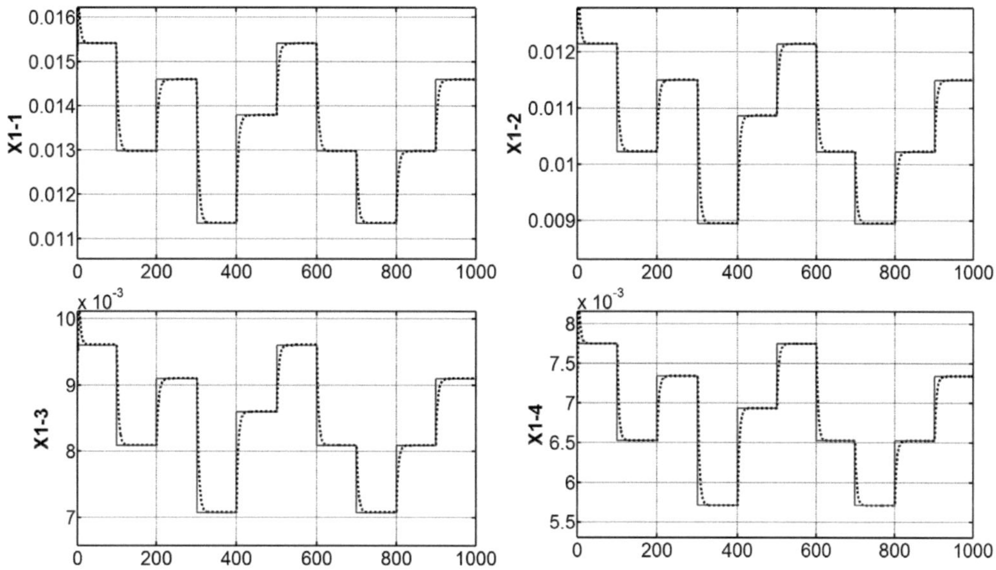

Fig. 23. Graphical simulation results of the I-term optimal control of the plant output X_1 vs. system reference in four measurement points for the total time of L-M learning: a) z=0.2H, b) z=0.4H, c) z=0.6H, d) z=0.8H

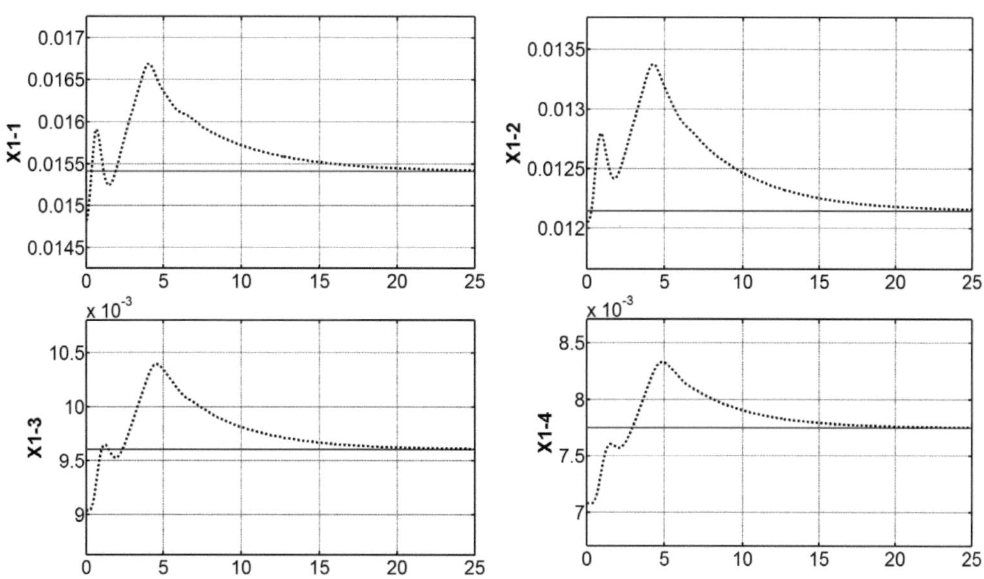

Fig. 24. Graphical simulation results of the I-term optimal control of the plant output X_1 vs. system reference in four measurement points for the beginning of L-M learning: a) z=0.2H, b) z=0.4H, c) z=0.6H, d) z=0.8H

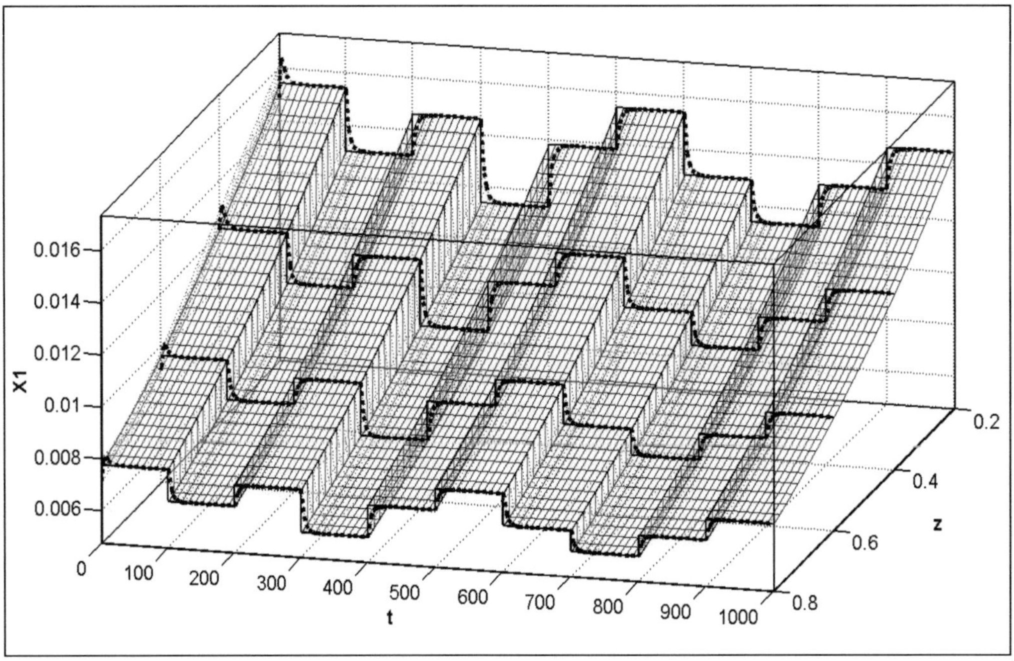

Fig. 25. Three dimensional plot of the I-term optimal control results of the plant output X_1 in four measurement points of L-M learning : z=0.2H, z=0.4H, z=0.6H, z=0.8H

The given on Fig. 23-25 graphical results of I-term optimal control showed smooth exponential behavior, fast convergence and the removal of the constant noise terms.

8. Conclusion

The paper proposed a new neural identification and control methodology for distributed parameter bioprocess plant. The simplification of the DPS given by PDEs is realized using the orthogonal collocation method in four collocation points, converting the PDE plant description in ODE one. The system is identified using RTNN model and BP and L-M learning, where a high precision of convergence is achieved (the final MSE% for both BP and L-M learning algorithms is of order of E-4 in the worse case). The comparative results showed a slight priority in precision and convergence of the L-M over the BP which could be seen in Figures 8, 11, and Tables 2, 3 (the worse case MSE for the L-M RTNN learning is 2.5476E-4 vs. BP RTNN learning which is 2.8282E-4). The obtained comparative simulation results of centralized adaptive direct, indirect SM and optimal control with I-term exhibited a good RTNN convergence and precise reference tracking. The MSE% of plant outputs tracking for the three considered methods of control is of order of E-5 in the worse case. The graphical simulation results showed that all control methods with I-term could compensate constant plant input noises and the I-term removal caused a system outputs deviation from the reference signals (see Fig. 21). The MSE study ordered the control methods used as: optimal, direct, and indirect, but the difference between them is little (see Tables 4.5.6 where worse case final MSE for DANC is 1.7568E-5; for SMC is 2.1347E-5; for the optimal control it is 1.4949E-5).

9. References

Aguilar-Garnica, F.; Alcaraz-Gonzalez, V. & Gonzalez-Alvarez, V. (2006). Interval observer design for an anaerobic digestion process described by a distributed parameter model, *Proceedings of the Second International Meeting on Environmental Biotechnology and Engineering: 2IMEBE*, pp. 1-16, ISBN 970-95106-0-6, Mexico City, Mexico, September 2006, CINVESTAV-IPN, Mexico

Baruch, I.S.; Flores, J.M.; Nava, F.; Ramirez, I.R. & Nenkova, B. (2002). An advanced neural network topology and learning, applied for identification and control of a D.C. motor. *Proceedings of the 1st Int. IEEE Symposium on Intelligent Systems*, Vol. 1, pp. 289-295, ISBN 0-7803-7601-3, Varna, Bulgaria, September 2002, IEEE Inc.,New York

Baruch, I.S.; Barrera-Cortes, J. & Hernandez, L.A. (2004). A fed-batch fermentation process identification and direct adaptive neural control with integral term. In: *MICAI 2004: Advances in Artificial Intelligence, LNAI 2972*, Monroy, R., Arroyo-Figueroa, G., Sucar, L.E., Sossa, H. (Eds.), page numbers (764-773), Springer-Verlag, ISBN 3-540-21459-3, Berlin Heidelberg New York

Baruch, I.S.; Georgieva P.; Barrera-Cortes, J. & Feyo de Azevedo, S. (2005a). Adaptive recurrent neural network control of biological wastewater treatment. *International Journal of Intelligent Systems, Special issue on Soft Computing for Modelling, Simulation and Control of Nonlinear Dynamical Systems, (O.Castillo, and P.Melin - guest editors)*, Vol. 20, No 2, (February 2005) page numbers (173-194), ISSN 0884-8173

Baruch, I.S & Garrido, R. (2005b). A direct adaptive neural control scheme with integral terms. *International Journal of Intelligent Systems, Special issue on Soft Computing for Modelling, Simulation and Control of Nonlinear Dynamical Systems, (O.Castillo, and P.Melin - guest editors)*, Vol. 20, No 2, (February 2005) page numbers (213-224), ISSN 0884-8173

Baruch, I.S.; Hernandez, L.A.; & Barrera-Cortes, J. (2007a). Recurrent neural identification and sliding mode adaptive control of an aerobic fermentation plant. *Cientifica, ESIME-IPN*, Vol. 11, No 2, (March-April 2007), page numbers (55-62), ISSN 1665-0654

Baruch, I.S.; Hernandez, L.A.; Mariaca-Gaspar, C.R. & Nenkova, B. (2007b). An adaptive sliding mode control with I-term using recurrent neural identifier. *Cybernetics and Information Technologies, BAS, Sofia, Bulgaria*, Vol. 7, No 1, (January 2007) page numbers 21-32, ISSN 1311-9702

Baruch, I. S., Mariaca-Gaspar, C.R., and Barrera-Cortes, J. (2008). Recurrent neural network identification and adaptive neural control of hydrocarbon biodegradation processes. In: *Recurrent Neural Networks*, Hu, Xiaolin, Balasubramaniam, P. (Eds.), Chapter 4, page numbers (61-88), I-Tech Education and Publishing KG, ISBN 978-953-7619-08-4, Vienna, Austria

Baruch, I.S. & Mariaca-Gaspar, C.R. (2009). A Levenberg-Marquardt learning algorithm applied for recurrent neural identification and control of a wastewater treatment bioprocess. *International Journal of Intelligent Systems*, Vol. 24, No 11, (November 2009) page numbers (1094-1114), ISSN 0884-8173

Baruch, I.S. & Mariaca-Gaspar, C.R. (2010). Recurrent neural identification and control of a continuous bioprocess via first and second order learning, *Journal of Automation, Mobile Robotics and Intelligent Systems*, Vol. 4, No 4, (December 2010) page numbers (37-52), ISSN 1897-8645 (print), ISSN 2080-2145 (on-line)

Bernard, O.; Hadj-Sadok, Z.; Dochain, D.; Genovesi, A. & Steyer, J.P. (2001). Dynamical model development and parameter identification for an anaerobic wastewater treatment process. *Biotechnology and Bioengineering*, Vol. 75, No 4, (June 2001) page numbers (424–438), ISNN 1097-0290

Bialecki, B. & Fairweather G. (2001), Orthogonal spline collocation methods for partial differential equations, *Journal of Computational and Applied Mathematics*, Vol. 128, No 1-2, (March 2001) page numbers (55-82), ISSN 0377-0427

Boskovic, J.D. & Narendra, K. S. (1995). Comparison of linear, nonlinear and neural-network-based adaptive controllers for a class of fed-batch fermentation processes. *Automatica*, Vol. 31, No 6, (June1995) page numbers (817-840), ISSN 0005-1098

Bulsari, A. & Palosaari, S. (1993). Application of neural networks for system identification of an adsorption column. *Neural Computing and Applications*, Vol. 1, No 2, (June 1993) page numbers (160-165), ISSN 0941-0643

Deng H. & Li H.X. (2003). Hybrid intelligence based modeling for nonlinear distributed parameter process with applications to the curing process. *IEEE Transactions on Systems, Man and Cybernetics*, Vol. 4, No. 4, (October 2003) page numbers (3506 - 3511), ISSN 1062-922X

Deng H., Li, H.X. & Chen G. (2005). Spectral-approximation-based intelligent modeling for distributed thermal processes. *IEEE Transactions on Control Systems Technology*, Vol. 13, No. 5, (September 2005) page numbers (686-700), ISSN 1063-6536

Gonzalez-Garcia, R; Rico-Martinez, R. & Kevrekidis, I. (1998). Identification of distributed parameter systems: a neural net based approach. *Computers and Chemical Engineering*, Vol. 22, No 1, (March 2003) page numbers (965-968), ISSN 0098-1354

Haykin, S. (1999). *Neural Networks, a Comprehensive Foundation*, Second Edition, Section 2.13, page numbers (84-89); Section 4.13, page numbers (208-213), Prentice-Hall, ISBN 0-13-273350-1, Upper Saddle River, New Jersey 07458

Padhi, R.; Balakrishnan, S. & Randolph, T. (2001). Adaptive critic based optimal neuro-control synthesis for distributed parameter systems, *Automatica*, Vol. 37, No 8, (August 2001) page numbers (1223-1234), ISSN 0005-1098

Padhi, R. & Balakrishnan, S. (2003). Proper orthogonal decomposition based optimal neuro-control synthesis of a chemical reactor process using approximate dynamic programming. *Neural Networks*, Vol. 16, No 5-6, (June 2003) page numbers (719 - 728), ISSN 0893-6080

Pietil, S. & Koivo, H.N. (1996). Centralized and decentralized neural network models for distributed parameter systems. *Proceedings of CESA'96 IMACS Multiconference on Computational Engineering in Systems Applications*, page numbers (1043-1048), ISBN 2-9502908-9-2, Lille, France, July 1996, Gerf EC Lille, Villeneuve d'Ascq, FRANCE

Ray, W.H. (1989). *Advanced Process Control*, page numbers (133-242), Butterworths Publ., ISBN 0-409-90231-4, Boston, London, Singapore, Sydney, Toronto, Wellington

Schoefs, O.; Dochain, D.; Fibrianto, H. & Steyer, J.P. (2004). Modelling and identification of a partial differential equation model for an anaerobic wastewater treatment process. *Proceedings of 10th World Congress on Anaerobic Digestion*, page numbers (343 - 347), ISBN 1-843-39550-9, Montreal, Canada

Wan, E. & Beaufays, F. (1996). Diagrammatic method for deriving and relating temporal neural networks algorithms. *Neural Computations*, Vol. 8, No.1, (January 1996) page numbers (182–201), ISSN 0899-7667

10

Optimization of Mapping Graphs of Parallel Programs onto Graphs of Distributed Computer Systems by Recurrent Neural Network

Mikhail S. Tarkov
A.V. Rzhanov's Institute of Semiconductor Physics
Siberian Branch, Russian Academy of Sciences
Russia

1. Introduction

A distributed computer system (CS) is a set of elementary computers (ECs) connected by a network that is program-controlled from these computers. Each EC includes a computing module (CM) (processor with a memory) and a system unit (message router). The message router operates under CM control and has input and output ports connected to the output and input ports of the neighboring ECs, correspondingly. The CS structure is described by the graph $G_s(V_s, E_s)$, where V_s is the set of ECs and $E_s = V_s \times V_s$ is the set of connections between the ECs.

The topology of a distributed system may undergo changes while the system is operating, due to failures or repairs of communication links, as well as due to addition or removal of ECs (Bertsekas, Tsitsiklis, 1989). The CS robustness means that failures and recoveries of the ECs bring only to increasing and decreasing time of a task execution. Control on resources and tasks in the robust distributed CS suggested solution of the following problems (Tarkov, 2003, 2005): the CS optimal decomposition to connected subsystems; mapping parallel program structures onto the subsystem structures; static and dynamic balancing computation load among CMs of the computer system (subsystem); static and dynamic message routing (implementation of paths for data transfer), i.e. balancing communication load in the CS network; distribution of program and data copies for organization of fault tolerant computations; subsystem reconfiguration and redistribution of computation and communication load for computation recovery from failures, and so on.

As a rule, all these problems are considered as combinatorial optimization problems (Korte & Vygen, 2006), solved by centralized implementation of some permutations on data structures distributed on elementary computers of the CS. The centralized approach to the problem solution suggests gathering data in some (central) EC, solving optimization problem in this EC with the following scattering results to all ECs of the system (subsystem). As a result we have sequential (and correspondingly slow) method for the problem solution with great overhead for gathering and scattering data. Now a decentralized approach is significantly developed for solution of problems of control resources and tasks in computer systems with distributed memory (Tel G., 1994), and in many cases this approach allows to parallelize the problem solution.

Massive parallelism of data processing in neural networks allows us to consider neural networks as a perspective, high-performance, and reliable tool for solution of complicated optimization problems (Melamed, 1994; Trafalis & Kasap, 1999; Smith, 1999; Haykin, 1999; Tarkov, 2006). The recurrent neural network (Hopfield & Tank, 1985; Wang, 1993; Siqueira, Steiner & Scheer, 2007, 2010; Serpen & Patwardhan, 2007; Serpen, 2008; da Silva, Amaral, Arruda & Flauzino, 2008; Malek, 2008) is a most interesting tool for solution of discrete optimization problems. A model of a globally converged recurrent Hopfield neural network is in good accordance with Dijkstra's self-stabilization paradigm (Dijkstra, 1974). This signifies that the mappings of parallel program graphs onto graphs of distributed computer systems, carried out by Hopfield networks, are self-stabilizing (Jagota, 1999). An importance of usage of the self-stabilizing mappings is caused by a possibility of breaking the CS graph regularity by failures of ECs and intercomputer connections.

For distributed CSs, the graph of a parallel program $G_p(V_p,E_p)$ is usually determined as a set V_p of the program branches (virtual elementary computers) interacting with each other by the point−to−point principle through transferring messages via logical (virtual) channels (which may be unidirectional or bidirectional) of the set $E_p = V_p \times V_p$. Interactions between the processing modules are ordered in time and regular in space for most parallel applications (line, ring, mesh, etc.) (Fig. 1).

For this reason, the maximum efficiency of information interactions in advanced high-performance CSs is obtained by using regular graphs $G_s(V_s,E_s)$ of connections between individual computers (hypercube, torus) (Parhami, 2002; Yu, Chung & Moreira, 2006; Balaji, Gupta, Vishnu & Beckman, 2011). The hypercube structure is described by a graph known as a m-dimensional Boolean cube with a number of nodes $n = 2^m$. Toroidal structures are m-dimensional Euclidean meshes with closed boundaries. For m = 2, we obtain a two-dimensional torus (2D-torus) (Fig. 2); for m = 3, we obtain a 3D-torus.

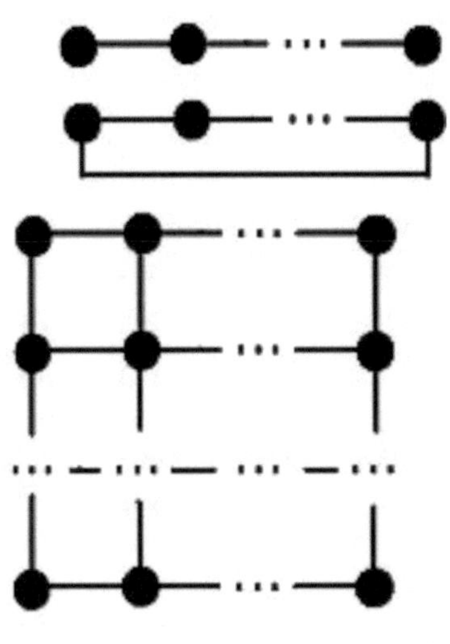

Fig. 1. Typical graphs of parallel programs (line, ring and mesh)

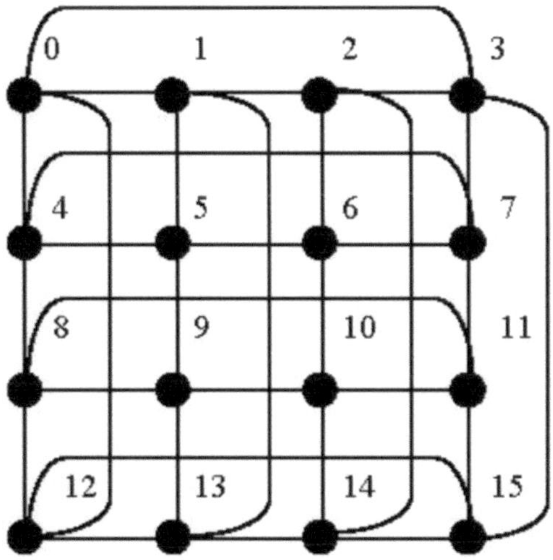

Fig. 2. Example of a 2D-torus

In this paper, we consider a problem for mapping graph $G_p(V_p,E_p)$ of a parallel program onto graph $G_s(V_s,E_s)$ of a distributed CS, where $n=|V_p|=|V_s|$ is a number of program branches (of ECs). The mapping objective is to map nodes of the program graph G_p onto nodes of the system graph G_s one-to-one to carry out mapping G_p edges onto edges of G_s (to establish an isomorphism between the program graph G_p and a spanning subgraph of the system graph G_s).

In section 2, we consider a recurrent neural network as a universal technique for solution of mapping problems. It is a local optimization technique, and we propose additional modifications (for example, penalty coefficients and splitting) to improve the technique scalability.

In section 3, we propose an algorithm based on the recurrent neural network and WTA ("Winner takes all") approach for the construction of Hamiltonian cycles in graphs. This algorithm maps only line- and ring-structured parallel programs. So, it is less universal than the technique proposed in section 2 but more powerful because it implements a global optimization approach, and hence it is very more scalable than the traditional recurrent neural networks.

2. Mapping graphs of parallel programs onto graphs of distributed computer systems by recurrent neural networks

Let us consider a matrix v of neurons with size $n \times n$, each row of the matrix corresponds to some branch of a parallel program and every column of the matrix corresponds to some EC. Each row and every column of the matrix v must contain only one nonzero entry equal to one, other entries must be equal to zero. Let the distance between the neighboring nodes of the CS graph is taken as a unit distance and d_{ij} is the length of the shortest path between nodes i and j in the CS graph. Then we define the energy of the corresponding Hopfield neural network by the Lyapunov function

$$L = C \cdot L_c + D \cdot L_d,$$
$$L_c = \frac{1}{2}\left[\sum_x \left(\sum_j v_{xj} - 1\right)^2 + \sum_i \left(\sum_y v_{yi} - 1\right)^2\right], \tag{1}$$
$$L_d = \frac{1}{2}\sum_x \sum_i \sum_{y \in Nb_p(x)} \sum_{j \neq i} v_{xi} v_{yj} d_{ij}.$$

Here d_{ij} is the distance between nodes i and j of the system graph corresponding to adjacent nodes of the program graph (a "dilation" of the edge of the program graph on the system graph), $Nb_p(x)$ is a neighborhood of the node x on the program graph.

The value v_{xi} is a state of the neuron in the row x and column i of the matrix v, C and D are parameters of the Lyapunov function. L_c is minimal when each row and every column of v contains only one unity entry (all other entries are zero). Such matrix v is a correct solution of the mapping problem (Fig. 3).

$$\begin{bmatrix} 1 & 0 & 0 & 0 & 0 & 0 & 0 & 0 & 0 \\ 0 & 1 & 0 & 0 & 0 & 0 & 0 & 0 & 0 \\ 0 & 0 & 1 & 0 & 0 & 0 & 0 & 0 & 0 \\ 0 & 0 & 0 & 0 & 0 & 0 & 0 & 0 & 1 \\ 0 & 0 & 0 & 0 & 0 & 0 & 0 & 1 & 0 \\ 0 & 0 & 0 & 0 & 0 & 0 & 1 & 0 & 0 \\ 0 & 0 & 0 & 1 & 0 & 0 & 0 & 0 & 0 \\ 0 & 0 & 0 & 0 & 1 & 0 & 0 & 0 & 0 \\ 0 & 0 & 0 & 0 & 0 & 1 & 0 & 0 & 0 \end{bmatrix}$$

Fig. 3. Example of correct matrix of neuron states

The minimum of L_d provides minimum of the sum of distances between adjacent G_p nodes mapped onto nodes of the system graph G_s (Fig. 4).

The Hopfield network minimizing the function (1) is described by the equation

$$\frac{\partial u_{xi}}{\partial t} = -\frac{\partial L}{\partial v_{xi}} \tag{2}$$

where u_{xi} is an activation of the neuron with indices x, i $(x, i = 1, \ldots, n)$,

$$v_{xi} = \frac{1}{1 + \exp(-\beta u_{xi})}$$

is the neuron state (output signal), β is the activation parameter.

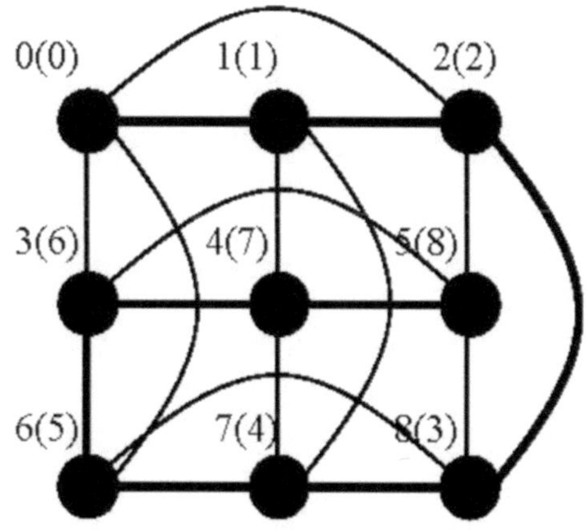

Fig. 4. Example of optimal mapping of "line"-graph onto torus (the mapping is distinguished by bold lines; the line-graph's node numbers are shown in brackets)

From (1) and (2) we have

$$\frac{\partial u_{xi}}{\partial t} = -C\left(\sum_j v_{xj} + \sum_y v_{yi} - 2\right) - D \sum_{y \in Nb_p(x)} \sum_{j \neq i} v_{yj} d_{ij}. \quad (3)$$

A difference approximation of Equation (3) yields

$$u_{xi}^{t+1} = u_{xi}^{t} - \Delta t \cdot \left[C\left(\sum_j v_{xj} + \sum_y v_{yi} - 2\right) + D \sum_{y \in Nb_p(x)} \sum_{j \neq i} v_{yj} d_{ij} \right], \quad (4)$$

where Δt is a temporal step. Initial values u_{xi}^{0} $(x, i = 1, \ldots, n)$ are stated randomly.

A choice of parameters $\beta, \Delta t, C, D$ determines a quality of the solution v of Equation (4). In accordance with (Feng & Douligeris, 2001) for the problem (1)-(4) a necessary condition of convergence is

$$C > D \frac{f_{\min}}{2(1-\alpha)}, \quad (5)$$

where $f_{\min} = \min\left\{ \sum_{y \in Nb_p(x)} \sum_{j \neq i} v_{yj} d_{ij} \right\}$, $\alpha \in [0,1)$ and α being a value close to 1. For a parallel program graph of a line type $f_{\min} = 1$. For example, taking $\alpha = 0.995$ for the line we have

$$C > 100 \cdot D.$$

From (4) and (5) it follows that the parameters Δt and D are equally influenced on the solution of the equation (4). Therefore we state $\Delta t = 1$ and have the equation

$$u_{xi}^{t+1} = u_{xi}^{t} - C \cdot \left(\sum_j v_{xj} + \sum_y v_{yi} - 2 \right) - D \cdot \sum_{y \in Nb_p(x)} \sum_{j \neq i} v_{yj} d_{ij}. \tag{6}$$

Let $\beta = 0.1$ (this value was stated experimentally). We will try to choose the value D to provide the absence of incorrect solutions.

2.1 Mapping by the Hopfield network

Let us evaluate the mapping quality by a number of coincidences of the program edges with edges of the system graph. We call this number a mapping rank. The mapping rank is an approximate evaluation of the mapping quality because the mappings with different dilations of the edges of the program graph may have the same mapping rank. Nevertheless, the maximum rank value, which equals to the number $|E_p|$ of edges of the program graph, corresponds to optimal mapping, i.e. to a global minimum of L_d in (1). Our objective is to determine the mapping algorithm parameters providing maximum probability of the optimal mapping.

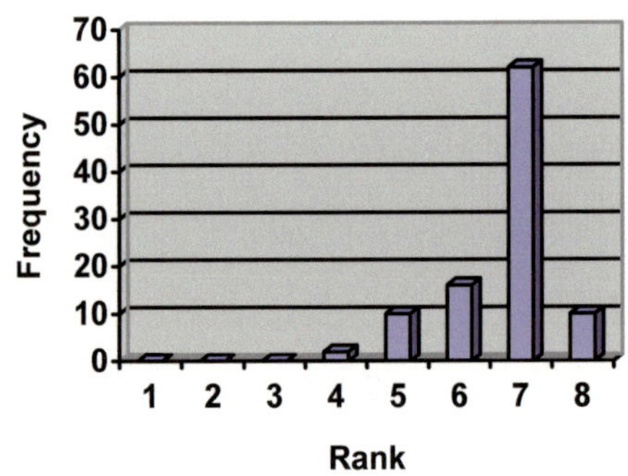

a) $n = 9$

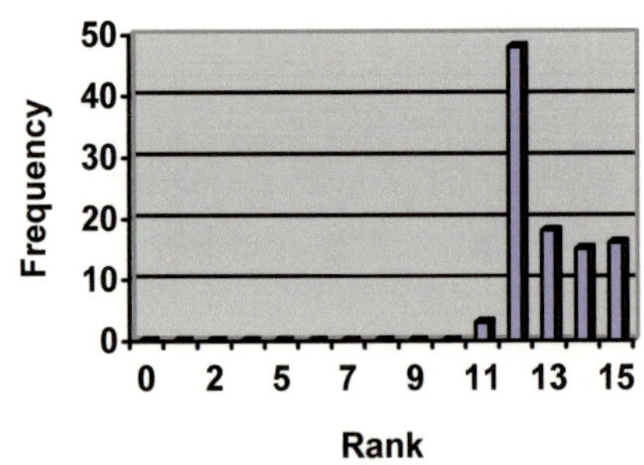

b) $n = 16$

Fig. 5. Histograms of mappings for the neural network (6)

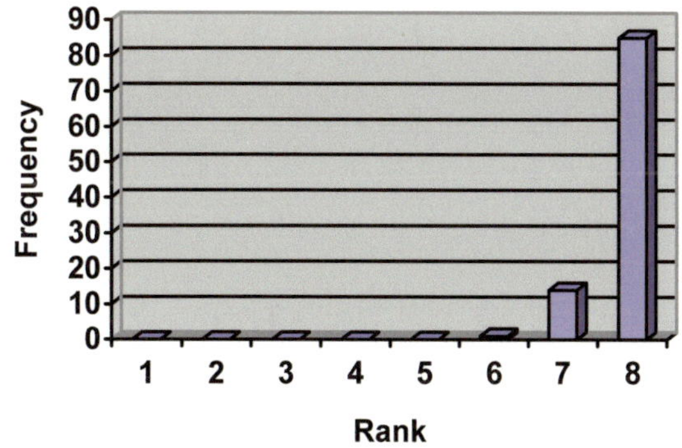

a) $n = 9$

b) $n = 16$

Fig. 6. Histograms of mappings for the neural network (8)

As an example for investigation of the mapping algorithm we consider the mapping of a line-type program graph onto a 2D-torus. Maximal value of the mapping rank for a line with n nodes is obviously equal to n-1.

For experimental investigation of the mapping quality, the histograms of the mapping rank frequencies are used for a number of experiments equals to 100. The experiments for mapping the line onto the 2D-torus with the number of nodes $n = l^2, l = 3,4,$ where l is the cyclic subgroup order, are carried out.

For $D \geq 8$ the correct solutions are obtained for $n = 9$ and $n = 16$, but as follows from Fig. 5a and Fig. 5b for $D = 8$, the number of solutions with optimal mapping, corresponding to the maximal mapping rank, is small.

To increase the frequency of optimal solutions of Equation (6) we replace the distance values d_{ij} by the values

$$c_{ij} = \begin{cases} d_{ij} & d_{ij} = 1 \\ p \cdot d_{ij} & d_{ij} > 1 \end{cases} \tag{7}$$

where p is a penalty coefficient for the distance d_{ij} exceeding the value 1, i.e. for non-coincidence of the edge of the program graph with the edge of the system graph. So, we obtain the equation

$$u_{xi}^{t+1} = u_{xi}^{t} - C \cdot \left(\sum_j v_{xj} + \sum_y v_{yi} - 2 \right) - D \cdot \sum_{y \in Nb_p(x)} \sum_{j \neq i} v_{yj} c_{ij}. \tag{8}$$

For the above mappings with $p = n$ we obtain the histograms shown on Fig. 6a and Fig. 6b. These histograms indicate the improvement of the mapping quality but for $n = 16$ the suboptimal solutions with the rank 13 have maximal frequency.

2.2 Splitting method

To decrease a number of local extremums of Function (1), we partition the set $\{1,2,...,n\}$ of subscripts x and i of the variables v_{xi} to K sets

$$I_k = \{(k-1)q, (k-1)q+1, ..., k \cdot q\}, \; q = n / K, \; k = 1,2,...,K,$$

and map the subscripts $x \in I_k$ only to the subscripts $i \in I_k$, i.e. we reduce the solution matrix v to a block-diagonal form (Fig. 7) and the Hopfield network is described by the equation

$$\begin{aligned} u_{xi}^{t+1} &= u_{xi}^{t} - C \cdot \left(\sum_{j \in I_k} v_{xj} + \sum_{y \in I_k} v_{yi} - 2 \right) - D \cdot \sum_{y \in Nb_p(x)} \sum_{j \neq i} v_{yj} c_{ij}, \\ v_{xi} &= \frac{1}{1 + \exp(-\beta u_{xi})}, \quad x, i \in I_k, k = 1,2,...,K. \end{aligned} \tag{9}$$

In this case $v_{xi} = 0$ for $x \in I_k, i \notin I_k, k = 1,2,...,n.$

$$\begin{bmatrix} v_{00} & v_{01} & v_{02} & 0 & 0 & 0 \\ v_{10} & v_{11} & v_{12} & 0 & 0 & 0 \\ v_{20} & v_{21} & v_{22} & 0 & 0 & 0 \\ 0 & 0 & 0 & v_{33} & v_{34} & v_{35} \\ 0 & 0 & 0 & v_{43} & v_{44} & v_{45} \\ 0 & 0 & 0 & v_{53} & v_{54} & v_{55} \end{bmatrix}$$

Fig. 7. Example of block-diagonal solution matrix for $K = 2$

In this approach which we call a splitting, for mapping line with the number of nodes $n = 16$ onto 2D-torus, we have for $K = 2$ the histogram presented on Fig. 8a.

From Fig. 6b and Fig. 8a we see that the splitting method essentially increases the frequency of optimal mappings. The increase of the parameter D up to the value $D = 32$ results in additional increase of the frequency of optimal mappings (Fig. 8b).

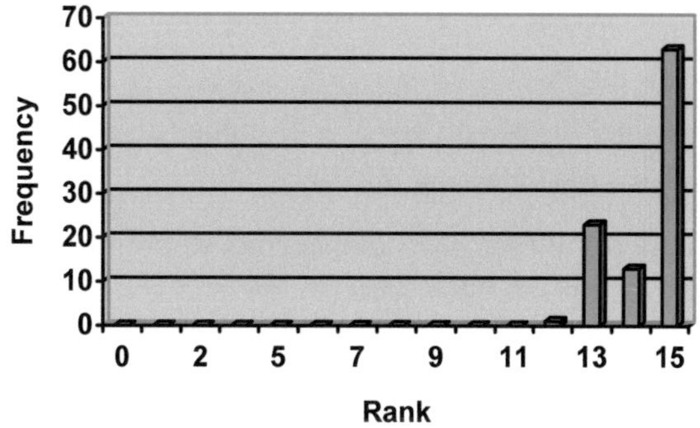

a) $n = 16$, $K = 2$, $D = 8$.

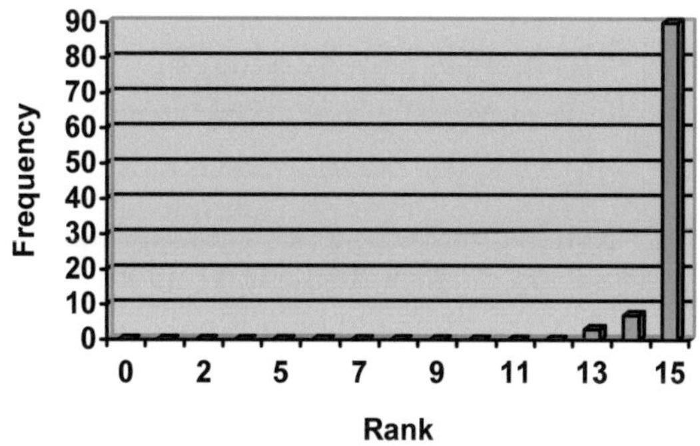

b) $n = 16$, $K = 2$, $D = 32$.

Fig. 8. Histograms of mappings for the neural network (9)

2.3 Mapping by the Wang network

In a recurrent Wang neural network (Wang, 1993; Hung & Wang, 2003) L_d in Expression (1) is multiplied by the value $\exp(-t/\tau)$ where τ is a parameter. For the Wang network Equation (9) is reduced to

$$u_{xi}^{t+1} = u_{xi}^{t} - C \cdot \left(\sum_{j \in I_k} v_{xj} + \sum_{y \in I_k} v_{yi} - 2 \right) - D \cdot \sum_{y \in Nb_p(x)} \sum_{j \neq i} v_{yj} c_{ij} \exp(-t/\tau),$$
$$v_{xi} = \frac{1}{1 + \exp(-\beta u_{xi})}, \quad x, i \in I_k, k = 1, 2, ..., K. \tag{10}$$

We note that in experiments we frequently have incorrect solutions if for a given maximal number of iterations $t_{\max}$ (for example, $t_{\max} = 10000$) the condition of convergence $\sum_{x,i} \left| u_{xi}^{t} - u_{xi}^{t-1} \right| < \varepsilon$, $\varepsilon = 0.01$ is not satisfied. The introduction of factor $\exp\left(-t/\tau\right)$ accelerates the convergence of the recurrent neural network and the number of incorrect solutions is reduced.

So, for the three-dimensional torus with $n = 3^3 = 27$ nodes and $p = n, K = 3, D = 4096, \beta = 0.1$ in 100 experiments we have the following results:

1. On the Hopfield network (9) we have 23 incorrect solutions, 43 solutions with Rank 25 and 34 optimal solutions (with Rank 26) (Fig. 9).
2. On the Wang network (10) with the same parameters and $\tau = 500$ we have all (100) correct solutions, where 27 solutions have Rank 25 and 73 solutions are optimal (with Rank 26) (Fig. 10).

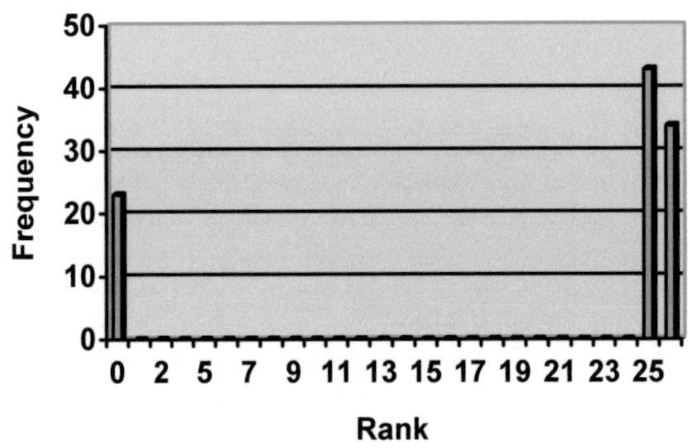

Fig. 9. Histogram of mappings for the Hopfield network ($n = 3^3 = 27$)

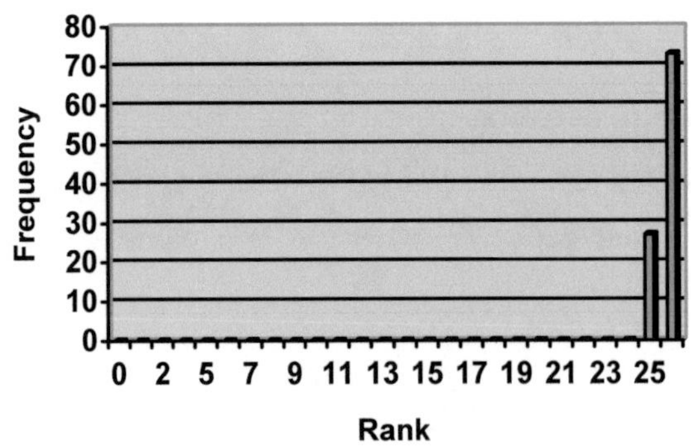

Fig. 10. Histogram of mappings for the Wang network ($n = 3^3 = 27$)

As a result we have high frequency of optimal solutions (for 100 experiments):

1. more than 80% for the two-dimensional tori ($n = 3^2 = 9$ and $n = 4^2 = 16$);
2. more than 70% for three-dimensional torus $(n = 3^3 = 27)$.

Further investigations must be directed to increasing the probability of getting optimal solutions of the mapping problem when the number of the parallel program nodes is increased.

3. Construction of Hamilton cycles in graphs of computer systems

In this section, we consider algorithms for nesting ring structures of parallel programs of distributed CSs, which are based on using recurrent neural networks, under the condition $n = |V_p| = |V_s|$. Such nesting reduces to constructing a Hamiltonian cycle in the CS graph and is based on solving the traveling salesman problem using the matrix of distances $d_{ij}\,(i,j = 1,...,n)$ between the CS graph nodes, with the distance between the neighboring nodes of the CS graph taken as a unit distance.

The traveling salesman problem can be formulated as an assignment problem (Wang, 1993; Siqueira, Steiner & Scheer, 2007, 2010)

$$\min \sum_{i=1}^{n} \sum_{j \neq i} c_{ij} x_{ij} \,, \tag{11}$$

under the constraints

$$\begin{gathered} x_{ij} \in \{0,1\}, \\ \sum_{i=1}^{n} x_{ij} = 1, j = 1,...,n, \\ \sum_{j=1}^{n} x_{ij} = 1, i = 1,...,n. \end{gathered} \tag{12}$$

Here, c_{ij}, $i \neq j$ is the cost of assignment of the element *i* to the position *j*, which corresponds to motion of the traveling salesman from the city *i* to the city *j*; x_{ij} is the decision variable: if the element *i* is assigned to the position *j*, then $x_{ij} = 1$, otherwise, $x_{ij} = 0$.

For solving problem (11) – (12), J. Wang proposed a recurrent neural network that is described by the differential equation

$$\frac{\partial u_{ij}(t)}{\partial t} = -C\left(\sum_{k=1}^{n} x_{ik}(t) + \sum_{l=1}^{n} x_{lj}(t) - 2 \right) - D \cdot c_{ij} \exp(-t/\tau) \,, \tag{13}$$

where $x_{ij} = g(u_{ij}(t))$, $g(u) = 1/[1 + \exp(-\beta u)]$. A difference approximation of Equation (13) yields

$$u_{ij}^{t+1} = u_{ij}^{t} - \Delta t \cdot \left[C\left(\sum_{k=1}^{n} x_{ik}(t) + \sum_{l=1}^{n} x_{lj}(t) - 2 \right) - D \cdot c_{ij} \exp\left(-\frac{t}{\tau} \right) \right], \tag{14}$$

Here $\beta, C, D, \tau, \Delta t$ are parameters of the neural network.

Siqueira et al. proposed a method of accelerating the solution of the system (14), which is based on the WTA ("Winner takes all") principle. The algorithm proposed below was developed on the basis of this method.

1. A matrix $\left\| x_{ij}(0) \right\|$ of random values $x_{ij}(0) \in [0,1]$ is generated. Iterations (14) are performed until the following inequality is satisfied for all $i, j = 1,...,n$:

$$\sum_{k=1}^{n} x_{ik}(t) + \sum_{l=1}^{n} x_{lj}(t) - 2 \le \delta ,$$

where δ is the specified accuracy of satisfying constraints (12).

2. Transformation of the resultant decision matrix $\left\| x_{ij} \right\|$ is performed:

2.1. $i = 1$.

2.2. The maximum element $x_{i,j_{\max}}$ is sought in the ith row of the matrix ($j_{\max}$ is the number of the column with the maximum element).

2.3. The transformation $x_{i,j_{\max}} = 1$ is performed. All the remaining elements of the ith row and of the column numbered $j_{\max}$ are set to zero. Then, there follows a transition to the row numbered $j_{\max}$. Steps 2.2 and 2.3 are repeated until the cycle returns to the first row, which means that the cycle construction is finalized.

3. If the cycle returns to the row 1 earlier than the value 1 is assigned to n elements of the matrix $\left\| x_{ij} \right\|$, this means that the length of the constructed cycle is smaller than n. In this case, steps 1 and 2 are repeated.

To ensure effective operation of the algorithm of Hamiltonian cycle construction, the following values of the parameters of system (14) were chosen experimentally (by the order of magnitude): $D = 1, C = 10, \tau \ge 1000, \beta = 0.1$. Significant deviations of these parameters from the above-indicated values deteriorate algorithm operation, namely:

1. Deviations of the parameter C from the indicated value (at a fixed value of D) deteriorate the solution quality (the cycle length increases).
2. A decrease in τ increases the number of non-Hamiltonian ring-shaped routes.
3. An increase in β deteriorates the solution quality. A decrease in β increases the number of iterations (14).

It follows from (Feng & Douligeris, 2001) that $\Delta t \le \Delta t_{\max}$, where $\Delta t_{\max} \le \dfrac{1}{\beta C} = \dfrac{1}{0.1 \cdot 10} = 1$.

The experiments show that it is not always possible to construct a Hamiltonian cycle at $\Delta t = 1$, but cycle construction is successfully finalized if the step Δt is reduced. We reduced the step Δt as $\Delta t / 2$ if a correct cycle could not be constructed after ten attempts.

The parameters $c_{ij}, i \neq j$, are calculated by the formula (7) where d_{ij} is the distance between the nodes i and j of the graph, and $p > 1$ is the penalty coefficient applied if the distance d_{ij} exceeds 1. The penalty coefficient was introduced to ensure coincidence of transition in the travelling agent cycle with the edges of the CS graph.

We studied the use of iterative methods (Jacobi, Gauss–Seidel, and successive overrelaxation (SOR) methods (Ortega, 1988)) in solving Wang's system of equations. With the notation

$$r_{ij}^t = -C\left(\sum_{k=1}^{n} x_{ik}^t + \sum_{l=1}^{n} x_{lj}^t - 2\right) - Dc_{ij}\exp(-t/\tau)$$

the Jacobi method (method of simple iterations) of solving system (14) has the form

1. $u_{ij}^{t+1} = u_{ij}^t + \Delta t \cdot r_{ij}^t, i,j = 1,...,n;$

2. $x_{ij}^{t+1} = g\left(u_{ij}^{t+1}\right), g\left(u_{ij}^{t+1}\right) = \dfrac{1}{1+\exp\left(-\beta u_{ij}^{t+1}\right)}, i,j = 1,...,n.$

According to this method, new values of x_{ij}^{t+1}, $i,j = 1,...,n$, are calculated only after all values u_{ij}^{t+1}, $i,j = 1,...,n$, are found. In contrast to the method of simple iterations, the new value of x_{ij}^{t+1} in the Gauss–Seidel method is calculated immediately after finding the corresponding value of u_{ij}^{t+1}:

$$u_{ij}^{t+1} = u_{ij}^t + \Delta t \cdot r_{ij}^t, \; x_{ij}^{t+1} = g\left(u_{ij}^{t+1}\right), \; i,j = 1,...,n.$$

In the SOR method, the calculations are performed by the formulas

$$u_{new} = u_{ij}^t + \Delta t \cdot r_{ij}^t,$$
$$u_{ij}^{t+1} = \omega \cdot u_{new} + (1-\omega) \cdot u_{ij}^t, \; \omega \in (0,2),$$
$$x_{ij}^{t+1} = g\left(u_{ij}^{t+1}\right), \; i,j = 1,...,n.$$

With $\omega = 1$, the SOR method turns to the Gauss–Seidel method.

Experiments on 2D-tori with the group of automorphisms $E_2 = C_m \otimes C_m$, $n = m^2$ show that the Jacobi method can only be used for tori with a small number of nodes ($m \in \{3, 4\}$).

The SOR method can be used for tori with $m \in \{3, 4, 6\}$ with appropriate selection of the parameter $\omega < 1$. For $m \geq 8$, it is reasonable to use the Gauss–Seidel method ($\omega = 1$). Figure 11 shows an example of a Hamiltonian cycle constructed by a neural network in a 2D-mesh with $n = 16$ (the cycle is indicated by the bold line).

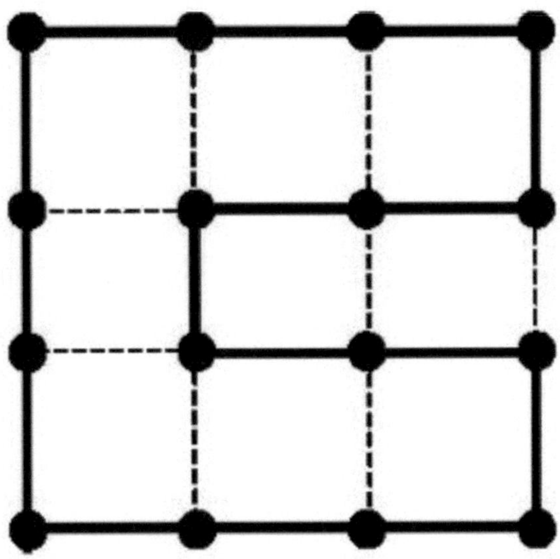

Fig. 11. Example of a Hamiltonian cycle in a 2D-mesh

In our experiments, we obtained Hamiltonian cycles (with the cycle length $L = n$) in 2D-meshes and 2D-tori for a number of experiments equals to 100 with up to $n = 1024$ nodes for $m = 2k$ and suboptimal cycle lengths $L = n + 1$ at $m = 2k + 1$, $k = 2, 3, \ldots, 16$. The penalty coefficients p and the values of Δt with which the Hamiltonian cycles were constructed for $n = 16$, 64, 256, and 1024, and also the times of algorithm execution on Pentium (R) Dual-Core CPU E 52 000, 2.5 GHz (the time equal to zero means that standard procedures did not allow registering small times shorter than 0.015 s) are listed in Tables 1 and 2.

n	$16 = 4^2$	$64 = 8^2$	$256 = 16^2$	$1024 = 32^2$
Δt	1	1	1	0,5
$p = n/2$	8	16	128	512
Time, s	0	0.015	0.75	73.36

Table 1. 2D-mesh

n	$16 = 4^2$	$64 = 8^2$	$256 = 16^2$	$1024 = 32^2$
Δt	1	1	1	0.5
$p = n$	16	64	256	1024
Time, s	0	0	4.36	73.14

Table 2. 2D-torus

In addition to the quantities listed in Tables 1 and 2, Tables 3 and 4 give the relative increase $\varepsilon = \frac{L-n}{n}$ in the travelling salesman cycle length, as compared with the Hamiltonian cycle length, for a 3D-torus and hypercube.

n	$64 = 4^3$	$216 = 6^3$	$512 = 8^3$	$1000 = 10^3$
Δt	0.012	0.1	0.1	0.1
p	64	32	32	32
L	64	218	520	1010
ε	0	0.01	0.016	0.01
Time, s	0.625	0.313	12.36	97.81

Table 3. 3D-torus

n	16	64	256	1024
Δt	0.1	0.1	0.1	0,1
p	32	32	32	32
L	16	64	262	1034
ε	0	0	0.016	0.023
Time, s	0	0.062	99.34	1147

Table 4. Hypercube

It follows from Tables 3 and 4 that:

1. In 3D-tori, the Hamiltonian cycle was constructed for n = 64. With n = 216, 512, and 1000, suboptimal cycles were constructed, which were longer than the Hamiltonian cycles by no more than 1.6%.
2. In hypercubes, the Hamiltonian cycles were constructed for n = 16 and 64 (it should be noted that the hypercube is isomorphous to the 2D-torus with n = 16). For n = 256 and n = 1024, suboptimal cycles were constructed, which were longer than n by no more than 2.3%.

3.1 Construction of Hamiltonian cycles in toroidal graphs with edge defects

The capability of recurrent neural networks to converge to stable states can be used for mapping program graphs to CS graphs with violations of regularity caused by deletion of edges and/or nodes. Such violations of regularity are called defects. In this work, we study the construction of Hamiltonian cycles in toroidal graphs with edge defects. Experiments in 2D-tori with a deleted edge and with n = 9 to n = 256 nodes for $p = n$ were conducted. The experiments show that the construction of Hamiltonian cycles in these graphs by the above-described algorithm is possible, but the value of the step Δt at which the cycle can be constructed depends on the choice of the deleted edge. The method of automatic selection of the step Δt is described at the beginning of Section 3. Table 5 illustrates the dependence of the step Δt on the choice of the deleted edge in constructing an optimal Hamiltonian cycle by the SOR method in a 2D-torus with n = 16 nodes for $\omega = 0.125$.

Examples of Hamiltonian cycles constructed by the SOR method in a 2D-torus with n = 16 nodes are given in Figs. 12a and 12b. Figure 12a shows the cycle constructed in the torus without edge defects for $\omega = 0.5$ and $\Delta t = 0.25$. Figure 12b shows the cycle constructed in the torus with a deleted edge (0, 12) for $\omega = 0.125$ and $\Delta t = 0.008$.

Edge	Δt	Edge	Δt
(0,12)	0,008	(5,9)	0,5
(0,3)	1,0	(6,7)	0,063
(0,1)	1,0	(6,10)	1,0
(0,4)	1,0	(7,11)	1,0
(1,13)	1,0	(8,11)	1,0
(1,2)	0,25	(8,9)	1,0
(1,5)	1,0	(8,12)	1,0
(2,14)	0,125	(9,10)	0,125
(2,3)	0,125	(9,13)	1,0
(2,6)	1,0	(10,11)	1,0
(3,15)	1,0	(10,14)	1,0
(3,7)	0,25	(11,15)	1,0
(4,7)	0,25	(12,15)	1,0
(4,5)	1,0	(12,13)	0,5
(4,8)	1,0	(13,14)	0,5
(5,6)	1,0	(14,15)	1,0

Table 5. Dependence Δt of the step on the choice of the deleted edge

Results discussed in this section should be considered as preliminary and opening the research field studying the relation between the quality of nesting of graphs of parallel algorithms to graphs of computer systems whose regularity is violated by node and edge defects and the parameters of neural network algorithms implementing this nesting.

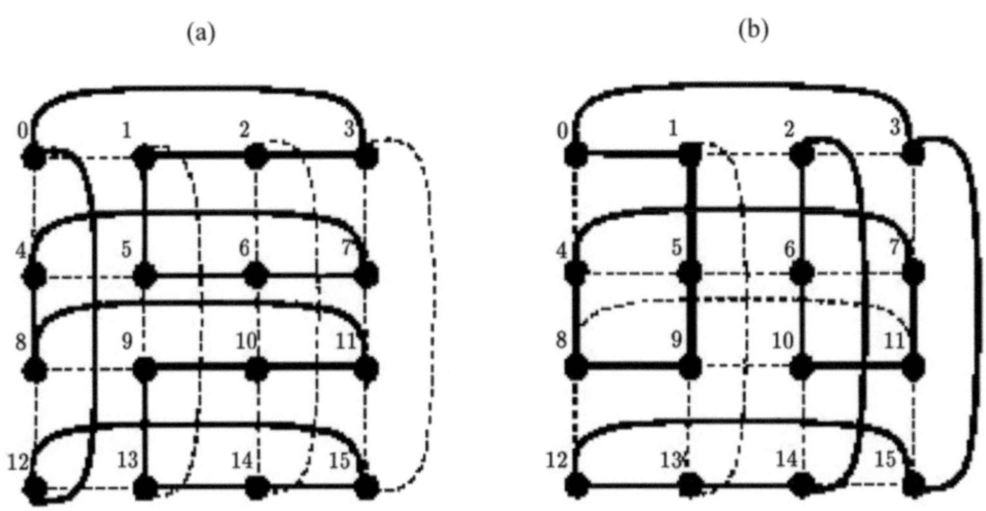

Fig. 12. Examples of Hamiltonian cycles in 2D-torus

3.2 Construction of Hamiltonian cycles by the splitting method

The time of execution of the above-described algorithm can be substantially reduced by using the following method:

1. Split the initial graph of the system into k connected subgraphs.
2. Construct a Hamiltonian cycle in each subgraph by the algorithm described above.
3. Unite the Hamiltonian cycles of the subgraphs into one Hamiltonian cycle.

For example, the initial graph of the system can be split into connected subgraphs by the algorithms proposed in (Tarkov, 2005).

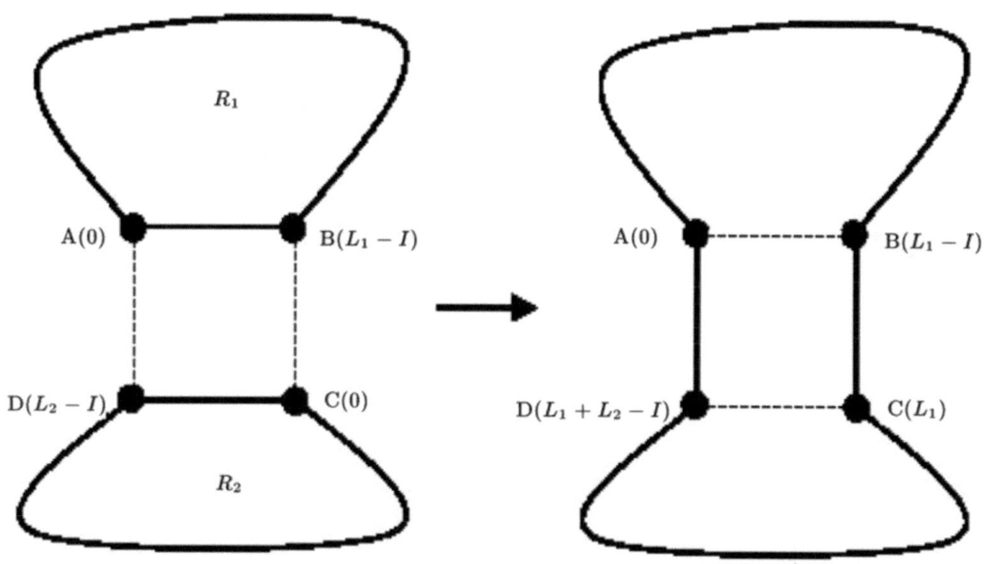

Fig. 13. Unification of cycles

For unification of two cycles R_1 and R_2, it is sufficient if the graph of the system has a cycle ABCD of length 4 such that the edge AB belongs to the cycle R_1 and the edge CD belongs to the cycle R_2 (Fig. 13).

The cycles R_1 and R_2 can be united into one cycle by using the following algorithm:

1. Find the cycle ABCD possessing the above-noted property.
2. Eliminate the edge AB from the cycle and successively numerate the nodes of the cycle R_1 in such a way that to assign number 0 to the node A and assign number $L_1 - 1$, where L_1 is the length of the cycle R_1, to the edge B. Include the edge BC into the cycle.
3. Eliminate the edge CD and successively numerate the nodes of the cycle R_2 so that the node C is assigned the number $L1$, and the node D is assigned the number $L_1 + L_2 - 1$, where L_2 is the length of the cycle R_2. Include the edge DA into the cycle. The unified cycle of length $L_1 + L_2$ is constructed.

The cycles R_1 and R_2, and also the resulting cycle are marked by bold lines in Fig. 12. The edges that are not included into the above-mentioned cycles are marked by dotted lines.

For comparison, Table 6 gives times (in seconds) of constructing Hamiltonian cycles in a 2D-mesh by the initial algorithm (t_1) and by the algorithm with splitting of cycle construction (t_2) with the number of subgraphs k = 2. The times are measured for p = n. The cycle construction time can be additionally reduced by parallel construction of cycles in subgraphs.

n	16	64	256	1024
t_1	0.02	0.23	9.62	595.8
t_2	0.01	0.03	2.5	156.19

Table 6. Comparison of cycle construction times in 2D-mesh

The proposed approach can be applied to constructing Hamiltonian cycles in arbitrary nonweighted nonoriented graphs without multiple edges and loops.

We can use the splitting method to construct Hamilton cycles in three-dimensional tori because the three-dimensional torus can be considered as a connected set of two-dimensional tori. So, the Hamilton cycle in three-dimensional torus can be constructed as follows:

1. Construct the Hamilton cycles in all of two-dimensional tori of the three-dimensional torus.
2. Unify the constructed cycles by the above unifying algorithm.

If the Hamilton cycles in all two-dimensional tori are optimal then the resulting Hamilton cycle in the three-dimensional torus is optimal too.

In the table 7 the times (in seconds) of construction of optimal Hamilton cycles in three-dimensional tori with $n = m \times m \times m$ nodes are presented: t_{seq} is the time of the sequential algorithm, t_{par} is the time of the parallel algorithm on processor Intel Pentium Dual-Core CPU E 52000, 2,5 GHz with usage of the parallel programming system OpenMP (Chapman, Jost & van der Pas, 2008), $S = t_{seq} / t_{par}$ is the speedup. The system of equations (14) was chosen for parallelization.

m	4	8	12	16	20	24	28	32
n	64	512	1728	4096	8000	13284	21952	32768
t_{seq}	0.125	0.062	0.906	6.265	31.22	133.11	390.61	2293.5
t_{par}	0.171	0.062	0.484	3.265	15.95	70.36	217.78	1397.6
S	0.73	1	1.87	1.92	1.96	1.89	1.79	1.64

Table 7. Construction of Hamiltonian Cycles in 3D-torus

So, the experiments show that the proposed algorithm:

1. Constructs optimal Hamilton cycles in 2D-tori with edge defects;
2. Allows to construct optimal Hamilton cycles in 3D-tori with tens of thousands of nodes (See Table 7).

4. Conclusion

A problem of mapping graphs of parallel programs onto graphs of distributed computer systems by recurrent neural networks is formulated. The parameter values providing the absence of incorrect solutions are experimentally determined. Optimal solutions are found for mapping a "line"-graph onto a two-dimensional torus due to introduction into Lyapunov function of penalty coefficients for the program graph edges not-mapped onto the system graph edges.

For increasing probability of finding optimal mapping, a method for splitting the mapping is proposed. The method essence is a reducing solution matrix to a block-diagonal form. The Wang recurrent neural network is used to exclude incorrect solutions of the problem of mapping the line-graph onto three-dimensional torus. This network converges quicker than the Hopfield one.

An efficient algorithm based on a recurrent neural Wang's network and the WTA principle is proposed for the construction of Hamiltonian cycles (ring program graphs) in regular graphs (2D- and 3D-tori, and hypercubes) of distributed computer systems and 2D-tori disturbed by removing an arbitrary edge (edge defect). The neural network parameters for the construction of Hamiltonian cycles and suboptimal cycles with a length close to that of Hamiltonian ones are determined.

Resulting algorithm allows us to construct optimal Hamilton cycles in 3D-tori with number of nodes up to 32768. The usage of this algorithm is actual in modern supercomputers having topology of the 3D-torus for organization of inter-processor communications in parallel solution of complicated problems.

Recurrent neural (Hopfield and Wang) network is a universal technique for solution of optimization problems but it is a local optimization technique, and we need additional modifications (for example, penalty coefficients and splitting) to improve the technique scalability.

The proposed algorithm for the construction of Hamiltonian cycles is less universal but more powerful because it implements a global optimization approach and so it is very more scalable than the traditional recurrent neural networks.

The traditional topology aware mappings ((Parhami, 2002; Yu, Chung & Moreira, 2006; Balaji, Gupta, Vishnu & Beckman, 2011)) are constructed especially for regular graphs (hypercubes and tori) of distributed computer systems. The proposed neural network algorithms are more universal and can be used for mapping program graphs onto graphs of distributed computer systems with defects of edges and nodes.

5. References

Balaji, P.; Gupta, R.; Vishnu, A. & Beckman, P. (2011). Mapping Communication Layouts to Network Hardware Characteristics on Massive-Scale Blue Gene Systems, *Comput. Sci. Res. Dev.*, Vol. 26, pp.247–256

Bertsekas, D.P. & Tsitsiklis, J.N. (1989). *Parallel and Distributed Computation: Numerical Methods*, Athena scientific, Bellmont, Massachusets: Prentis Hall

Chapman, B., Jost, G. & van der Pas, R. (2008). *Using OpenMP : portable shared memory parallel programming* , Cambridge, Massachusetts :The MIT Press

da Silva, I. N.; Amaral, W. C.; Arruda, L. V. & Flauzino, R. A. (2008). Recurrent Neural Approach for Solving Several Types of Optimization Problems, *Recurrent Neural Networks*, Eds. Xiaolin Hu and P. Balasubramaniam, Croatia: Intech, pp. 229-254

Dijkstra, E.W. (1974). Self-stabilizing Systems in Spite of Distributed Control. *Commun. ACM*, Vol.17, No.11, pp. 643-644

Feng, G. & Douligeris C. (2001). The Convergence and Parameter Relationship for Discrete-Time Continuous-State Hopfield Networks, *Proc. of Intern. Joint Conference on Neural Networks*

Haykin, S. (1999). *Neural Networks. A Comprehensive Foundation*, Prentice Hall Inc.

Hopfield, J.J. & Tank, D.W. (1985). Neural Computation of Decisions in Optimization Problems, *Biological Cybernetics*, Vol.52, pp.141-152

Hung, D.L. & Wang, J. (2003). Digital hardware realization of a recurrent neural network for solving the assignment problem, *Neurocomputing*, Vol. 51, pp.447-461

Jagota, A. (1999). Hopfield Neural Networks and Self-Stabilization, *Chicago Journal of Theoretical Computer Science*, Vol.1999,Article 6, http://mitpress.mit.edu/CJTCS/

Korte, B. & Vygen, J. (2006). *Combinatorial optimization. Theory and algorithms.* Bonn, Germany: Springer

Malek, A. (2008). Applications of Recurrent Neural Networks to Optimization Problems, *Recurrent Neural Networks*, Eds. Xiaolin Hu and P. Balasubramaniam, Croatia: Intech, pp. 255-288

Melamed, I.I. (1994). Neural networks and combinatorial optimization, *Automation and remote control*, Vol.55,No.11, pp.1553-1584

Ortega, J.M. (1988). *Introduction to Parallel and Vector Solution of Linear Systems*, New York: Plenum

Parhami, B. (2002). *Introduction to Parallel Processing. Algorithms and Architectures*, New York: Kluwer Academic Publishers

Serpen, G. & Patwardhan, A. (2007). Enhancing Computational Promise of Neural Optimization for Graph-Theoretic Problems in Real-Time Environments, *DCDIS A Supplement, Advances in Neural Networks*, Vol. 14, No. S1, pp. 168--176

Serpen, G. (2008). Hopfield Network as Static Optimizer: Learning the Weights and Eliminating the Guesswork, *Neural Processing Letters*, Vol.27, No.1, pp. 1-15

Siqueira, P.H., Steiner, M.T.A., & Scheer, S. (2007). A New Approach to Solve The Travelling Salesman Problem, *Neurocomputing*, Vol. 70, pp.1013-1021

Siqueira, P.H., Steiner, M.T.A., & Scheer, S. (2010). Recurrent Neural Network With Soft 'Winner Takes All' Principle for The TSP, *Proceedings of the International Conference on Fuzzy Computation and 2nd International Conference on Neural Computation*, pp. 265-270, SciTePress, 2010

Smith, K. A. (1999). Neural Networks for Combinatorial Optimization: A Review of More Than a Decade of Research, *INFORMS Journal on Computing*, Vol.11,No.1, pp.15-34.

Tarkov, M.S. (2003). Mapping Parallel Program Structures onto Structures of Distributed Computer Systems, *Optoelectronics, Instrumentation and Data Processing*, Vol. 39, No. 3, pp.72-83

Tarkov, M.S. (2005). Decentralized Control of Resources and Tasks in Robust Distributed Computer Systems, *Optoelectronics, Instrumentation and Data Processing*, Vol. 41, No. 5, pp.69-77

Tarkov, M.S. (2006). *Neurocomputer systems*, Moscow, Internet University of Inf. Technologies: Binom. Knowledge laboratory (in Russian)

Trafalis T.B. & Kasap S. (1999). *Neural Network Approaches for Combinatorial Optimization Problems*, Handbook of Combinatorial Optimization, D.-Z. Du and P.M. Pardalos (Eds.), pp. 259-293, Kluwer Academic Publishers

Tel, G. (1994). *Introduction to Distributed Algorithms*, Cambridge University Press, England, 1994

Wang, J. (1993). Analysis and Design of a Recurrent Neural Network for Linear Programming, *IEEE Trans. On Circuits and Systems-I: Fundamental Theory and Applications*, Vol. 40, No.9, pp.613-618

Yu, H.; Chung, I.H. & Moreira, J. (2006). Topology Mapping for Blue Gene/L Supercomputer, *Proceedings of the 2006 ACM/IEEE conference on Supercomputing*, ACM Press, New York, NY, USA, pp. 52–64

11

Detection and Classification of Adult and Fetal ECG Using Recurrent Neural Networks, Embedded Volterra and Higher-Order Statistics

Walid A. Zgallai[1,2]
[1]*Wokingham*
[2]*Dubai*
[1]*U. K.*
[2]*U. A. E.*

1. Introduction

The fetal heart rate (FHR) is a useful tool in the assessment of the condition of the fetal before and during labour. Fetal Electrocardiography (FECG) (Sureau, 1996) uses non-invasive surface electrodes placed on the maternal abdomen is another tool for FHR recording (Sureau, 1996). The fetal signal is weak relative to the maternal signal and to the competing noise. Widrow et al. (Widrow et al., 1975) proposed an adaptive filtering and adaptive noise cancellation method to extract the FECG from the composite maternal ECG signal. Auto-correlation and cross correlation techniques (Van Bemmel, 1968) and spatial filtering techniques (Van Oosterom, 1986, and Bergveld and Meijier 1981) have been proposed. These methods require multiple maternal thoracic ECG signals. Other methods were proposed for the rejection of the disturbing maternal ECG signal (Sureau, 1996). The automated long-term evaluation of FECG is regarded as less robust than CTG. A failure rate of approximately 30% is quoted as an almost unanimous norm (Herbert et al., 1993). The advantage of FECG is that it can be implemented in small and relatively low-cost devices (Lin et al., 1997).

A proposed technique employing wavelet transform (Khamene and Negahadariapour, 2002) exploits the most distinct features of the signal, leading to more robustness with respect to signal perturbations. The algorithm is validated using high SNR data. Dynamic modelling has been proposed (Schreiber, and D Kaplan, 1996). The data has comparatively high SNR and the fetal heartbeats can be detected by an adaptive matched filter and requires much shorter data samples than the dynamic modelling. The dynamic modelling apparent success at high SNR is offset by the required lengthy data. Due to the beat-to-beat fluctuations of the shape and duration of the ECG waveform, the normal ECG cannot be considered to be deterministic. Determinism is found in adult and fetal ECGs for data lengths of 10,000 samples (Rizk et al., 2002). The independent component analysis (ICA) has been carried out under assumptions (Lathauwer et al., 2000), the validity of each has been challenged (Rizk et al., 2001).

This chapter investigates the application of recurrent neural networks to the detection and classification of ECG signals. Third-order cumulants, bispectrum, polyphase, and embedded Volterra are utilised. The chapter develops methodology for adult ECG detection using the higher-order statistics. It extends that to non-invasive fetal heartbeat detection, during labour. The work is also extended to classify adult heart abnormalities based on the phases of the higher-order statistics. The chapter is organised as follows; Sections 2 and 3 employ third-order cumulant slices and bispectrum contours, respectively, to detect adult and fetal ECG signals. Section 4 introduces a method of ECG abnormality detection using polyphase. Section 5 shows how third-order cumulants could be utilised for the detection of late potentials. Section 6 summarises the conclusions.

2. ECG third-order cumulant slices classification

2.1 Background

Many techniques have been introduced to detect fetal heartbeats during labour. The advances in higher-order statistics, non-linear filtering, and artificial neural networks are exploited to propose a hybrid technique to improve the non-invasive detection of fetal heartbeats during labour. A third-order cumulants (TOCs) technique for non-invasive fetal heartbeat detection has been proposed (Zgallai et al., 1997). The ECG signal is processed using a Volterra filter. To improve the performance of the Volterra filter, quadratic and cubic LMF Volterra filters have been proposed (Zgallai et al., 2007). The proposed system uses the mother and fetal third-order cumulants (TOCs), which carry the signature imprints of their respective QRS-complexes, in the signal processing phase.

Quadratic and cubic Volterra filters with LMF updates have been employed to synthesise the signal into linear, quadratic, and cubic parts, and retain only the linear part. The classification phase employs an LMS-based single-hidden-layer perceptron. This section proposes incorporating an adaptive cubic LMF Volterra and an artificial neural network classifier to improve the detection rate (Zgallai, 2010). The cubic Volterra filter has been shown to improve the performance of some biomedical signals such as electromyographic signals during labour (Zgallai et al., 2009). Cross validation has been done by comparing the results of the detection to QRS peaks of the fetal heartbeat extracted from the fetal scalp electrode which is the goldstandard.

2.2 Third-order cumulants

A non-Gaussian signal {X(k)} has TOCs given by (Nikias and Petropulu, 1993):

$$c_3^x(\tau_1,\tau_2) = \mathrm{Cum}\{X(k), X(k+\tau_1), X(k+\tau_2)\}\,. \tag{2.1}$$

The calculations of the TOCs are implemented off-line due to the large CPU time required to calculate the lags. One way of reducing this load is to use 1-d slices of the TOCs. One-dimensional slices of $c_3^x(\tau_1,\tau_2)$ can be defined as (Nikias and Petropulu, 1993):

$$r_{2,1}^x(\tau) \underline{\underline{\nabla}} \mathrm{Cum}\{X(k), X(k), X(k+\tau)\} = c_3^x(0,\tau) \tag{2.2}$$

$$r_{1,2}^{x}(\tau)\underline{\underline{\nabla}}\mathrm{Cum}\{X(k),X(k+\tau),X(k+\tau)\}=c_{3}^{x}(\tau,\tau) \tag{2.3}$$

where $r_{2,1}(\tau)$ and $r_{1,2}(\tau)$ represent 1-d wall and diagonal slices, respectively. The former can be obtained from Eq. (2.1) by assuming $\tau_1 = 0$. The later obeys the condition $\tau_1 = \tau_2$. Employing 1-d slices will have the effect of reducing the CPU time by reducing the complexity of the operations. The calculations of TOC slices are comparable to those of autocorrelation and take CPU time of approximately 1 msec unlike TOCs, which take 1 sec to calculate. For a sampling rate of 0.5 KHz and an FHR of the order of 120 bpm, a real-time system can be implemented. An algorithm which calculates any arbitrarily chosen off diagonal and off wall one-dimensional slice, and hence reduce the CPU time by 99%, has been developed (Zgallai, 2007).

Adequate knowledge of the TOC of both the maternal and fetal ECG signals must first be acquired in order to pave the way for fetal QRS-complex identification and detection. There are several motivations behind using TOC in processing ECG signals; (i) ECG signals are predominantly non-Gaussian (Rizk and Zgallai, 1999), and exhibit quadratic and higher-order non-linearities supported by third- and fourth-order statistics, respectively. (ii) Gaussian noise diminishes in the TOC domains if the data length is adequate (Nikias and Petropulu, 1993). It is possible to process the ECG signal in Gaussian noise-free domains. For ECG signals a minimum length of 1 sec is adequately long to suppress Gaussian noise in the TOC domains, whilst not long enough to violate Hinich's criterion of local stationarity (Brockett et al., 1988). In general, ECG signals are non-stationary in the statistical sense, but relatively short data can be successfully treated with conventional signal processing tools primarily designed for stationary signals. When dealing with individual cardiac cycles, non-stationarity is not an issue but when one takes on board the heart rate time series which is chaotic and multi-dimensional then it is not wise to assume stationarity for analysis purposes. (iii) In the TOC domain all sources of noise with symmetric probability density functions (pdfs), e.g., Gaussian and uniform, will vanish. The ECG signals are retained because they have non-symmetric distributions (Zgallai et al., 1997). (iv) ECG signals contain measurable quantities of quadratic and, to a lesser extent, cubic non-linearities. Such measurable quantities of non-linearity, if not synthesised and removed before any further processing for the purpose of signal identification and classification, could lead to poor performance with regard to fetal QRS-complex detection rates.

2.3 LMF quadratic and cubic volterra

The Volterra structure is a series of polynomial terms (Schetzen, 1980) which are formed from a time sequence {y(k). The output of the filter is expressed as

$$y(n)=\sum_{i_1=1}^{N} a_{i_1}^{1} x_{k-i_1+1}+\sum_{i_1=1}^{N}\sum_{i_2=1}^{N} a_{i_1,i_2}^{2} x_{k-i_1+1}x_{k-i_2+1}+\ldots \tag{2.4}$$

Adaptive conventional Volterra is updated using the Least-Mean Squares (LMS) criterion. The LMS algorithm minimises the expected value of the squared difference between the estimated output and the desired response. A more general case is to minimise $E\{e(n)^{2N}\}$ (Wallach and Widrow, 1984). N = 2 is the Least-Mean-Fourth (LMF). The LMF algorithm updates the weights as follows:

$$\mathbf{a}_i(n+1) = \mathbf{a}_i(n) + 2\mu_i \,.e^3(n).x(n)\,. \tag{2.5}$$

The LMF has a faster convergence than the LMS algorithm. It has generally a lower weight noise than the LMS algorithm, with the same speed of convergence. It was shown to have 3 dB to 10 dB lower mean-squared error (MSE) than the LMS algorithm (Wallach and Widrow, 1984). Adaptive LMF-based quadratic and cubic Volterra structures have been developed and shown to outperform LMS-based Volterra by 6-7 dBs (Zgallai, 2007).

2.4 Neural network classifiers

A major limitation of the back-propagation algorithms is the slow rate of convergence to a global minimum of the error-performance surface because the algorithm operates entirely on the gradient of the error-performance surface with respect to the weights in the single-hidden-layer perceptron. The back-propagation learning process is accelerated by incorporating a momentum term. The use of momentum introduces a feedback loop which prevents the learning process from being stuck at a local minimum on the error-performance surface of the single-hidden-layer perceptron. The classifier is a single-hidden-layer perceptrion based on a modified Back-Propagation technique. The modified back-propagation algorithm has a momentum term which helps to avoid local minima. One hundred and sixty one-dimensional TOC slices have been used as templates for the desired signals in the Artificial Neural Network (ANN) classifier.

2.5 The proposed algorithm

2.5.1 TOC detection

1. *Create ECG cumulant database*
2. *Detect the maternal QRS-complexes* – Read the ECG recording sequentially, and process each of the 90% overlapping windows (length 250 msec) to compute the diagonal or wall slice TOC. The slice is matched to the templates until a maternal QRS-complex is detected. An auxiliary subroutine is used to pinpoint the position of the R-wave. If the second successive segment detects a maternal QRS-complex then it is discarded because it is the same complex detected in the adjacent window. The whole process of TOC template matching is repeated until the second maternal QRS-complex is detected and its R-wave is pinpointed. The maternal heart rate is accurately calculated from the knowledge of the current and previous R-wave positions.
3. *Detect the fetal cardiac cycles* – The search begins from the position of the detected maternal R-wave. Window overlapping, each with fetal cumulant template matching, continues until the first, second, and possibly third fetal ECG TOC diagonal and wall slice signatures have been matched to one template for each one of them. Once the slices have been matched, the window will be flagged as a detection window. If the next overlapping window detects a fetal heartbeat, it will be discarded because it is the same fetal heartbeat that has just been detected in the previous window. The number of fetal heartbeats detected within the maternal cardiac cycle is counted. The instantaneous maternal heart rate is previously known with some degree of accuracy, and the relative fetal to maternal heartbeat is also known within the maternal cardiac cycle. Hence, the averaged fetal heart rate can be calculated within each maternal cardiac cycle. Operations 2 and 3 are repeated for all individual maternal cardiac cycles.

2.5.2 Window minimum length and ECG segmentation

The duration of the fetal cardiac cycle varies from 250 msec to 500 msec for a range of fetal heart rate between 240 bpm and 120 bpm. The fetal QRS-complex itself occupies between 50 msec and 70 msec. The fetal heartbeat is detected in a flag window of length 250 msec. This window length serves two criteria; (i) it is the minimum length yielding an acceptable upper threshold of both the deterministic and stochastic noise types inherent in the higher-order statistics of the ECG signals encountered, and (ii) this window length allows the detection of one, two, three, or four fetal heartbeats (FHBs) within one maternal transabdominal cardiac cycle. For example, for maternal heartbeat of 60 bpm, the R-wave-to-R-wave = 1000 msec, and four segments x 250 msec = one maternal cardiac cycle = possible four fetal cardiac cycles.

2.5.3 Overlapping window

When detecting the fetal heartbeat within the maternal transabdominal cardiac cycle, 90% overlapping windows, each of 250 msec duration, are scanned at a rate of 100 Hz with a sampling rate of 0.5 KHz. The overlapping percentage should be carefully chosen to compensate for the apparent loss of temporal resolution due to a lengthy window which is dictated by the maximum threshold of the variance of the TOCs. The average fetal QRS-complex duration is 60 msec. This may be encountered at the beginning, middle, or end of the flag window. Hence by using a window overlapping of 90%, any fetal QRS-complex which may be missed because it starts to evolve, say, 20 msec before the end of a window, can definitely be picked up by the next one or two overlapping windows when it completes its full duration of 60 msec and has definitely reached its full peak (the R-wave). If this particular QRS-complex has enough strength to be picked up by two successive overlapping windows, the algorithm will count it as one FHB. It has been found that reducing the overlapping below 90% yielded missed fetal heartbeats.

2.5.4 Averaged fetal heart rate calculation

The instantaneous fetal heart rate is calculated by measuring the interval between two successive R-waves. This requires pinpointing accurately the R-point of the QRS-complex. Although the ECG TOC template matching technique is very effective in detecting the occurrence of the QRS-complex as a whole even when it is completely buried in noise, it cannot locate the R-wave over a window length of 250 msec which satisfies the criterion for the variance threshold. In most transabdominal ECG recordings (85%), the fetal QRS-complexes cannot be seen as they are completely masked by other signals and motion artefact. This obscurity accounts for the lower success rate of fetal heartbeat detection in other assessed fetal heartbeat detection techniques (Sureau, 1996). The adult heartbeats can be measured accurately and the instantaneous heart rate for adults can be calculated. Hence, by counting the number of fetal heartbeats (FHBs) that have occurred between two successive maternal R-waves, one can easily calculate the averaged FHR within the maternal cardiac cycle. On average, the maternal cardiac cycle is 1000 msec. Two maternal cardiac cycles measure 2 sec. So, detecting and displaying up to eight FHBs will take less than 2.000030 sec which is well within the manufacturers' detection-to-display interval of 3.75 sec.

2.6 Data collection and results

2.6.1 Data collection

Data was obtained from pregnant women at various stages of gestation (Zgallai, 2007). This was achieved, with the consent of women, using a pair of electrodes, Sonicaid 8000, a Pentium IV PC and an interface card. The software used for the attractor calculations was MATLAB 8.0. Ag-AgCl Beckman electrodes of 8 cm in diameter, and 25-cm spaced centres were positioned on the abdominal wall after careful preparation of the skin, which lowers the interelectrode impedance of 10 kΩ. The electrode pair is set over the umbilicus, and lined up with the median vertical axis of the uterus. The ground electrode is located on the woman's hip. The training data involves using third-order cumulants and their slices of segments of fetal scalp electrode measurement. These are used to compare with results obtained from the transabdominal ECG recording. The testing data is the transabdominal ECG recording.

2.6.2 Results

2.6.2.1 TOCs and their diagonal and wall slices

An optimised third-order Volterra structure is employed to decompose the ECG signal into its linear, quadratic, and cubic parts and retain only the linear part. Fig. 2.1 depict a maternal transabdominal ECG signal with segmentation and the corresponding TOCs and their diagonal and wall slices for predominantly maternal QRS-complexes, the first fetal heartbeats with maternal contribution, QRS-free ECGs, and the second fetal heartbeats with maternal contribution. The diagonal and wall TOC slices of the maternal QRS-complexes, segment (I) in Fig. 2.1, are easily distinguished from the diagonal and wall TOC slices of segments (II), (III), and (IV). Furthermore, the diagonal and wall TOC slices of the fetal heartbeat segments, (II) and (IV) in Fig. 2.1, are distinguishable from the corresponding diagonal and wall TOC slices of the QRS-free ECG segments (III). However, in some cases, those of segments (II) and (IV) could be mistaken for QRS-free ECG segments. The peaks of the QRS-free ECG segments are much narrower and more related to motion artefact than a signal.

2.6.2.2 The NN classifier

A single-hidden-layer perceptron is used for the classification of the TOC slices of the maternal QRS-complexes, the first fetal heartbeat with maternal contribution, QRS-free ECG, and the second fetal heartbeat with maternal contribution from maternal transabdominal ECG segments. This is achieved using a standard back-propagation with momentum algorithm (Caudill and C. Butler, 1992). Each of the input and output layers have a dimension of 8 x 8 and the hidden layer has a dimension of 5 x 5. The input to the first layer is the TOCs diagonal and wall slices. The network is trained using TOC slice templates obtained from the maternal chest and fetal scalp electrode ECGs as well as previously detected and earmarked transabdominal ECG segments. The latter training sequences are templates of the diagonal and wall slices of the TOCs of four segments from maternal transabdominal full cardiac cycles. The input to the network is eight template patterns. These are the TOC diagonal and wall slices of four segments from one transabdominal cardiac cycle. For example the first pair are maternal slices, the second pair are fetal slices, the third pair are QRS-free slices, and the fourth pair are fetal slices. The network is trained over the eight patterns. The training terminates when the worst error in all patterns in one pass is less than 0.1. Typically the average error will be in the range of 0.001.

The TOC slice templates are used as input to the classifier. Each one of the 10 templates in each set is used as an input and the weights of each neuron in the classifier are optimised by changing the learning rate and the momentum constant until the error is minimised. Then the transabdominal ECG signal with 250-msec window is used as an input to the classifier. The instantaneous weights of the input signal are compared to those of the templates which are stored in the memory. The two sets of parameters are correlated. Once a signal is classified the output will be set to 1. The classification of the four segments involves a pattern-by-pattern updating rather than batch updating for the weight adjustments. This is more suitable to speed up the performance. Pattern-by-pattern updating tends to be orders of magnitude faster than batch updating. However, it should be noted that pattern-by-pattern updating is harder to parallelise. Fig. 2.2 summarises the results of the optimisation process.

Parameters of the single-hidden layer perceptron: The network has been optimised in terms of its learning rate, momentum constant, and hidden layer size to achieve the minimum mean-squared error. The optimum learning rate is found to be 0.8. The optimum momentum constant is found to be 0.99 and 0.90 for the maternal QRS-complex and the fetal heartbeat with maternal contribution segments, respectively. The single-hidden-layer has an optimum dimension of 5 x 5. The input to the first layer is the TOCs diagonal and wall slices. The network is trained using TOC slice templates. The input to the network is eight template patterns. These are the TOC diagonal and wall slices of four segments from one transabdominal cardiac cycle. The network is trained over the eight patterns. The training terminates when the worst error in all patterns in one pass is less than 0.1. Typically the average error will be in the range of 0.001.

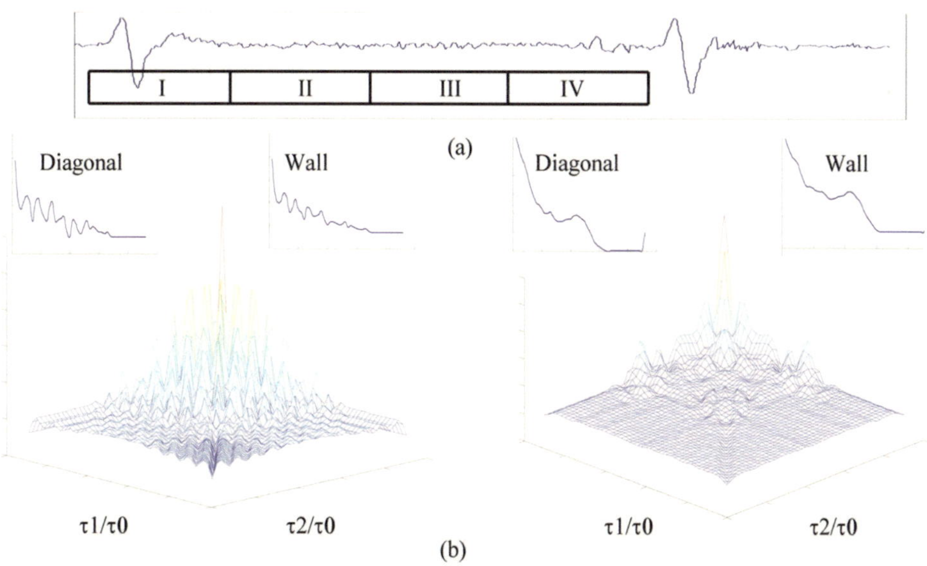

Fig. 2.1. (a) Transabdominally-measured ECG (Code: 16-23) showing segmentation (segments I, II, III, and IV, 250 msec each). (b) The TOCs and their diagonal and walll slices (insets) for the QRS-free ECG (l.h.s.) and the second fetal heartbeat with maternal contribution (r.h.s.). τ_0, τ_1 and τ_2 are, respectively, the reference, first and second time lags of the TOCs.

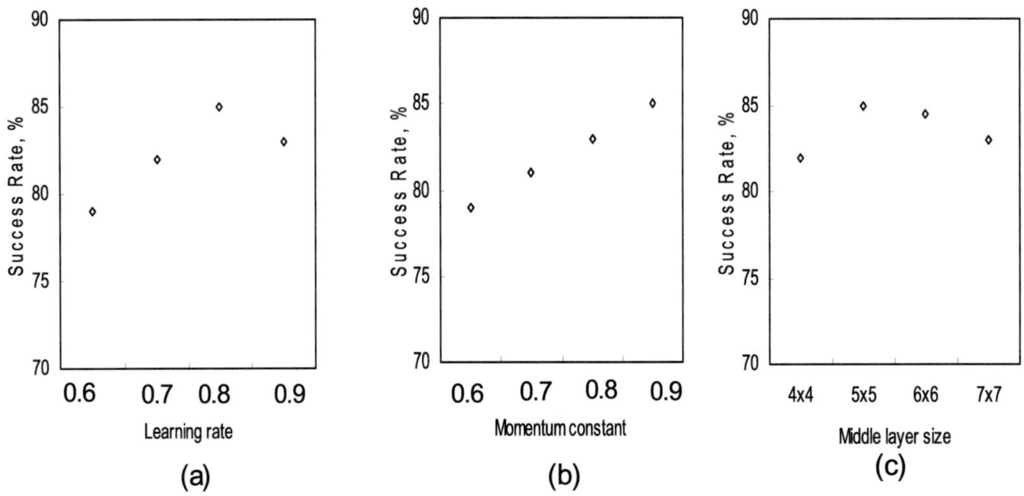

Fig. 2.2. The effect of changing (a) the learning rate, (b) the momentum constant, and (c) the middle layer size, on the classification rate of the fetal heartbeats with maternal contribution from transabdominally-measured ECG signals and employing TOC diagonal slices and their templates to be matched using a single-hidden-layer perseptron back-propagation with momentum. Segment length is 250 msec each. The optimised parameters are: learning rate = 0.8, momentum constant = 0.9, and middle-layer size = 5 x 5.

2.6.2.3 Cumulant matching of the fetal heartbeats

Each one of the four transabdominal ECG segments (Data length = 250 msec) has ten corresponding templates used for matching. An optimised cubic Volterra structure is employed to synthesise the four transabdominal ECG segments and the corresponding templates.

2.6.2.4 The maternal heartbeat classification rates

The classification rate is 100% for maternal QRS-complexes using the TOC template matching technique with single-hidden-layer classification. To calculate the maternal heart rate an auxiliary method to pinpoint the R-wave employing an adaptive thresholding has been used. Note that this is not accurate when one deals with deformed QRS-complexes in heart patients. The data obtained include all mothers' ECGs exhibiting normal-to-the-patient QRS-complexes. The instantaneous maternal heart rate is calculated by dividing 60 by the R-to-R interval (in seconds). The application of this auxiliary routine leads to a maternal heart rate with an accuracy of 99.85%.

2.6.2.5 Classification rate for the hybrid technique

Definitions

1. The Sensitivity (Se) is defined as the ratio of the True Positives (TP) to the sum of the True Positives and the False Negatives (FN). The sensitivity reports the percentage of true beats that are correctly classified by the algorithm.
2. The Specificity (Sp) is defined as the ratio of the True Positives (TP) to the sum of the True Positives (TP) and the False Positives (FP). It reports the percentage of classified heartbeats which are in reality true beats.
3. The classification rate: The mean value of the sensitivity and the specificity is used as the criterion for the effectiveness of the technique.

Table 2.1 shows the fetal heart detection quality and classification rate using transabdominally-measured ECGs and their respective TOC diagonal or wall slices with and without linearisation. The combined diagonal and wall slices improve the classification rate by about 1% over and above that achieved by either slice. A further improvement of about 1% is achieved by using two off-diagonal and off-wall slices. A second-order Volterra synthesiser results in a higher detection rate of 83.49%.

The highest achievable classification rate for non-invasive fetal heartbeat detection using the first hybrid system is 86.16% when a third-order Volterra synthesiser is employed in conjunction with single-hidden-layer classifiers. Note that the classification rate for coincident maternal and fetal QRS complexes is 0%. The classification rate of non-coincident maternal and fetal QRS-complexes is 95.55%.

TOC matching template slice type	**Sensitivity (%)**	**Specificity (%)**	**Classification Rate (%)**	**False Positives**	**False Negatives**
TOC Diagonal/Wall slice	76.24	79.38	77.81	24744	28512
TOC Diagonal and Wall slices	77.13	80.24	78.74	23712	27444
TOC Diagonal, wall, diagonal & wall, & 22.5^{o} slice	78.04	81.18	79.69	22584	26352
Diagonal/Wall slice 2nd order LMF Volterra	82.37	84.61	83.49	18468	21156
Diagonal/Wall slice 3rd order LMF Volterra	84.46	87.85	86.16	14500	18648

Table 2.1. Fetal heart detection quality and classification rate using transabdominally-measured ECG and their respective TOC diagonal or wall slices with and without linearisation. The total number of fetal heartbeats is 120,000 and the total number of maternal ECG recordings. is 30. The performance was assessed against synchronised fetal scalp heartbeats. All mothers were during the first stage of labour at 40 weeks of gestation.

3. ECG bispectrum contour classification

3.1 Background

This section describes a hybrid system using the mother and fetal ECG bispectral contours (BIC), which carry the signature imprints of their respective QRS-complexes, in the signal processing phase. The classification phase employs LMS-based single-hidden-layer classifiers. The maternal chest ECGs and the fetal scalp electrode ECGs have been used as templates or the HOS representatives in the classification phase. The bispectral contour matching technique is used to identify the signatures of both the maternal and fetal QRS-complexes. It will be shown that the highest achievable Fetal Heartbeat (FHB) classification rate using the BIC template matching technique is 90.12% with reduced false positives and negatives associated with the power spectrum-based FHB classification rate of 70%. Furthermore, the BIC has a marginally improved classification performance over and above the TOC during episodes of overlapping fetal QRS-complexes and maternal T-waves. This is achieved at the expense of complexity and computation time. The hybrid bispectral contour matching technique is an extension to the hybrid cumulant matching technique. Therefore, the choice of the NN classifier is based on the general discussion presented previously. *Prior information* remain as valuable assets and are exploited herein. It is the matching of the horizontal 2-d bispectral contours that has been used in the BIC template matching technique instead of the 1-d polar bispectral slices. Because in order to use the 1-d polar bispectrum slices effectively, one needs to use a minimum of 24 polar slices to facilitate capturing the most rapid changes in the bispectrum including null features that could be used as discriminant patterns. Whereas for BIC contours, provided that they are horizontally cut at a maximum number of 10 levels, a good quality discriminant picture can be made available for the neural network classifier. For example, it is very unlikely that maxima and troughs are missed because of any changes in their respective positions.

The same procedure of Section 2 is applied with the replacement of the third-order cumulant slices by the bispectral contours (usually 10 contours including the tip of the peak and are spaced by approximately 1 dB). The CPU time for the bispectrum computation is almost twice that for cumulants and 2000 times that for individual TOC slices. The Detection key operations are exactly the same as those described in Section 2 except that the third-order cumulant slices are now going to be replaced by the bispectral contours (Zgallai, 2012).

3.2 ECG bispectrum

The nth-order cumulant spectrum of a process {x(k)} is defined as the (n-1)-dimensional Fourier transform of the nth-order cumulant sequence. The nth-order cumulant spectrum is thus defined as (Dogan and J. M. Mendel, 1993):

$$C_n^x(\omega_1,\omega_2,\ldots,\omega_{n-1}) = \sum_{\tau_1=-\infty}^{+\infty} \cdots \sum_{\tau_{n-1}=-\infty}^{+\infty} c_n^x(\tau_1,\tau_2,\cdots,\tau_{n-1})\, e^{-j(\omega_1\tau_1+\omega_2\tau_2+\ldots+\omega_n\tau_{n-1})} \tag{3.1}$$

where

$$|\omega_i| \le \pi \quad \textit{for} \quad i = 1,2,\ldots n-1, \;\; \textit{and} \quad |\omega_1 + \omega_2 + \ldots + \omega_{n-1}| \le \pi$$

The bispectrum, n = 3, is defined as:

$$C_3^x(\omega_1,\omega_2) = \sum_{\tau_1=-\infty}^{+\infty} \sum_{\tau_2=-\infty}^{+\infty} c_3^x(\tau_1,\tau_2)\ e^{-j(\omega_1\tau_1+\omega_2\tau_2)} \tag{3.2}$$

where $c_3^x(\tau_1,\tau_2)$ is the third-order cumulant sequence. The computational complexity of the bispectrum is of the order of N^3.

3.3 Typical examples of bispectra and their contours

Linearisation is a key step in the signal processing and it is applied using an optimised third-order Volterra synthesiser to all the results included. Fig. 3.1 depict dual-band-pass filtered bispectra and their contours normalised to the maternal QRS-complex spectral peak for the transabdominally-measured ECG segments I, II, III, and IV. Segment I: predominantly maternal QRS-complex, segment II: the first fetal heartbeat with maternal contribution; segment III: QRS-free ECG, and segment IV: the second fetal heartbeat with maternal contribution. The dual-band-pass filter consists of two fifth-order Butterworth filters with cut-off frequencies of 10 Hz to 20 Hz, and 25 Hz to 40 Hz, respectively, a pass-band attenuation of 0.5 dB, and a stop-band attenuation larger than 70 dB. The sampling rate is 500 Hz. Optimised Kaiser weighting coefficients are used for the fetal and maternal ECGs to enhance their spectral peaks at 30 Hz and 17 Hz, respectively. The Kaiser windows are centred at frequencies of 15 Hz, 16 Hz, 17 Hz, 18 Hz, and 19 Hz for the maternal QRS-complex, and at frequencies of 28 Hz, 29 Hz, 30 Hz, 31 Hz, 32 Hz, 33 Hz, 34 Hz, 35 Hz, 36 Hz, 37 Hz, and 38 Hz for the fetal heartbeat.

Fig. 3.1 (I) shows the maternal QRS-complex principal bispectral peaks and contours centred at the frequency pairs (18 Hz, 5 Hz) and (18 Hz, 16 Hz). These maternal frequency pairs with a frequency peak at 18 Hz slightly deviate from the actual frequency of 17 Hz (Rizk et al., 2000), which is due to the BIC bias. The maternal optimised Kaiser window centred at 18 Hz will help to detect this deviated peak. Fig. 3.1 (II) shows the first fetal heartbeat principal bispectral peaks and contours at the frequency pairs (30 Hz, 5 Hz), (30 Hz, 18 Hz), and (30 Hz, 30 Hz). The fetal optimised Kaiser window centred at 30 Hz will help to detect these peaks. Note that these peaks are sharp. Fig. 3.1 (III) shows the QRS-free ECG bispectral peak and contours centred at the frequency pair (27 Hz, 15 Hz). Note that the BIC of the QRS-free ECG is at approximately -12 dB which is 3 dB and 6 dB lower than that of the first and second fetal heartbeats, respectively. Fig. 3.1 (IV) shows the second fetal heartbeat principal bispectral peak and contours centred at the frequency pairs (30 Hz, 5 Hz), and (30 Hz, 28 Hz). The fetal optimised Kaiser window centred at 30 Hz will help to detect these peaks.

3.4 Estimation of the bispectral contour matching variance

The variance of the BIC is defined as the expected value of the squared difference in frequency (in Hz) between the computed BIC of the 250 msec flag window of the transabdominal ECG signal and the computed BIC from the synchronised fetal scalp electrode ECG 250 msec window.

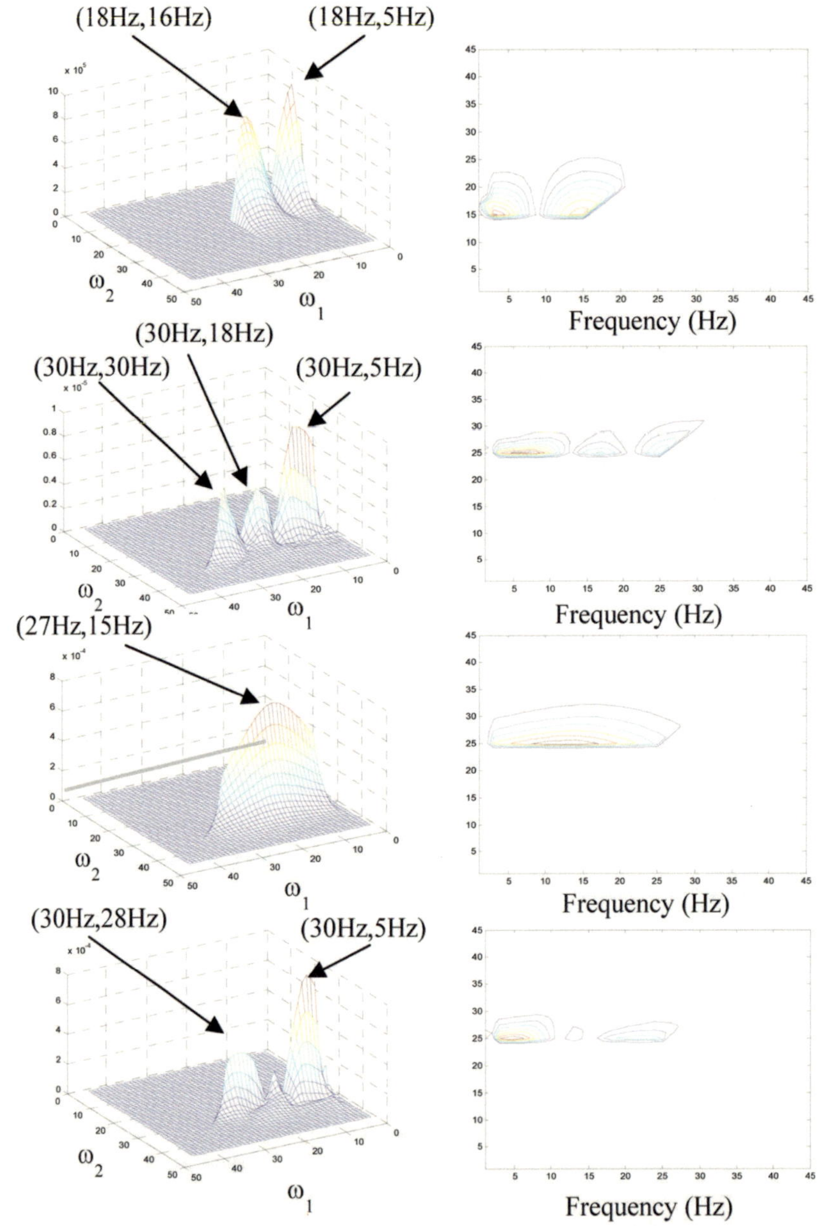

Fig. 3.1. Dual-band-pass filtered bispectra, Kaiser shaped window, (l.h.s.) and their contour maps normalised to the maternal QRS spectral peak (r.h.s.) for the transabdominally-measured ECG segments I, II, III, and IV of Fig. 2.1. Segment I: maternal QRS-complex, Segment II: the first fetal heartbeat with maternal contribution; Segment III: QRS-free ECG; and Segment IV: the second fetal heartbeat with maternal contribution. The dual band-pass filter consists of two fifth-order Butterworth filters with cut-off frequencies of 10 Hz to 20 Hz, and 25 Hz to 40 Hz, respectively, and a pass-band attenuation of 0.5 dB, a stop-band attenuation larger than 70 dB. The sampling rate is 500 Hz.

$$\mathrm{Var_b} = E\,[(\mathrm{Bis}(\omega_1, \omega_2)_{\text{Transabdominal}} - \mathrm{Bis}(\omega_1, \omega_2)_{\text{fetal scalp}}\,]^2 \qquad (3.3)$$

The above variance ranges from 0.47 - 3.3, average = 1.716, when calculated for 120,000 FHBs. The variance indicates the deviation of the frequency of the BIC (in Hz) of the transabdominal ECG signal from that of the fetal scalp electrode around 30 Hz.

3.5 The back-propagation with momentum algorithm in single-hidden-layer perceptron

Single-hidden-layer perceptron classifiers are trained in a supervised manner with the back-propagation algorithm which is based on the error-correction learning rule. The back-propagation algorithm provides a computationally efficient method for the training of the classifiers. The back-propagation algorithm is a first-order approximation of the steepest descent technique. It depends on the gradient of the instantaneous error surface in weight space. The algorithm is therefore stochastic in nature. It has a tendency to zigzag its way about the true direction to a minimum on the error surface. Consequently, it suffers from a slow convergence property. A momentum term is employed to speed up the performance of the algorithm. The classifier used here is exactly the same as that used in Section 2.

3.6 Optimisation of the parameters of the back-propagation algorithm

Fig. 3.2 shows the effect of changing the learning rate (β), the momentum constant (α) and the middle layer size on the classification of the maternal QRS-complexes and the fetal heartbeats using the BIC template matching technique. The effect of changing the learning rate on the classification rate is shown in Fig. 3.2 (a). Small values of β are not able to track the variations in the bispectral contours. For classification of the bispectral contours, β reaches its optimum value at 0.2. For values larger than 0.2, the output values are too large so that the difference with respect to the reference signal (template) will increase. This leads to larger error that will be fed back to the network, which will lead to slower convergence. The network will take long time to converge, or it might not converge at all. The optimum value of the momentum constant is found to be 0.2, as depicted in Fig. 3.2 (b). Smaller values are not enough to push the adaptations to avoid local minima. While larger values tend to affect the routine detrimentally by bypassing the global minimum. The performance deteriorates significantly as the learning rate and the momentum constant diverge from their optimum values. The number and size of the middle layers were investigated by trial and error. There is a trade off between networks that should be small enough to allow faster implementation, and larger networks in size and number of hidden layers which are very slow and can not be implemented on-line using the current technology. Large networks could have complex relationships that represent non-linearities that might not exist in the real signals at all. The optimum parameters indicated in Fig. 3.2 are calculated without considering the CPU time factor which might render those parameters undesirable for real-time applications. The CPU time for training is in the range of 17 to 60 sec. The average mean-squared error (MSE) is 0.04. The worst error is 0.1, which is the criterion for convergence. The implemented neural network has a single middle layer size of 6 x 6 as shown in Fig. 3.2 (c). The number of passes (epochs) required for training varied from 6 to 14.

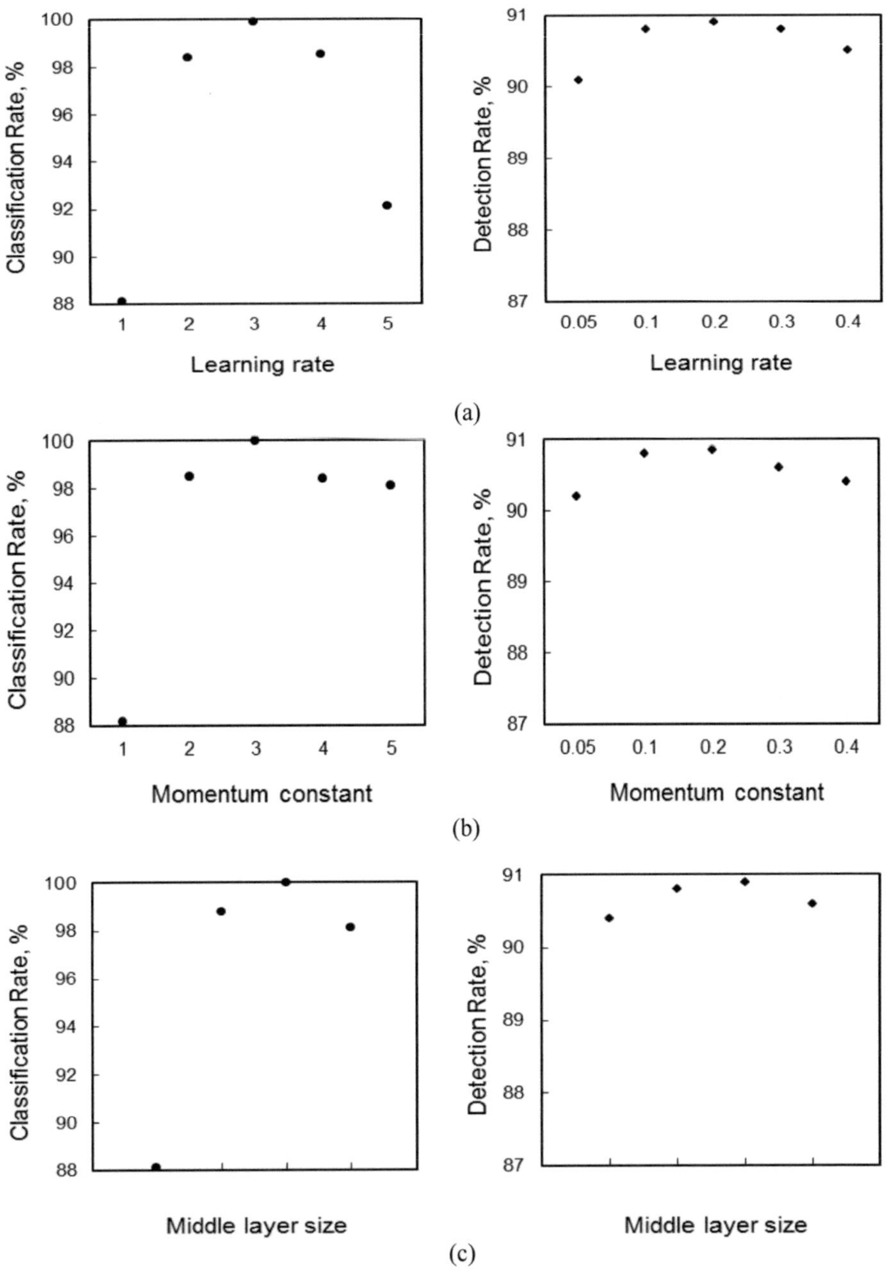

Fig. 3.2. The effect of changing (a) the learning rate, (b) the momentum constant, and (c) the middle layer size on the classification rate of the maternal QRS-complexes (l.h.s.) and fetal heartbeats (r.h.s.) from transabdominally-measured ECG signals using bispectral contours and their templates to be matched using a single-hidden-layer perceptron back-propagation algorithm with momentum. Data length = 250 msec. The optimised parameters for the BIC classification are: learning rate = 0.2, momentum constant = 0.2, and middle-layer size = 6 x 6. (Code: 5-1-100).

3.7 Bispectral contour matching of the maternal QRS-complex and fetal heartbeat

The bispectral contour template matching technique works with only 10 templates of maternal transabdominal QRS-complexes and 20 templates of fetal heartbeats with maternal contribution. The classification of the four segments involves a pattern-by-pattern updating rather than batch updating for the weight adjustments. This is more suitable to speed up the performance. Pattern-by-pattern updating tends to be orders of magnitude faster than batch updating. However, it should be noted that pattern-by-pattern updating is harder to parallelise (Zgallai, 2012).

3.8 The maternal QRS-complex and the fetal heartbeat classification rates

3.8.1 The maternal QRS-complex classification rate

Table 3.1 shows a top classification rate of 100% for maternal QRS-complexes using bispectral contours for signal processing and single-hidden-layer perceptron classification. The 100% maternal QRS-complex classification rate has been achievable with or without linearisation. It makes no difference to the results. A brief description of the optimised parameters required for the linearisation process is given. To calculate the maternal heart rate an auxiliary method to pinpoint the R-wave is needed. For this application an adaptive thresholding method has been employed. Note that this is not very accurate when one deals with deformed QRS-complexes in heart patients. All maternal ECGs, however, exhibit normal-to-the-patient QRS-complexes. The instantaneous maternal heart rate is calculated by dividing 60 by the R-to-R interval (in seconds). The application of this auxiliary routine leads to a maternal heart rate with an accuracy of 99.85%.

Parameters: The second-order Volterra parameters are: filter length = 6, step-size parameters = 0.005, and 0.0004 for linear and quadratic parts, respectively, delay = 3. The third-order Volterra parameters are: filter length = 6, step-size parameters = 0.001, 0.0002, and 0.0004 for linear, quadratic and cubic parts, respectively, delay = 4. A dual-band-pass filter is applied to the bispectrum, the first has a band-pass of 10 Hz to 20 Hz and the second has a band-pass of 25 Hz to 40 Hz. Optimised Kaiser windows centred at frequencies of 15 Hz, 16 Hz, 17 Hz, 18 Hz, and 19 Hz for the maternal spectrum, and at frequencies of 28 Hz, 29 Hz, 30 Hz, 31 Hz, 32 Hz, 33 Hz, 34 Hz, 35 Hz, 36 Hz, 37 Hz, and 38 Hz for the fetal spectrum are used in both the power spectrum and the BIC.

3.8.2 Fetal heartbeat detection quality and classification rate for the bispectral contour template matching technique

Table 3.2 summarises the results of the fetal heartbeat detection using the power spectrum method (second-order statistics), and the bispectrum contour template matching technique. Optimised adaptive LMF-based second- and third-order Volterra synthesisers are employed. The power spectrum method has a classification rate of 71.47%. Using the second hybrid system, the classification rate increased to 87.72% without linearisation, and to 88.28% and 90.12% using second- and third-order Volterra synthesisers with LMF update, respectively. The second hybrid method has an improvement of 19% and 4% in the classification rate over and above that achieved with the second-order statistics and the TOC template matching technique, respectively. The classification rate of the coincident maternal and fetal QRS-complexes is 0%. The classification rate of non-coincident maternal and fetal QRS-complexes is 99.21%.

*Parameters:*The second-order Volterra parameters are: filter length = 6, step-size parameters = 0.005, and 0.0004 for linear and quadratic parts, respectively, delay = 5. The third-order Volterra parameters are: filter length = 6, step-size parameters = 0.001, 0.0002, and 0.0004 for linear, quadratic and cubic parts, respectively, delay = 5. A dual-band-pass filter is applied to the bispectrum, the first has a band- pass of 10 Hz to 20 Hz and the second has a band-pass of 25 Hz to 40 Hz. Optimised Kaiser windows centred at frequencies of 15 Hz, 16 Hz, 17 Hz, 18 Hz, and 19 Hz for the maternal spectrum, and at frequencies of 28 Hz, 29 Hz, 30 Hz, 31 Hz, 32 Hz, 33 Hz, 34 Hz, 35 Hz, 36 Hz, 37 Hz, and 38 Hz for the fetal spectrum are used in both the power spectrum and the BIC.

Spectral matching template with ANN classifiers	**The power spectrum**	**The bispectrum contours**
Classification rate	99.84	100.00

Table 3.1. The classification rate for the maternal QRS-complex using maternal transabdominally-measured ECGs and their respective power spectrum and bispectral contours.

Spectral matching template type with and without linearisation using Volterra and in conjunction with ANN classifiers	**Se (%)**	**Sp (%)**	**FP, out of 120000**	**FN, out of 120000**	**Classification rate (%)**
Power spectrum with linearisation	71.29	71.44	34272	34537	71.37
Bispectral contour without linearisation	87.97	87.46	15048	14436	87.72
Linearised bispectral contour using 2nd order adaptive LMF Volterra synthesiser	88.53	88.04	14352	13764	88.28
Linearised bispectral contour using 3rd order adaptive LMF Volterra synthesiser	90.53	89.73	12324	11364	90.12

Table 3.2. Fetal heart detection quality and classification rate using transabdominally-measured ECG and their respective power spectrum and bispectral contours with and without linearisation. The total number of fetal heartbeats is 120,000 and the total number of maternal ECG recordings is 30. The performance was assessed against synchronised fetal scalp heartbeats. All mothers were during the first stage of labour at 40 weeks of gestation.

3.9 Discussion

The bispectral contour matching technique is an extension to the cumulant matching technique. Therefore, the choice of the NN classifier is based on the discussion presented previously. *Prior information* remain as valuable assets and are very much exploited herein. It is the matching of the horizontal 2-d bispectral contours that has been used in the BIC template matching technique instead of the 1-d polar bispectral slices. Because in order to use the 1-d polar bispectrum slices effectively, one needs to use a minimum of 24 polar slices to facilitate capturing the most rapid changes in the bispectrum including null features that could be used as discriminant patterns. Whereas for BIC contours, provided that they are horizontally cut at a maximum number of 10 levels, a good quality discriminant picture can be made available for the neural network classifier. For example, it is very unlikely that maxima and troughs are missed because of any changes in their respective positions. Approximately 50,000 maternal cardiac cycles have been included in the analysis. The numbers of bispectral contours compound templates are 10 for the maternal chest, 10 for the fetal scalp, and 140 for the transabdominally-measured 250 msec segments, respectively. Each bispectral compound template is made of 10 horizontal templates at different levels. Starting from a normalised 0 dB and going down in steps of 1 dB each to a - 10 dB.

The maternal transabdominal ECG signal is linearised using an optimised LMF-based second- or third-order Volterra synthesiser. The second-order Volterra synthesiser parameters are: filter length = 6, step-size parameters = 0.005, and 0.0004 for linear and quadratic parts, respectively, delay = 5. The third-order Volterra synthesiser parameters are: filter length = 6, step-size parameters = 0.001, 0.0002, and 0.0004 for linear, quadratic and cubic parts, respectively, delay = 5. The transabdominal ECG signal is segmented into four segments containing; (I) The maternal QRS-complex, (II) the first fetal heartbeat with maternal contribution, (III) QRS-free ECG, and (IV) the second fetal heartbeat with maternal contribution. To segment the transabdominal ECG signals, the window length is carefully chosen to; (i) Yield an acceptable upper threshold of both the deterministic and stochastic noise types inherent in the higher-order statistics of the ECG signals encountered, and (ii) allow the detection of one, two, three, or four fetal heartbeats (FHBs) within one maternal transabdominal cardiac cycle.

The classification procedure starts by matching the bispectral contours of the segments to those of the templates until the first and the second maternal QRS-complexes are detected and their R-waves are pinpointed. The maternal heart rate is accurately calculated from the knowledge of the current and previous R-wave positions. Then, the search for the fetal heartbeat starts at 50 msec before the first maternal R-wave and continues until the second maternal R-wave is reached. Although the ECG bispectral contour template matching technique is very effective in detecting the occurrence of the fetal heartbeats as a whole in the frequency domain even when it is completely buried in noise, it cannot locate the R-wave in the time domain over a window length of 250 msec. However, the maternal heartbeats can be measured fairly accurately and calculate the instantaneous heart rate for the mother. Hence, by counting the number of fetal heartbeats that have occurred between two successive maternal R-waves, one can easily calculate the averaged FHR within the maternal cardiac cycle;

The average FHR = MHR x Number of FHBs / number of maternal heartbeats

the instantaneous maternal heart rate is previously known with some degree of accuracy, and the relative fetal to maternal heartbeat is also known within the maternal cardiac cycle. Hence, the averaged fetal heart rate can be calculated within each maternal cardiac cycle.

3.9.1 The effect of window length on the bispectral contour variance

The variance of the bispectrum for the optimum window length of 250 msec with FHB occurrence ranges from 0.47 to 3.3 with an average value of 1.716. The variance of the bispectrum is smaller than that of the third-order cumulants. A further 15% increase in the variance of the bispectrum is due to an increase in the maternal heartbeat from 60 bpm to 100 bpm. The latter has resulted in an 30% decrease in segment size.

3.9.2 Parameters of the single-hidden layer perceptron

The network has been optimised in terms of its learning rate, momentum constant, and hidden layer size to achieve the minimum mean-squared error. The optimum learning rate is found to be 0.2. The optimum momentum constant is found to be 0.2. The single-hidden-layer has an optimum dimension of 6 x 6. The input to the first layer is the bispectral contours of the four transabdominally-measured ECG segments. The network is trained using the BIC templates. During the training phase, the input to the network is four template patterns. These are the BIC of four segments from one transabdominal cardiac cycle. For example the first is the maternal QRS-complex BIC, the second is the first fetal heartbeat BIC, the third is the QRS-free ECG BIC, and the fourth is the second fetal heartbeat BIC. The network is trained over ten templates of each of the four segments. The training terminates when the worst error in all patterns in one pass is less than 0.1. Typically the average error will be in the range of 0.001.

4. ECG abnormality classification using polyphase

The main motivations behind the use of HOS are their ability to (i) preserve the phase of the signal frequency components (ii) suppress Gaussian noise, (iii) characterise and separate motion artefact (Nikias and Petropulu, 1993), and other non-Gaussian low frequency components, and (iv) detect and classify non-linearities. HOS algorithms are employed to develop discriminant contour patterns in the multi-dimensional phase of the polyspectra (polyphase) of normal looking ECGs in outpatients having weariness and general malaise or have recently had suspected angina. Similar polyphase patterns have been found in the ECGs of acute myocardial infarct patients with or without diagnostic S-T segment and T-wave changes. The polyphase computation is done in milliseconds but a temporal window of 10 ECG cycles is necessary in each of the polyspectral averaging process. The polyphase patterns can be displayed every 10 seconds. A high resolution three-lead ECG is adequate for polyphase discrimination. The results of a pilot study show that this is a potential diagnostic technique. Particularly in those 50% Pre-Infarction Syndrome cases which show perfectly normal 12-lead ECGs and will not be identified early enough to prevent them from developing acute myocardial infarction (AMI), (Struebe and Strube, 1989). The standard 12-lead ECG has poor sensitivity for the early detection for (AMI). Only 40-50% patients presenting with AMI show S-T segment and T-wave changes on the initial ECG. The rest might not receive the benefit of acute interventional therapies in the first hours after the event. The application of HOS to ECGs has shown fruition in positively identifying ischemic heart diseases (Strube and Strube, 1989, Zgallai, 2011a, Zgallai, 2011b, and Zgallai 2011c). The methodology involved decomposing the ECGs into linear and several non-linear component waves prior to identification and classification. Methods of validation employed clinical diagnoses and other apriori clinical information spanned over a number of years. Using other HOS discriminant patterns, the focus is on the identification of coronary artery disease, solely from its polyphase contour patterns. Polyphase patterns are obtained using the standard three-lead ECG, a multi-channel low-noise amplifier, an interface card and a PC. Sampling frequency is 0.5 KHz and a resolution of 12 bits. Recurrent neural networks have been used to classify the patterns in Fig 4.1 c and d, respectively (**Rizk et al., 1999b**). The employed neural network has an input layer, a middle layer, and an output layer. The input layer has 64 neurons, the middle layer has 16 neurons, and the output layer has 8 neurons. The network size has been optimised using trial and error with an MSE threshold of 0.001. The learning rate and momentum constant are, respectively, 0.7 and 0.9.

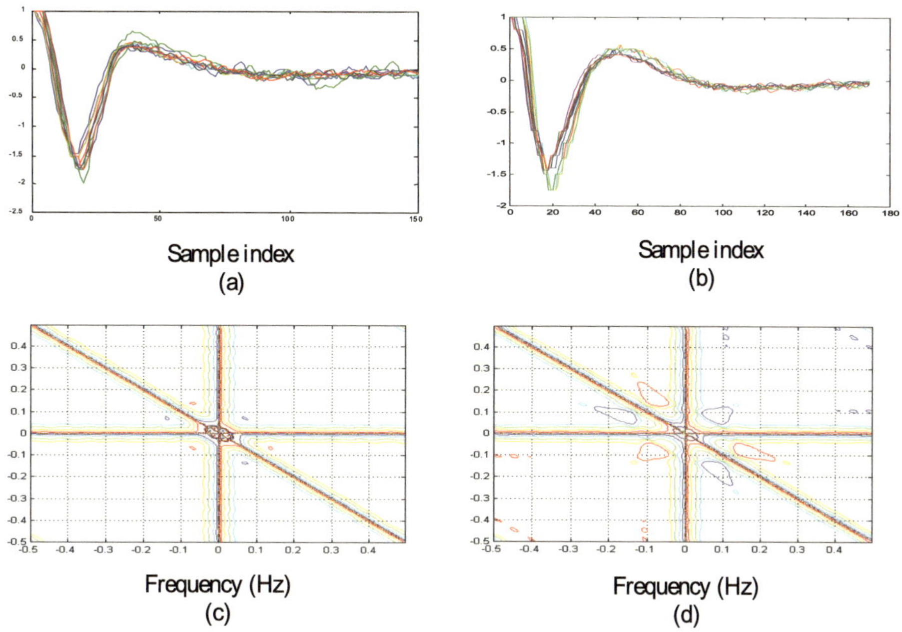

Fig. 4.1. Typical electrocardiogram biphase signature of an Acute myocardial infarction (AMI) presented with a normal looking 12-lead ECG without S-T segment and T-wave changes and normal sinus rhythm. (a) and (b) are ECGs of normal and AMI subjects, respectively. (c) and (d) are the corresponding bispectral phases using the direct method with frequency domain smoothing and Kaiser window. The bispectrum is the average of 10 ST bispectra, the S-T segment is 150 samples starting from the R peak (**Rizk et al., 1999b**).

5. ECG abnormality classification using cumulants

This section describes a simple and accurate multi-layer recurrent neural network classifier specifically designed to successfully distinguish between normal and abnormal higher-order statistics features of electrocardiogram (ECG) signals. The concerned abnormality in ECG is associated with ventricular late potentials (LPs) indicative of life threatening heart diseases. LPs are defined as signals from areas of delayed conduction which outlast the normal QRS period (80-100 msec). The QRS along with the P and T waves constitute the heartbeat cycle. This classifier incorporates both pre-processing and adaptive weight adjustments across the input layer during the training phase of the network to enhance extraction of features pertinent to LPs found in 1-d cumulants. The latter is deemed necessary to offset the low SNR ratio in the cumulant domains concomitant to performing short data segmentation in order to capture the LPs transient appearance. The procedures of feature selection for neural network training, modification to the back propagation algorithm to speed its rate of conversion, and the pilot trial results of the neural ECG classifier are summarised.

5.1 Background

The relationship between myocardial infarction (MI) and short-duration high-frequency components occurring around the terminal end of the QRS complex in the cardiac cycle of the ECG has been investigated by a number of dedicated research workers (Gomis et al., 1997). The high frequency components are associated with late potentials (LPs) emanating from areas of delayed conduction and outlast the normal QRS period (80-100 msec). LPs are linked with malignant ventricular tachycardia (VT) after a myocardial infarction (dead zone or scar tissue in the ventricular muscle). The later is highly correlated with sudden cardiac death. Common methodology for detecting LPs in the time domain involves temporal scanning of the S-T region of the cardiac cycle and relies upon accurate identification of the QRS boundaries (Li et al., 1995). The detection problem is exacerbated by the fact that LP's are relatively weak (mv) and often below the noise floor. In the frequency domain, second-order statistics can offer a limited success. The shapes of power spectra of normal and abnormal (malignant VT) ECGs are invariably broadly similar and without significant features above the noise floor, at approximately -70 dB (Rizk et al., 1998). LPs are essentially non-linear transient events (Gomis et al., 1997) and consequently interact with the inherent non-linearity of the cardiac waves as well as certain class of recursive non-linearly attributed to external factors such as motion artefact (Zgallai et al., 1997).

Previous work (Zgallai et al., 1997) showed that results obtained using HOS offer some empirical evidence that: (i) ECG signals contain intrinsic as well as quadratic and higher-order non- linearities, (ii) the QRS wave is predominantly linear non-Gaussian, the P and T waves are characterized by having quadratic and cubic non-linearities, (iii) the QRS wave can be totally resolved from the motion artifact in the bispectrum domains and (iv) disproportionately high-frequency non-linearity in the bicoherence squared is indicative of abnormality in an otherwise innocent looking ECG. However, non-linear filtering and a high resolution technique such as the spectral MUSIC incorporates an optimised window must be applied to a short duration data sample (without compromising the variance), prior to the application of HOS (Zgallai et al., 1997). Third-order Volterra filtering applied to raw data can be beneficial in isolating quadratic and cubic non-linearity in the higher-domains (Zgallai et al., 2007).

The higher-order statistical features are selected and enhanced using sampled weights of a non-linear function based on a priori information about distinguished abnormality signatures in the higher domains. The function is modified adaptively during the training of the neural network which employs ten 1-d cumulants every 1000 or less cycles per patient. After this the updated version of the function parameters are fixed over the next 1000 cardiac cycles. Subsequently, a simple neural network classifier based on a modified version (Jacobs, 1988, and Hush and Salas, 1988) of the back-propagation algorithms performs accurate LPs and even ischemic ECG classification (Zgallai, 2011 a, Zgallai, 2011 b, and Zgallai, 2011 c).

5.2 Higher-order statistics feature selection and enhancement

The experimental setup consists of an ECG monitor, interface card and a workstation. Raw ECG data are measured using three orthogonal surface electrodes, sampled at 500 Hz and fed to the computer which performs the following operations. Accurate on-line QRS detection. This involves Volterra whitening filters in the time domain or / and the high-resolution spectral MUSIC in the frequency domain. Positions of ECG peaks are pinpointed in the time domain. The MUSIC algorithm incorporates two sliding sets of three overlapping Kaiser windows and adaptive thresholding operations which not only pinpoint the high-level low-frequency QRS spectral peaks (LFQRSSPs) per cycle, but also performs the preliminary spotting of the low-level high-frequency late potential components over a range of frequencies from 100-250 Hz. Detection of late potential high-frequency spectral peaks is carried out off-line every 5 LFQRSSPs to allow appropriate segmentation between the R-R marking in the time domain processing which runs almost synchronisingly with the MUSIC routine. A detailed procedure for segmentation involves calculating the bicoherence squared and mapping a particular region for each individual segment to confirm existence of quadratic non-linearity before moving on to interrogate another segment or skip a few segments up to the next R peak. This controlled skipping helps to avoid the highly non-linear T wave of the present cycle and the P wave of the adjacent one.

The Volterra filtering can be used to partially suppresses motion artifact only in those cases of missing LFQRSSPs and the MUSIC routine is repeated over the same cardiac cycle for confirmation of the presence or absence of QRSs. This has been found to be necessary in extreme cases and in the absence of QRS waves (ventricular fibrillation). Off-line calculations of the cumulant diagonal and wall 1-d slices are performed on those segments suspected of having LPs as depicted in Fig. 5.1. It is clearly seen that abnormality is manifested in the eminent petal pattern (a horizontal slice has a petal shape) in the cumulant domains. Five thousand cardiac cycles of normal and abnormal ECGs were put to the test. An arbitrarily chosen non-linear function modifies the envelope of the so-called 'petal pattern' to enhance its peculiarity against background artifact. The non-linear function is then sampled across the input layer of the neural network.

5.3 Design of the neural classifier

Fig. 5.2 shows the network preceded by a preprocessing unit which performs the task of determining a set of meaningful and representative features in the HOS domains. A sigmoid logistic function is used to describe the input-output relation of the non-linear device. The neural network is designed to classify two classes; normal and abnormal third-order cumulants. The combined use of skewness and kurtosis can provide more accuracy in difficult cases.The utility of the diagonal slice of the fourth-order cumulant can be of more help when used in the desired response for the third output. The use of higher than the third-order statistics adds more complexity to the network.

5.3.1 Block adaptive weight adjustment

Initially the classification was attempted by feeding cumulant slices of short ST segments of the order of 10 to 30 samples at 500 Hz sampling rate. This attempt was 80% successful as the network missed low profile petal patterns with low levels of signal-to-noise ratios in their vicinity as a result of short data segmentation. A function was introduced to strengthen the relative magnitude of the discriminant cumulant slice features. The function is sampled across the input layer and its parameters (α,β) can be adaptively changed for each cumulant slice fed during the training phase which usually takes up to 10 modified cumulant slices every 1000 cardiac cycles. Obviously the shape of function can be changed to cater for other types of abnormalities.

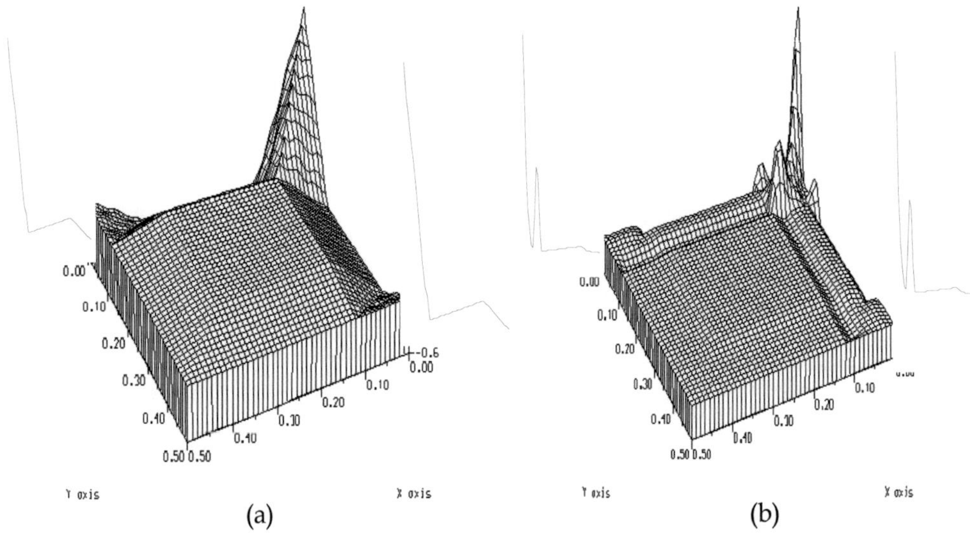

Fig. 5.1. Typical third-order cumulants and their 1-d diagonal and wall slices shown in insets (left, right) of (a) a normal subject and (b) a subject having infarction in the ventricular muscle.

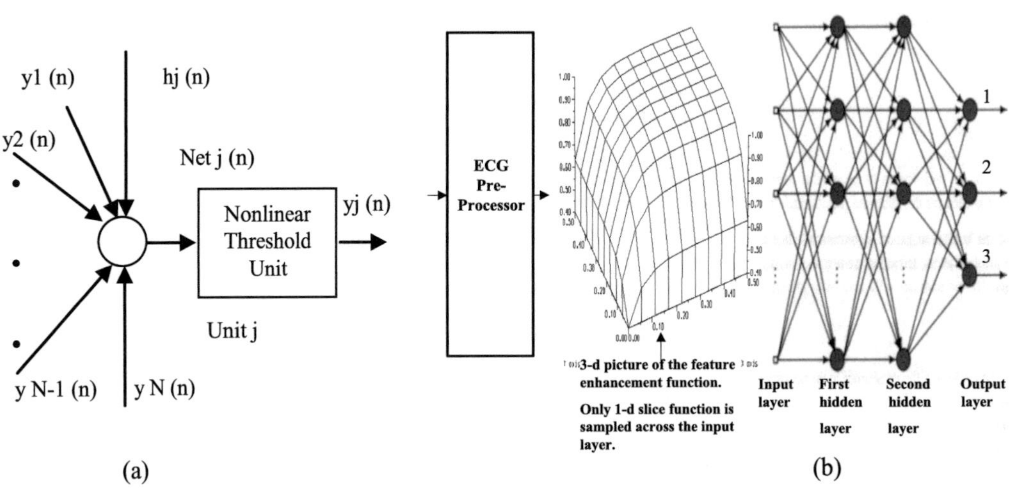

Fig. 5.2. Architecture of the four-layerd neural network. (a) Neuron or processing unit in the network. (b) The four-layer neural network. Only 1-d slice of the weight function modifies the corresponding cumulant slice.

5.3.2 Modification to the back-propagation algorithm

The back propagation method (Hush and Salas, 1988) used in the supervised learning of a multi-layer neural network is basically a gradient descent method. Although this method has become the most popular learning algorithm for multi-layer networks, its rate of convergence is often found to be too slow for practical applications. Well established methods have been adopted (Hush and Salas, 1988). In the modified back-propagation method, every weight w_{ij} in the network is given its own learning rate η_{ij}, and the training data set is divided into a number of epochs each containing K training patterns (training patterns are 1-d cumulants from overlapping segments of the ST region). The weight w_{ij} and learning rate η_{ij} are updated every time after an entire training epoch (10 cumulants) has been presented to the network. The weight and learning rate updating rules of the modified back-propagation algorithm can be summarized as follows (Hush and Salas, 1988).

$$w_{ij}(n+1) = w_{ij}(n) + \eta_{ij}(n+1)\sum_{k=1}^{K} \delta_{kj}(n) y_{ki}(n) + \tau \Delta w_{ij}(n-1) \tag{5.1}$$

$$\eta_{ij}(n+1) = \eta_{ij}(n) + \Delta\eta_{ij}(n) \tag{5.2}$$

$$\Delta\eta_{ij}(n) = \begin{cases} \Omega, & if \quad S(n-1)D(n) > 0 \\ -\phi\eta_{ij}(n), & if \quad S(n-1)D(n) < 0 \\ 0, & otherwise \end{cases} \tag{5.3}$$

$$D(n) = \sum_{k=1}^{K} \frac{\partial \varepsilon_k(n)}{\partial w_{ij}(n)} \tag{5.4}$$

$$S(n) = (1-\Theta)D(n) + \Theta S(n-1). \tag{5.5}$$

The index n refers to the nth epoch in the training data; the index k refers to the kth pattern in an epoch containing K patterns; δ_{kj} is the modulated error signal of neuron j with the kth pattern in an epoch; y_{ki} refers to the actual computed output of neuron I with the kth pattern in an epoch; ε_k is the index performance to be minimised by the weight update rule with the kth input pattern; finally, Ω, Φ, and Θ (all of which have values between 0 and 1) are the control parameters.

5.4 Experimental results

Three orthogonal leads ECG were recorded from several subjects confirmed of having VT with a prior myocardial infarction (MI). Two subjects suspected of having MI but time- and frequency-domains analysis had not shown any abnormality, and several normal subjects. A total of 3,000 cardiac cycles for this pilot study. Their feature extraction and enhancement were performed. The parameter α and β of the exponential weight function applied across the input layer were chosen to fall in the region of 1-2 and 0.25 - 0.5 for α and β, respectively. The initial learning rates $\eta_{ij}(0)$ were all chosen to be 0.06. The momentum factor, α, was fixed at 0.09. The control parameters β, Φ and Θ were chosen to be 0.03, 0.1 and 0.5 respectively. The classifier described here achieved very high (90%) classification rate. The remaining 10% failure mainly arose because the MI suspected cases were not invasively examined and confirmed.

6. Statistical analysis of ECG detection methods

ECG signals are predominantly non-Gaussian (Rizk and Zgallai, 1999 and Rizk et al., 1995), and exhibit quadratic and higher-order non-linearities supported by third- and fourth-order statistics, respectively. ECG signals do contain measurable quantities of quadratic and cubic non-linearities. Such quantities if not synthesised and removed before any further processing for the purpose of signal identification and classification could lead to poor performance with regard to fetal QRS-complex detection rates. The non-linearity in the ECG signal can be detected using the bicoherence squared. The bicoherence squared has peaks at the frequency pairs of (6 Hz,15 Hz) and (14 Hz,14 Hz) for the fetal scalp cardiac cycle, (15 Hz,15 Hz) for the maternal chest cardiac cycle, and (7.5 Hz,7.5 Hz) for the maternal transabdominal cardiac cycle. These bicoherence peaks support non-linearity (Zgallai, 2007). There is a general consensus that individual cardiac cycles are locally stationary. However, when applying a highly dimensional signal such as the transabdominal ECG that have several individual non-linear and deterministic signals overlapping both in the time and frequency domains, all coexisting in a cocktail of noise and motion artefact, it is prudent to re-examine the validity of the stationarity assumption in relation to such signals. It is only natural to expect that the proximity of two non-linear signals such as the maternal and fetal QRS-complexes would result in non-linear (quadratic and higher-order) coupling and this in turn would invoke non-stationarity. The bispectral OT region is insepcted (Nikias and Petropulu, 1993) for the maternal bispectral contour maps at a level of -30 dB. When the two R-waves of the maternal and fetal QRS-complexes are separated by 200 msec, the resultant bispectrum does not support the OT region (Zgallai, 2007). However, the situation is totally different when the two R-waves are as close as 35 msec. The OT region of the bispectrum is fully occupied and non-stationary (Zgallai, 2007). Hence, conventional signal processing techniques to separate the maternal and fetal QRS-complexes cannot be used. This problem has been adequately solved by linearising (at least removing quadratic coupling) the transabdominal signal before attempting to separate individual QRS-complexes.

Correlartion-based second-order statistics do not show any distinguishable features that could be used to differentiate between maternal QRS-complex, fetal heartbeat with maternal contribution, and QRS-free ECG contributions. The FFT method reveals a fetal scalp electrode ECG principal spectral peak at 30 Hz (Zgallai, 2007). The FFT method for the transabdominal cardiac cycle reveals the maternal principal spectral peak of 15 Hz (Zgallai, 2007). However, the FFT does not clearly show fetal spectral peak from the segmented transabdominal signal. There could be a shallow peak as low as 28 Hz or a shifted peak as high as 42 Hz (Zgallai, 2007).

Statistical analysis of ECG data, including Pearson's correlation analysis and higher order moments have been carried out (Rizk and Zgallai, 1999). The value of Pearson's product-moment correlation coefficient for both the third-order cumulant and the bispectral contour method is within the range of -0.1 to +0.1.

The Receiver Operating Characeteristics (ROC) analysis has been used to statistically analyse the results of the two propsoed detection methods, third-order cunulant and bispectral contour, compared to the second-order statistics method. The Area Under Curve (AUC) has been used as a measure for diagnostic accuracy and discriminating power. The second-order statistics-based, third-order cumulant slice, and the bispectral controue methods have AUC values of 0.731, 0.794, and 0.843, respectively. This suggests that the third-order cumulant is a better detection method than second-order statistics-based, and that the bispectral contour method outperforms the third-order cumulant method.

Youden's index, defined as sensitivty + specificity - 1, has also been used for the detection methods. The second-order statistics-based methods have indices in the range of 0.42 to 0.55. The third-order cumulant method has an index of 0.72. The bispectral contour method has an index of 0.80. This suggests that the third-order cumulant is a better detection method than second-order statistics-based, and that the bispectral contour method outperforms the third-order cumulant method.

Also, the Partial Area Under Curve (PAUC) measure has been used for a False-Positive Rate (FPR) of 10% and sensitivty larger than 75%. The second-order statistics-based method gives a PAUC of 0.043. The third-order cumulant method has a corresponding value of 0.125 whilst that of the bispectral contour method is 0.137. This suggests that the third-order cumulant is a better detection method than second-order statistics-based, and that the bispectral contour method outperforms the third-order cumulant method.

7. Conclusion

The sensitivity, specificity and classification rate for the third-order slice cumulant matching hybrid system have been calculated . The technique has been evaluated for diagonal, wall, or arbitrary TOC slices, employing both the LMF-based quadratic and cubic Volterra filters. The results indicate that a linear combination of diagonal and wall slices of the TOC can improve the detection rate by up to 1% over and above the 77.8% obtainable using only either slice. Using two more arbitrary slices off-diagonal and off-wall would result in a further improvement of up to 1%. Using two slices instead of only one results in an two-fold increase in the CPU time of 1 msec using Unix WS. Further improvement of 6% to 8% is attainable with maternal transabdominal ECG signal linearisation employing second- and third-order Volterra synthesisers, respectively. Based on the first hybrid system using TOC slices for signal processing and subsequent single-hidden-layer classification, 100% and 86.16% classification rates have been achieved for maternal QRS-complex and fetal heartbeats, respectively. Note that the classification rates for coincident and non-coincident maternal and fetal QRS-complexes are 0% and 95.55%, respectively. The remaining undetected 13.84% fetal heartbeats include 9.8% overlap with the maternal QRS-complexes and 4% occur during depolarisation of the maternal T-waves. Those events unavoidably lead to significant distortion of the fetal TOCs. This means that the cumulant signatures will not be close to the TOC template signature stored in the database. Examples of false negatives and false positives have been found in the following cases, respectively, (i) a fetal heartbeat with maternal contribution TOC diagonal slice was wrongly matched to a QRS-free ECG TOC diagonal slice template, and (ii) a QRS-free ECG TOC diagonal slice was wrongly matched to a fetal heartbeat with maternal contribution TOC diagonal slice template.

Results obtained for the bispectral contour matching hybrid system from 30 cases using the non-invasive transabdominally-measured ECG signal, with the simultaneous fetal scalp electrode ECG signal as a reference, show that the method has a classification rate of 100% for normal, healthy maternal QRS-complexes and 90.12% for fetal heartbeats. It has been shown that an improvement of 1% to 3% is attainable with ECG signal linearisation employing second- and third-order Volterra synthesisers, respectively. Conventional methods (based on the power spectrum) of fetal heartbeat detection have a success rate in the range of 70%. The second hybrid system has a significantly higher classification rate. The classification rate of fetal heartbeats for non-coincident maternal and fetal QRS-complexes is 99.21%. The classification rate of fetal heartbeats for coincident maternal and fetal QRS-complexes is 0%. This means that the hybrid bispectral contours technique fails to resolve the fetal beat when both the mother and fetal QRS-complexes are synchronised. The bispectral contour template matching technique improved the classification rate by approximately 4% over and above that of the third-order cumulant template matching technique. The difference in performance is not due to better resolvability of the latter over the former in the case of coincident maternal and fetal QRS-complexes, as both techniques fail in this respect. But, it is due to the fact that the BIC template matching technique can resolve a few of the fetal QRS-complexes occurring within the T-wave region of the mother.

Non-invasive classification of a particular type of ECG abnormality, late potentials, was investigated. This has been achieved by the prudent use of their third-order cumulant 1-d slices. A four-layer neural network classifier based on modified back-propagation algorithm and incorporating adaptive feature enhancement weights applied to its input layer during its learning phase has been successfully tested. Classification rate obtained from 3000 cardiac cycles of normal, confirmed, and suspected abnormal subjects is 90%. In a separate study conducted on the same data a sophisticated recurrent back-propagation network achieved less that 80% success rate. However, the instability issues of the latter network have not been fully investigated.

8. References

Bentley, J. M., Grant, P. M., and McDonnel, J. T. E. (1998). Time-frequency and time-scale techniques for the classification of native and bioprosthetic heart valve sounds. *IEEE Transactions on Biomedical Engineering*, Vol. 45, pp. 125-128.

Bergveld, P. and Meijier, W. J. H. (1981) A New Technique for the Suppression of MECG. *IEEE Transactions on Biomedical Engineering*, vol. 28, pp. 348-354.

Brockett, P. L., Hinich, M. J., and Patterson, D. (1988) Bispectral-Based Tests for the Detection of Gaussianity and Linearity in Time Series. *Journal of the American Statistical Association*, vol. 83, No. 403, pp. 657-664.

Caudill, M. & Butler, C. (1992) *Understanding Neural Networks: Computer Explorations*, MIT press.

Crowe, J. A. et al., (1995) Sequential recording of the abdominal fetal electrocardiogram and Magnetogram. *Physiological Measurements*, vol. 16, pp. 43-47.

De Lathauwer, K., De Moor, B., and Vandewalle, J. (2000) Fetal electrocardiogram extraction by blind source separation. *IEEE Transactions on Biomedical Engineering*, Vol. 47, No. 5, pp. 567- 572, May.

Dogan, M. C. and Mendel, J. M. (1993) Antenna Array Noise Re-conditioning by Cumulants. *Proceedings of the IEEE Signal Processing Workshop on Higher Order Statistics*, CA.

Gomis, P. et al., (1997). Analysis of abnormal signals within the QRS complex of the high-resolution electrocardiogram. *IEEE Transactions on Biomedical Engineering*, Vol. 44, No. 8, pp. 681-693, August.

Herbert, J. M. et al., (1993) Antepartum Fetal Electrocardiogram Extraction and Analysis. *Proceedings of Computers in Cardiology*, pp. 875-877.

Hush, D. R., and Salas, J. M. (1988). Improving the learning rate of back-propagation with the gradient reuse algorithm. *Proceedings of the 2nd International conference on neural networks.* Vol. 1, pp. 441-447.

Jacobs, R. A. (1988). Increased rates of convergence through learning rate adaptation. *Neural Networks*, Vol. 1, pp. 295-307.

Khamene, A. and Negahadariapour, S. (2002) A new method for the extraction of fetal ECG from the composite abdominal signal. *IEEE Transactions on Biomedical Engineering*, Vol. 47, No. , pp. 507–511, April.

Kovaes, E., Torok, M., and Habermajer, I. (2000) A rule-based phonocardiogrphic method for long- term fetal heart rate monitoring. *IEEE Transactions on Biomedical Engineering*, Vol. 47, pp. 124-130.

Li, C., Zheng, C., and Tai, C. F. (1995). Detection of ECG characteristic points using wavelet transforms. *IEEE Transactions on Biomedical Engineering*, Vol. 42, January.

Lin, C. et al., (1997) A portable monitor for fetal heart rate and uterine contraction. *IEEE Engineering in Medicine and Biology Socierty (EMBS) Magazine*, pp. 80-84, Nov./Dec.

Longini, R. L., Reichert, T. A., Yu, J. M. and Crowley, J. S. (1977) Near orthogonal basis functions: A real time fetal ECG technique. *IEEE Transactions on Biomedical Engineering*, Vol. 24, pp. 39-43.

Moody, G. (1997), MIT/BIH database distribution. MIT, Massachusets Avenue, Room 20A-113, Cambridge, MA 02139, USA.

Nikias, C. L. and Petropulu, A. P. (1993). *Higher Order Spectral Analysis: A Nonlinear Signal Processing Framework.* A. V. Oppenheim Series editor.

Rizk, M., Zgallai, W. A., Carson, E., MacLean, A., & Grattan, K. (2002) Multi-fractility in Fetal Heart Beat Dynamics. The *2nd European Medical and Biological Engineering Conference*, Austria, December.

Rizk M., Zgallai W. A., , McLean, A., Carson, E., and Grattan, K. (2001) Virtues and Vices of Source Separation Using Linear Independent Component Analysis for Blind Source Separation of Non-linearly Coupled and Synchronised Fetal and Mother ECGs. *IEEE Engineering in Medicine and Biology Conference*, USA.

Rizk, M., Zgallai, W., Morgan, C., ElKhafif, S., Carson, E., & Grattan, K. (2000) Novel decision strategy for P-wave detection utilising nonlinearly synthesised ECG components and their enhanced pseudospectral resonances. *IEE Proceedings Science, Measurement & Technology*, Special section on Medical Signal Processing, vol. 147, No. 6, pp. 389-397, November.

Rizk M. and Zgallai, W. (1999) "Higher Order Statistics Are Indispensable Tools in The Analysis of Electrocardiogram Signals," IEE Colloquium on Statistical Signal Processing, January.

Rizk, M, Zgallai, W. A., ElKhafif, S., Carson, E., Grattan, K., Thompson, P. (1999). Highly accurate higher-order statistics based neural network classifier of specific abnormality in electrocardiogram signals. *International Conference on Acoustics, Speech, & Signal Processing, ICASSP99*, USA, 13/3.

Rizk, M., Zgallai, W. A., El-Khafif, S., Carson, E., Grattan, K. (1998) "Higher- Order Ambulatory Electrocardiogram Identification and Motion Artifact Suppression With Adaptive Second- and Third-Order Volterra Filters," SPIE '98 Advanced Signal Processing Algorithms, Architectures, and Implementations VIII Vol. 3461 pp. 417-431, San Diego, USA, 19-24 July.

Rizk, M., Romare, D., Zgallai, W. A., Grattan, K., Hardiman, P., and O'Riordan, J. (1995) "Higher order statistics (HOS) in signal processing: Are they of any use?," IEE colloquium, digest #111, pp. 1/1-1/6, London, May.

Schetzen, M. (1980) *The Volterra Wiener theory of the non- linear systems*. New York: Wiley.

Schreiber, T. and Kaplan, D. (1996) Signal separation by nonlinear projections: The fetal Electrocardiogram. *Physics Review E*, Vol. 53, p. R4326.

Spiegl, A., Steinbigler, Schmueking, P. I., Knez, A. and Haberl, R. (1998). Analysis of beat-to-beat variability of frequency contents in the electrocardiogram using two-dimensional Fourier transform. *IEEE Transactions on Biomedical Engineering*. Vol. 45, No. 2, pp. 235-241, February.

Strube, G. and Strube, G. (1989), *Commonsense Cardiology*, Kluwer Academic Publishers.

Sureau, C. (1996) Historical perspectives: forgotten past, unpredictable future. *Baillier's Clinical obstetrics and gynaecology, international practice and research, intrapartum surveillance*, (J Gardosi, ed.), vol. 10, No. 2, pp. 167-184.

Van Bemmel, J. H. (1968) Detection of weak electrocardiograms by autocorrelation and cross correlation envelopes. IEEE *Transactions on Biomedical Engineering*, Vol. 15, pp. 17-23.

Van Oosterom, A. (1986) Spatial filtering of the fetal electrocardiogram. *Journal of Perinatal Medicine*, vol. 14, pp. 411-419.

Wallach, E. and Widrow, B. (1984) The Least-Mean Fourth (LMF) adaptive algorithm and its Family. *IEEE Transactions on Information Theory*, Vol. IT-30, No. 2, pp. 275-283, March.

Widrow, B. et al., (1975) Adaptive Noise Cancellation: Principles and Applications. *Proceedings of IEEE*, Vol. 63, No. 12, pp. 1692-1716, December.

Zgallai, W. A. (2012) Non-Invasive Fetal Heartbeat Detection Using Bispectral Contour Matching. International Conference on Electronics and Biomedical Engineering Applications, UAE.

Zgallai, W. A. (2011a) A novel super-resolution MUSIC-based pseudo-bispectrum. *The IEEE 17th International Conference on Digital Signal Processing (DSP)*, Greece, 6-8/07.

Zgallai, W. A. (2011b) A polycoherence-based ECG signal non-linear detector. *The IEEE 17th International Conference on Digital Signal Processing (DSP)*, Greece, 6-8/07.

Zgallai, W. A. (2011c) MUSIC pseudo-bispectrum detects ECG ischaemia. *The IEEE 17th International Conference on Digital Signal Processing (DSP)*, Greece, 6-8/07.

Zgallai, W. A. (2010) Non-invasive fetal heartbeat detection using third-order cumulant slices matching and ANN classifiers. *The 7th International Association of Science and Technology for Development (IASTED), International Conference on Biomedical Engineering, IASTED*, Austria, 17/02.

Zgallai, W. A. (2009) Embedded Volterra for Prediction of Electromyographic Signals During Labour. *The 16th IEEE International Conference on Digital Signal Processing (DSP)*, Greece, 05/07.

Zgallai, W. A. (2007) *Advanced Robust Non-Invasive Fetal Heart Detection Techniques During Active Labour Using One Pair of Transabdominal Electrodes*, PhD Thesis, City University London, UK.

Zgallai, W. A. Et al., (1997) MUSIC-Based Bispectrum Detector: A Novel Non-Invasive Detection Method For Overlapping Fetal and Maternal ECG Signals. *Proc 19th IEEE International Conference Engeering in Medicine and Biology*, EMBS, pp. 72-75, USA, October.

Zgallai W. A. et al., (1997) Third-order cumulant signature matching technique for non-invasive fetal heart beat identification. *IEEE International Conference on Acoustics, Spech, and Signal Processing (ICASSP)*, vol. 5, pp 3781-3784, Germany.

M. Sabry-Rizk, S. El-Khafif, E. Carson, W. Zgallai, K. Grattan, C. Morgan and P. Hardiman (1999b), "Suspicious Polyphase Patterns of Normal Looking ECGs Provide Fast Early Diagnoses of a Coronary Artery Disease," IEEE Proceedings of the joint EMBS/BMES conference, pp. 979, 13-16 October 1999.

12

Artificial Intelligence Techniques Applied to Electromagnetic Interference Problems Between Power Lines and Metal Pipelines

Dan D. Micu[1], Georgios C. Christoforidis[2] and Levente Czumbil[1]
[1]*Technical University of Cluj-Napoca,*
[2]*Technological Educational Institution of West Macedonia, Kozani,*
[1]*Romania*
[2]*Greece*

1. Introduction

European ecological regulations meant to protect nature and wild life along with construction cost reduction policies generated a set of government regulations that limit the access to new transmission and distribution corridors. As a result, gas, water or oil supply pipelines are forced to share the same distribution corridors with Electrical Power Lines (EPL), AC Railway Systems or Telecommunication Lines (figure 1).

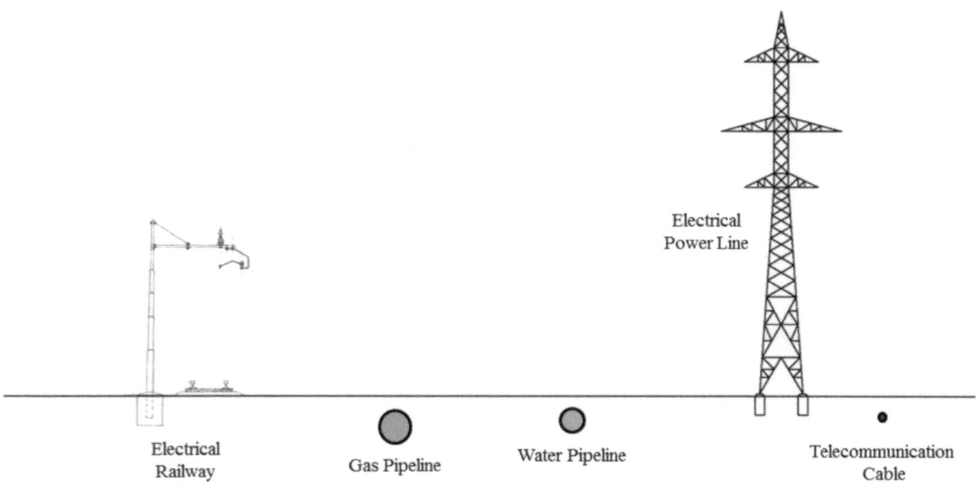

Fig. 1. Common distribution corridor. Right of way.

The electromagnetic fields generated by high voltage electrical power lines produce AC interference in the nearby metallic structures. Therefore, in many cases these underground or above ground utilities supply Metal Pipelines (MP) are exposed to effects of induced AC currents and voltages (CIGRÉ 1995, Dawalibi & Southey 1989). Especially in case of power line faults, the resulting AC voltage in unprotected pipelines may reach thousands of volts.

This could be dangerous on both the operating personnel (that may be exposed to electric shocks), and to the structural integrity of the pipeline, due to corrosion. Underground steel pipelines are in permanent contact with the electrolyte solution from the soil, so proper protection measures are necessary in order to limit the induced current densities, which are the cause of electrochemical corrosion. Uncontrolled corrosion of supply pipelines may cause gas or/and oil spills with very serious ecological and economic implications. (Baboian 2002, Collet et al. 2001)

In order to provide proper protection for pipelines the AC interference has to be well known. Normally, the electromagnetic interference between electrical power lines and nearby metallic pipelines could be generated by any of the following three types of couplings (CIGRÉ 1995):

- **Inductive Coupling**: Aerial and underground pipelines that run parallel to or in close proximity to transmission lines or cables are subjected to induced voltages by the time varying magnetic fields produced by the transmission line currents. The induced electromotive forces (EMF) causes current circulation in the pipeline and voltages between the pipeline and surrounding earth.
- **Conductive Coupling**: When a ground fault occurs in the electrical power system the current flowing through the grounding grid produce a potential rise on both the grounding grid and the neighbouring soil with regard to remote earth. If the pipeline goes through the "zone of influence" of this potential rise, then a high difference in the electrical potential can appear across the coating of the pipeline metal.
- **Capacitive Coupling**: Affects only above ground pipelines situated next to overhead power lines. It occurs due to the capacitance between the power line and the pipeline. For underground pipelines the effect of capacitive coupling may be neglected, because of the screening effect of the earth.

In case of interferences between EPLs under normal operating conditions and underground pipelines, only the inductive coupling described by the self and mutual impedance matrix has to be taken into consideration. Conductive and capacitive interference may be, also, neglected when a ground fault happens significantly away from the common corridor.

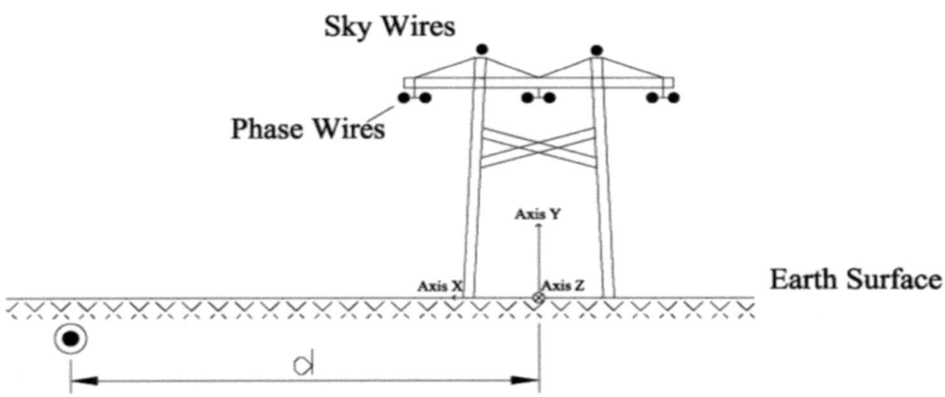

Fig. 2. Cross section of an interference problem between an EPL and an underground MP.

To evaluate the self and mutual impedance between the conductors (phase wires, sky wires and pipelines) the magnetic vector potential has to be evaluated on the cross section (figure 2) of these conductors as presented in (Christoforidis et al. 2003, 2005).

Thus, taking into account the cross section of the studied problem, the *z*-direction component of the magnetic vector potential A_z and of the total current density J_z are described by the following system of differential equations:

$$\begin{cases} \dfrac{1}{\mu_0\mu_r}\cdot\left[\dfrac{\partial^2 A_z}{\partial x^2}+\dfrac{\partial^2 A_z}{\partial y^2}\right]-j\omega\sigma A_z+J_{sz}=0 \\ -j\omega\sigma A_z+J_{sz}=J_z \\ \iint\limits_{S_i} J_z ds = I_i \end{cases} \quad (1)$$

where σ is the conductivity, ω is the angular frequency, μ_0 is the magnetic permeability of free space ($\mu_0 = 4\cdot\pi\cdot10^{-7}$ H/m), μ_r is the relative permeability of the environment, J_{sz} is the source current density in the *z*-direction and I_i is the imposed current on conductor *i* of S_i cross section.

To solve this differential equation system, the finite element method (FEM) is recommended to be used. FEM effectively transforms the electromagnetic interference problem into a numerical one. Although FEM yielded solutions are very accurate, regarding to the problem complexity, the computing time of this method increases with the geometry, its mesh, material characteristics and requested evaluation parameters.

The FEM calculations are used in the described method, as a means of calculating the self and mutual impedances of the conductors present in the configuration. Generally, if there exist *n* conductors in the configuration and assuming that the per unit length voltage drop on every conductor is known for a specific current excitation, the mutual complex impedance between conductor *i* and another conductor *j* carrying a certain current, where all other conductors are imposed to carry zero currents, is given by:

$$Z_{ij}=\frac{V_i}{I_j}\ (i,j=1,2,\ldots,n) \quad (2)$$

Similarly, the self-impedance of conductor *i* may be calculated using (2), by setting *i*=*j*.

The procedure is summarized below (Papagiannis et. al. 2000):

- By applying a sinusoidal current excitation of arbitrary magnitude to each conductor, while applying zero current to the other conductors, the corresponding voltages are calculated.
- The self and mutual impedances of the j conductor may be calculated using (2).

The above procedure is repeated *n* times, so as to calculate the impedances for *n* conductors.

Applying FEM calculations for the solution of linear electromagnetic diffusion equation (first relation from system (1)), the values for source current density in the *z*-direction (J_{szi}) on each conductor *i* having a conductivity of σ_i are obtained. Therefore, equation (2) becomes:

$$Z_{ij} = \frac{V_i}{I_j} = \frac{J_{szi} / \sigma_i}{I_j} \quad (i,j = 1,2,\ldots,n) \tag{3}$$

Following the above procedure, effectively linking electromagnetic field variables and equivalent circuit parameters, the self and mutual impedances per unit length of the problem are computed.

By using FEM to calculate the impedances of the problem instead of classic formulae, (e.g. Carson's formulae), one can deal effectively with more complex situations, such as multilayer earth or terrain irregularities.

Nevertheless, the study of electromagnetic interference between power lines and underground pipelines using FEM for different system configurations requires expensive computing time. This is because each new problem geometry taken under consideration involves a new mesh development and new calculations. To solve system equation (1) for a given problem geometry (EPL-MP separation distance, soil resistivity) with an Intel Core2 Duo T6400 (2.0 GHz/2.0 GHz) processor PC it takes from 20 to 50 minutes depending on mesh discretization. Therefore, any scaling method of the results from one configuration case to another may be of interest if it provides less computing time.

A first attempt in applying artificial intelligence techniques to scale EPL-MP interference results was made in (Satsios et al. 1999a, 1999b). A Fuzzy Logic Block (FLB) was implemented to evaluate the Magnetic Vector Potential (MVP) for an EPL-MP interference problem where phases to earth fault occurred. The input values were the geometrical parameters of the studied problem configuration (separation distance, soil resistivity) and the coordinates of the point where the MVP should be calculated. However, the implemented FLB provide relatively good results for MVP, the main disadvantage of this method consists in determination of the optimal parameters, which describes the fuzzy logic rule base. An iterative technique based on conjugate gradient has been used to optimize the fuzzy rule base parameters. Later on a Genetic Algorithm technique had been proposed in (Damousis et al. 2002) to determine the optimal parameters and rule base configuration

Another approach in using artificial intelligence techniques in the study of electromagnetic interferences between power lines and underground metal pipelines was introduced by Al-Badi (Al-Badi et al. 2005, 2007). A feed-forward Neural Network with one output layer and one hidden layer was proposed to evaluate the induced AC interference in an underground pipeline exposed to electromagnetic fields generated by an electrical power line in case of a phase to earth fault. The input values of this Neural Network were the fault current, the soil resistivity, the separation distance and a fourth parameter which indicates the presence of mitigation wires. The main advantage of this NN solution was that it provided directly the value of the induced AC voltages. However, the limitation of this model consists in the fact that the results are obtained for a specific common distribution corridor length.

In this chapter two artificial intelligence techniques are presented. These were applied by the authors in some EPL-MP electromagnetic interferences studies (Micu et al. 2009, 2011). The first one is a neural network alternative to the EPL-MP interference problem presented in (Satsios et al. 1999a, 1999b). The advantage of the proposed alternative consists in the accuracy of the obtained results and in the shorter training time. The second is a neural network solution used to evaluate the self and mutual impedance matrix, which describe the inductive coupling between an electrical power line and an underground pipeline in the presence of a three vertical layer earth. For such a case, no analytical formula exists so far, and this means that lengthy calculations using FEM must be made. The obtained impedance matrix can be used to build and solve the equivalent electrical circuit model and thus evaluate the induce AC voltage. This equivalent electrical circuit approach permits to solve more complex problem geometries where for example the separation distance between EPL and MP varies along the common distribution corridor.

2. Magnetic vector potential evaluation using neural networks

The first attempt of the authors to use neural networks based artificial intelligence techniques in the study of electromagnetic interference problems was focused on finding an easier method to identify the optimal solution to scale the results from a set of known problem geometries to any other new problem geometries in case of specific EPL-MP interference problems.

2.1 Studied electromagnetic interference problem

The studied electromagnetic interference problem, presented in figure 3, refers to an underground metallic gas pipeline which shares for 25 km the same distribution corridor with a 145 kV EPL at 50 Hz frequency. The power line consists of two steel reinforced aluminium conductors per phase. Sky wire conductors have a 4 mm radius and the gas pipeline has a 0.195 m inner radius, a 0.2 m outer radius and a 0.1 m coating radius. The characteristics of the materials in this configuration have the following properties: the soil is assumed to be homogeneous; MP and sky wires have an σ =7.0E+05 S/m conductivity and a μ_r=250 relative permeability.

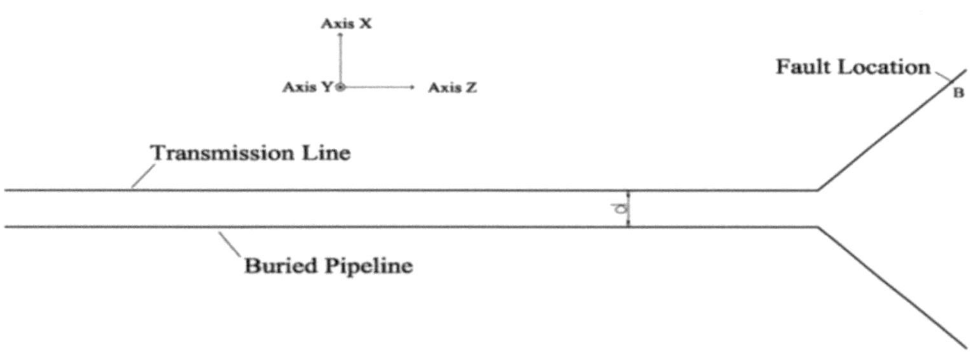

Fig. 3. Top view of the parallel exposure.

It is assumed that a phase to ground fault occurs at point B, far away outside the common EPL-MP distribution corridor. The earth current associated with this fault has a negligible action upon the buried pipeline. This fact allows us to assume only the inductive coupling caused by the flowing fault current in the section where the power lines runs parallel to the buried gas pipeline. End effects are neglected, leading to a two dimensional (2D) problem, presented in figure 4, were the magnetic vector potential has to be evaluated.

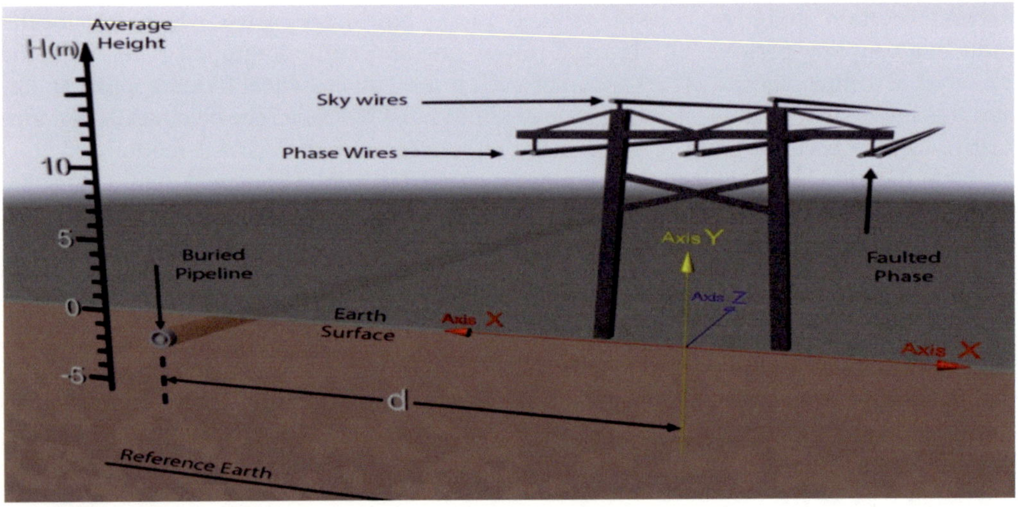

Fig. 4. Cross section of the studied EPL-MP interference problem.

2.2 Fuzzy logic implementation

A first attempt in applying artificial intelligence techniques to reduce the computational time needed by FEM to evaluate the MVP values for different problem geometries have been made in (Satsios et al. 1999a, 1999b). The presented Fuzzy Logic Block had as input values the separation distance, *d*, between EPL and MP, the soil resistivity, *ρ*, and the coordinates *(x,y)* of the point where MVP is wanted to be evaluated:

$$\begin{aligned}&\text{The } j^{th} \text{ rule from the presented Fuzzy Logic Block's rule base:}\\ &R^j: \textbf{IF}\, d,x,y \text{ and } \rho \text{ belong to the } j^{th} \text{ membership function, } \mu_d^j, \mu_x^j\, \mu_y^j \text{ and}\\ &\mu_\rho^j \text{ correspondingly}\\ &\textbf{THEN}\, A^j = \lambda_0^j + \lambda_d^j \cdot d + \lambda_x^j \cdot x + \lambda_y^j \cdot y + \lambda_\rho^j \cdot \rho\end{aligned} \tag{4}$$

The proposed Fuzzy Logic Block showed relatively good results for MVP's amplitude and phase evaluation according to the training database created by calculating MVP with FEM for a set of known problem geometries (figure 5):

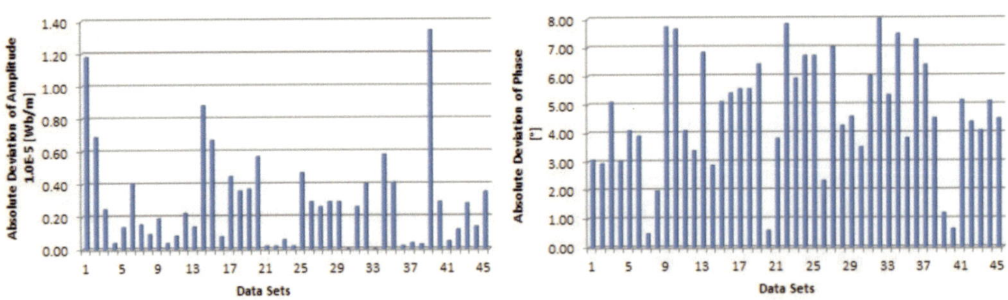

Fig. 5. Absolute evaluation error provided by the presented Fuzzy Logic Block.

To identify the proper rule base and the optimal parameters for each rule an iterative technique has been applied using gradient based relations like:

$$\nabla_{\overline{\alpha_{\Delta}^{j}}} J^{P} = \frac{\mu^{j}}{\sum_{j} \mu^{j}} \left[A^{p}(d,x,y,\rho) - A_{FEM}^{p}(d,x,y,\rho) \right] \cdot \left[A^{j} - A^{p}(d,x,y,\rho) \right] \cdot \frac{\Delta^{p} - \overline{\alpha_{\Delta}^{j}}}{\left(\sigma_{\Delta}^{j}\right)^{2}} \tag{5}$$

and

$$\nabla_{\overline{\sigma_{\Delta}^{j}}} J^{P} = \frac{\mu^{j}}{\sum_{j} \mu^{j}} \left[A^{p}(d,x,y,\rho) - A_{FEM}^{p}(d,x,y,\rho) \right] \cdot \left[A^{j} - A^{p}(d,x,y,\rho) \right] \cdot \frac{\Delta^{p} - \overline{\alpha_{\Delta}^{j}}}{\left(\sigma_{\Delta}^{j}\right)^{3}} \tag{6}$$

where $\Delta \in \{d,x,y,\rho\}$ and $A_{FEM}^{p}(d,x,y,\rho)$, $A^{p}(d,x,y,\rho)$ are the MVP values obtained with FEM and respectively.

In the following, in order to improve the accuracy of the obtained results and to simplify the implementation process of the applied artificial intelligence technique, the authors propose an alternative by using a Neural Network solution instead of the presented Fuzzy Logic Block presented in (Satsios et al. 1999a, 1999b).

2.3 MatLab implementation of prosed neural networks

To identify the optimal neural network solution different feed-forward and layer recurrent architectures were evaluated. To implement these neural network architectures the *Neural Network Toolbox* of the *MatLab* software application was used. This software was chosen because it enables the creation of almost all types of NN from perceptrons (single layer networks used for classification) to more complex architectures of feed-forward or recurrent networks. To create a feed-forward neural network in *MatLab* the following function can be called from command line:

net = newff(P,T,S,TF,BTF,BLF,PF) (7)

where:

- P - is a RxQ1 matrix of Q1 representative R-element input vectors;
- T - is a SNxQ2 matrix of Q2 representative SN-element target vectors;
- S - is a vector representing the number of neurons in each hidden layer;
- TF - is a vector representing the transfer function used for each layer;
- BTF - is the back propagation function used to train the NN;
- BLF - is the weight/bias learning function;
- PF - is performance evaluation function.

A similar function can be called to create a layer recurrent neural network:

net = newlrn(P,T,S,TF,BTF,BLF,PF) (8)

Once a neural network is created, to train it, the following *Matlab* function can be used:

train(net,P,T) (9)

where:

- net – is the neural network that has to be trained;
- P – is a RxQ1 matrix of Q1 representative R-element input vectors;
- T – is a SNxQ2 matrix of Q2 representative SN-element target vectors;

These to functions also provide a pre-processing of the four input parameters: *d* the separation distance between EPL and MP (which varies between 70 m and 2000 m), ρ the soil resistivity (which varies between 30 Ωm and 1000 Ωm) and *(x,y)* the coordinates of the point where the MVP is wanted to be evaluated (which varies between 0 and 2100 m, respectively between 0 m and -30 m); by scaling them in the range of [-1,+1].

To train the different NN architectures the Levenberg-Marquardt training method and the descendent gradient with momentum weight learning rule has been implemented. As training data base a set of MVP values evaluated with FEM and presented in (Satsios et al. 1999a, 1999b) were used. These MVP values were calculated in different points up to 15 different problem geometries (soil resistivity, separation distance) obtaining a set of 37 input/output pairs used to train the proposed NN. Table 1 presents some of the training data sets.

No	*d* [m]	*x* [m]	*y* [m]	ρ [Ω*m]	MVP	
					Amp. 10^{-5} [Wb/m]	**Phase [°]**
1	70	70	-15	30	36.1	-22.8
5	800	818.25	-13.5	30	3.88	-82.61
9	400	384.81	-7.82	70	17.2	-44.46
14	70	40	0	100	55.9	-18.53
18	1000	1022.5	0	100	7.23	-67.27
23	300	290.26	-15.8	500	35.5	-26.74
28	700	670	-22.5	700	26	-33.74
30	150	150.55	-16.99	900	53	-19.7
33	1500	1499.1	-17.48	900	15.6	-46.35
37	2000	2030	-5	1000	12.2	-52.73

Table 1. Training data sets.

Once the NN are trained they can provide automatically the corresponding output values for any combination of input parameters by applying the following *MatLab* function:

$$\text{sim(net,X)} \tag{10}$$

where *net* is the implemented neural network and *X* is a set of input values.

2.4 Results obtained with feed-forward neural networks

To determine precisely the magnetic vector potential in each point of the studied domain, the amplitude and the phase of the MVP has to be evaluated. Considering the different variation range: $10^{-6} \div 10^{-4}$ [Wb/m] for amplitude, and -180°÷180° for phase, the authors chose to implement two different neural networks - one for amplitude and one for phase -

instead of implementing a single NN that would provide both amplitude and phase. Also the output values for NN which returns the MVP amplitude were scaled from $10^{-6}\div10^{-4}$ to $0.1\div100$, so the final output values has to be multiplied by 10^{-5} to obtain the actual MVP amplitude value in [Wb/m].

Initially, feed-forward neural networks with one output layer and one hidden layer were tested (figure 6). Some of the obtained results were already presented in (Micu et al. 2009) and (Czumbil et al. 2009). In the following a more detailed study is presented.

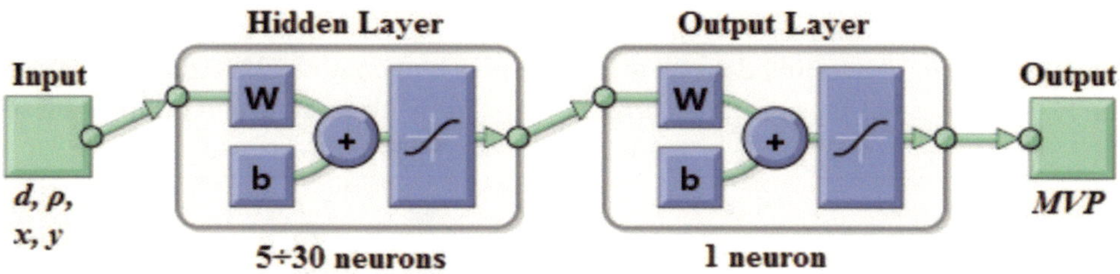

Fig. 6. Implemented feed-forward network architecture.

The number of neurons in the hidden layer was varied from 5 to 30 with a step of 5 neurons. The transfer function of the output layer was set to *purelin* (the linear transfer function) and the transfer function on the hidden layer was varied between *tansig* (the hyperbolic tangent sigmoid function), *logsig* (the logarithmic sigmoid function) and *purelin*. Also, the performance evaluation function was varied between *mse* (mean square error), *msereg* (mean square error with regularization performance) and *sse* (sum squared error).

After the implementation and training, the proposed feed-forward networks were submitted to a testing process. The error between the output values generated by NN and the magnetic vector potential evaluated with FEM for the training data sets was determined. Analysing the obtained errors, it was concluded that none of the tested architectures having the *purelin* transfer function on the hidden layer, had provided acceptable results. The average evaluation error was around 10% and the achieved maximum error was greater than 25%. For all the other NN architectures, the evaluation error for the training data sets was neglectable.

No	*d* [m]	*x* [m]	*y* [m]	*ρ* [Ω*m]	MVP	
					Amp. 10^{-5} **[Wb/m]**	**Phase [°]**
1	70	40	-15	100	53.8	-19.34
2	70	81.66	-27.03	30	32.90	-25.57
3	400	392.25	-25.56	70	16.7	-46.05
4	300	281.66	-27.03	500	37.5	-25.93
5	700	690.36	-15.80	700	25.6	-34.07
6	1000	1007.50	0	70	5.68	-72.98
7	1000	1015	-30	100	7.16	-69.22
8	1500	1524.77	-6.93	900	15.40	-46.56

Table 2. Testing data sets.

Since the main goal was the implementations of a suitable NN, that would provide accurate solutions for any new problem geometry, a second testing database was used to select the optimal NN architecture. This second database is a totally new set of data, which was not applied to NN during the training process (table 2).

Analyzing the average and maximum evaluation errors obtained for the testing data sets, in case of the neural network which would evaluate the amplitude of the magnetic vector potential, two possible NN architectures were determined (AmpFfNN2 and AmpFfNN7). The first one (AmpFfNN2) has 10 neurons with *tansig* transfer function on the hidden layer and uses an *mse* performance evaluation function. In this case the obtained average evaluation error for the testing data set is 0.71% with a maximum 1.72% achieved evaluation error. Figure 7 presents the evaluation error obtained for both training and testing data sets.

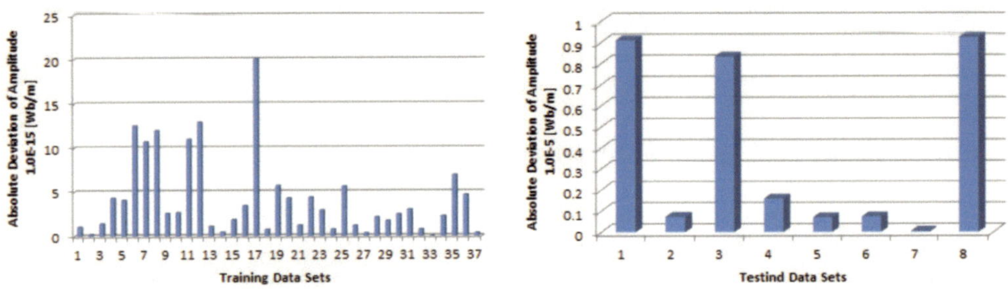

Fig. 7. Absolute evaluation error for AmpFfNN2 network.

The second possible solution (AmpFfNN7) for the amplitude network has 5 neurons with *logsig* transfer function on the hidden layer and uses an *mse* performance evaluation function. In this case the obtained average evaluation error for the testing data set is 0.77% with a maximum 2.50% achieved evaluation error. Figure 8 presents the evaluation error obtained for both training and testing data sets.

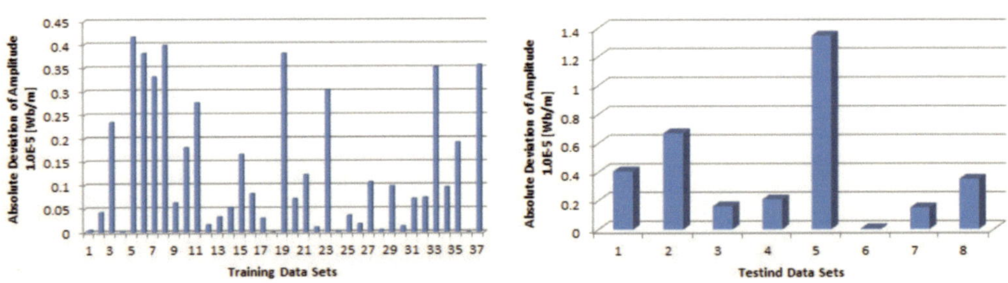

Fig. 8. Absolute evaluation error for AmpFfNN7 network.

Comparing the result for both possible amplitude NN architectures it can be observed that AmpFfNN2 provides better results for both training and testing data sets.

Based on the obtained maximum and average evaluation errors for neural networks implemented for MVP phase evaluation, two possible optimal NN architectures were determined (PhaseFfNN38 and PhaseFfNN43). The first one (PhaseFfNN38) has 10 neurons with *tansig* transfer function on the hidden layer and uses an *sse* performance evaluation function. In this case the obtained average evaluation error for the testing data set is 1.55% with a maximum 4.02% achieved evaluation error. Figure 9 presents the evaluation error obtained for both training and testing data sets.

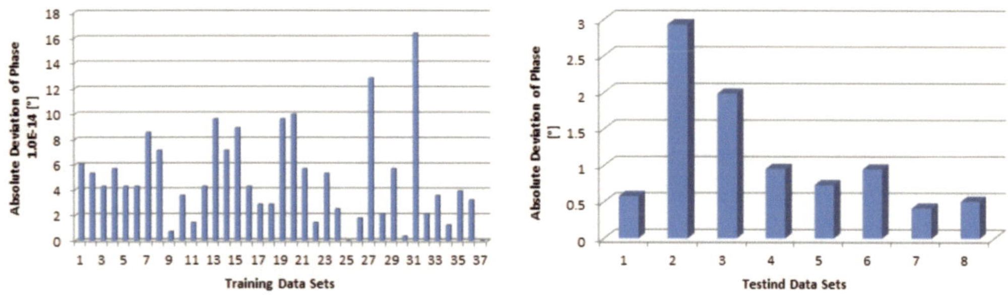

Fig. 9. Absolute evaluation error for PhaseFfNN38 network.

The second possible solution (PhaseFfNN43) for the amplitude network has 5 neurons with *logsig* transfer function on the hidden layer and uses an *sse* performance evaluation function. In this case the obtained average evaluation error for the testing data set is 1.19% with a maximum 5.47% achieved evaluation error. Figure 10 presents the evaluation error obtained for both training and testing data sets.

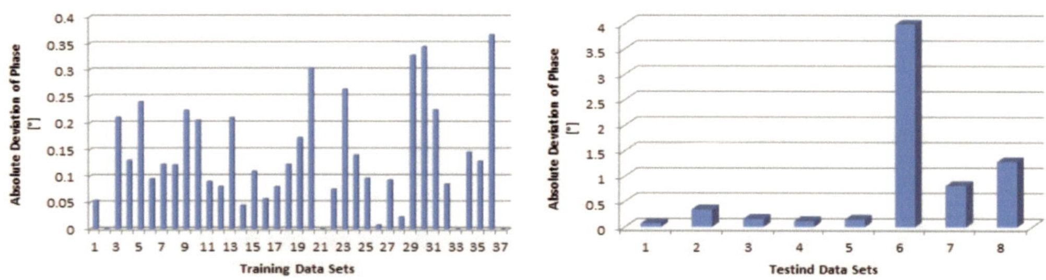

Fig. 10. Absolute evaluation error for PhaseFfNN43 network.

Comparing the result for both possible phase NN architectures it can be observed that generally PhaseFfNN43 provides better results for the testing data sets. However, considering the fact that for the training data sets PhaseFfNN43 provides evaluation errors in range of 0.25 degrees while PhaseFfNN38 provides almost none existing evaluation errors, the optimal NN solution could be considered PhaseFfNN38.

2.5 Results obtained with recurrent neural networks

To find the best NN solution which would provide the most accurate results different layer recurrent architecture were also tested. Some of the results were presented in (Micu et al. 2011) but a more detailed study is given in the following.

A layer recurrent feed-forward neural network with one output layer and one hidden layer is considered (figure 11). The number of neurons in the hidden layer was varied from 5 to 30 with a step of 5 neurons. The transfer function of the output layer was set to *purelin* (the linear transfer function) and the transfer function on the hidden layer was varied between *tansig* (the hyperbolic tangent sigmoid function) and *logsig* (the logarithmic sigmoid function). Also performance evaluation function was varied between *mse* (mean square error), *msereg* (mean square error with regularization performance) and *sse* (sum squared error).

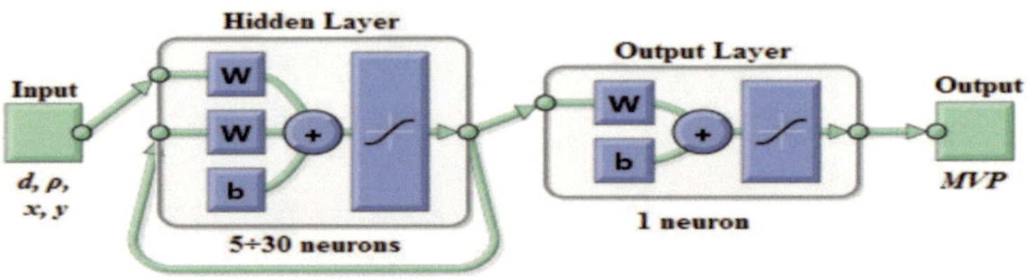

Fig. 11. Implemented layer recurrent network architecture.

Comparing the average and maximum evaluation errors obtained for the testing data sets, in case of the neural network which evaluates the amplitude of MVP, three different NN architectures (AmpLrnNN8, AmpLrnNN19 and AmpLrnNN43) were determined as possible solutions.

The first one (AmpLrnNN8) has 10 neurons with *logsig* transfer function on the hidden layer and uses an *mse* performance evaluation function. In this case the obtained average evaluation error for the testing data set is 0.35% with a maximum 1.08% achieved evaluation error. Figure12 presents the evaluation error obtained for both training and testing data sets.

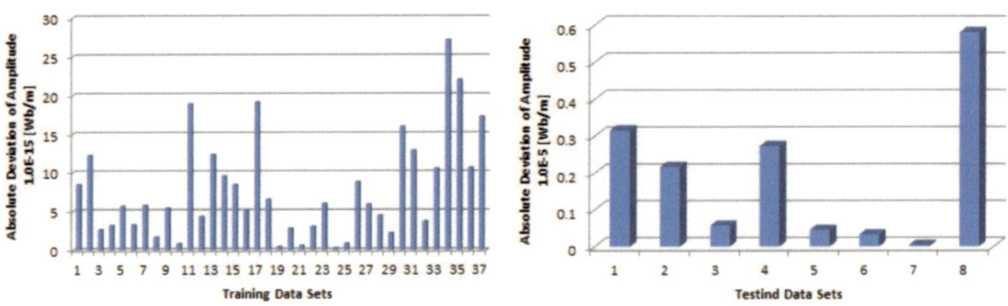

Fig. 12. Absolute evaluation error for AmpLrnNN8 network.

The second possible solution (AmpLrnNN19) for the amplitude network has 5 neurons with *logsig* transfer function on the hidden layer and uses an *msereg* performance evaluation function. In this case the obtained average evaluation error for the testing data set is 0.65% with a maximum 1.12% achieved evaluation error. Figure 13 presents the evaluation error obtained for both training and testing data sets.

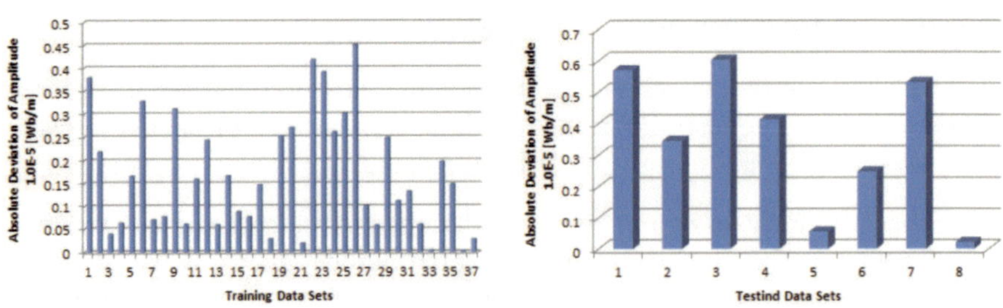

Fig. 13. Absolute evaluation error for AmpLrnNN19 network.

The third possible solution (AmpLrnNN43) for the amplitude network has 5 neurons with *tansig* transfer function on the hidden layer and uses an *sse* performance evaluation function. In this case the obtained average evaluation error for the testing data set is 0.47% with a maximum 1.26% achieved evaluation error. Figure 14 presents the evaluation error obtained for both training and testing data sets.

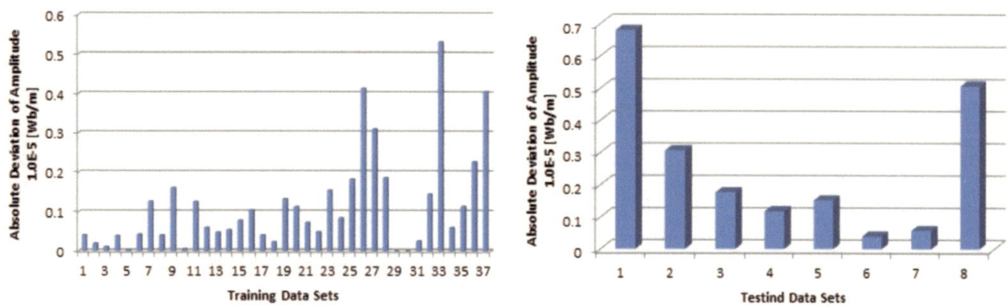

Fig. 14. Absolute evaluation error for AmpLrnNN43 network.

Comparing the results from figures 12, 13 and 14 it can be observed that the most accurate solutions will be obtained for AmpLrnNN8 neural network.

Studying the maximum and average evaluation errors obtained for neural networks implemented to evaluate the phase of MVP, three NN architectures (PhaseLrnNN8, PhaseLrnNN19 and PhaseffNN44) were determined as possible optimal solution.

The first one (PhaseLrnNN8) has 10 neurons with *logsig* transfer function on the hidden layer and uses a *mse* performance evaluation function. In this case the obtained average evaluation error for the testing data set is 1.16% with a maximum 4.21% achieved evaluation error. Figure 15 presents the evaluation error obtained for both training and testing data sets.

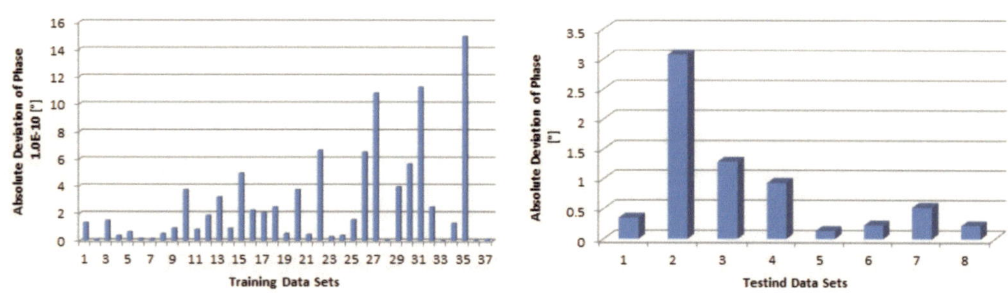

Fig. 15. Absolute evaluation error for PhaseLrnNN8 network.

The second possible solution (PhaseLrnNN19) for the amplitude network has 5 neurons with *tansig* transfer function on the hidden layer and uses a *msereg* performance evaluation function (ffNN2). In this case the obtained average evaluation error for the testing data set is 1.19% with a maximum 3.02% achieved evaluation error. Figure 16 presents the evaluation error obtained for both training and testing data sets.

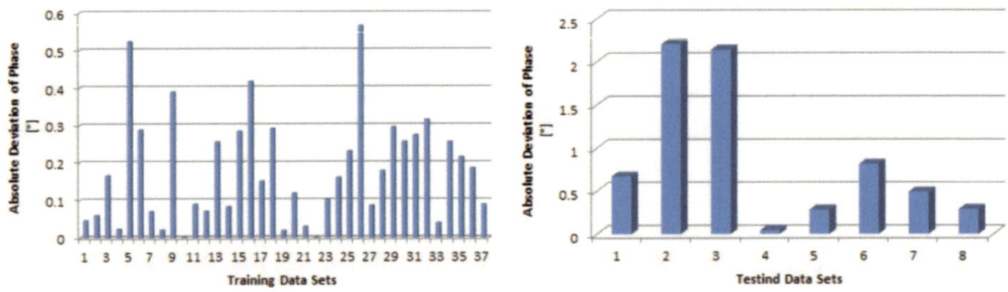

Fig. 16. Absolute evaluation error for PhaseLrnNN19 network.

The third possible solution (PhaseLrnNN44) for the amplitude network has 10 neurons with *logsig* transfer function on the hidden layer and uses a *sse* performance evaluation function. In this case the obtained average evaluation error for the testing data set is 1.18% with a maximum 3.58% achieved evaluation error. Figure 17 presents the evaluation error obtained for both training and testing data sets.

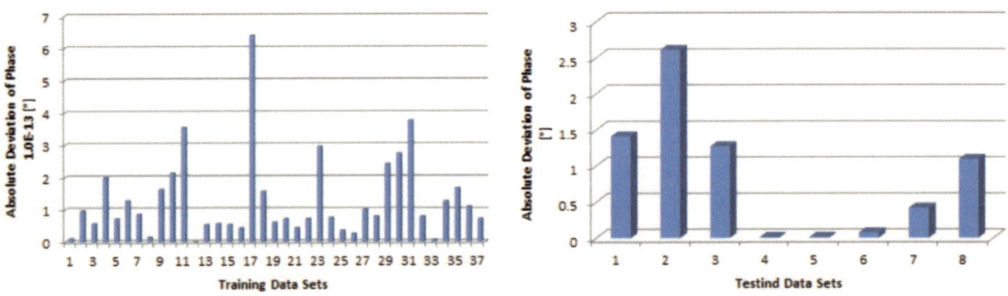

Fig. 17. Absolute evaluation error for PhaseLrnNN43 network.

Analysing the results shown in figures 15, 16 and 17 the authors concluded that the optimal layer recurrent NN architecture solution to evaluate the phase of the magnetic vector potential it is PhaseLrnNN19 network structure.

2.6 Discussions

Based on the maximum and average evaluation errors obtained for the implemented NN architectures the authors has concluded that it should be used a NN structures that have even *tansig* either *logsig* transfer function implemented on the hidden layer. Generally, a *tansig* transfer function will provide much better training results then a *logsing* function, but for totally new input values could provide less accurate results. Also it was observed that a higher number of neurons did not necessary provide more accurate results and instead of predicting the MVP values for new problem geometries it would identify the closest training input/output pair.

Studying the results provided by the identified optimal NN architectures in case of layer recurrent networks (AmpLrnNN8 for MVP amplitude evaluation, respectively PhaseLrnNN19 for MVP phase evaluation) and comparing to the MVP solutions provided by the optimal feed-forward architectures (AmpFfNN2 and respectively PhaseFfNN38) it can be observed that even if the studied problem does not necessary require the implementation of recurrent neural networks, we can get more accurate solutions by using recurrent networks.

Comparing the results obtained with the implemented neural networks (figure 7÷10 and 12÷15) with those provided by the fuzzy logic block presented in (Satsios et al. 1999a, 1999b) (figure 5) we can observe a 50% or more accuracy increase in determining MVP amplitude and phase, depending on the implemented neural network architecture.

Once the magnetic vector potential is evaluated, the self and mutual impedance matrix, which describes the inductive coupling between the electrical power line and underground pipeline, can be evaluated using the relationships presented in (Christoforidis et al. 2003, 2005). After that the equivalent electrical circuit of the studied EPL-MP problem can be solved to obtain the induced AC voltage.

3. Self and mutual inductance matrix evaluation in case of a three layer earth

Considering the accuracy of the results for the MVP obtained from the implemented neural networks, the authors started to develop a neural network solution to evaluate directly the self and mutual impedance matrix, which describe the inductive coupling. In this case a more complex EPL-MP interference problem had been chosen for study.

3.1 Studied electromagnetic interference problem

An underground gas transportation pipeline runs in the same right of way with a 220kV/50Hz electrical power line (figure 18). In order to study more realistic problem geometries is considered a multilayer soil (three vertical layers) with different resistivities.

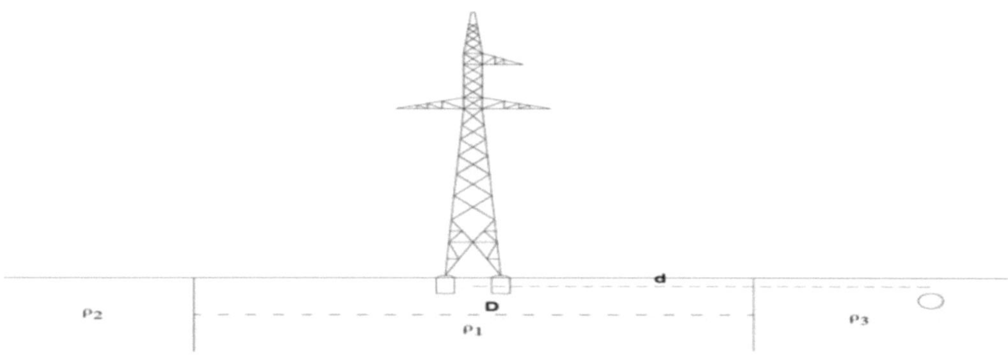

Fig. 18. Right of way configuration

The pipeline is considered to be buried at 2 m depth and having an 0.195 m inner radius, 5 mm thickness and 5 cm bitumen coating. The EPL phase wires are placed on triagonal single circuit IT.Sn102 type towers with one sky wire.

3.2 Neural network implementation

In order to do not redo each time the finite element calculation when different problem geometry has to be studied, the authors had decided to implement a neural network solution to evaluate the self and mutual inductance matrix for any possible problem geometries. As input values the following geometrical parameters has been selected:

- d - distance between EPL and MP (which varies between 0 m and 1000 m);
- ρ_1 - resistivity of middle layer earth (which varies between 30 Ωm and 1000 Ωm);
- ρ_2, ρ_3 ($\rho_2 = \rho_3$) - resistivity of left and right side earth layer (which varies as ρ_1);
- D - earth middle layer width (which varies between 50 m and 1100 m).

During the pre-processing stage of the proposed neural network solutions implementation all the input parameters were automatically scaled by MatLab in the [-1,+1] range.

The outputs of the proposed neural network will be the impedance matrix elements. Considering the fact that the impedance matrix is a symmetrical matrix, the output values are the matrix elements above the main diagonal. For the proposed EPL-MP problem with one pipeline, three phase wires and one sky wire the matrix elements will be: $Z_{11}, Z_{12}, Z_{13}, Z_{14}, Z_{15}, Z_{22}, Z_{23}, Z_{24}, Z_{25}, Z_{33}, Z_{34}, Z_{35}, Z_{44}, Z_{45}, Z_{55}$, where Z_{ii} represents the self impedance of conductor i and Z_{ij} the mutual impedance between conductor i and j ($i = \overline{1,3}$ represents EPL phase wires, $i = 4$ represents EPL sky wire and $i = 5$ represents MP).

After analysing in detail the impedance matrices for different EPL-MP problem geometries the authors concluded that in order to increase NN results accuracy and to reduce training time it will be better to implement different NN for the real and imaginary part of each impedance. Also for accuracy improvement were implemented 3 different networks for the impedance matrix elements: NN1 for all conductors self impedances ($Z_{11}, Z_{22}, Z_{33}, Z_{44}, Z_{55}$), NN2 for the mutual impedances between the pipeline and the conductors($Z_{15}, Z_{25}, Z_{35}, Z_{45}$), NN3 for the other mutual impedance elements.

Case No.	d [m]	D [m]	ρ_2 [Ω*m]	ρ_1 [Ω*m]	ρ_3 [Ω*m]	Case No.	d [m]	D [m]	ρ_2 [Ω*m]	ρ_1 [Ω*m]	ρ_3 [Ω*m]
8	5	60	500	50	500	2301	20	550	30	250	30
373	100	60	500	750	500	2532	100	550	100	500	100
875	20	120	100	750	100	2914	5	1050	10	250	10
1231	500	120	100	30	100	3274	100	1050	500	1000	500
1391	0	240	50	10	50	3545	750	1050	30	750	30
1891	250	240	500	30	500	4320	750	1500	50	10	50
2134	0	550	50	250	50	4442	1000	1500	250	1000	250

Table 3. Training EPL-MP problem geometries.

To train the proposed NN a training data base was created based on the impedance matrices obtained using FEM for different EPL-MP problem geometries. In order to create a useful training database approximately 5000 different EPL-MP problem geometries were simulated varying the EPL-MP separation distance from 0 m to 1000 m, the earth layers resistivity from 10 Ωm to 1000 Ωm and the middle layer width from 50 m to 1500 m. Table 3 presents some of the different EPL-MP problem geometries used to train the proposed NN.

Case No.	d [m]	D [m]	ρ_2 [Ω*m]	ρ_1 [Ω*m]	ρ_3 [Ω*m]	Case No.	d [m]	D [m]	ρ_2 [Ω*m]	ρ_1 [Ω*m]	ρ_3 [Ω*m]
1	310	800	900	850	900	16	490	1100	300	400	300
2	15	400	850	450	850	17	170	700	300	350	300
3	105	1100	550	550	550	18	150	700	500	500	500
4	350	900	500	800	500	19	240	500	80	750	80
5	250	800	150	150	150	20	125	800	300	600	300
6	60	800	500	900	500	21	420	100	550	20	550
7	340	400	600	150	600	22	75	400	350	700	350
8	65	400	650	350	650	23	105	1200	250	950	250
9	170	800	650	750	650	24	100	700	650	850	650
10	55	1000	900	400	900	25	85	400	140	160	140
11	40	200	600	800	600	26	300	400	900	100	900
12	115	800	800	800	800	27	145	300	350	900	350
13	120	900	750	350	750	28	15	500	140	700	140
14	135	400	180	500	180	29	100	1300	300	180	300
15	310	800	900	850	900	30	10	1000	200	750	200

Table 4. Training EPL-MP problem geometries.

In order to find the optimal neural network solution which will provide the most accurate results, the authors have implemented and tested different NN architectures. To test the implemented neural networks, the training database and a totally different data set that was not applied during the training process, were used. The error between the solutions provided by each implemented NN and the self and mutual impedance matrices are determined to identify the optimal architecture. Table 4 presents the randomly generated EPL-MP problem geometries used to test the implemented NN

3.3 Tested feed-forward architectures

To identify the optimal solution for each of the proposed neural networks, different feed-forward architectures with one output layer and two hidden layers were implemented (figure 19). Based on the experience gained after implementing the neural network for MVP calculation, the transfer function for the output layer has been chosen to be *purelin* (linear function) and *tansig* (hyperbolic tangent sigmoid function) for the hidden layers. The number of neurons was varied from 5 to 30 for the first hidden layer and from 5 to 20 for the second hidden layer. The performance evaluation function was set to *mse* (mean square error) and the descendent gradient with momentum weight learning rule was selected to train the neural networks using the Levenberg-Marquardt method.

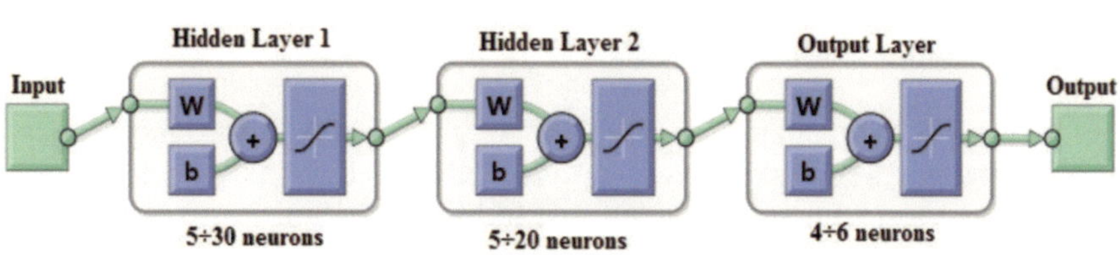

Fig. 19. Implemented feed-forward network architecture.

The training process took around 1 to 5 minutes for each implemented neural network. Once the proposed neural network architectures were trained, to identify the optimal solution, the error between the output values provided by NN and the finite element solutions was calculated and compared for each NN.

In case of NN used to evaluate the real part of the self-impedances, the optimal NN1 architecture is a feed forward NN with two hidden layers: 30 neurons on the first hidden layer and 10 neurons in the second hidden layer. The average error is 0.048% for the training data set and respectively 0.064% for the testing data set, with a maximum achieved error of 0.8% and 0.3% for the training and respectively the testing data sets. Figure 20 presents the error distribution for training and testing problem geometry data sets.

Fig. 20. Percentege error distribution for Real Part NN1.

For the NN used to evaluate the imaginary part of the self-impedances, the optimal NN1 architecture is a feed forward NN with two hidden layers: 20 neurons on the first hidden layer and 20 neurons in the second hidden layer. The average percentage error is 0.14% for the training data set and respectively 0.129% for the testing data set, with a maximum achieved percentage error of 5.24% and 0.85% for the training and respectively the testing data sets. Figure 21 presents the percentage error distribution for training and testing problem geometry data sets.

Fig. 21. Error distribution for Imaginary Part NN1.

In case of NN used to evaluate the real part of the mutual impedances between EPL conductors (phase wires and sky wires), optimal NN3 architecture is a feed forward NN with two hidden layers: 20 neurons on the first hidden layer and 20 neurons on the second hidden layer. The average error is 0.014% for the training data set and respectively 0.034% for the testing data set, with a maximum achieved error of 3.12% and 0.14% for the training and respectively the testing data sets. Figure 22 presents the error distribution for training and testing problem geometry data sets.

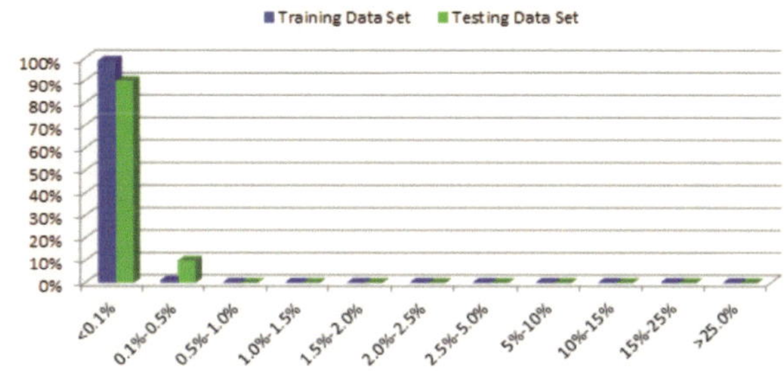

Fig. 22. Error distribution for Real Part NN3

For the NN used to evaluate the imaginary part of the mutual impedances between EPL conductors (phase wires and sky wires) optimal NN3 architecture is a feed forward NN with two hidden layers: 30 neurons on the first hidden layer and 20 neurons in the second hidden layer. The average error is 0.073% for the training data set and respectively 0.097% for the testing data set, with a maximum achieved error of 2.98% and 0.46% for the training and respectively the testing data sets. Figure 23 presents the error distribution for training and testing problem geometry data sets.

Unfortunately in case on the NN used to evaluate the real part of the mutual impedances between MP and other conductors, none of the tested NN architectures provided acceptable results. This was caused by the fact that the real part of mutual impedances between MP and other conductors varies in a very large range from 1E-11 to 1E-6.

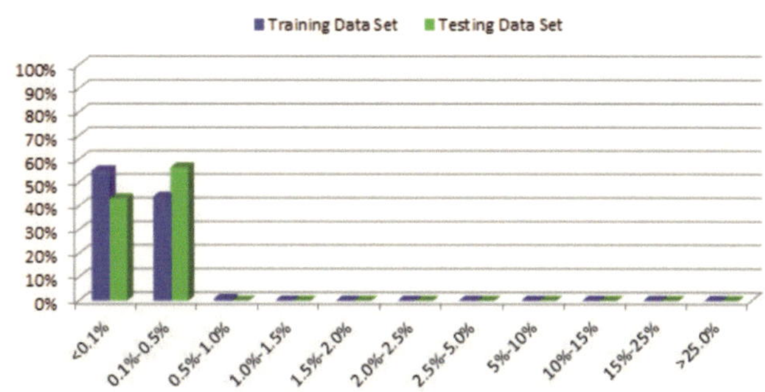

Fig. 23. Error distribution for Imaginary Part NN3.

After a complete analysis of the real and imaginary part of the mutual impedance between MP and other conductors another approach was used; two NN were implemented to evaluate the amplitude and argument of the mutual impedances, instead of the impedance real and imaginary part.

In case of NN used to evaluate the amplitude of the mutual impedances between MP and other conductors the optimal NN2 architecture it was identified as a feed forward NN with two hidden layers: 30 neurons on the first hidden layer and 25 neurons in the second hidden layer. The average error is 0.066% for the training data set and respectively 0.087% for the testing data set, with a maximum achieved error of 17.95% and 0.43% for the training and respectively the testing data sets. Figure 24 presents the error distribution for training and testing problem geometry data sets.

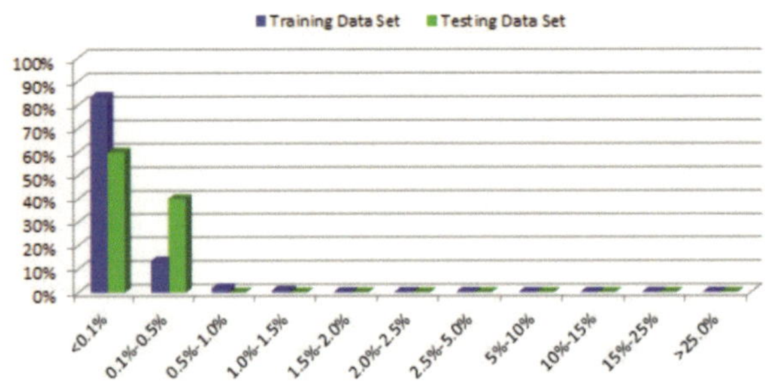

Fig. 24. Error distribution for Amplitude NN2.

For the NN used to evaluate the argument of the mutual impedances between MP and the other conductors the optimal NN2 architecture is a feed forward NN with two hidden layers: 20 neurons on the first hidden layer and 20 neurons in the second hidden layer. The average error is 0.249% for the training data set and respectively 0.313% for the testing data set, with a maximum achieved error of 6.71% and 1.43% for the training and respectively the testing data sets. Figure 25 presents the error distribution for training and testing problem geometry data sets.

Fig. 25. Error distribution for Argument NN2.

After identifying the optimal architecture of the neural networks these two NN were unified in a virtual black box in order to evaluate mutual impedances real and imaginary part. This unification procedure has as secondary unwanted result a change in the final complex mutual impedance evaluation error. Thus the average error become 0.665% for the training data set and respectively 0.407% for the testing data set, with a maximum achieved error of 18.728% and 1.107% for the training and respectively the testing data sets. Figure 26 presents the global evaluation error distribution of complex mutual impedance for both training and testing problem geometry data sets.

Also, the authors implemented and tested some layer recurrent neural network architectures. But unfortunately because of the large training database with very different output values the training process proved to be very time consuming (more than one hour) and the obtained results had the same accuracy as the previous feed-forward networks.

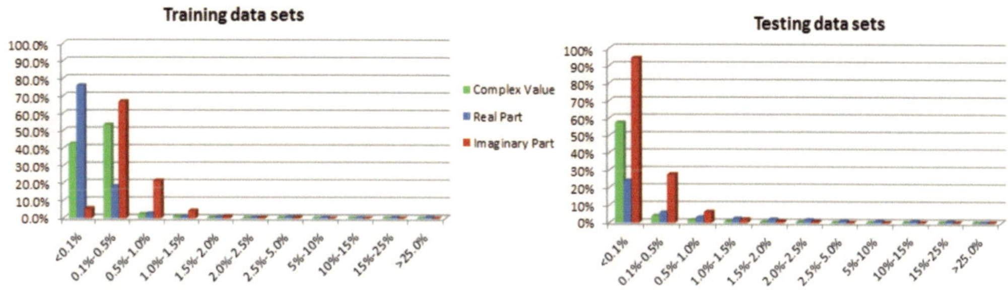

Fig. 26. Global error distribution for NN2 optimal networks.

4. Conclusions

In this chapter the authors implement neural networks based artificial intelligence techniques in the study of electromagnetic interference problems (right of way EPL-MP) focusing on finding an easier method to identify the optimal solution.

To solve the differential equation which describes the couplings between EPL and nearby MP usually a finite element method is used. This FEM calculation needs excessive computational time especially if different problem geometries of the same interference problem have to be studied.

In order to reduce computation time the authors proposed two neural networks based artificial intelligence techniques to scale the results from a set of known problem geometries to any new problem geometry. The proposed neural networks were implemented for specific EPL-MP interference problems. The first one evaluates the magnetic vector potential in case of a phase to earth EPL fault and second one determines the self and mutual impedance matrix in case of a three vertical layer earth.

The obtained results with the proposed neural network solutions proved themselves to be very accurate. Thus ad shown neural network based solution to study EPL-MP interference problems could be a very effective one, especially if we take into account the fact that the solutions provided are obtained instantaneously ones they are properly trained.

Also it has been shown that even there is a special requirement to use recurrent neural networks, these NN architectures could provide more accurate solutions than the basic feed-forward structures.

5. Acknowledgment

The work was supported by TE_253/2010_CNCSIS project - "Modelling, Prediction and Design Solutions, with Maximum Effectiveness, for Reducing the Impact of Stray Currents on Underground Metallic Gas Pipelines", No. 34/2010.

6. References

Al-Badi, A., Ellithy, K. & Al-Alawi, S., (2005), "An Artificial Neural Network model for Predicting gas pipeline Induced Voltage caused by Power Lines under Fault

Conditions", *COMPEL: The International Journal for Computation and Mathematics in Electrical and Electronic Engineering*, Vol. 24, No. 1, (2005), pp. 69-80,ISSN: 0332-1649.

Al-Badi, A., Ellithy, K. & Al-Alawi, S., (2007), "Prediction of Voltage on Mitigated Pipelines Paralleling Electric Transmission Lines using an Artificial Neural Network", *The Journal of Corrosion Science and Engineering*, Vol. 10, Preprint 28, (March 2007), ISSN: 1466-8858.

Baboian, R. (Ed.), (2002), *NACE Corrosion Engineer's Reference Book*, NACE International, ISBN: 1-57590-139-0, Huston, USA.

Christoforidis, G. C., Labridis, D. P. & Dokopoulos, S., (2003), "Inductive Interference Calculation on Imperfect Coated Pipelines due to Nearby Faulted Parallel Transmission Lines", *Electric Power Systems Research*, Vol. 6, No. 2., (August 2003), pp. 139-148, ISSN: 0378-7796.

Christoforidis, G. C., Labridis, D. P. & Dokopoulos, S., (2005), "A Hybrid method for calculating the Inductive Interference caused by Faulted Power Lines to nearby Buried Pipelines", *IEEE Trans. on Power Delivery*, Vol. 20, No. 2, (April 2005), pp. 1465-1473, ISSN: 0272-1724.

Czumbil, L. , Micu, D. D. & Ceclan, A., (2009), "Artificial Intelligence Techniques Applied to Electromagnetic Interference Problems", *IFMBE Proceedings*,ISBN:978-3-642-22585-7, Vol. 26, Cluj-Napoca, Romania, September 23-26, 2009

CIGRÉ Working Group 36.02, (1995), *Guide on the Influence of High Voltage AC Power Systems on Metallic Pipelines.*

Collet, E., Delores, B., Gabillard, M. & Ragault, I., (2001), "Corrosion due to AC Influence of Very High Voltage Power Lines on Polyethylene-Coated Steel Pipelines Evaluation of Riks-Preventive Measures", *Anti-Corrosion Methods and Materials*, Vol. 48, No. 4, (August 2001), pp. 221-226, ISSN: 0003-5599.

Damousis, I. G., Satsios, K. J., Labridis, D. P. & Dokopoulos, P. S., (2002), "Combiend Fuzzy Logic and Genetic Algorithm Techniques - Application to an Electromagnetic Field Problem", *Fuzzy Sets and Systems*, Vol. 129, No. 3, (August 2002), pp. 371-386, ISSN: 0165-0114.

Dawalibi, F. P. & Southey, R. D., (1989), "Analysis of electrical interference from power lines to gas pipelines. Part I - Computation methods", *IEEE Trans. on Power Delivery*, Vol. 4, No. 3, (July 1989), pp. 1840-1849, ISSN: 0272-1724.

Micu, D. D., Czumbil, L., Christoforidis, G., Ceclan, A., Darabant, L. & Stet, D. (2009), "Electromagnetic interferences between HV power lines and metallic pipelines evaluated with neural network technique", *Proceedings of the 10th International Conference on Electrical Power Quality and Utilization (EPQU)*,ISBN: 978-1-4244-5171-5 , Lodz, Poland, September 15-17, 2009.

Micu, D. D., Czumbil, L., Christoforidis, G., & Ceclan, A. (2011), "Layer Recurrent Neural Network Solution for an Electromagnetic Interference Problem", *IEEE Trans. on Magnetics*, Vol. 47, No. 5, (May 2011), pp. 1410-1413, ISSN: 0018-9464.

Papagiannis, G. K., Triantafyllidis, D. G., Labridis, D. P., (2000) "A One-Step Finite Element Formulation for the Modelling of Single and Double Circuit Transmission Lines", *IEEE Trans. On Power Systems*, vol. 15, Nr. 1, 2000, pp.33-38.

Satsios, K. J., Labridis, D. P. & Dokopoulos, P. S., (1999), "An Artificial Intelligence System for a Complex Electromagnetic Field Problem: Part I - Finite Element Calculations and Fuzzy Logic Development", *IEEE Trans. on Magnetics*, Vol. 35, No. 1, (January 1999), pp. 516-522, ISSN: 0018-9464.

Satsios, K. J., Labridis, D. P. & Dokopoulos, P. S., (1999), "An Artificial Intelligence System for a Complex Electromagnetic Field Problem: Part II - Method Implementation and Performance Analysis", *IEEE Trans. on Magnetics*, Vol. 35, No. 1, (January 1999), pp. 523-527, ISSN: 0018-9464.

13

An Application of Jordan Pi-Sigma Neural Network for the Prediction of Temperature Time Series Signal

Rozaida Ghazali, Noor Aida Husaini,
Lokman Hakim Ismail and Noor Azah Samsuddin
Universiti Tun Hussein Onn Malaysia
Malaysia

1. Introduction

Temperature forecasting is mainly issued in qualitative terms with the use of conventional methods, assisted by the data projected images taken by meteorological satellites to assess future trends (Paras *et al.*, 2007). Several criteria that need to be considered when choosing a forecasting method include the accuracy, the cost and the properties of the series being forecast. Considering those criteria, it is noted that such empirical approaches that has been conducted for temperature forecasting is intrinsically costlier and only proficient of providing certain information, which is usually generalized over a larger geographical area (Paras *et al.*, 2007). Despite of involving sophisticated mathematical models to justify the use of empirical rules, it also requires a prior knowledge of the characteristics of the input time-series to predict future events. Not only that, most temperature forecasts today have limited information about uncertainty. Yet, meteorologists often find it challenging to communicate uncertainty effectively. Regardless of the extensive use of the numerical weather method, they are still restricted by the availability of numerical weather prediction products, leading to various studies being conducted for temperature forecasting (Barry & Chorley, 1982; Paras *et al.*, 2007)

Due to that inadequacy, Neural Network (NN) has been applied in such temperature forecasting. NN mimic human intelligence in learning from complicated or imprecise data and can be used to extract patterns and detect trends that are too complex to be perceived by humans and other computer techniques (Mielke, 2008). NN which can be described as an adaptive machine that has a natural tendency for storing experiential knowledge, are able to discover complex nonlinear relationships in the meteorological processes by communicating forecast uncertainty that relates the forecast data to the actual weather (Chang *et al.*, 2010). However, when the number of inputs to the model and the number of training examples becomes extremely large, the training procedure for ordinary neural network, especially the Multilayer Perceptron (MLP) becomes tremendously slow and unduly tedious. Indeed, MLP are prone to overfit the data (Radhika & Shashi, 2009) and adopts computationally intensive training algorithms. On the other hand, MLP also suffer long training times and often reach local minima (Ghazali & al-Jumeily, 2009).

Considering the limitations of MLP, therefore in this work, the intention of utilizing the use of higher order neural networks (HONN) which have the ability to expand the input representation space is considered. The Pi-Sigma Neural Network (PSNN) (Shin & Ghosh, 1991-a), a class of HONN, is able to perform high learning capabilities that require less memory in terms of weights and nodes, and at least two orders of magnitude less number of computations when compared to the MLP for similar performance levels, and over a broad class of problems (Ghazali & al-Jumeily, 2009; Shin & Ghosh, 1991-b).

In conjunction with the benefits of PSNN, a new model called Jordan Pi-Sigma Neural Network (JPSN) which posses a Jordan Neural Network architecture (Jordan, 1986) is proposed to perform temperature forecasting. In this regard, the JPSN that managed to incorporates feedback connections in their structure and having the superior properties of PSNN is mapped to function variable and coefficient related to the research area. Consequently, this work is conducted in order to prove that JPSN is suitable for one-step-ahead temperature prediction.

2. Pi-sigma neural network (PSNN)

PSNN is a type of HONN and was first introduced by Shin & Ghosh (1991-a). The basic idea behind the network is due to the fact that a polynomial of input variables is formed by a product ("pi") of several weighted linear combinations ("sigma") of input variables. That is why this network is called pi-sigma instead of sigma-pi. The PSNN exhibits fast learning while greatly reducing network complexity by utilising an efficient form of polynomials for many input variables. This special polynomial form helps the PSNN to dramatically reduce the number of weights in its structure. Figure 1 shows the architecture of PSNN:

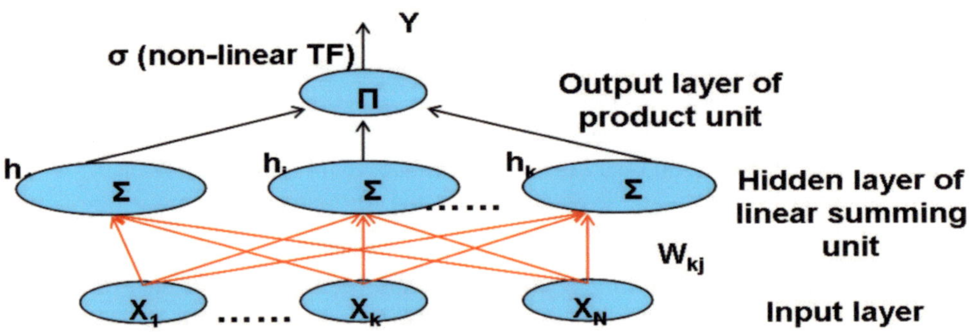

Fig. 1. Structure of Kth Order PSNN

Input x is an N dimensional vector and x_k is the kth component of x. The weighted inputs are fed to a layer of K linear summing units; h_{ji} is the output if the jth summing units for the ith output y_i, viz:

$$y_i = \sigma\left(\prod_j\left(\sum_k w_{kji}x_k + \theta_{ji}\right)\right) \tag{1}$$

where w_{kji} and θ_{ji} are adjustable coefficients, and σ is the nonlinear transfer function (Shin & Ghosh, 1991-a). The number of summing units in PSNN reflects the network order. By using an additional summing unit, it will increase the network's order by 1 whilst preserving old connections and maintaining network topology.

In PSNN, weights from summing layer to the output layer are fixed to unity, resulting to a reduction in the number of tuneable weights. Therefore, it can reduce the training time. Sigmoid and linear functions are adopted in the output layer and summing layer, respectively. The use of linear summing units makes the convergence analysis of the learning rules for the PSNN more accurate and tractable (Ghazali & al-Jumeily, 2009; Ghazali *et al.*, 2006). Compared to other HONN models, Shin and Ghosh (1991-b) argued that PSNN can contribute to maintain the high learning capabilities of HONN, needs a much smaller number of weights, with at least two orders of magnitude less number of computations when compared to the MLP for similar performance levels, and over a broad class of problems (Ghazali *et al.*, 2006). Moreover, the PSNN is superior to other HONN in approaching precision computation complexity and has a highly regular structure. Since weights from hidden layer to the output are fixed at 1, the property of PSNN drastically reduces the training time. The applicability of this network was successfully applied for image processing (Hussain and Liatsis, 2002), time series prediction (Knowles, 2005; Ghazali *et al.*, 2011), function approximation (Shin & Ghosh, 1991-a; Shin & Ghosh, 1991-b), pattern recognition (Shin & Ghosh, 1991-a), Cryptography (Song, 2008), and so forth.

3. The properties and structure of Jordan pi-sigma neural network (JPSNN)

The structure of JPSN is quite similar to the ordinary PSNN. The main difference is the architecture of JPSN is constructed by having a recurrent link from output layer back to the input layer. This structure gives the temporal dynamics of the time-series process that allows the network to compute in a more parsimonious way (Hussain & Liatsis, 2002). The architecture of the proposed JPSN is shown in Figure 2 below.

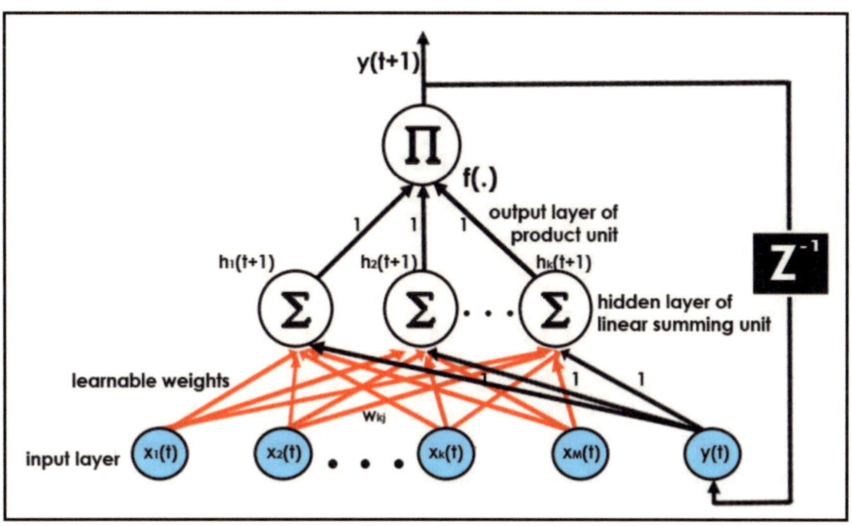

Fig. 2. The architecture of JPSN

where

$x(t)$	-	the input nodes at *t-th* time
w_{kj}	-	the trainable weights
$h_k(t+1)$	-	the summing unit
$y(t+1)$	-	the output at time $t+1$
$y(t)$		the output at time *t*
$f(\cdot)$		the activation function

Weights from the input layers $x(t)$ to the summing units layer are tunable, while weights between the summing unit layers and the output layer are fixed to 1. The tuned weights are used for network testing to see how well the network model generalizes on unseen data. Z^{-1} denotes time delay operation.

Let the number of external inputs to the network be M and the number of the output be 1. Let $x_m(t)$ be the m *-th* external input to the network at time *t*. The overall input at time *t* is the concatenation of $y(t)$ and $x_k(t), where(k=1,...,M)$, and is referred to $z(t)$ where:

$$z_k(t)=\begin{cases} x_k(t) & if \quad 1\le k\le M \\ 1 & if \quad k=M+1 \\ y_k(t) & if \quad k=M+2 \end{cases} \tag{2}$$

Meanwhile, weights from $z(t)$ to the summing unit are set to 1 in order to reduce the complexity of the network.

The proposed JPSN combines the properties of both PSNN and Recurrent Neural Network (RNN) so that better performance can be achieved. When utilizing the newly proposed JPSN as predictor for one-step-ahead prediction, the previous input values are used to predict the next elements in the data. Since network with recurrent connection holds several advantages over ordinary feedforward MLP especially in dealing with time-series problems, therefore, by adding the dynamic properties to the PSNN, this network may outperform the ordinary feedforward MLP and also the ordinary PSNN. Additionally, the unique architecture of JPSN may also avoid from the combinatorial explosion of higher-order terms as the network order increases.

3.1 Learning algorithm of JPSN

The supervised learning used in JPSN can be solved with the standard backpropagation (BP) gradient descent algorithm (Rumelhart *et al.*, 1986), with the recurrent link from output layer back to the input layer nodes. Since the same weights are used for all networks, the learning algorithm starts by initialising the weights to a small random value before training the weights. The JPSN is trained adaptively in which the errors produced are calculated and the overall error function *E* of the JPSN is defined as:

$$e_j(t)=d_j(t)-y_j(t) \tag{3}$$

where $d_j(t)$ denotes the target output at time $(t-1)$. At each time $(t-1)$, the output of each $y_j(t)$ is determined and the error $e_j(t)$ is calculated as the difference between the actual value expected from each unit i and the predicted value $y_j(t)$.

Generally, JPSN can be operated in the following steps:

For each training example:

1. Calculate the output.

$$y(t)=f\left(\prod_{L=1}^{k} h_L(t)\right) \tag{4}$$

$h_l(t)$ can be calculated as:

$$h_L(t)=\sum_{m=1}^{m} w_{Lm}x_m(t)+w_{L(m)}+w_{L(m+1)}\, y(t-1)=\sum_{m=1}^{m+1} w_{Lm}z_m(t-1) \tag{5}$$

where $h_L(t)$ represents the activation of the L unit at time *t*, and *y(t)* is the previous network output. The unit's transfer function *f* sigmoid activation function, which bounded of output range of [0,1].

2. Compute the output error at time *(t)* using standard Mean Squared Error (MSE) by minimising the following index:

$$E_k=\frac{1}{n_{tr}}\sum_{i=1}^{n_{tr}}\left(y_i-z_{ki}\right)^2 \tag{6}$$

where z_{ik} denotes the output of the *k*-th node with respect to the *i*-th data, and n_{tr} is the number of training sets. This step is completed repeatedly for all nodes on the current layer.

3. By adapting the BP gradient descent algorithm, compute the weight changes:

$$\Delta w_j=\eta\left(\prod_{j\neq 1}^{m} h_{ji}\right)x_k \tag{7}$$

where h_{ji} is the output of summing unit and η is the learning rate.

4. Update the weight:

$$w_i=w_i+\Delta w_i \tag{8}$$

5. To accelerate the convergence of the error in the learning process, the momentum term, α is added into Equation 3.6. Then, the values of the weight for the interconnection on neurons are calculated and can be numerically expressed as

$$w_i=w_i+\alpha\Delta w_i \tag{9}$$

where the value of α is a user-selected positive constant $(0\le\alpha\le 1)$

6. The JPSN algorithm is terminated when all the stopping criteria (training error, maximum epoch and early stopping) are satisfied. If not, repeat step 1)

The utilisation of product units in the output layer indirectly incorporates the capabilities of JPSN while using a small number of weights and processing units. Therefore, the proposed JPSN combines the properties of both PSNN and JNN so that better performance can be achieved. When utilising the newly proposed JPSN as predictor for one-step-ahead, the previous input values are used to predict the next element in the data. Since network with recurrent connection holds several advantages over ordinary feedforward networks especially in dealing with time-series problems, therefore, by adding the dynamic properties to the PSNN, this network may outperformed the MLP and also the ordinary PSNN. Additionally, the unique architecture of JPSN may also avoid from the combinatorial explosion of higher-order terms as the network order increases. The JPSN has a topology of a fully connected two-layered feedforward network. Considering the fixed weights that are not tuneable, it can be said that the summing layer is not "hidden" as in the case of the MLP. This is by means; such a network topology with only one layer of tuneable weights may reduce the training time.

4. Temperature prediction with JPSN

Temperature forecasting is the essence of traceability for weather forecasting. Certainly, temperature is a kind of atmospheric time-series data where the time index takes on a predetermined or unlimited set of values. The temperature can have a greater influence in daily life than any other single element on a routine basis. Therefore, some great observation are needed to obtain accuracies for the temperature measurement (Ibrahim, 2002). Temperature forecasting undoubtedly is the most challenging task in dealing with meteorological parameters. It represents not only a very complex nonlinear problem, but also extremely difficult to model.

A great interest in developing methods for more accurate predictions for temperature forecasting has led to the development of several methods which employ the use of physical methods, statistical-empirical methods and numerical-statistical methods (Barry & Chorley, 1982; Lorenc, 1986). These methods, however, constitutionally complex and are limited and restricted to that of numerical weather prediction products (Paras *et al.*, 2007). Considering the downside of those methods, Neural Networks have placed such sophisticated models within the reach of practitioners, and therefore have been successfully applied in many problems. Therefore, in this work, JPSN is used for temperature perdiction in Batu Pahat.

The forecasting horizon for temperature prediction is a one-step-ahead, whereas the output variable represents the temperature measurement of one-day ahead of temperature data. A univariate data of a 5-years daily temperature measurement in Batu Pahat Malaysia, ranging from 2005 to 2009 was used for the simulation (please refer to Table 1). The data was obtained from the Central Forecast Office, Malaysian Meteorological Department (MMD).

Size	Maximum (°C)	Minimum (°C)	Average (°C)
1826	29.5	23.7	26.75

Table 1. The properties of Batu Pahat Temperature signal

To purify the data for further processing, it is needed to identify and remove the contaminating effects of the outlying objects on the data. Therefore, in this study, a Max-Min Normalization technique was used so that the data can be distributed evenly and scaled into an acceptable range. In order to avoid computational problems, the range was set between the upper and lower bound of the network transfer function, which often to be the monotonically increasing function, $1/(1+e^{-x})$ (Cybenko, 1989) between [0, 1]. The Max-Min Normalization can be implemented using the following equation:

$$v' = \frac{v - \min A}{\max A - \min A}(new\_\max A - new\_\min A) + new\_\min A \tag{10}$$

Let A be the temperature data of Batu Pahat region and *min A, max A* indicate the minimum and maximum values of data A. Max-Min Normalization maps a value v of data A to v' in the range $\{new\_\min A, new\_\max A\}$.

In data normalization, the statistical distribution values for each input and output are roughly uniform. Therefore, removing the outliers should make the data more accurate. Figure 3 shows the daily temperature data of Batu Pahat region before normalization while Figure 4 shows the daily temperature data of Batu Pahat region after normalization.

Meanwhile, Figure 5 shows the frequency of temperature distribution data for 5-years after normalization process. From Figure 5, it can be seen that the histogram of the transformed data is symmetrical. Therefore, it can be said that the temperature data for Batu Pahat (after normalization) is relatively uniform, and closely follow the normal distribution, thus suitable as the network inputs.

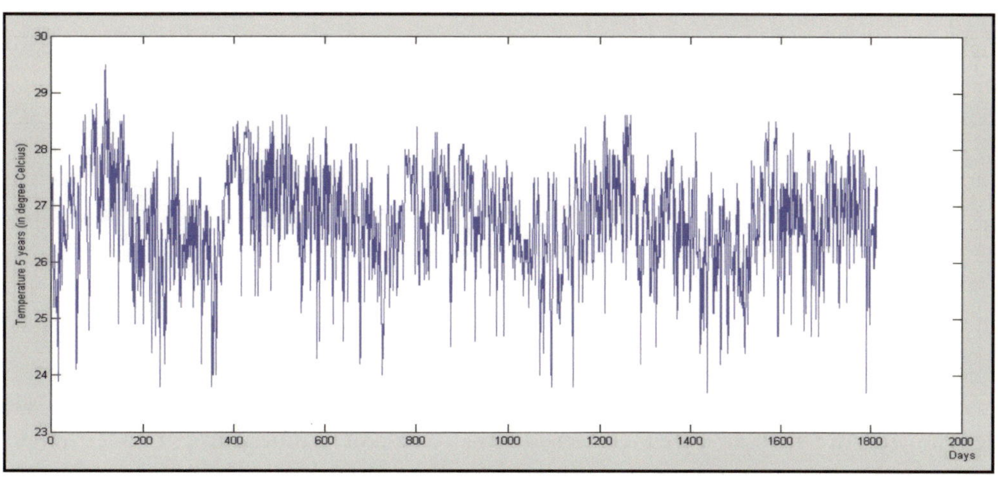

Fig. 3. Daily Temperature Data of Batu Pahat Region (before normalization)

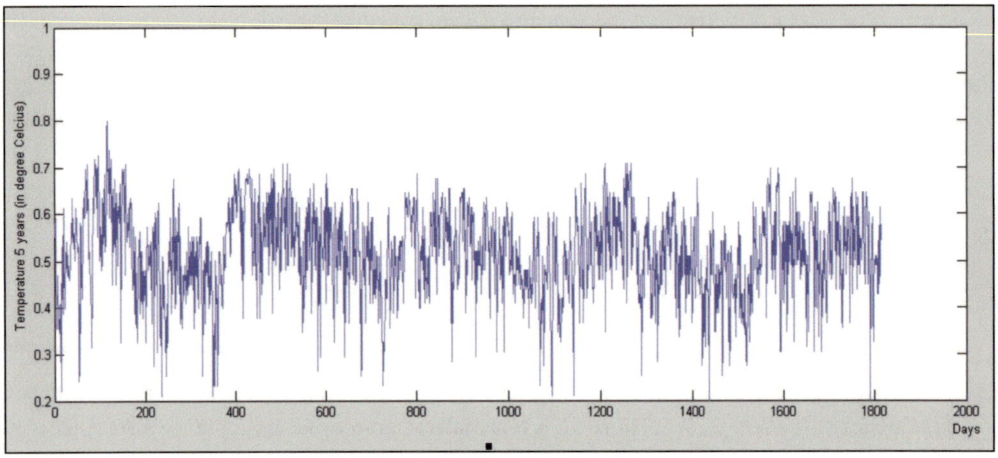

Fig. 4. Daily Temperature Data of Batu Pahat Region (after normalization)

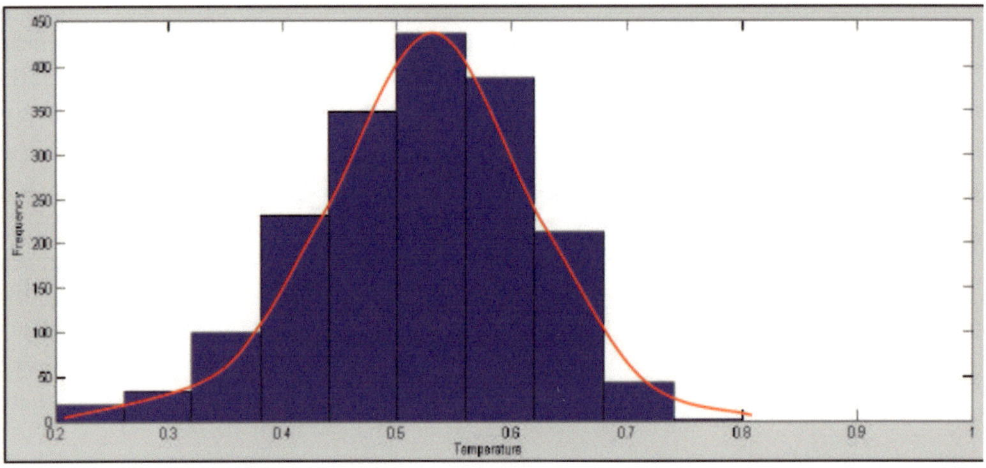

Fig. 5. Normal Distribution of Temperature Data (after normalization)

For simulation purposes, the data was segregated into time order and was divided into three sets; 50% for training, 25% for testing and 25% for validation, as shown in Table 2.

Training	Validation	Testing
914	456	456

Table 2. Summary of Temperature Dataset Segregation

For comparison purposes, the JPSN performances on temperature prdiction will be benchmarked againts that of the ordinary PSNN and the widely known MLP. As there is no rule of thumb for identifying the number of input, a trial-and-error procedure was determined. All networks were built considering 5 different number of input nodes ranging from 4 to 8. A single neuron was considered for the output layer. The number of hidden nodes (for MLP), and the higher order terms (for PSNN and JPSN) were initially started with 2 nodes, and increased by one until a maximum of 5 nodes.

5. Simulation results

The temperature dataset collected from MMD was used to demonstrate the performance of JPSN by considering a few different network parameters. Generally, the factors affecting the network performance include the learning factors, the higher order terms, and the number of neurons in the input layer. Extensive experiments have been conducted for training, testing and validation sets, and average results of 10 simulations/runs have been collected. Two stopping criteria were used during the learning process; the maximum epoch and the minimum error, which were set to 3000 and 0.0001 respectively. In order to assess the performance of all network models, four measurement criteria, namely the number of epoch, Mean Squared Error, Normalized Mean Squared Error, and Signal to Noise Ratio are used. Convergence is achieved when the output of the network meets the earlier mentioned stopping criteria. By considering all in-sample dataset that have been trained, the best value for the momentum term $\alpha = 0.2$ and the learning rate $\eta = 0.1$, were chosen based on extensive simulations done by trial-and-error procedure.

The above discussions have shown that some network parameters may affect the network performances. In conjunction with that, it is necessary to illustrate the robustness of JPSN by comparing its performance with the ordinary PSNN and the MLP. Table 3 to Table 5 show the average results from 10 simulations for the JPSN, the ordinary PSNN and the MLP, respectively.

Input Nodes	Network Order	NMSE on Testing Dataset	MSE on Testing Dataset	SNR	Number of Epoch
4	2	0.7710	0.0065	18.7557	1460.9
	3	0.7928	0.0066	18.6410	1641.1
	4	0.8130	0.0068	18.5389	1209.9
	5	0.8885	0.0074	18.1574	336.8
5	2	0.7837	0.0066	18.6853	193.5
	3	0.8253	0.0069	18.4705	287.6
	4	0.8405	0.0070	18.3910	214.5
	5	0.8632	0.0072	18.2762	117.2
6	2	0.7912	0.0066	18.6504	285.3
	3	0.8329	0.0070	18.4333	292.8
	4	0.8522	0.0071	18.3341	238
	5	0.8850	0.0074	18.1691	97.1
7	2	0.7888	0.0066	18.6626	236.3
	3	0.8310	0.0070	18.4425	178.8
	4	0.8206	0.0069	18.4954	182.2
	5	0.8751	0.0073	18.2213	116.7
8	2	0.8005	0.0067	18.5946	185.9
	3	0.8166	0.0069	18.5106	283.9
	4	0.8468	0.0071	18.3515	149.4
	5	0.8542	0.0072	18.3147	152

Table 3. Average Result of JPSN for One-Step-Ahead Prediction.

Input Nodes	Network Order	NMSE on Testing Dataset	MSE on Testing Dataset	SNR	Number of Epoch
4	2	0.7791	0.0065	18.7104	1211.8
	3	0.7792	0.0065	18.7097	1302.9
	4	0.7797	0.0065	18.7071	1315.3
	5	0.7822	0.0066	18.6935	1201.0
5	2	0.7768	0.0065	18.7234	1222.5
	3	0.7769	0.0065	18.7226	1221.6
	4	0.7775	0.0065	18.7193	1149.9
	5	0.7806	0.0065	18.7023	916.9
6	2	0.7758	0.0065	18.7289	961.3
	3	0.7770	0.0065	18.7222	852.5
	4	0.7775	0.0065	18.7192	1155.6
	5	0.7832	0.0066	18.6880	948.0
7	2	0.7726	0.0065	18.7470	1064.0
	3	0.7733	0.0065	18.7432	911.6
	4	0.7760	0.0065	18.7277	922.1
	5	0.7766	0.0065	18.7244	1072.2
8	2	0.7674	0.0064	18.7688	719.3
	3	0.7677	0.0064	18.7671	877.0
	4	0.7693	0.0065	18.7579	861.4
	5	0.7694	0.0065	18.7574	970.9

Table 4. Average Result of PSNN for One-Step-Ahead Prediction.

Input Nodes	Hidden Nodes	NMSE on Testing Dataset	MSE on Testing Dataset	SNR	Number of Epoch
4	2	0.7815	0.0065	18.6971	2849.9
	3	0.7831	0.0066	18.6881	2468.2
	4	0.7825	0.0066	18.6918	2794.2
	5	0.7827	0.0066	18.6903	2760.9
5	2	0.7803	0.0065	18.7037	2028.6
	3	0.7792	0.0065	18.7097	2451.8
	4	0.7789	0.0065	18.7114	2678.1
	5	0.7792	0.0065	18.7097	2565.8
6	2	0.7750	0.0065	18.7335	2915.1
	3	0.7763	0.0065	18.7261	2837.2
	4	0.7776	0.0065	18.7188	2652.4
	5	0.7783	0.0065	18.7152	2590.8
7	2	0.7742	0.0065	18.7378	2951.2
	3	0.7780	0.0065	18.7164	2566.6
	4	0.7771	0.0065	18.7217	2796.4
	5	0.7786	0.0065	18.7131	2770.0
8	2	0.7734	0.0065	18.7350	2684.8
	3	0.7749	0.0065	18.7268	2647.2
	4	0.7747	0.0065	18.7278	2557.1
	5	0.7753	0.0065	18.7242	2774.6

Table 5. Average Result of MLP for One-Step-Ahead Prediction.

As it can be noticed, Table 3 which shows the results for temperature prediction using JPSN reveals that the 2nd order network, with 4 inputs demonstrates the best results using all measuring criteria except for the number of epochs. Meanwhile, Table 4 shows the results that were produced by PSNN on temperature prediction. It demonstrates that the combination of 8 input nodes and PSNN of Order 2 shows the best performance for all measuring criteria. Same thing goes to the MLP, which signifies that MLP with 2 hidden nodes and 8 input nodes attained the best results for all measuring criteria except for SNR and number of epochs (refer to Table 5).

Network Models	NMSE on Testing Dataset	MSE on Testing Dataset	MAE on Testing Dataset	SNR	Number of Epoch
JPSN	0.771034	0.006462	0.063458	18.7557	1460.9
PSNN	0.779118	0.006529	0.063471	18.71039	1211.8
MLP	0.781514	0.006549	0.063646	18.69706	2849.9

Table 6. Comparison on the Best Single Simulation Results for JPSN, PSNN and MLP.

In order to compare the predictive performance of the three models, Table 6 presents the best simulation results for JPSN, PSNN and MLP. Over all the training process, JPSN obtained the lowest MAE, which is 0.063458; while the MAE for PSNN and MLP were 0.063471 and 0.063646, respectively. By considering the MAE, it shows that JPSN is able to make a very close forecasts to the actual output in analysing the temperature. In this respect, JPSN outperformed PSNN by a ratio of 1.95×10^{-4}, and 2.9×10^{-3} for the MLP. Moreover, it can be seen that JPSN reached higher value of SNR. Therefore, it can be said that the network can track the signal better than PSNN and MLP. Apart from the MAE and SNR, it is verified that JPSN exhibited lower prediction errors, in terms of NMSE and MSE on the out-of-sample dataset. This indicates that the network is capable of representing nonlinear function better than the two benchmarked models. In the case of learning speed, particularly on the number of epoch utilized, PSNN converged much faster than the JPSN and MLP. However, JPSN reached a smaller number of epoch when compared to the MLP. On the whole, the performance of JPSN gives a gigantic comparison when compared to the two benchmarked models.

For demonstration purpose, the models' performance on their NMSE is depicted in Figure 6. It shows that JPSN steadily gives lower NMSE when compared to both PSNN and MLP. This by means shows that the predicted and the actual values which were obtained by the JPSN are better than both comparable network models in terms of bias and scatter. Consequently, it can be inferred that the JPSN yield more accurate results, providing the choice of network parameters are determined properly. The parsimonious representation of higher order terms in JPSN assists the network to model successfully.

The plots depicted in Figures 7 to 9 present the temperature forecast on the out-of-sample dataset for all network models. As shown in the plots, the blue line represents the trend of the actual values, while the red line represents the predicted values. The predicted values of daily temperature measurement made by all network models almost fit the actual values with minimum error forecast. On the whole, JPSN practically beat out PSNN and MLP by 1.038% and 1.341%, respectively. It is verified that JPSN has the ability to perform an input-output mapping of temperature data as well as better performance when compared to both network models. Besides, the evaluations on MAE, NMSE, MSE, and SNR over the temperature data demonstrated that JPSN were merely improved the performance level compared to the two benchmarked network models, PSNN and MLP. The better performance of temperature forecasting is allocated based on the vigour properties it contains. Hence, it can be seen that the thrifty representation of higher order terms in JPSN assists the network to model effectively.

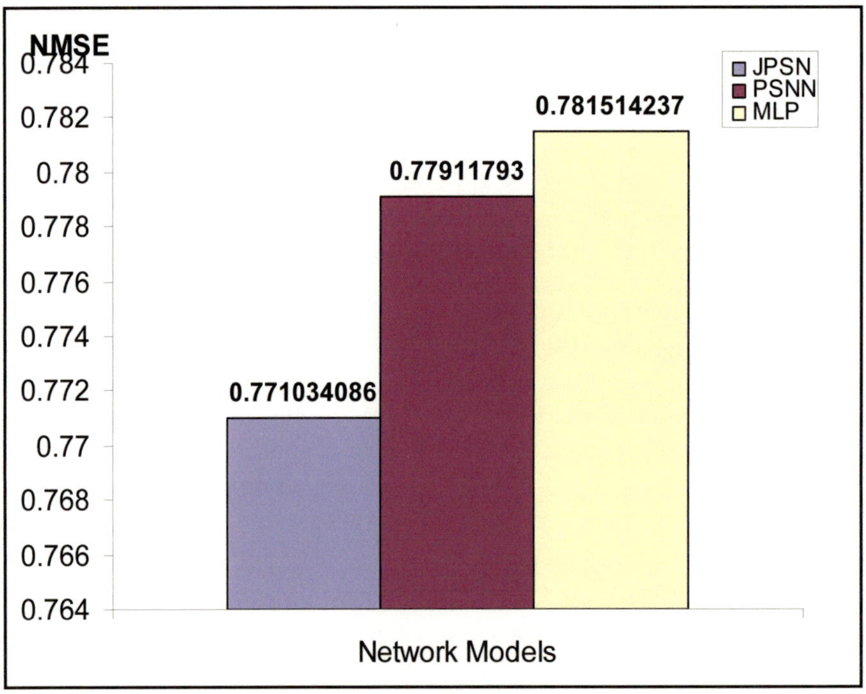

Fig. 6. The NMSE for JPSN, PSNN, and MLP.

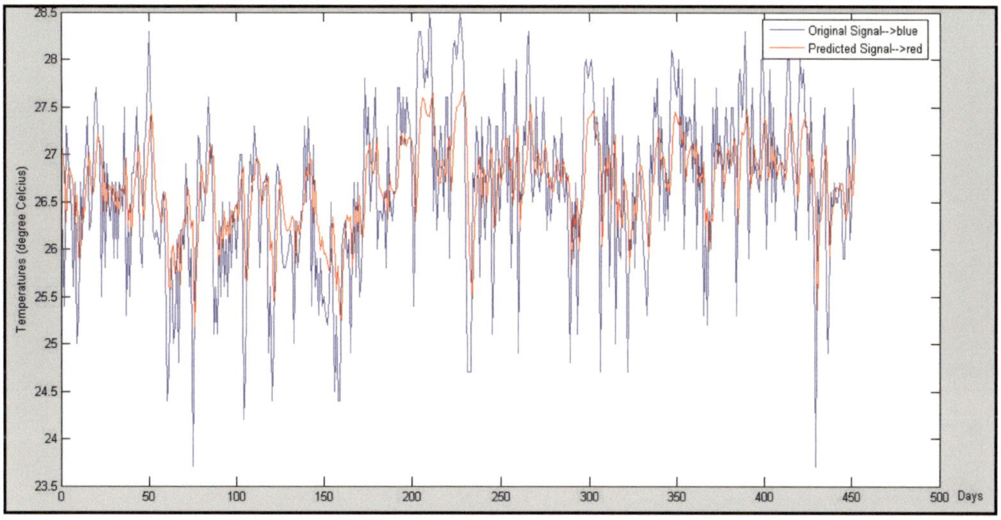

Fig. 7. Temperature Forecast made by JPSN on Out-of sample Dataset.

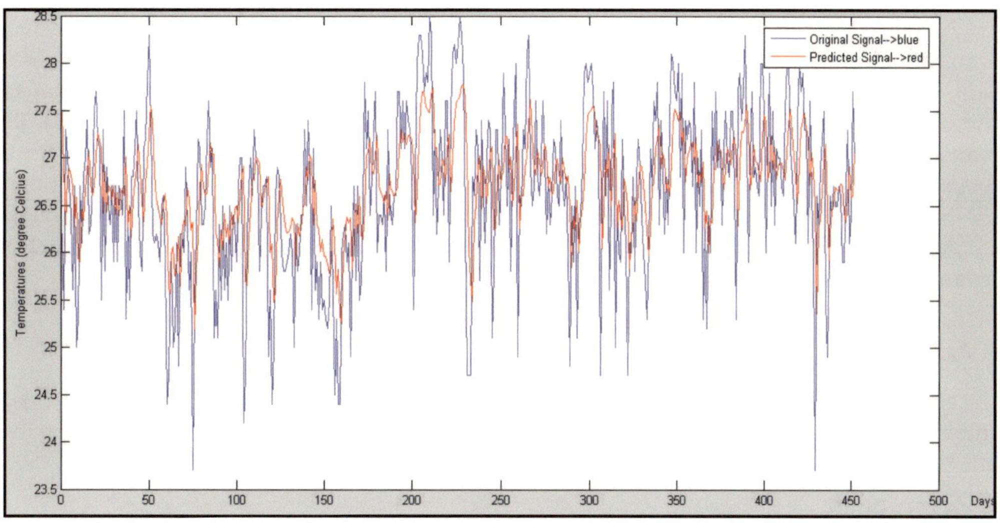

Fig. 8. Temperature Forecast made by PSNN on Out-of sample Dataset.

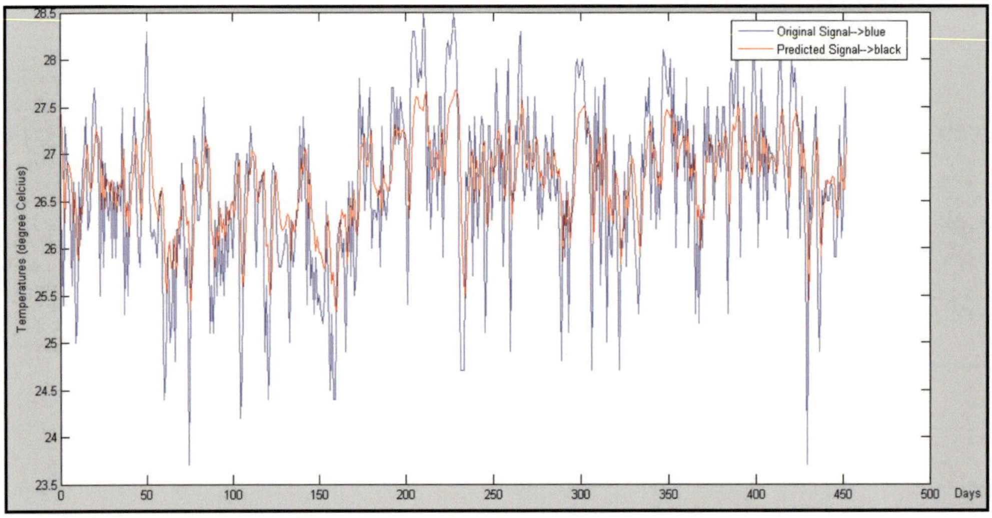

Fig. 9. Temperature Forecast made by MLP on Out-of sample Dataset.

6. Conclusion

There are many applications and techniques on temperature that was developed in the past. However, limitations such as the accuracy and complexity of the models make the existing system less enviable for some applications. Therefore, improvement on temperature forecasting requires continuous efforts in many fields, including NN. Several methods related to NN, particularly have been investigated and carried out. However, the ordinary feedforward NN, the MLP, is prone to overfitting and easily get stuck into local minima. Thus, to overcome the drawbacks, a new model, called JPSN is proposed as an alternative mechanism to predict the temperature event. The JPSN which combines the properties of PSNN and RNN can benefits the temperature prediction event, which may overcome such drawbacks in MLP. In this chapter, JPSN is used to learn the historical temperature data of Batu Pahat, and to predict the temperature measurements for the next-day ahead. Simulations for the comprehensive evaluation of the JPSN were presented, and the evaluation covering several performance criteria: the NMSE, MSE, SNR, and number of epoch were discussed. Experimental results of JPSN were compared with the ordinary PSNN and the MLP. Results obtained from each model were presented, and on the whole, the proposed JPSN has shown to outperform the ordinary PSNN and MLP on the prediction errors and convergence time.

7. Acknowledgment

The work of R. Ghazali is supported by Ministry of Higher Education (MOHE) Malaysia, under the Exploratory Research Grant Scheme (ERGS).

8. References

Baboo, S. S. & Shereef, I. K. (2010). An Efficient Weather Forecasting System using Artificial Neural Network. *International Journal of Environmental Science and Development,* Vol.1, No.4, pp.321-326.

Barry, R. & Chorley, R. (1982). *Atmosphere, Weather, and Climate*: Methuen.

Chang, F.-J.: Chang, L.-C., Kao, H.-S. & Wu, G.-R. (2010). Assessing the effort of meteorological variables for evaporation estimation by self-organizing map neural network. *Journal of Hydrology, 384*(1-2), 118-129.

Cybenko, G. (1989). Approximation by Superpositions of a Sigmoidal Function. *Signals Systems, 2 (303)*, pp. 14.

Ghazali, R. & al-Jumeily, D. (2009). Application of Pi-Sigma Neural Networks and Ridge Polynomial Neural Networks to Financial Time Series Prediction. In *Artificial Higher Order Neural Networks for Economics and Business* (pp. 271-293). Hershey, New York: Information Science Reference.

Ghazali, R.: Hussain, A. & El-Deredy, W. (2006). Application of Ridge Polynomial Neural Networks to Financial Time Series Prediction. *In Proceedings of the International Joint Conference on Neural Networks, IJCNN 2006,* part of the IEEE World Congress on Computational Intelligence, WCCI 2006, Vancouver, BC, Canada, 16-21 July 2006. pp. 913-920, IEEE, 2006.

Ghazali, R.: Hussain, A. J. & Liatsis, P. (2011). Dynamic Ridge Polynomial Neural Network: Forecasting the univariate non-stationary and stationary trading signals. *Elsevier: Expert Systems with Applications.* 38, pp. 3765-3776.

Hussain, A. J. & Liatsis, P. (2002). Recurrent Pi-Sigma Networks for DPCM Image Coding. *Neurocomputing, 55*, pp. 363-382.

Ibrahim, D. (2002). Temperature and its Measurement. In *Microcontroller Based Temperature Monitoring & Control* (pp. 55-61). Oxford: Newnes.

Jordan, M. I. (1986). *Attractor Dynamics and Parallelism in a Connectionist Sequential Machine.* Paper presented at the Proceedings of the Eighth Conference of the Cognitive Science Society, New Jersey, USA.

Lorenc, A. C. (1986). Analysis Methods for Numerical Weather Prediction. *Quarterly Journal of the Royal Meteorological Society, 112*(474), pp. 1177-1194.

Mielke, A. (2008). Possibilities and Limitations of Neural Networks. Retrieved August 24, 2009, from http://www.andreas-mielke.de/nn-en-1.html

Paras, Mathur, S., Kumar, A. & Chandra, M. (2007). *A Feature Based Neural Network Model for Weather Forecasting.* Paper presented at the Proceedings of World Academy of Science, Engineering and Technology.

Radhika, Y. & Shashi, M. (2009). Atmospheric Temperature Prediction using Support Vector Machines. *International Journal of Computer Theory and Engineering, 1*(1), pp. 55-58.

Rumelhart, D. E.: Hinton, G. E. & Williams, R. J. (1986). Learning Representations by Back-Propagating Errors. *Nature, 323 (9)*, pp. 533-536.

Shin, Y. & Ghosh, J. (1991-a). The Pi-Sigma Networks: An Efficient Higher-order Neural Network for Pattern Classification and Function Approximation. *Proceedings of International Joint Conference on Neural Networks, Vol.1*, pp.13-18.

Shin, Y. & Ghosh, J. (1991-b). Realization of Boolean Functions using Binary Pi-Sigma Networks. In Kumara & Shin, (Ed.), *Intelligent Engineering Systems Through Artificial Neural Networks, Dagli*, (pp. 205-210). ASME Press.

Song, G. (2008). Visual Cryptography Scheme Using Pi-sigma Neural Networks. *Proceedings of the* pp. 679-682.